The
Central Estate
and the
Hartlepools
(1800-2000)

by

JACK WOOLFORD

Published by Printability Publishing Ltd. of Wolviston
on behalf of Jack Woolford.

Designed and Typeset by Steve Franks.
Printed by Atkinson Print Ltd.,
10/11 Lower Church Street, Hartlepool TS24 7DJ.
Tel: (01429) 267849 Fax: (01429) 865416
ISDN No: (01429) 894231
e-mail: printability@atkinsonprint.co.uk • www.atkinsonprint.co.uk

ISBN No. 1 872239 34 X

First Edition September, 2002

TO JOHN WARD
AND ALL MY CENTRAL ESTATE,
HARTLEPOOL (AND WEST HARTLEPOOL)
NEIGHBOURS AND FRIENDS 1917-2001

ACKNOWLEDGEMENTS

I am indebted to my grandfather, George Woolford, who moved from Darwen, Lancs. to Hartlepool for skilled employment at Gray's shipyard in 1911, and to my parents from Blackburn, Lancs., who followed him in 1916. I am also indebted to my history teachers, notably to Mr. H. L. Rees of the Henry Smith School Hartlepool (1933-35) and at Christ's College, Cambridge and Cambridge University (1935-38). I am indebted to my colleagues in the Adult Education Departments of the Universities of Oxford (1946-78) and Kent at Canterbury (1975-78) who taught me the value of local history, and in particular to Dr. H.C.F. Lansberry.

My first debt for the history of the Central Estate is to Miss Mary Hoban, Reference Librarian of the Hartlepool Public Library who, in the early 70s, introduced and guided me to and through the archives of Hartlepool newspapers, directories, books, maps and pictures, a never-failing source of information and support. My second, and even greater debt is to Mr. John Ward (Plate 89 p. 250) to whom, as then Secretary of the Hartlepool Society, I was introduced by Miss Hoban and who for the thirty years of my research has been my friend and mentor, making it possible for me, also born on the Central Estate but resident in Kent since 1946 and in Dover since 1949, to pursue my Hartlepool studies by correspondence, photocopying of sources and by his own publications and video compilations (see Bibliography). I am also much indebted to Mr. George Colley, himself a major contributor to the historiography of the Hartlepools with his seven published collections of pictures and comments (see Bibliography), from which he has so generously permitted me to borrow for my own illustrations, and for his advice and encouragement. I am also indebted to Councillor Douglas Ferriday, to Hartlepool Borough Council for illustrations and to the "Hartlepool Mail" formerly "Northern Daily Mail" for both text and illustrations.

I must also thank those Central Estatians whose memories I tape-recorded in the 1970s whose names are recorded in my text, and those old friends and schoolmates who reminisced and argued with me: Mr. Harry Elliott, Mr. Alec Gray, Mr. Jack Robson, Mr. Bert Cox, Mr. Charles Kettlewell, Mr. Alec Cowan, and to those who have replied to my letters in "The Mail". I am indebted to Dorothy Smith (née Borrowdale) for West Hartlepool variations and for Hartlepool variations to Edgar Lightfoot. Finally I am deeply indebted to Steve Franks of Deal, Kent, whose professional computing skills have produced this book from my manuscript and illustrations .

Preface

I myself was born on the Central Estate, at 68 Arch St. on June 12th 1917, and lived at 54 Stephenson Street from 1922-27 and at 72 Arch Street until 1945. I went to Hart Road School from age 5 to 11 and regularly attended the Primitive Methodist Chapel in Hart Road from age 5 to 15. It was on the Central Estate that I became a Hartlepudlian, despite the facts that my parents and grandparents were Lancastrians, and learned the dialect and the values, learned how and what to play, and how and when to fight, and although there came a time when I was glad to get away to earn my living elsewhere, I was drawn back after twenty years of separation by an increasingly strong wish to return to my roots and an even stronger wish to understand and explain them.

Although it was no more than a triangle of streets, the Central Estate had both a magnificent beach and pleasant countryside less than half a mile away, and two towns with all their shopping and entertainment attractions only half a mile more. Moreover there was a street culture of games and a way of life built from school, church/chapel, sporting and employment associations which I now recognise as having been characteristic of a living community - that is to say a group of people who, however scattered their origins, had a way of life in common, the joys and burdens of which they shared, which I incorporate into my history in due chronological course as it occurred.

Jack Woolford

Contents

Illustrations

Tables

Chapter 1: Origins

To those who, like me, were born on the Central Estate, Hartlepool, when it was already established as a community in the early years of the 20th century, it was taken for granted to mean "central" between Hartlepool and West Hartlepool, which geographically indeed it was. As I grew up I became aware that it was part of the Throston Ward of the Borough of Hartlepool, which schooled and policed us and to which our parents paid rates and elected councillors. West Hartlepool, though adjacent, indeed almost contiguous, was different; bigger and better for shopping or entertainment but different, if not hostile. We shared our Member of Parliament and our tramways, gas and water, but not our Town Council, Councillors or Mayor, and we exchanged bitter insults about: "Who hung the monkey?" (Appendix G)(Plates 1-5 pp. 19-21).

Had we thought about it we should have regarded the Central Estate as the natural expansion of the ancient town of Hartlepool, chartered by King John in 1201, beyond the original Headland and the newer railways and docks. Yet it was not so simple or self-evident and, moreover, finding out what really happened proved to be a difficult as well as an interesting task.

Hartlepool was Anglo-Saxon in origin, dating from the middle of the 7th century AD, and it achieved medieval importance as Port to the Bishopric of the County Palatine of Durham, with both naval and military importance in the wars between English and Scottish kings(Plate 3 p. 20). After the 16th century Reformation it declined into an 18th century fishing port and minor watering place. Its history is well told in Sir Cuthbert Sharp's famous *History of Hartlepool* of 1816 and its *Supplemental History*, by John Procter in 1851. The story is further updated in Robert Wood's *West Hartlepool* of 1967, in Eric Waggott's *Jackson's Town* of 1978 and in Walter Gill's *Hartlepool Story* of 1990, but, although all account for the fateful rise and rivalry of West Hartlepool from 1844, none mentions the Central Estate.

The history may briefly be summarised. The revival of Hartlepool, and the consequential foundation of the Central Estate, resulted from the Industrial Revolution which, in the last quarter of the 18th century transformed agricultural, commercial and colonial Britain into the industrial workshop of the world. Increasing demand for the new industrial products, made possible by inventors like Hargreaves, Arkwright, Watt and Stephenson - spinning jennies, looms, pumping and steam engines and then locomotives, railways and iron ships - greatly increased the demand for coal. This, in turn, greatly stimulated the mine owners of the Durham coalfields (who dated back at least to the 1300s), the landowners over whose properties the railways ran or might run, and the seaports of the Tyne, Wear and Tees, to increase their trade and profits, especially from exporting coal. Their efforts were competitive, not collaborative, and it was their cutthroat rivalries for sales, rents, tolls and dues (measured in pounds, shillings and pence) and routes (measured in miles) which revived Hartlepool, created West Hartlepool, and led to the development of the land between them.

In the 1820s, Hartlepool, with a population of little more than a thousand(Map 2 p. 63), was governed by neighbouring landowners who were not interested in industry, and it was left to enterprising outsiders, to perceive that the harbour formed by the Headland (in which, surprisingly, corn was grown from 1808 to 1813 and which was also a rubbish dump) made it possible to compete for exporting coal brought by newly invented railways from newly sunk collieries. Hartlepool's superiority was not only that it was nearer to some of the collieries, notably Haswell, Thornley and Wingate. If its tidal harbour were cleared, deepened and enclosed, it could accommodate much larger ships and charge much smaller dues than Teesside Port Clarence on the (1825) Stockton and Darlington Railway. (Map 1 Coal Railways c1840 p. 62)

The pioneers were, first, in 1823, Arthur Mowbray of the Hetton Coal Company and then, in 1830, Rowland Burdon of Castle Eden, and Christopher Tennant of Stockton. Tennant and Burdon collaborated in the establishment of the Hartlepool Dock and Railway Company in 1831 which, by 1835, successfully exported coal from Haswell, Thornley and Wingate. Tennant already had an interest in the Stockton and Darlington Railway but, as a Stockton man, he was angered by a proposal in 1827 to extend it to a new Port Darlington, which in fact became the new town of Middlesbrough. He therefore constructed a new railway, the Clarence, from shallow riverside Port Clarence to Hartlepool. The Hartlepool Dock and Railway Company, equally angered by the threat of competition, prevented him from constructing a rival dock by pre-emptively purchasing the land at Middleton on which it could have been built. A compromise followed by which wagons from the Clarence Railway could use the Hartlepool staiths (railway landing stages from which coal was tipped down from wagons into the holds of ships berthed below) by paying a toll to pull them up an inclined plane, but the toll for this made them uncompetitive. After three years, during which only an eighth of the promised tonnage materialised and during which the Clarence Railway itself obstructed the use of an alternative route from more new collieries to the Hartlepool Railway, the agreement lapsed. It may reasonably be judged in retrospect that there were faults on both sides(Plate 12 p. 24).

Tennant's successor to the control of the Clarence and Hartlepool Railway in 1839, was Ralph Ward Jackson(Plate 13 p. 25), another outsider, determined not only to compete for railway tolls on coal transport but to create a new town ("the Liverpool of the east coast") as well as a new dock, and also to compete for shipbuilding, which by now was successfully established in Hartlepool. Thus the Hartlepool West Harbour and Dock Act of 1844 created, in effect, the rival town of West Hartlepool, whence the enmity between the two Hartlepools and (most probably) the insult about "who hung the monkey!" (Appendix G, p. 287).

In retrospect it seems strange that Jackson was content that his creation should merely be named "West" Hartlepool. Waggott's brilliant and fascinating biography, published by the (united) Borough Council in 1980, is rightly entitled "Jackson's Town". It might well, and equally rightly, have been named "Jacksonville", of which the future Central Estate, however named, might have been a part!

The enmity, which in 1845 caused Ralph Ward Jackson to close the railway linking the two towns, ended only (if indeed it did) a century and a quarter later with the merger of the two Hartlepools in 1967, despite the much earlier union of Poor Law in 1857, the reunion of the railway link to Hartlepool in 1862, the ownership of both railways and docks by the North Eastern Railway in 1865, the creation of a joint parliamentary seat in 1867 and the union of the docks themselves in 1880.

The Central Estate was built on the sandy and tussocky land between the two towns - Hart Warren, in the Parish of Throston (Map 3, p. 137)- but the drawing of the boundary in old Hartlepool's favour was only settled in 1882 after forty years of enmity. As Eric Waggott points out in his 1967 article (in the Hartlepool Central Library) on "The Hartlepools and Their Identity Problem", from 1850 Hartlepool was a Municipal Borough with charters dating back to 1201 (King John) and even earlier, whereas West Hartlepool which did not exist at all until 1844, was a mere Improvement District from 1854, and did not achieve Municipal Borough status until 1887.

When I first investigated the origins of the Central Estate in the 1970s I imagined that information would be readily available in the Minutes of Town Council meetings, but to my amazement they were not available. I was allowed to search the old Town Hall to no effect, and was even more amazed to be told by a former Hartlepool Councillor that they had disappeared after the 1967 amalgamation of the Hartlepools and, he suspected, might have been destroyed. The implication was that disconcerting truths might otherwise have come to light.

In fact they were merely in prolonged and delayed transit, and re-emerged in the County Archives of the new county of Cleveland into which Hartlepool was reluctantly relocated in the local government reorganisation of 1974. The Hartlepool Borough Council Court and Election Book records borough boundary extension and division into wards on May 6th 1868, and on June 3rd, that the proposed polling districts should be Throston, Stranton and Seaton Carew. Waggott says that in early 1869 Hartlepool Councillor Groves suggested inviting West Hartlepool to join "the parent town" but, perhaps because Ralph Ward Jackson, though sacked from the West Hartlepool Harbour and Dock Co. in 1862 for alleged financial malpractices, was still influential, nothing came of it. Jackson's own Petition to the Queen for Incorporation in 1872 was rejected but in 1881 the West Hartlepool Improvement Commissioners applied for the inclusion, no less, of both Middleton and Throston as well as Seaton Carew into their district.

The Hartlepool reply was more than equal and opposite. Not only did they ask for Middleton, Throston and Seaton Carew. They asked for West Hartlepool, too, and in 1882 the Local Government Board, the responsible government department, gave its blessing. Nevertheless it was Hartlepool which, on second thoughts, rejected amalgamation. Waggott speculates that Hartlepool rejected what could have been subordination to the larger and wealthier West Hartlepool, and accordingly the government regretfully gave Middleton and Throston (including the site of the future "Central Estate") to Hartlepool, and Seaton Carew to West. Hartlepool rejected as inopportune a further West Hartlepool offer of incorporation and the Northern Daily Mail of Thursday December 6th headlines "VICTORIOUS HARTLEPOOL" and reported that "The Mayor... has declared Wednesday next a general holiday in the borough for the purpose of celebrating their recent extension". Thus was the municipal future of the Central Estate decided seven years before it was born. It would have been born in any case but, as will emerge, had it been as a ward of the Borough (1887) or County Borough (1902) of West Hartlepool it would have differed in status and loyalties, rates and schools, if not in design and housing.

Meanwhile there had been a most intriguing suggestion. An undated map (Map 5, p. 139) of the "Port of Hartlepool in the County of Durham showed the towns of

Hartlepool and West Hartlepool *and the projected New Town to be called Middle Hartlepool* (my italics throughout) on the estate of the trustees under the will of the late Duke of Cleveland and of Frederick Acclom Milbank Esq., as divided into building sites by Martin and Fenwick, Civil Engineers, Land Agents and Values of No 1 Park Place Leeds, the agents for sale". Martin in his (1924) "Historical Notes of West Hartlepool and its Founder", states that "In the early fifties, the prospects of West Hartlepool were so promising, that the Trustees of the late Duke of Cleveland, who was a large landowner in the district, instructed their agents to prepare a plan for the building of a town to be called 'Middle Hartlepool'". This was to be built on the Dyke House Estate.

He goes on to say that "The idea must have been abandoned previous to 1859 for in that year part of the estate was offered for sale to the Guardians for the building of a workhouse". It does not necessarily follow that the sale of a part meant the abandonment of the whole plan, and it is also strange because the map itself, which is superimposed on the Ordnance Survey map of 1857, with Cleveland Road, the Cement Works and the Ropery etc. already existing, clearly shows the `Workhouse of the Hartlepool Poor' also in existence (just north of Howbeck House) and this was built in 1861. This suggests that the concept of 'Middle Hartlepool' may have continued into the sixties. In any case it was within the area of contention between the rival towns and must have been known, at least, to Ralph Ward Jackson and to the members of the West Hartlepool Improvement Commission. Had it materialised it would either have killed the Central Estate before it was conceived, or developed the area earlier as part of a larger whole and without a distinct and separate identity. What was needed at a time of rapidly rising population and industrialisation was the simultaneous availability of land, of capital for investment in industry or commerce and in housing, all with favourable prospects, and of suitably friendly local government. This last ingredient was patently, fortunately or unfortunately, absent.

The Middle Hartlepool plan proposed Sites for Manufactories adjacent to the Old Cemetery and for the whole area south of Warren Hall to Cleveland Road and as far as the point where it was to be crossed by the proposed railway which was actually built later. It accurately forecast that the land east of Cleveland Road to the Slake should be Boat Builders' Yards, Workshops and Timber Ponds, but beyond the point where the railway bridged across the road, it proposed domestic housing accompanied by a Market, a Church, Botanical Gardens and a Cemetery. The site for the proposed Market later became a gasworks and the site for the Botanical Garden a waterworks; but the Church, St. Oswald's, was later built, and so were the Brougham and Wharton Terraces which the plan actually named. It is of interest to note that a Milbank Road parallel with and between Cleveland and Raby Roads was built and that there was already a Millbank Crescent in Hartlepool. It is likelier that spelling was variable or careless than that two families with such similar names and worthy of such commemoration coexisted. Irrespective of parish or municipal boundaries, it was the same family which owned all the land. It is of further interest to note that both the proposed Hart and Warren Roads were actually later built and that the triangle between Cleveland and Hart Roads on which the Central Estate was later built, was contemplated.

Rising population and increasing concern with public health greatly increased the demand for more and better housing from the 1830s onwards, thanks to growing awareness of the links between hygiene and health. The quadrupling of the Hartlepool population, from less than a thousand in 1801 to more than 5000 in 1841, and its redoubling to almost 10,000 by 1851 indicates the scale of housing demand. The fact that it was overtaken by West Hartlepool by 1861, and which was twice as big by 1891, indicates the dwarfing in size of old Hartlepool by new West Hartlepool. The Central Estate was only a small part of the equation.

As to quality, the author of the *Supplemental History* of 1851 was scathing: "the extension of Hartlepool cannot, without a great stretch of candour, be called improvements... In an age when, for purposes of defence and protection, the clustering together of dwellings was a principle, an excuse might be found in the state of society and the exigencies of the times. But Hartlepool, springing up in the middle of the nineteenth century, and with the warning of a terrible pest (cholera) which, in 1832 and again in 1849, made fearful havoc among its population, presents an example of the worst nuisances of the worst towns of the kingdom". He added that the worst examples were to be found on Corporation property and contrasted them with the open and spacious roads and the neat and commodious houses and shops of West Hartlepool.

According to the Preface to the *Supplemental History*, its author was John Procter, printer and publisher, as before mentioned. According to Robert Wood's *West Hartlepool* the author was Thomas Wood, Secretary of the Hartlepool Dock and Railway Company. Whoever was the author, he may well have been prejudiced, for in 1850 the revised Hartlepool Town charter included Public Health Act duties, and in the same year public baths had been opened and a report had been made to the General Board of Health into the Sewerage, Drainage and Supply of Water. However insanitary the accommodation may have been, the population had nevertheless boomed. Moreover, it was obviously easier to build a brand-new town from scratch than to rebuild and extend a very old one in a restricted area, however similar they may later have seemed (Map 4, p. 138).

The Central Estate was, thirty years later, built in conformity with the Artisan and Labourers' Dwellings Act of 1868, the Public Health Act of 1872, the Artisans and Labourers' Dwellings Improvement Act and Public Health Acts of 1875, and progressively stricter model bye laws, a response to both health and housing problems. "The rapid increase of the population", added Procter or Wood, "and the limited quantity of ground available... induced the inhabitants and trustees to look at the charity-lands as a means of supplying the deficiency, and at the same time benefiting both said estate and the borough".

Meanwhile, in 1855, there was a race course on the Warren. According to the "Hartlepool Free Press" of July 1855:

> *"A few of the sporting gentlemen of the Borough met at Hart Warren for the purpose of cutting the first sod for the improvement of the ground for the new race course. I. Lawrenson Esq., to whom we are indebted for his strenuous exertions in obtaining for us the use of the ground, cut the first sod, after which the healths of the Lord and Lady of the Manor, Mr. Bolam the Steward, and Mr. Story the tenant of the farm, were drank (sic) on the spot. We understand from the elastic nature of the ground and the clear run there will be, that the course will not be equalled in the north.*

Consequently we may anticipate upon having the best horses and unprecedented sport".

An advertisement on Sept. 1st 1855 said that the Hartlepool Races were "to be run on the new course, on Hart Warren (about five minutes walk from the town of Hartlepool) on Monday and Tuesday the 3rd and 4th September". On September 8th it reported that the races "came off on Mon and Tues last on the new course situate on Hart Warren at the north end of the town. Mon Sept 3rd trial Stakes 5 sovs (sovereigns i.e. pounds sterling) and 20 sovs 2 runners - about one mile. Hartlepool Handicap - no runners. Corporation Plate 2 runners - 5 sovs. Racing Stakes 3 sovs and 2 sovs 5 ran - 1 1/2 miles".

The turnout of horses, at least, was not numerically impressive. Perhaps humbler fare was more suited to local taste. The "South Durham Herald" reported on January 5th 1867 that "A rabbit coursing handicap and sweepstakes got up by Mr. Wm. Graham of the Commercial Inn, Commercial Street, Hartlepool came off on Hart Warren on New Year's Day and was well attended".

Nevertheless "Hartlepool and West Hartlepool Races" were advertised on a poster dated May 18 1859 (now in the new Hartlepool Museum on the Marina) to be run on 18th and 19th July 1859 on "New Racecourse, Hart Warren Farm". Subscriptions were solicited "to publish the programme" by "John Lawrenson, Secretary and Treasurer". All cannot have gone quite well, for in 1861 a similar poster states: "The Racecourse has undergone considerable improvements within the last twelve months, being greatly enlarged and the objectionable turns eliminated. The course is flat, of an oval or egg shape about one mile round, with a straight run in of about two furlongs". The grandstand, not mentioned as an improvement, must already have been there. For "Hartlepool Meeting 186" John Lawrenson, now "Clerk of the Course", offered grandstand tickets at 2s. 6d. for one day or 4s. 0d. for two, sums well beyond the reach of any but the prosperous. Presumably the grandstand was a temporary erection on an otherwise working farm.

According to Robert Wood's 1967 "Victorian Delights", on some Saturday March 13, which by my calculation must have been the selfsame 1855, "Mr. Barr the Celebrated Scotch Falconer will fly his Peregrine Falcons on the Warren Near Hartlepool... Admission to the field 1/-".

A shilling, now but 5p, was then very far from cheap. "John O'Heugh" (NDM 1959) dates a racecourse at least 14 years earlier than 1855, locates it on the future Watson Street and says that in 1841 Robert Stephenson who farmed Low Warren and for whom Stephenson Street is said later to have been named, was steward of the course and later its clerk(Plate 16 p. 26). He does not identify his source of information, but it may well be that the 1855 course, described as "new", was the second of its kind. Now that the former Warren Cement Works, less than two hundred yards from Watson Street, is now designated as "Park", the Central Estate has come full circle as an amenity area.

In another NDM article, "John O'Heugh" says that "the first house on the Central Estate is dated 1889" and there was indeed a block of stone above the lintel of the house-and-shop at the junction of Beaumont and Watson Streets, deeply incised

"1889" (Plate 17 p. 27), although as noted below, there is no recorded planning application for Watson Street until 1892. The advertisement for the Brougham Street, Hartlepool, Methodist Chapel on Saturday July 12th 1890 contains a notice for the "Central Estate Methodist Chapel", although the Trustees did not get their building permit until September 21st 1893. Perhaps a house or hut was used.

In the apparent absence of municipal records, the obvious alternative was the files of the "Northern Daily Mail" and other local papers, and as will appear, the "Northern Daily Mail" ultimately, if almost incidentally or accidentally, yielded the answer.

According to the lists of Borough of Hartlepool planning applications, now in Cleveland County Archives Department, there were no applications for buildings on the Central Estate until November 1888 when J. Burn applied to build 10 double houses in Cleveland Road and M. Gray an unspecified number in Cleveland and Hart Roads. The NDM of February 7th 1889 reports that Councillor M'Donald of the Improvement Committee:

> ... *"wished to be informed of what had been done towards keeping the footpath open between Cleveland-road and the Workhouse* ***as a large number of houses were now being built in the vicinity****"* *(my emphasis). The Surveyor replied: "a new street goes right across the footpath, so that it is now diverted".*

Nothing similar is recorded in the NDM until October 6th 1892 when R. J. Marshall's application to build nine houses in Bell and Watson Streets and C. Pounder's application for two in Union Road were both rejected, although this was apparently almost a formality at first application. On December 8th 1892 plans were approved for R. J. Marshall to build four houses in Hart Road, W. Rennie a double house and a butcher's shop in Cleveland Road, and C. T. Watson stables in Watson Street. From then onwards the applications, time after time by the same C. T. Watson, R. J. Marshall, J. J. Rennie and other builders, multiplied and, as we shall see, by 1897 the Central Estate was largely built and occupied (Map 6 p. 67).

Even more interesting, on that same October 6th 1892 M. Gray's "deviation from the "*estate plan*" was granted. Since various streets, as yet unbuilt, were successively named there must indeed have been a plan, although it had not previously been reported. It was, in fact, ultimately located in the Cleveland County Archive.

On June 8th 1893 the NDM reported "SMELLS ON THE CENTRAL ESTATE". "A letter was read from Messrs. Turnbull and Tilly on behalf of Mr Matthew Gray as to the flushing of drains on the Central Estate, and stating that the Corporation were liable to do the same. It was resolved that the (Improvement) Committee adhere to the resolutions passed, repudiating liability... Councillor M'Donald said the stench from the drains on the Central Estate was abominable... Councillor Gilooly substantiated... Surely they had not to wait until half-a-dozen died before attending to the drain... Ald(erman) Graham said they must be maintained by the owners until taken over".

On July 27th 1893 the Improvement Committee resolved "that the *owner* of the Central Estate be requested to cover the manholes thereon" and on March 7th 1895 J. Garry was permitted another deviation from the Central Estate Plan. The next revelation came in the report of the Improvement Committee held on October 17th

1895. "Resolved that the Town Clerk write Major Gray, *owner of the Central Estate*, and Mr Garry the architect, as to the stagnant pools of water on the Estate and request that the same be at once filled in". Mr Garry's name often appears as agent for other applicants for building permits: but who was M. Gray and was he the same person as Matthew Gray and Major Gray?

It was through the kindness of Mr. and Mrs. Cowley, whom I met by the good offices of Bob Moore who had taken over Tommy Newton's newsagent and confectionery shop in Arch Street, in 1978, that I learned from the deeds of their house at 23 Rokeby St. that one of the vendors of the land on which it was built was 'M. Gray'. In 1992 the Hartlepool Borough Council Court and Election Book 1866-83 was made available to me by courtesy of the Cleveland County Archivist David Tyrell, and although disappointed to find a mere record of decisions, rather than the Minutes with proposers, seconders, discussion and resolutions, I was interested indeed to learn that in January 1867 the Farwell Field site, immediately to the west of the original Headland, was sold to *William Gray* and others by Robert Asquith (Map 2 p. 136).

It was unlikely that there were two William Grays at the same time, able and willing to buy land, presumably for housing, and the one and only William Gray, a draper from Blythe, Northumberland, had come to Hartlepool in 1843, had gone into partnership with a Hartlepool shipbuilder, John Denton, in 1863, was by 1867 the most successful local shipbuilder and in 1862 had been Mayor of Hartlepool. In 1869 he acquired a shipyard in West Hartlepool and in 1887, he became the first Mayor of the new Borough of West Hartlepool. In 1890 he was knighted and although he died in 1898, the firm he had established, three times won the Blue Ribbon for launching the greatest UK tonnage of the year, and survived until 1962. In other words Sir William Gray was a successful entrepreneur and it is neither surprising nor sinister that he should have indulged in land speculation in 1867. With his interests in and connections with both Hartlepools, the Middle Hartlepool proposal cannot have been unknown to him, or, likewise indeed, to Ralph Ward Jackson (Plate 14 p. 25).

The Ordnance Survey map of 1857 (Map 3 p. 137), which however may later have been overprinted, shows that Durham St. was already expanding westward, and that Trinity Church and Millbank Crescent had already been built. In 1868 Farwell Field plots were sold as building sites. Moreover the 1857 map also shows that the Warren Cement Works (1852) and the Rope Walk (1855), later integral parts of the Central Estate, already existed. Hartlepool was expanding both for housing and industry and it could only go westwards.

Sir William Gray married in 1849 and in 1855 had a son, Matthew. Matthew Gray, named after his paternal grandfather, inherited his father's business acumen and as well as mastering the technicalities and commerce of shipbuilding, he negotiated the purchase in 1881 of the West Hartlepool Ironworks which became the famous Steelworks. He was also, like his father, involved in local politics, successively an Improvement Commissioner and then both a Borough and a County Councillor for West Hartlepool. Like his father he was a generous benefactor to religious and other good causes and his wife's contribution to the foundation of St. Oswald's Church (Plate 15 p. 26)as a memorial to him is recorded in the fabric. He died aged only 40 on June 16th 1896, predeceasing his father by more than two years, and the NDM obituary, which confirms his parentage, was followed on July 2nd by a condolence expressed by the Hartlepool Borough Council which specifically refers to him as 'Major Gray'. Since he was never a regular soldier and certainly not a member of the Salvation Army he must have acquired his military title through service in the Militia which preceded the Territorial Army.

In the Hartlepool Reference Library there is also a brief biography of James Garry (1850-1918. He was practising as an architect in West Hartlepool in 1870 and designed a school, a church, a bank and shops including Gray Peverell's (later Binns') (Plate 10 p. 23) and the Grand Hotel (Plate 11 p. 24) which survive. At the time of his plans for the Central Estate in 1888 he was already a West Hartlepool Borough Councillor. Whether or not he was responsible for more than the layout of the Estate is not clear and it did not contain anything as grandiose as Middle Hartlepool's Botanical Garden, or Market, although a chapel, a church, two schools and a public house ultimately appeared, as well as houses and shops.

My search for the origins of the Central Estate was concluded by access to the deeds of 41 Stephenson Street, by courtesy of Mrs. Jean (née Scott) which traces ownership of the land backwards from July 20th 1920 through its sale by Sir William's widow in 1899 to Dec. 21st, 1883:

'Abstract of the Title of Matthew Gray esquire to Freehold Land in the Borough of Hartlepool in the County of Durham known as the Central Estate': Matthew Gray purchased from Andrew and James Montagu and from Sir Frederick and William Harry Vane Milbank 12 acres 'bounded on the North-East by a road called Harte or Hart Road on the South by a road called Cleveland Road on the East or South-East by land of the Vendors intended to be converted into a street 36 feet wide and on the West or North-West by the middle of an intended street also 36 feet wide which said piece or parcel of land was delineated on the plan drawn on the back of the now abstracting Indenture and thereon coloured round with red... at the price of £6,000'. Matthew Gray undertook to fence the land, to make and maintain a 'Proposed Street forty feet wide' coloured yellow on the plan, with proper footpaths on either side and a sewer if required to points A and B on the plan, and to widen Hart Road, etc. etc.

The title is further traced back through Montagus and Milbanks in 1871, to Henry Lord Brougham in 1853 and to Sir Frederick Milbank in 1844. It must earlier have been a part of the estate of William Harry Vane, 1st Duke of Cleveland (1766-1842), whose son-in-law was Mark Milbanke. His trustees endowed the Prissick Street schools in 1836, gave the land on which Trinity Church was built in 1850 and owned the land on which Middle Hartlepool had been projected. Earlier still it had been part of the Hart estate of Sir George Pocock and earlier still of the Lumley Earls of Scarborough...

Consequently it was the Gray family, father and son, who begat the Central Estate and it is improbable that there was any deliberate, still less sinister, concealment of the fact that the Central Estate had an owner and an architect. It may well have been such common knowledge as to make it unworthy of special mention. Presumably all the deeds of all the houses on the Estate contained the same information. It cannot have been connected with the apparent disappearance of the Minutes of the Hartlepool Borough Council, which, as seen, did not in fact occur, although the crucial years 1883-1904 have still not been located.

Government and influence, if not corruption, are eternally associated and conspiracy accusations abound. At the same time sea-green incorruptibles are rare and may also be dangerous. In any case nods and winks are never recorded and I am assured by a friendly county archivist that what is remarkable is not that so many local government records have disappeared but that so many have managed to survive generations of careless or criminal handling and transfer. Except for Hansard's records of parliamentary proceedings, it was only the press which (fortunately) recorded and printed debates, although reporters could be (and frequently were) excluded from committees. Minutes recorded decisions only.

"John O'Heugh", in the NDM extract from which I have already quoted, says that the Central Estate was so named because of its connection with Gray's Central Marine Engineering works and as I have shown, the connection with the Grays, father and son, was close. Furthermore, and curiously enough, it was in 1883 that the Central Marine Engine Works, as well as the Central Estate, began its life. Bearing in mind, however, that as will be shown in Chapter 2, many Central Estate houses were occupied from the outset by people who did *not* work for Grays, unlike many of the residents of the already existing Warren Terrace who nearly all worked at Warren Cement Works, there was clearly no concept of tied houses. Gray's shipyards in both Hartlepool (Middleton) and West Hartlepool long predated the engine works. The "Central" Estate seems, as suggested above, to have been named for its equidistance from both Hartlepool and West Hartlepool.

The Grays, father and son, were interested in profitable investment and the borough in which it occurred was probably not important to them. Their political involvement in the affairs of both boroughs was doubtless convenient and neither necessarily sinister or corrupt. If not disinterestedly benevolent, in the Central Estate they nevertheless created something well worth creating.

Plate 1 - Tram in Northgate c. 1902

Plate 2 - High Street c. 1890

Plate 3 - 14th century Sandwell Gate, Old Sea Wall, Hartlepool

Plate 4 - Borough Buildings, Hartlepool

Plate 5 - Brougham Street, Hartlepool c. 1905

Plate 6 - Church Street West Hartlepool 1910

Christ's Church, the gift of Ralph Ward Jackson, is now an art gallery

Plate 7 - Lynn Street, West Hartlepool, 1900

Plate 8 - CWS Central Stores, Stockton Street, West Hartlepool, 1915

Plate 9 - Wesleyan Church and Town Hall, West Hartlepool c. 1900

Plate 10 - Gray Peverell (later Binns), West Hartlepool, 1902

Plate 11 - Grand Hotel, West Hartlepool, 1920

Plate 12 - Engine House, Throston Bridge, 1834

Plate 13 - Ralph Ward Jackson c. 1850

Plate 14 - William (later Sir William) Gray c. 1860

Plate 15 - St. Oswald's Church c. 1900

HARTLEPOOL RACES.

Fellow Townsmen,

Having, at your request, applied to the Mayor and Corporation for a grant to have the use of that part of the Moor which is considered Corporate property for the Races. I am sorry to inform you that I have met with a refusal;—the question being negatived by a majority of two.

Noes	- - -	6
Ayes	- - -	4
Majority	-	2

In thanking the worthy Mayor and the 3 Aldermen for responding to your wishes in advocating the Races, I am happy to state that several Gentlemen have come forward and are making application in another quarter with every probability of success.

I have the honour to be
Gentlemen,
Your Obt. Servant

JOHN LAWRENSON.

Hartlepool, 11*th July*, 1842.

J. Proctor, Printer, Hartlepool.

Plate 16 - Hartlepool Races, 1842

Plate 17 - Central Estate's First House (Watson Street) 1889
Converted to a shop in 1902, demolished 1970

Chapter 2: The 1891 Census

Although the original boundaries of the Central Estate were clearly delineated by the triangle of streets bounded by Hart, Cleveland and Union Roads, it would be pedantic to exclude the Warren Cement Works (Plate 22 p. 59) and the Ropery (Plate 82 p. 249), already mentioned, not to mention the Old and Jewish Cemeteries and the adjacent Fever (originally Cholera) Hospital, all between the railway to Hartlepool and the sandbanked seashore. If the western boundary with West Hartlepool was the railway line from the docks to the propyard at (so-called) Greenland just short of the railway bridge (Plate 19 p. 37), it is not unreasonable to suggest that the 'natural' eastern boundary with Hartlepool was Throston (also railway) Bridge (Plate 18 p. 37) and although the kipper houses, coal depot and sawmill on Cleveland Road were part of the extension of Hartlepool, the children of Clyde Place and Clyde Terrace were schooled (and some of them Sunday-schooled) on the Central, and their parents voted for Throston Ward councillors. The Lord Clyde Hotel was also a Central pub by anticipation. The Estate later expanded, first between Hart Road and the railway embankment, and then along Hart Road, beyond the triangle of railway embankments which enclosed Warren Hall, and which was named West View, in the early 1920s. Romaine Park in the 1930s was an "internal" expansion, also between Hart Road and the railway embankment, and there was also some infilling in existing streets.

The 1891 census (of the Parish of Throston), only two years into the life of the Estate, published in 1991, gives the first information about the peopling of the Central Estate and a fascinating source it turns out to be.

It is important to recall that the census was *de facto* and not *de iure*, which is to say that it recorded those actually in residence on the night of enumeration and not those who might have been or, indeed, ought to have been, there. Consequently the figures may be a slight underestimate. On the other hand, as will appear below, even more people would have meant even more overcrowding. As to ages and statuses, birth and marriage certificates were not required and some answers may have been some distance from "nothing but the truth". Unmarried mothers and illegitimate fathers, for instance, were not on oath, nor were atheists nor agnostics, of which there must have been at least a few. The enquiry forms were not preserved and what survive are the enumerators' summaries.

The enumerator is not always legible, there are apparent erasures and some of the entries are difficult to understand. Both man and wife are recorded as married (no single parents) and what, for example, is the difference between a boarder and a lodger? Presumably the boarder was fed and watered but the lodger catered for himself. Why are some children (e.g. boys of 3, 5, 8, 10 and 11 and girls of 11 and 12) given marital status as single? Why were one or two children not recorded as 'scholars' although of school age? Assuming, reasonably, that the system had not basically changed by the next census in 1901, according to the NDM of March 11, the duties of enumerators were as follows:

> *"During the week ending March 30 he has to leave a schedule with every occupier of a house or tenement, taking note in an especially prepared memorandum book as he*

goes along of every person who receives a schedule, and of every uninhabited house or building at the time.

On Monday April 1st he has to collect the schedule, seeing that all he left are accounted for, and where necessary giving assistance in the filling up of the schedules. Between April 1st and 8th he has to copy every particular from the schedules into an enumeration book...

It will be the duty of every householder and every lodger who occupies separate rooms and boards by himself to fill up the particulars on the census paper and have it ready... It is very important also to distinguish every person's trade or occupation... (e.g.) at a shipyard whether a "ship plater", "ship plater's helper" or "boilersmith", or "ship painter" or "shiprivetter.. Shopkeepers and their assistants must be classified... Labourers must state the class of labour they follow... and those who have retired must give their former occupation...

Unless he was a very well informed local resident, the enumerator must have accepted the job descriptions given to him: although there was a dictionary of occupations, jobs must have been self-ascribed, and open to exaggeration. The occupational tables (Appendix I) give many examples. Class-consciousness as manifested in job descriptions was deeply engrained. Not only did it persist. It continues to do so.

Both husband and wife are recorded as married and, of course, neither wifehood nor motherhood are regarded as employment. Every man, including 70- and 80-year olds, one sole army pensioner excepted, in the absence of a statutory age of retirement, had both a trade and a job, for there appears to have been full employment! Although the year 1890 was the peak of an economic boom which was resumed in 1893 and lasted into the new century, this was quite extraordinarily exceptional in contemporary England and it implies that the Estate was built for the prosperous and successful. On the other hand, only 8 women were recorded as formally employed: 1 companion, a dressmaker's apprentice, 5 domestic servants and one waitress. By way of contrast, all those of "independent means" (4) were women, including a youngster of only 17. The remaining females were infants or scholars.

However, give or take a few minor errors, on or about the night of April 1st, 1891 there were 85 households (including more than 1 family per house in some cases) and also including houses outside the Estate Plan (e.g. at the Fever Hospital and in the former brickfield) with 465 inhabitants, 243 male and 222 female. These ranged from 2 or 3 persons in 2-4 rooms (13 examples); 6 persons in 3-4 rooms (20 examples); 8 in 4 rooms (7 examples); 9 in 4 rooms (3 examples); 10 in 4 rooms (3 examples); and 14 in 3 rooms (1 example: husband and wife, 5 daughters, 3 sons, a grandfather, 2 boarders and a domestic servant). Bearing in mind differences of age and sex, the presence of relatives including in-laws (30 in 17 households), boarders and lodgers (31 in 20 households) and 5 with both relatives and boarders, together with a total of 9 servants and 4 visitors, there must have been considerable overcrowding even by the standards of the time.

Of the Heads of Family, 74 were married men with their wives, 4 were widowers and 1 was single. There were 5 widows as Heads of Family and 1 female Head of Family was single. No man under the age of 21 was married and no woman under 20. There were 7 childless families of childbearing age, 4 one-child families, 12 two-child, 12 three-child, 8 four-child, 7 five-child, 6 six-child and 2 eight-child families.

The average age-gap between children of the same family seems to have been about two years which presumably implies prudential birth control practices. According to R. C. K Ensor in the Oxford History of England: 1870-1914 (1936), population was growing rapidly because of the fall in the death-rate and despite the fall in the birth rate from the 1870s which he attributes to increasing knowledge and availability of contraceptive techniques, made the more desirable by improving living standards and increasing wages. It is noteworthy that there were recorded only 5 deaf-and-dumb, blind, lunatic, imbecile or idiot - although we are not told what were the criteria: 1.2%.

Age	Sex		Total		
	M	F		Male	Female
0-5	44	51	95	////////////////////	/////////////////////////
6-10	20	27	47	/////////	////////////
11-15	22	23	45	//////////	///////////
16-20	22	26	48	//////////	////////////
21-30	61	37	98	/////////////////////////////	/////////////////
31-40	31	25	56	////////////////	/////////////
41-50	24	14	38	///////////	//////
51-60	14	13	27	///////	///////
61-70	3	5	8	///	/////
71-80	1	1	2	/	/
81-90		1	1		/
Total	243	222	465		

Table 1 - 1891 Census

One of the social consequences of the Industrial Revolution was formerly said to have been the break-up of the extended family in which grandparents, parents, children and grandchildren lived together under one roof, mutually dependent and supportive. The so-called nuclear family, of parents and children only, was said to have taken its place. Seven Central Estate families, however, included nieces and nephews or cousins, 13 families included fathers- mothers- brothers- and sisters-in-law, 3 families included grandchildren, and 2 families included grandparents. This totals 23, or just over 25%, of all households; convincing testament to the survival, whether by design or absence of choice, at least in part, of the extended family. The profile of ages is interesting. One of the children of 2 years and under must have been the Central Estate's first-born.

The highest category is of children (142) and teenagers (93), compared with only 192 adults under 50, 27 in their 50s, 10 in their 60's and 70's and only one over 80. The smaller number of females in each group over 5 years old, superficially surprising except at the senior end, must have resulted from the inferior opportunities of women for employment in a heavy-industrial area. It would have been different in a cotton or woollen mill town, where women were employed in mills. Moreover, many of the 21-30 males were probably "engaged" to marry. At that time marriage was a serious business, a full-time occupation for "respectable" men as well as women. Twenty six boys and 46 girls were classed as scholars, some of them under 5: and there were one or two under-14s who apparently did not attend school. As there were still no schools on the Estate, all must have walked to Hartlepool and back.

It is not, of course, a representative sample of the general population because only people in work could afford mortgage or rental payments, but it is significant in highlighting the enormous social changes which occurred during the lifetime of the Central Estate. When it was demolished in the 1970s and 80s, the age profile was almost reversed and the expectation of life almost doubled, with many more older than younger people, and at least as many pensioners as infants.

The Central Estate from beginning to end was predominantly working class, and it is not surprising that in 1891 there were only 4 men who might have been classifiable as 'professional'. I say 'might' because the employments recorded were self-ascribed and a 'retired civil engineer' whose children were a fitter and a dressmaker and whose boarder was a shipyard labourer may not have been professionally qualified; an 'army pensioner' with young children and a boarder had probably been a ranker; and a 'customs officer' may have been no more than a clerk. Only the solitary farmer was unquestionably middle class.

More meaningful in social and economic terms are the distinctions between service and manufacturing employment and between skilled and unskilled industrial workers.

In service employment there were a barman, 2 caretakers, a cartman, 2 clerks, a companion, an errand boy, a nightwatchman, 2 office boys, a seaman, a storekeeper, a tram conductor, a vanman and 6 (female) domestic servants. There were 2 butchers, a coal merchant, a general dealer, a grocer's assistant, a fishmonger, 4 marine engineers (including a chargeman), a milkman and a publican. In retirement there were a civil engineer, a customs officer and a soldier, making 36 in all. Apart from the 25 cement workers and a single compositor, everyone else worked in the shipyards or the marine engineering works, many, if not most of them, presumably at Gray's, which was the nearest.

Of skilled workers, including apprentices, there were 2 dressmakers, 7 blacksmiths and a forgeman, a brass finisher, 4 cement millers, a compositor and a driller, 2 engine-men, 12 fitters including a foreman, 6 joiners (but no carpenters), 2 millwrights, 5 moulders, 5 platers, a plumber, a shipwright, 7 turners (including machinists) and a wire-rope maker, totalling 59, although only 2 of them were supervisory. There were only 48 labourers, subdivided between coal, dock, engineer, fitter, horse, iron, paint, striker and waterworks (1 each), boilermakers (2), cement (17), farm (4), platers (holders-up) (2) and shipyard (13), which implies the predominantly skilled, and therefore better paid, social character of the early Central Estate. A further point of interest is the persistence of families and sons in occupations, a reminder of the importance of influence. There were 5 cement-making families, a glass works and a fitter father and son, 2 boilermaking and one blacksmithing families and a shipyard labourers' family. Boarders tended to board with workers in the same employment (10 examples).

The only employees whose workplace is definitely identifiable worked at the Cement Works which a German, Otto Trechmann, had founded in 1852. They were of typically mixed origins. There were an engineman (German), a millwright (Scot), a watchman (Irish), 4 millers (one each from Hartlepool, Stockton, North. Shields and Somerset), and 18 labourers (one each from Scotland, Lancashire, Norfolk, Suffolk and Somerset, two each from Ireland, Devonshire and Yorkshire, three from Durham County and four from Hartlepool. All but three of the householders in Warren Road and Terraces were cement workers, which implies that they may not have been company houses, and 4 cement workers lived in three other streets. Most certainly there were no Central Marine Engine Works tied houses. Matthew Gray sold land, not houses.

At least as significant as the trades are the birthplaces, surprisingly widespread in view of the subsequent rapid growth of a homogenous community, of the inhabitants. The evidence of what sociologists call 'horizontal social mobility' is indeed substantial. There were 1 Canadian and 5 Germans, 1 Welsh, 13 Scots and 17 Irish. There were 1 each from Essex, Gloucestershire, Huntingdonshire, Staffordshire and Sussex; 2 each from Birmingham, Cornwall, Derbyshire, Northamptonshire and Oxford; 3 each from Cumberland and Westmorland; 4 each from Kent and Lincolnshire; 5 each from Norfolk and Suffolk; 6 from Devon and Somerset, 7 from Nottinghamshire, 8 from London and 18 from Lancashire. The numbers increase from closer counties: 36 from Northumberland, 65 from Yorkshire and 71 from other parts of County Durham. The largest number, 185 (43%), was, not unnaturally, from Hartlepool itself, although how long they had been there is not revealed.

Older 'immigrants' brought their wives and families with them, from Germany, from Ireland, from Somerset and Devon, Norfolk and Suffolk, Newcastle, Nottingham, Sussex, Lancashire and Yorkshire. Many others had moved far from home to find their wives and husbands, with husbands and wives from, for example, Germany and Suffolk, Canada and Middlesex, Scotland and Yorkshire, Devon and Gloucester, Norfolk and Somerset, Bradford and Oxford, Yorkshire and Cornwall, Birmingham and Ireland; and Chatham and Darlington. The Hartlepool gene pool was widely, perhaps deeply, enriched. The social experience of some newcomers included periods of residence in two or three scattered places before residence in Hartlepool. Many, however, had settled and bred in Hartlepool before the move to the Central Estate and at least 7 intermarried with Hartlepudliennes.

Some of the religious denominations are, like the Irish, presumably guessable and one may infer that the majority was Protestant. As with the children to school, worshippers must have walked to church or chapel.

There were some eccentricities in first names: 'Barnard', 'Granger' and 'Peller', together with the odd 'Lancelot' and 'Septimus' for males and 'Clearion', 'Francesca' and 'Selinia' for females. The vast majority were conventional with clear majorities of 34 Johns, 26 Williams, 24 Marys and 13 Elizabeths. Over a hundred had second names (and none had more) but these are recorded only by initials.

A number or surnames persisted into the 1920s and 30s. I myself recognise, from the 1920s and 30s, Arkley, Cox, Danby, Dixon, Gooch, Green, King, Lower, Metcalf, Mitchell, Pearson, Place, Prosser, Spence, Ward and Winn, not to mention Brown and Smith, and it will be interesting subsequently to trace continuities - and discontinuities - of family and residence.

The Fever Hospital and Wire Rope House, Warren Farm and Warren Road, Warren Terrace and Back Warren Terrace, like Clyde Terrace and Clyde Place, already existed. Occupation of the new Estate began at the eastern end, in Pease and Watson Streets and Cleveland Road. The streets had already been named on the October 1888 Plan, presumably by Matthew Gray and James Garry. Cleveland Road, was already and obviously named from the former dukely owner of the land, and Hart Road obviously led to the old village of Hart from which Hartlepool derived its name. Union Road formed the base of the triangle linking Hart and Cleveland Roads: it cannot have been related to the Union Workhouse, also already existent, because it was remote, although Union Roads and Union Streets with workhouse connections were common in other places at the time. It did, in fact, unite the two main roads.

What was named in the Plan as Brunel St., obviously named after the great engineer of the Clifton Suspension Bridge and the Great Western Railway etc., was renamed Watson St. at the request of the builder C. T. Watson in January 1890. Pease St. was presumably named after the Edward Pease who was the chief promoter and financier of the Stockton and Darlington Railway of 1825 and it would have been consistent to name other streets after James Watt and George Stephenson, other Industrial Revolution luminaries, likely to have been honoured by the Grays. As already noted, however, Stephenson could have celebrated or commemorated the steward of the earlier racecourse. His widow Eleanor still lived in Warren Hall in 1881. Lambton was the family name of the earldom of Durham and Sir Isaac Bell was MP for Hartlepool 1875-80. Beaumont may have been another local worthy.

According to Tommy Newton, hairdresser and newsagent in Arch St., 1895-1967: "... when the Central Estate was to be built... the road we know as Hart Road... was intended to go along Arch St., the name Arch St. indicating that it led to... the Second Arch. This was to be the main road out of the town". This suggestion was independently made to me in 1992 by William Hunter. It is true that there were two arches through the railway embankment on the seaward side of Hart Road leading to the beach before the Estate was designed or built, and that the Second, as it continued to be called, was emphatically arch-shaped. It was, however, almost a mile away, deeply set into the embankment and thus barely visible from Hart Road, still less from Arch Street, and it was a road rather than a street for more than three quarters of its length. Moreover the 1888 plan definitively marks "Hart or Harte" Road which, if only a footpath, must long have led to Hart Village. There was, however, what could well have been named another "Second Arch", very narrowly separated from another "First", piercing the railway embankment from West Hartlepool to Sunderland, close to what later became Montague Road, much more directly aligned with Arch Street, although not visibly so after the construction of the later propyard fence. Had it not been so then "Arch" Street would have been curved and upper Union Road and Stephenson, Watt and Bell Streets would have needed another road to join them. The solution actually built was both more economical and more symmetrical, though it may have resulted as much from accident as design.

John O'Heugh's assertion that Watson Street was named for the C. T. Watson who built it is further substantiated by the fact that he is named on the plan itself for the ownership or building of houses in several places, including shops at the junctions of Stephenson Street with both Watson Street and Cleveland Road. Since similar blocks were earmarked for Allison, Burn, Marshall and Pounder, all subsequent builders, it is perhaps surprising that they, too did not give their names to streets. Even more surprising is the modesty of the Grays and John Garry. C. T. Watson may have been, as we shall see, rather more than a mere speculative builder, but why were not the only begetter of the Central Estate, his even more illustrious father nor the architect himself, also immortalised in street names? Presumably it was modesty rather than concealment.

There was one detached house, "Sandfield", for the manager of the Ropery. All other houses were terraced, fronting immediately on the street (no front garden, of course) but with separate back entrance and enclosed backyard. Some had three bedrooms, a 'front room' (parlour) and an upstairs (only) bay window. Most had two bedrooms, with only a large kitchen and scullery on the ground floor. They were designed and built by speculative builders at affordable prices or rents for working class family units. There were no back-to-backs.

In addition to ordinary two-storey houses with a staircase there were so-called 'double-tenanted' or 'up and downer' houses with upstairs and downstairs flats which each had a separate entrance but which shared a backyard with one or two privies. One was built above the other so that a smaller plot of land could be used than for two vertical houses. All houses were supplied with gas, water and sewerage and also with a well in the backyard, filled with rain water from drainpipes from the roof and supplying a pump over the kitchen sink. This was for 'soft' water, in contrast to the mains supply which was very, very hard. Unfortunately the pumped water, though good for the complexion and needing less soap and no washing soda, was dirty from the soot and other effluents in the local atmosphere.

Living rooms had a fireplace with an oven on one side and a water tank on the other. There might also be a separately coal-fired 'copper' for clothes washing and heating water for bathing. Upstairs there were two or three bedrooms. There were few bathrooms. According to Tommy Newton's daughter Mary, the only two were 20 Bell St. and 29 Cleveland Road. The rest either used the sink or a portable galvanised larger or smaller bath. In some of the bedrooms there were small fireplaces and gas lights consisting of flared burners, but candles in candle sticks were more often used. The living room and parlour lights had incandescent gas mantles and were therefore very well lit.

The width of streets and backstreets, like the sanitary requirements, the provision of bedrooms to keep the sexes apart, the ban on cellars or basements, the provision of a coalhouse rather than a coalhole and a backyard shed were all statutory. So, too, was the separation of house from place of work. Trades, crafts and domestic animals other than pets were forbidden and shops and workshops were confined to corner sites.

With full employment, flourishing family life and modern housing and despite the need to walk to shops, churches and schools, one may say that the Central Estate got off to a good start. According to Mrs. Jenny Robson "they were sold as fast as they were put up" and "you were lucky to get a house in Stephenson Street". According to Dr. Gibb (see below) she said: "The Central Estate was the aristocracy of the working class".(!)

Comparison with the 1881 Census of the selfsame Parish of Throston is obviously interesting. There were, indeed, some unemployed at that time. Before 1891 Warren Farm had changed hands from Stephensons to Hardys and the Cholera Hospital had changed its name to Fever Hospital and its tenant from a gardener to a caretaker. No patients - unlike the entry for the Workhouse - are named in either year. There had been a cottage at the (Old) Cemetery which may have become unoccupied. There had been 12 Railway Cottages listed between the Cemetery and Clyde Place. Demolition is not very likely to have occurred, and the 1897 map records a row of at least 8 houses between the railway embankment and the sand banks. More than half of their male inhabitants were railway workers, but as with Warren Road and Terrace there is doubt as to whether they were company-owned by the Cement Works or by the North Eastern Railway Company. Were they omitted from the 1891 census? It is most unlikely. Renaming of streets is much more probable.

In 1881 Clyde Place contained the Lord Clyde Hotel (Plate 22 p. 59), which had changed hands, and two unnumbered houses, but with one exception the names do not tally with any 1891 occupants, although this is by no means unusual. Clyde Terrace had 15 houses/households, also not numbered, and Clyde Place with 3, totalling 98 inhabitants. In 1891, however, the hotel is located in Clyde Terrace with 6 numbered houses if we include Back Clyde Terrace, which must have been adjacent, and 6 in Clyde Place. The total is 13, with 67 inhabitants.

In 1881 Warren Terrace had only 4 houses, one of which passed from father to namesake son, who followed his father's trade though only as a labourer. Cleveland Road already had 5 households, one with the same occupants and one with the same family name and place of origin. They were numbered 1 and 5.

In all this, in one sense, there was nothing novel. Urban industrialisation was now at least a century old, and working class housing and working class communities with factory-based work patterns had been created or had sprung up since the 1780s. Although facilitated by transport improvements, notably the railway, recruitment to factories had always been from far and wide. By the 1880s a working class culture of mutual aid associations (e.g. unions, friendly and cooperative societies), of characteristic political and religious affiliations, and entertainments, already existed. In another sense, because it was recruited at a particular time and in particular, if not peculiar, economic and geographical circumstances, what became the Central Estate was unique, with its own and peculiar combination of people, whose accents merged into a dialect, and whose shared experiences of work and leisure, boom, slump, war, peace - and weather - united them into a community.

Plate 18 - Throston Railway Bridge, 1967

Plate 19 - Cleveland Road Railway Bridge, 1905

Chapter 3: Central Estate 1889-1900

The Central Estate was a slow starter. There is as yet no explanation of the delay between Matthew Gray's purchase of the land in 1883, and the dating of the Plan no less than five years later in 1888. Economic circumstances may have been responsible. The beginning of construction followed in 1889 but, once started, construction was very rapid. In only eleven years from the beginning, and seven years after the Census, the Estate was more than half built.

There will be no more detailed information, household by household, until publication of the 1901 census in 2001 (and onwards at decennial intervals to the demolition and reconstruction of the 1970s and 80s in the 2070s and 80s) but meanwhile enough editions of Ward's Directories survive to offer snapshots of 1900, 1902-3, 1912-13, 1921-22, 1924-25, 1927-28, 1929-30, 1930-34 and 1935. They record only householders and their trades. The wives (or husbands), children, relatives, visitors or lodger/boarders do not appear. There are enough obvious errors, notably the disappearance of some streets for more than ten years, to cast considerable doubt on the accuracy of the survey and, as with the census, it is not clear if the entries were made by Ward's staff or compiled by them from forms filled in by householders. They might have been compiled from electoral or ratepayers' lists, or payment for inclusion may have been mandatory. Indeed, it is not clear in whose interest - apart from the publisher's and the advertisers' and posterity's - it was to publish them at all. The shops, factories, chapels and schools etc. were obviously known and had, where required, other and more direct means of advertisement in the local press and on billboards etc. Nevertheless they uniquely make available some material for a social portrait.

In 1900 there were 450 households, as compared with 1891 when there were 85: a more than fivefold increase. If the average number per household remained, as it probably did, at the 1891 level of 5, the population was now well over 2000. Assuming that those without a specified occupation were retired if male, widowed if female and of independent means if unmarried, there were 8 men, 17 widows (6) and 5 spinsters (4).

As to streets, Cleveland Road had expanded from 20 to 75 households, Clyde Place, Street and Terrace from 16 to 26, Pease Street from 4 to 9, and Watson St from 28 to 85: C. T. Watson was obviously prospering. In addition, in previously unbuilt Arch Street there were 26 households, in Bell Street 25, in Hart Road, in addition to a coal depots, the Cement Works, the Ropery, galvanising works and the Primitive Methodist Chapel, there were 37. Warren Road, Warren Terrace and Back Warren Terrace with 16 appears to have become Wilster Terrace (cement workers still) and Warren Terrace with 13. Lambton Street had 10, Stephenson Street had 51, Union Road 42 and Watt Street 36 (Household table Appendix I).

Some households continued from 1891. Robt. Ward, cement works labourer, seems to have moved from Warren Road to Clyde Place. Thomas Spence remained in Watson St. but had promoted himself from coal trimmer to shopkeeper. John Adams had progressed from shipyard labourer to coal trimmer. Granger McBeath remained a machinist. In Cleveland Rd., William Robson, trimmer, had retired and James McMahon had graduated from boilermaker to boilersmith. William Deer's 3 Clyde

Place had become 12 Clyde St and John Black, labourer's, 6 Clyde Place had become Clyde St. It is noteworthy indeed, and a comment on Ward's Directory, that in 1891 houses were numbered which appear as unnumbered in 1900. Eight survivors in nine years is impressive only as evidence of a mobile population.

None of the houses in Arch and Bell Streets were recorded as having been numbered, none in Cleveland Road, Clyde Place or Terrace, and none in Pease Street or Watt Street. All houses in Lambton Street were numbered, just over half in Watson Street, all but 6 in Hart Road, all but 14 in Union Road but only 21 in Stephenson Street. This must have been a great inconvenience to would-be callers as well as to postmen. Presumably it was the Borough Council which was laggard. It was not until 1900 that the Improvement Committee resolved that all houses should be numbered.

As to occupations and trades (Table 8 - Appendix I p. 102), in direct comparison with the 1891 census (numbers in brackets), in service employment there were still only 1 barman (although there were now 2 pubs), 4 bricklayers (2) and 1 caretaker (2), two cartmen (1), a tram conductor (1), 1 engine-man (1), 5 mariners (1), a mate and a mooring man, 3 storekeepers (1), a vanman (1), 2 watchmen (1); and 2 waitresses but no domestic servants! (6). This last statistic is notable, suggesting that the revolt from domestic service predated the First World War 1914-18. Presumably preference (snobbery?) and (relative) prosperity created other options.

In shops there were 5 butchers (2), a clothier (1) a general dealer (1), 8 grocers (1), an innkeeper as well as a publican (1), 2 lodging house keepers (1) but no longer a fishmonger, a milkman, an office boy or a seaman. Additionally there were a beer retailer, 4 bootmaker/repairers, 3 confectioners, 3 dairymen, 4 drapers, 4 dressmakers, 2 fried fish dealers, 2 fruiterers, a hairdresser, a hardwareman, a hosier, a plumber, a post officer, 5 shopkeepers, a stonemason and a watchmaker.

There were also, in service employment, a fireman and 2 policemen, one of these resident and the other a railway employee. In land transport there were 5 cranemen, 2 engine drivers, 2 guards, 2 shunters and 3 signalmen: at sea there was a marine engineer (1), 5 mariners and a mooring man.

In clerical employment there were 5 clerks (2), together with an assistant overseer, an insurance agent and a secretary. In management there were 4 builders (including R. J. Marshall and C. T. Watson), 2 managers and a manageress and no less than 12 foremen (1). At the professional level, the Cement Works now employed an analyst, and there were 2 surgeons, although they merely held surgeries in Cleveland road premises and resided elsewhere. There was still the one farmer, surprisingly now recording only one 'hind' in place of the former 4 'farm servants'. Since there was no great current improvement in agricultural productivity the others may been housed in farm buildings or elsewhere in the town. The tied cottages, which I recall, beyond the second railway arch, must have been built later.

As in service employment, so in manufacturing. The proportion of the more skilled was rising. There were 10 blacksmiths (7), 18 boilersmith (15), and 3 brass finishers (1), but only 1 cement miller in place of 4: improved technology may have increased productivity. There were 10 coal trimmers (1), 4 dressmakers (2), 4 drillers (2), 26 fitters (12), 5 forgemen (1), 11 joiners (2) and 14 machinists (4) but only 1 millwright (2). There were 16 moulders (5), 13 platers (4), 3 shipwrights (1), 8 turners (2) but only 1 wire rope maker (1).

Newcomers were 4 boatbuilders, 4 carpenters, 6 caulkers, a cooper, 3 coppersmiths, a cutter, a diesinker, an electrician, an engineman, 8 engineers,, 3 furnacemen, a galvaniser, a marker off, 9 patternmakers, a platelayer, 13 riveters, a shipsmith, a tinsmith, a teemer, a waterman and 4 wiredrawers.

The 48 labourers in 1891 were a third of the 134 service and skilled employees: 33%. In 1900 the 66 labourers were only a fifth of the 348 service and skilled employees: 19%. The increasing proportion of skilled working class and of lower middle class service employees, as they would have regarded themselves, confirms the earlier impression and also connotes social respectability. There was certainly at that time a clear distinction between 'respectable' and 'rough' working class, although not all the skilled were necessarily respectable and not all the labourers were necessarily rough.

In addition to the Cement Works (Plate 22 p. 59), the Ropery (Plate 82 p. 249) and the Creosote Works, there was only a galvanising works (by the railway arch on later Heortnesse Road) in the immediate vicinity, providing alternatives to shipyard employment - although only handfuls.

We do not know where the barman, coal merchant, the milkman, the butchers the fishmonger and the publican recorded in the 1891 census worked, and not all shop workers in 1900 can have worked on the Estate. Shopkeeping, however, flourished and the nation of shopkeepers derided by Napoleon were represented in Arch Street, which had become and remained the main shopping street, at least by the beer retailer, the bootmaker, the dairyman, the general dealer, one of the fried fish (and chips, with salt and vinegar, no doubt) dealers, the hairdresser and 2 grocers. The names of Hutchinson, Middleton and Newton will be recalled by many later inhabitants. Bell Street had a grocer and a butcher as well as R J Marshall the builder, whilst Cleveland Road housed C. T. Watson himself (Plate 38 p. 134), now the innkeeper of the Central Hotel (Plate 20 p. 58) as well as builder. Cleveland Road had also a bootmaker and a butcher, a confectioner and a draper, a fruiterer and the Post Office. Clyde Terrace had a shopkeeper and an innkeeper (the same man as in 1891), presumably of the Lord Clyde, and Hart Road a dairyman, a hay and corn dealer and a shopkeeper. Stephenson Street had a bootmaker, a butcher (Wade), dressmakers, a fruiterer and an insurance agent. Watson Street had 2 confectioners, a draper (Redshaw), the other fried fish dealer, a grocer (Banks), a lodging house, a newsagent and a shopkeeper (Spence). The 1900 total is 35. Only Lambton, Pease and Watt Streets were (as yet) shopless.

The increase of Central Estate shopping facilities was immense. In addition there may also have been 'house shops', houses whose front rooms were converted with a counter and some shelves. In later years many streets had one, some selling sweets and groceries, some cooking and selling pies and peas, pease pudding and 'ducks' (dumplings), toffee apples or toffee cake. They appear not to have sought or needed any kind of permission and the rateable value of the property may not have been affected. I am reliably informed by Mrs. Mary White (née Shires) that her mother, who opened a house-shop in Stephenson St when widowed in 1919, merely asked Mrs. Dando, already shopkeeping on the Stephenson Street/Hart road corner, if she minded. Her kindly reply was that there was enough business for both of them.

It would be interesting to know to what extent shops were planned, built on speculation, or built to order. There were examples of houses for sale and to let, whilst some prospective owners, like the G. E. Fowler who secured permission for a house in Arch St in 1899 which my parents bought in 1926, applied for permission themselves. Many if not all purchases were financed by building society mortgages. In 1895 there were no less than 5 Hartlepool 'model building societies' and that builder C. T. Watson should have been President of one of them suggests a natural alliance of interests. In 1900 Sir William Gray's widow sold a building plot to R. J. Marshall (with a restrictive covenant against the sale of alcohol) for £21/16/8 for a house to sell at £168. The 4%(!) mortgage with the Hartlepools Cooperative Society was for £145, making the cash deposit £23 or 13.7% of the purchase price. The quarterly payments were £2/5/6, i.e. 11/4d per week. Only a regularly employed skilled worker could have afforded it.

The grants or denials of permission recorded in the NDM under Improvements Committee give no more information other than the name of the applicant, usually a builder. Nearly all the shops were corner shops and the Estate was certainly full of corners: no less than 30. That shopkeeping was a desired occupation and a status symbol is not open to doubt. There was as yet no pharmacist, newsagent, pawnbroker, tobacconist(!) or undertaker. The Arch St Cooperative Society grocery and butchery shops were sanctioned in 1900.

The hairdresser's shop at the corner of Bell St and Arch St was built in 1895 by R.J. Marshall for Isaac Newton, who already had a saloon in Hartlepool, and who took out a mortgage to pay for it, for use by his nephew, Tom, then 17, whom he had trained. The shop on the opposite Arch St/Bell St corner, which became Newton Watson's the fruiterer and greengrocer, was a year later. The Newtons and Watsons were related and the latter was nephew to no less than C. T. Watson himself (Plate 38 p. 134).

The Newtons, uncle and nephew, were not merely hairdressers. On Sept 13 1900 the NDM reported:

> *The conclusion of the season for Hartlepool Swimming Club was marked last night at the breakwater by a championship race won by J. Robertson, followed by a display of ornamental swimming by Messrs A. Belk, G. W. E. Easson and T. and I. Newton. These gentlemen walked down the pier in their ordinary clothes, and then, to the consternation of the bystanders, suddenly jumped over into the water, and swam to a cable moored some distance away. Here they dived and undressed, appearing on the surface in the customary bathing attire. They then formed a ring, expansion and contraction, keel-hauling, boat-rowing, three-reel waltzing etc.*

The "Tommy" Newton I knew as a child, hairdresser, newsagent and confectioner, was a serious, rather formidable man over six feet in height who served customers with a remote, uninterested air as though preoccupied with higher things. He regarded himself as and was, in fact, a middle-class intellectual.

On August 10th 1889 the 'South Durham Herald and Stockton Journal' reported that Hartlepool Councillor M'Donald wanted suitable backyard space for clothes drying, instead of using back streets. Cllr. M'Donald may have been radical in attitude, but as an architect and surveyor as well as headmaster of Church Close Schools and a governor of the Henry Smith School, he was no mere populist agitator. He did not succeed, and all backstreets had head-height hooks outside each backdoor around which clothes lines were fastened crisscross. Backstreets took horses and carts which delivered coal etc. and collected refuse (mainly ashes), so that washing days, always Mondays, were a torment both to wives and cartmen because the washing had to be folded round and round over the washing lines for every delivery or collection (Plate 21 p. 58).

Shortly after building began in any street, the Improvement Committee would publish plans and estimates for flagging, paving, kerbing and channelling, locally known as 'streetage', and adjacent properties were charged 'apportionments'. Disputes inevitably followed and were settled by arbitration. In 1893 the average charge was £21 per site: at least £500 in 1990s terms. That there were vacant lots for many years at some street corners is simply explained by the fact that double streetage payments would have been exacted and householders, unlike shopkeepers, could not afford to pay. Consequently there were playing 'fields' galore for football and cricket, with goal posts or stumps chalked on end-house walls, for marbles, bullikers and other games. Other areas, as yet unbuilt, bordering on Cleveland and Hart Roads, were subdivided into small gardens and housed chickens, rabbits and racing pigeons as well as growing vegetables and flowers.

Gas street lamps began to be provided from 1893 onwards: initially one each in Arch and Bell Streets and in Cleveland and Union Roads. What wonderful 'bays' they made for the headquarters of street games by day as well as night, and what convenient cross bars they offered for gymnastic displays! Adjacent householders and their wives consequently waged an endless, hopeless war for quietness (Plate 26 p. 61) .

Improvements on the ground improved during the decade. I have already recorded in Chapter 1 the disputes in 1893 and 1895 between Matthew Gray and the Borough Council about manholes, smells and drain-flushing and the fact that the disputes then ceased indicates that the problems of manholes, ventilating shaft, flushings and connections to outfalls were solved. Current theories relating contemporary Throston typhoid outbreaks to privies (earth closets) doubtless helped. The NDM reported on June 8th 1893 that Councillor M'Donald said that "the stench from the drains on the Central Estate was abominable" and Councillor Gilooly added that "surely they did not have to wait until half a dozen died before attending to the drains".

Main sewers ran down the middle of the backstreets between the parallel rows of houses and the backstreets(Plate 21 p. 58) were paved with stones. The smell from the refuse destructor reported (NDM June 8,1893) was also cured by a new destructor in 1898 on the site of the old glassworks and the 'foul effluvia' from the Hart Road Artificial Manure depot received only one mention: on May 5th 1892. If it was the factory adjacent to Throston Bridge, which made manure from fish guts, it remained a nuisance for many years. Fortunately the houses in Clyde Place and Clyde Terrace were at least partially sheltered by the upwind kipper houses which, though odoriferous, not to say smelly, were much less unpleasant.

In 1891 the new iron Throston Bridge (Plate 18 p. 37), with pavements protected by railings on both sides of the road and an (iron) Gentlemen's public convenience, was erected and connected to Clyde Place with an asphalt footpath. In the same year a portion of the road to the cemetery on the sandbanks was to be macadamised, although this was only 4 years before the need for a new cemetery was announced.

By 1894 there was clear need for a Post Office and in 1895 a resident policeman was appointed. In 1897 there was even a suggestion for a 2-cell lockup but nothing seems to have been done. The recorded crime rate was low indeed. Three young persons, not necessarily from the Central Estate, damaged the graveyard in 1893, a milkman was fined for watering his milk in 1896 and there was a suicide in 1897. In that year, too, the Northern Daily Mail opened an office in Watson Street.

The Central Estate received two more and larger amenities in the 90s. The first was the Cemetery Battery. National concern for safety against possible French or German invasion led to the construction of a coastal battery of six inch guns on the land immediately east of the Old Cemetery, a gruesomely suggestive propinquity, completed in 1894. This was in addition to the battery on the Heugh (Map 7 p. 141).

On December 8th, 1892 the NDM reported that "The new battery about to be erected by the War Office on the south side of the cemetery raises a question of right of way in which the Town Council is interested. Councillor Gilooly raised the point. He said there was a door opening from the south side of the cemetery, and added it would be very inconvenient now if the right of way that the public claimed was done away with". In fact it would have doubled the distance to the graves near the wall because the only entrance was several hundred yards further from the town. "The Town Clerk is to look into the matter and report to the next meeting, a resolution to that effect having been moved by Ald. Horsley. A suggestion by Councillor Hall that a door at the opposite side of the cemetery would answer as well was disposed of by the Town Clerk saying that they had no right of way there". Presumably the Town Clerk did his best: but the right of way never materialised.

In 1896 six-inch guns were installed and, on January 7th 1897, fired, and caused enough damage to require compensation. Except to small boys it was probably an occasionally noisy nuisance, which also partially blocked access to the beach and further emphasised the proximity of the iron works' slag heap on Spion Kop and the Refuse Destructor chimney. The seaward aspect of the Estate was not improving. (Map 6 p. 140) More civilised, although much more immediately controversial, was the new pub, the Central Hotel in Cleveland Road. In 1892 the builder C. T. Watson, for whom Watson Street was named, had already been in trouble with the Borough Council for 'opening Cleveland Road without permission' (whatever that meant) and in 1893 he had tried but failed to be elected Councillor. He had, however, permission to erect the hotel and to add stabling and a cellar in September 1892 but obtaining a license at the Brewster Sessions was much more difficult (Plate 20 p. 58).

On Sept 4th 1895 the NDM reported in surprising and unusual detail, under the headline 'THE CENTRAL HOTEL', a meeting of the Licensing Committee of the Borough Council in Brewster Sessions. All but two of the members were alderman or councillors and all were presumably Justices of the Peace.

"... Mr Bell, on behalf of Mr C. T. Watson, made an application for an innkeeper's license for a house on Cleveland Road known by the sign of the Central Hotel.
Mr C. T. Watson having given formal evidence, Mr Bell addressed the justices. The last application in regard to this house, he said, was really for a provisional license, for the house was not then built. Now the house was built, and a glance at the building was sufficient to show one that the accommodation provided in it was of no inferior class. People living on the Central Estate now had to go a considerable distance for their refreshments or amusement. They did not all stay in their houses, but, like everybody else, took their own course, rightly or wrongly. Mr Watson had been told over and over again by people living in the neighbourhood that were a license granted to his house it would be the very thing that was required, since the distance from the Central Estate into the town was great and the way to the Lord Clyde objectionable. The district, moreover, was growing rapidly. Mr Bell, in conclusion, pointed out that if hotels were to be so far separated, there was a very great chance of clubs springing up, and it was, he submitted, better to have the drink under the control of the law than to have it in clubs which were not under inspection.
Mr T. H. Tilly stated he appeared to support the application on behalf of 186 inhabitant householders on the Central Estate, 11 property owners on the estate, and the owner of the estate as well.
Mr J. F. Latimer of Darlington, appeared on behalf of Messrs Spence, Andrews and Firth, owners of property on the Central Estate, to oppose the granting of the license.
Reuben Schofield was called by Mr Bell to give evidence. He stated that he had been living on the Estate for four years. He thought the house of Mr Watson would be a great benefit to the district. There were altogether 308 householders on the estate. He considered there being no licensed house nearer than the Lord Clyde a great inconvenience.
Mr Latimer: Why don't you move nearer the Lord Clyde if you feel the inconvenience?
Mr Schofield: It would not do for me to keep moving about.
Mr Thomas Place, a shopkeeper on the.Central Estate, said he had heard many complaints about the lack of a public house. It would be a great advantage to him if the license were granted, for the commercial travellers with whom he dealt would have somewhere to go when he was buying from them. It would be a benefit to the public at large.
Mr Bell was about to call a third witness when Dr. Rawlings and the Chairman remarked that they thought they had heard a sufficient number.
Mr Bell: Very well.
Dr. Rawlings went on to say that last time the license was applied for there was an engagement that an old license would be abolished.
Mr Bell: We are prepared to make the same engagement now.
Dr. Rawlings said that to his mind that was the great point in the matter. They had enough licensed premises in the borough, but a redistribution of them was doubtless desirable.
Councillor Withy: I think we were to have two licenses given up.
The Chairman: No.
Mr Latimer asked what was the name of the house to be abolished?

Mr Bell: The Blue Anchor in Hartlepool
Mr Tilly spoke a few words in favour of the granting of the license.
Mr Latimer, in opposing the granting of the license, pointed out that West Hartlepool, with double the population of Hartlepool, had 11 fewer licensed houses at the present time. He presented a petition signed by 47 of the 70 owners of property on the estate against the granting of the license.
James Andrews, who had built a house in close proximity to the house to which it was asked license might be granted, said he would not have done so had he anticipated that he might have a public house so near to his property.
Mr Henry Firth objected to the granting of the license on similar grounds.
In answer to questions by Mr Bell, Mr Firth admitted that he had a shop near a public house. He did, not, however, take so much objection to the nearness of a public house to his property in this instance.
Mr Bell: How is it that you do not mind a public house being near a shop and yet object to one being near house property?
Mr Firth: Respectable people will not live in the houses.
Mr Bell: There are no respectable people living in shops then? (Laughter)
Mr Firth: I happen to occupy it myself. (More laughter) It is a lockup shop, though.
This concluded the evidence, etc., in regard to this application.

Although there are references in the report to 'house', the building must visibly have been a public house or hotel with planning permission and it is unlikely to have been built by C. T. Watson as a pure (or impure) speculation. Indeed, as Mr Bell said, he had applied for a provisional license before building commenced. This suggests that the proceedings were largely formal, a public compliance with laws, byelaws and regulations. Temperance, however, was and long had been a social issue with massive economic, church/chapel and party-political vested interests, and the battleground was precisely that of reducing or maintaining existing licenses. This helps to account for the rival petitions, whose numbers (186 householders pro & 47 property owners con) imply wide and deep rival partisanship.

On the other hand the quality of the evidence and of the witnesses in favour was derisory. The distance to the town was a kilometre rather than a mile, and the distance to the Lord Clyde, however allegedly objectionable to a thirsty man, at most two or three hundred yards (or metres). The objectors had a better case on property values, although Bell, presumably a lawyer, scored heavily against them in laughter. It may be noteworthy that the Tilley who represented Watson's petitioners, was presumably a member of the law firm (Turnbull and Tilley) which represented Matthew Gray on the issue of the "smells on the Central Estate" in 1893. Mr Latimer was presumably hired (or volunteered) from Darlington because of his commitment to the temperance cause. Mr Bell was the Hartlepool Town Clerk. C. T. Watson was presumably well connected to be so loftily represented.

Of the committee members and witnesses mentioned, a T. Place, marine engineman, now shopkeeper (pro) and a T. Spence, coal trimmer, (con) may have been identical with residents from 1891. By 1900, apart from C. T. Watson himself, only R(euben?) Schofield, a moulder from Watson Street, and T. Spence, now also a shopkeeper, may also have been identical. There was an F. R. Spence, a barman, an unlikely objector, and no less than three other R. Spences, coopers and blacksmiths, both thirstier occupations than shopkeeping. Some at least of the property owners were nonresident.

Two months later - a long delay - on November 6th, 1895 the NDM reported "The Decision of the Magistrates".

> *"At Hartlepool Petty Sessions today, the question of the confirmation of the license granted by the licensing Justices to Mr C. T. Watson... came up for consideration for the third time... Very considerable interest was evinced in the matter, the Court being crowded to its utmost capacity. Mr H. W. Bell appeared on behalf of Mr C. T. Watson; Mr Latimer of Darlington for Mr Firth and other property owners on the estate; and Mr J. Strover on behalf of Mr Matthew Gray, the owner of the estate.*
> *Mr Watson gave formal evidence. He further said that he was the owner of 53 houses on the estate...*
> *Mr Latimer: You have offered to give up the license of the Blue Anchor?*
> *Mr Watson: Yes. I can close the Blue Anchor in an hour's time if the license is confirmed.*
> *Is the Blue Anchor your property? - No.*
> *Your purchase of the Blue Anchor is conditional on your getting the license? Yes, certainly.*
> *Who is the owner of the property? Colonel Cameron.*
> *What did you agree to give in return? £700 for the Blue Anchor.*
> *Nothing beyond that? No.*
> *Do you mean to say that the owners of the Blue Anchor are going to sell the property to you if you get another license? Yes.*
> *Reuben Schofield gave evidence in support.*
> *Mr Latimer: You seem to have taken a good deal of interest in this matter. Have you received any remuneration?*
> *Reuben Schofield: I answered the question last time - none.*
> *Who has asked you to go around with the petition which has been put in. No one.*
> *Who wrote that petition: I did.*
> *And you signed it? Yes.*
> *Is this (pointing to the petition) your writing? Yes.*
> *Mr Latimer: I will put that in for your worships' notice.*
> *Mr Bell: The petition has already been put in. Mr Bell re-examining witness:*
> *You take a little interest in public matters? Yes.*
> *And you considered you were taking interest in a public matter by getting up the petition? Yes.*
> *Mr Strover stated that he appeared to support the application on behalf of Mr Matthew Gray, the owner of the estate.*
> *Mr Latimer objected to Mr Strover taking any part in the matter. He considered it a most improper course.*

The Magistrates decided to hear Mr Strover.

Mr Strover briefly stated that Mr Gray requested that the license should be confirmed.

Mr Latimer then addressed the Court. He put in a petition against the granting of the license signed by 47 of the 70 owners of property on the estate. He also put in a memorial signed by Sir William Gray who as the head of a firm who were large employers of labour in the vicinity of the Central Hotel believed that the granting of the license would result in positive injury to the interests of both the workmen and the firm, and prayed that the license might not be confirmed.

The reading of this memorial was received with applause.

Mr Latimer further put in petitions against the license signed by 544 members of Nonconformist churches, 77 office-bearers in Nonconformist churches, Messrs Mowbray and Macfarlane, Mr Waites and Mr Fox.

The Bench then retired. On returning after a short time, The Mayor said that he had to announce that the bench decided that the license be not confirmed. (Applause.)

Mr Latimer made an application for his costs, but the Magistrates decided that they would not allow the costs.

On the previous occasion the Bench had numbered 6. This time it was no less than 14. This was apparently a cause célèbre. The magistrates included Otto Trechmann, the owner of the Cement Works, and ex-mayor Ald. Rowe, formerly a grocer in Arch Street who went on to become a wine & spirits merchant in Hartlepool (and who sold "Special Adore" Whisky, 9 yrs. old at 3/6d per bottle). He may have had at least a fellow-feeling for Mr Watson. This time, however, the honours went to Mr Latimer of Darlington. He won a trick by eliciting from Mr Watson that he was prepared to pay Col. Cameron, the owner of the local brewery no less than £700 (now something like £42,000) for the license of the Blue Anchor which he would close in favour of the Central Hotel. He trumped the backing of C. T. Watson's Matthew Gray, the owner of the estate, with the veto of no less than Sir William Gray himself, the owner of the shipyard and the Central Marine Engineering Works and Matthew's father to boot. Here indeed was a breakdown of either family communications, family principles, or both. How could it be resolved?

The answer was instantaneous. On the following day, November 27th, the NDM editor published this letter:

> *Dear Sir, - I was not present at the Hartlepool Borough Court this morning… and consequently am indebted to the local press for a knowledge of what transpired. Will you kindly allow me to state that until I read the Mail this morning, I was totally unaware that I had been professionally represented, and I may add that I have had no communication, either verbally or in writing with anyone interested in the granting of a license or contrariwise. The somewhat unwarranted use of my name therefore comes upon me in the nature of a surprise. It must be obvious to all that I would never contemplate opposing a memorial signed by Sir Wm. Gray in the interests of works with which I am also largely connected. I have never interfered in matters of this kind and I should not dream of ever endeavouring to influence the decision of a local licensing bench, as the magistrates must of necessity know better than I can possibly do what are and what are not the requirements of a particular district. Yours Truly, M. Gray.*

Was someone being economical with the truth? It is scarcely credible that Mr Strover should have misunderstood his brief. Matthew Gray's filial piety and appetite for humble pie did him credit but as the owner of the Estate he not only knew C. T. Watson and his plans, but through Mr Tilley had announced his support for the license at the September hearing in precisely the same words as Mr Strover.

A lively correspondence followed in the columns of the NDM with rival statistics on the number of petitionary signatories and what the answer would and should have been if powers of local veto over licences had been vested in voters and not magistrates. Reuben Schofield, the petitioner in favour of the pub, had the better of the numerical argument if he had truly polled 202 out of 312 occupiers and 32 owners, an even larger vote than the 186 and 12 quoted by Mr Tilley. On the other hand his adversary W. Armstrong (of Hartlepool, not the Estate), who counted only owners, not occupants in his figures, scored a palpable hit in his concluding paragraph:

> *... I maintain too, sir, that to transfer the license from the Blue Anchor is virtually the granting of a new license. For it is a well-known fact that the Blue Anchor is not a paying concern. If there had been an offer to transfer the license from one of the Northgate Hotels (say Councillor Derry's) to the Central Hotel, then I grant you there would have been some reason in it. But as it is it is like the giving of a dead horse for a living one...*

If this were true, then the brewery owner, Col. Cameron, (who also owned the Lord Clyde) was selling the dead horse for £700!

On Monday December 2nd 1895 Messrs Turnbull and Tilley, not mentioned at the second hearing, revealed an interesting detail.

> *SIR - Our instructions were to appear for thirty two owners of property on the Central Estate exclusive of Mr Watson, and for 212 inhabitant householders (inclusive of owners) on the estate, in favour of the confirmation of the license, and this we did. In addition to this we were instructed that at a previous Brewster Sessions property owners on the estate had given evidence that they bought their sites from Major Gray on the express condition that no license would be permitted on the estate, and that they hinted that Major Gray was breaking faith with them. This we were in a position and were authorised to contradict, and further our representative should not have committed Major Gray.*
> *Mr Watson was not and is not precluded under his contract with Major Gray from holding a license in respect of the property for which the application was made. We shall be glad if you will publish this letter in your next issue. - Your obedient servants, TURNBULL and TILLEY.*

So Mr Strover was a member of the Turnbull and Tilley firm employed by Matthew Gray, and it was he who took the blame. Who was being economical with the truth between the property owners and Major Gray is not determinable from available evidence, but for a leading local businessman the Major was either remarkably careless and forgetful or remarkably naive.

Before the issue of the Central Hotel license was settled, a similar issue arose. On September 1st 1896, a year after Mr Watson's second application, the NDM reported:

> *Mr M. Harrison applied on behalf of Mr J. W. S. Hayes for a "beer off". He said that the applicant was the oldest, or second oldest, resident on the Central Estate.*

He had the branch Post Office but this would be partitioned off from the other part if the license were granted. The house was quite distant from the Lord Clyde Hotel and from a house to which an off-license was some time ago granted... He had gone amongst his neighbours in the district to see what were the views and feelings of the locality on the matter and he had obtained a memorial signed by them in favour of the granting of the license...

Mr Hayes then gave evidence. He stated that his shop was 400 yards *(366 metres)* from the Lord Clyde and 300 yards *(274 metres)* from the house holding the off-license *(on the corner of Arch and Stephenson Streets: Mrs. Middleton)*. He put in the memorial, offering it as evidence of the views of the residents in the vicinity.

Mr Latimer objected to the memorial being put in unless the signatures were proved.

The Mayor asked the applicant how he was going to partition off the part of his premises used for postal business.

Mr Hayes replied that he would either use the back kitchen for the beer business or else make structural alterations in the shop. He would make the arrangements the police considered most satisfactory.

Mr Latimer then rose to speak in opposition to the granting of the license. The proposition, he pointed out in the first place, was in respect to the shop: not to the back kitchen at all. In the second place, he submitted that the shop being used as a post office, it was not a desirable place for an off-license. This was undoubtedly a question for the postal authorities, but at the same time it was one for their worships to consider.

Mr Harrison at this point asked for whom Mr Latimer might be appearing.

Mr Latimer replied that he was instructed by Mr Firth, a ratepayer in the town and an owner of property on the Central Estate. In conclusion he submitted that the Lord Clyde and the other off-license house were amply sufficient to supply the legitimate wants of the district.

The Rev. Harvey Field said he wished to object as a ratepayer.

The Justices refused to grant the license...

Like Mr Watson, Mr Hayes was rather unrealistic in his estimate of the walking capacity of the thirsty. An off-license and a pub were, reasonably, enough for 500 people living within 500 yards. Mr Latimer, the Darlington solicitor, who appeared to specialise in the profession of kill-joy, nevertheless had a point and was also right about the incompatibility of post office and beer in the climate of 1895, as indeed it apparently continues to be. As on previous occasions, the Lord Clyde was not represented, nor on this occasion, was the off-licensee. They must have been interested but may have been dissuaded by their employers, including Col. Cameron in the case of the Lord Clyde. The Rev. H. Field, presumably Nonconformist , was not a local resident.

Another year later, on September 1st 1897 the NDM reported:

The annual Brewster Sessions of the Borough of Hartlepool was held today... The Court -room was crowded, the greatest interest being felt in the application which was to be made in respect to the Central Hotel by Mr Watson. The various contending interests were well represented. Amongst those present were Mr T. Tweddell, JP, Ald. Kirby, Mr Thompson, a large contingent of publicans and the owners of li-

censed houses; also the following members of the Free Church Council: the Rev. H. Field, the Rev. G. G. Nicholson, Mr H. T. Lee (Secretary), M E. Oliver, Mr S. Buck, Mr D. Mitchell, Mr J. Ainsley, Mr H. Firth, and Miss Greenshields…
Mr Bell appeared on behalf of the applicant.
Mr Watson gave formal evidence. He had 66 houses of his own on the Central Estate and he was building 17 more now. He put in a petition signed, he said, by residents on the Central Estate.
Mr Latimer (Darlington) in cross examining Mr Watson asked, When did you first make your application for this license?
Mr Watson: Four or five years ago.
And your application has been made continuously from that time? No.
I believe you omitted last year? Yes.
How was it there was no application last year? Well, I did not get my notice in on time.
Is that your sole reason? My sole reason.
Are you not aware that there is an Adjourned Session, at which you could have made application? Yes.
Why didn't you enter your application then? I think the first Sessions are the best.
I believe there is already some accommodation on this estate as regards licensed premises? Not that I am aware of.
There is the Lord Clyde for instance?
That is not on the Central Estate.
Mr Latimer, proceeding, asked various questions about the distance of the Lord Clyde from Mr Watson's proposed hotel, a beer house on the estate, etc.
Alderman White, however, interrupted, intimating that he did not see the necessity for these points to be gone into. They had, he said, had all these points before them again and again, and he thought that the proper thing to do was to put to the vote the question of whether or not the license should be granted, at once, and not sit there.
Mr Latimer replied that they must have evidence before they could sit on the case, and he was entitled to ask the questions he was putting to the applicant.
The Justices decided to go on with the hearing and Ald. White got up a moment later and retired.
On the justices retiring, the MAYOR said: I have to announce that the Licensing Committee decided to decline the application for the place that was proposed to be called the Central Hotel, and in doing so I want to mention to Mr Watson that the decision may have been influenced by the fact that he has not made the same offer this time that he did before, of giving up another full license in the town.
In any case, that is the decision, that the license be not granted.

So C. T. Watson was a landlord as well as builder and would-be innkeeper. It is not likely that any other landlord had anywhere near 83 houses and he was in a sense succeeding Matthew Gray as owner of the estate. It is clear that he was a man of parts if not of stature and it is consequently difficult to credit, unless he had too many other irons in the fire, that he had forgotten to apply in the previous year or was ill-informed about Adjourned Brewster Sessions. He may well have been advised or judged that impatience might be counterproductive. His failure to offer an old license in exchange is also strange but can hardly have been mere carelessness. That the issue was locally regarded as one of substance is obvious from the turnout and it must have contributed to the growth of a Central Estate consciousness and sense of identity. If C. T. Watson was right the Estate did *not* include the Lord Clyde.

A month later on September 28th 1897 the NDM reported yet again.

> *The adjourned Brewster Sessions were held at Hartlepool today. There were two applications for new licenses as follows:*
> *John William Sigger Hayes, application for an off beer license to premises situated at the corner of Cleveland Road and Pease Street.*
> *Charles Thomas Watson, application for an innkeeper's license to premises known as the Central Hotel in Cleveland Road.*
> *The members of the Licensing Committee present were Ald. White (in the chair), Dr. Rawlings, ex-Ald. Black, Ald. Horsley, Ald. Rowe and Councillor Withy. The other member of the committee (the mayor) was not present.*
> *There were a number of magistrates on the Bench during the hearing of the application. There were Ald. Sir Thomas Richardson, Ald. Hunter, ex-Ald. Graham, Councillor Yeoman, Councillor Foxton, Councillor Murray, Mr J. Pinder and Mr Trechmann. Amongst those present in the Court were the Revs C. W. Vaughan, R. Shields, Walton Armstrong and G. C. Nicholson, Mr E. Oliver etc.*
> *Mr HARRISON made the application on behalf of Mr Hayes, who, he said, had been for 20 years a trimmer, and during the same period had also carried on grocery business in Hermit Street. For the past five years he had occupied the house and shop in respect of which he was making the application. It belonged to him. Mr Hayes, he added, had considerably improved the house since he made his application at the last licensing sessions.*
> *Mr Hayes, in evidence, stated he had a sub-post office attached to these premises.*
> *Mr Latimer, solicitor, Darlington, who opposed on behalf of Mr Spence and others, asked: Are you aware that the Postmaster objects to licensed premises at post offices?*
> *Mr Hayes: It may be so.*
> *Mr Latimer: What are you going to do then?*
> *Mr Hayes: I could do without the post office if I got the license.*
> *Mr Latimer: Oh, if you could get a license you would give up the post office?*
> *Mr Hayes: Yes.*
> *MR HARRISON: There are plenty of other suitable places for a post office?*
> *Mr Hayes: Yes.*
> *Mr Watson then submitted his application. Having given formal evidence as to the posting of the notices, etc., Mr Watson, referring to what was said at the annual licensing day, handed in a slip of paper on which, he said, were the names of two houses, either of which he was in a position to close if the license for the Central Hotel were granted.*
> *Ald. HORSLEY (reading): The Blue Anchor and the Railway Tavern. Ald Horsley asked Mr Watson if he proposed to keep the house a free house.*
> *Mr Watson: Yes; buy my beer and spirits wherever I mind.*
> *Ald. HORSLEY asked the Magistrates Clerk (Mr Belk) if the Justices could not insert a condition in the license to the effect that the house should remain a free house.*
> *The CLERK replied in the negative.*
> *Ald. HORSLEY stated that should the house ever become a tied house he would object to the renewal of the license should it ever be granted.*
> *Mr Watson: I intend to keep it a free house.*

Councillor WITHY, referring to the licenses Mr Watson was offering, said they should have three such as they had given up.
Mr Latimer then proceeded to cross-examine Mr Watson. In reply to his opening questions, Mr Watson said he was prepared to give up either one or the other of the houses named.
Mr Latimer: Are you the owner of these properties? No.
Mr Latimer: Then you are not in a position to give them up?
Mr Watson: Yes I am: by a private arrangement of mine.
Mr Latimer: What is the private arrangement?
Mr Watson: I am not disposed to divulge it. I have given the Bench a guarantee to give up either the one or the other of these houses, and that the house will be free.
Mr Latimer: But I want to know what this arrangement is.
Mr Watson: And I decline to tell you.
Mr LATIMER (appealing to the Bench): I ask for an answer to my question.
Ald. HORSLEY: The Bench are satisfied that Mr Watson will give up one of these houses.
Mr LATIMER: But your Worships cannot be satisfied?
Ald. HORSLEY: Excuse me, we are satisfied.
Mr LATIMER: Mr Watson says he is not the owner of these houses, and unless he is not in a position to give them up.
Dr. RAWLINGS: He cannot open the other house until he has given up one of these, so it is broad as it is long.
In answer to further questions by Mr Latimer, Mr Watson stated that the Blue Anchor was in Sandwell Chase and the Railway Tavern in Bond Street.
Mr LATIMER: What do you consider is the value of the Blue Anchor?
Mr Watson: I don't know.
What is your own idea? - I don't know. I never went through it.
Can you not give us a rough estimate? - I cannot.
Can you give us an estimate of the value of the Railway Tavern? - No, I cannot.
Are they premises in any way the same quality as the Central Hotel? - They are not so modern.
Do you consider them anything so valuable?
Ald. HORSLEY: We know all the premises.
Mr LATIMER: I must get these facts.
Ald. WHITE: We know all about it. We've had it trailed over and over again.
Mr LATIMER: We have had these offers made before.
Ald. HORSLEY: Don't keep us sitting here all day. We know all the circumstances surrounding the case. We know better than you know.
The Justices were preparing to leave the Bench, but Mr LATIMER said: I am going to take a technical objection. Several of the Justices still continued to make their way towards the retiring-room, but Ald. ROWE observed that they should hear what Mr Latimer had to say.
Ald. HORSLEY: Get your technical objection in.
Mr LATIMER: I am going to put it in now. Mr Latimer then proceeded to refer to a section of the Act having reference to the removal of a license from one house to another, and pointed out that they had not before them any person to say that it was not proposed to apply for a renewal of the licenses which Mr Watson offered to give up.

Dr. RAWLINGS: You are never satisfied with anything at all. (Laughter)...
Mr LATIMER concluded by putting in a petition signed by 284 residents upon the Central Estate, and another signed by 54 property owners on the estate - both in opposition to the granting of the application.
THE DECISION
On the Justices returning after a brief retirement to the retiring-room, Ald. WHITE announced that Mr Hayes's application was declined. The Justices had decided to accept Mr Watson's offer of the Blue Anchor, and his application would be granted on the understanding that the house was closed.

Mr Hayes was an enterprising man. To be a trimmer was to crawl about in the hold of a ship shovelling coal newly tipped from the staiths so that the vessel resumed an even keel (which the fall of the coal from railway wagons above on one side of the ship inevitably disturbed). It was a dusty, dirty job from which the trimmer returned home as much in need of a bath as a miner. To have been at the same time a grocer argues hygienic versatility at least, for Hermit Street can scarcely have run to bathrooms. To have aspired to run postmastership in parallel with beer-retailing or to get the beer license by abolishing the post office counter when there was already an off-license two streets away, however, argues extraordinary, not to say daft, optimism. One hopes in retrospect that he did not lose too much money on the improvements he had commissioned. Perhaps C. T. Watson the builder had done them on the cheap.

C. T. Watson, the would-be innkeeper, was harder headed, with two licenses, not one, up his sleeve, and obliging readiness to run a free rather than a tied (to a brewery) house. He did not own the two pubs, had no idea what they were worth and would not divulge how, therefore, he could give a license up. Mr Latimer had much the better of the arguments, and the number of his petitioners had jumped by over 100: but the Bench was clearly and emphatically not on his side. Had Mr Latimer objected that Aldermen White and Horsley and Dr. Rawlings appeared to be somewhat partisan he would have been right. Justice may have been done but was certainly not seen to have been done. The audience, however, had undoubtedly been dramatically and forensically entertained. If thirsty they could then have adjourned to the Lord Clyde - to Col. Cameron's profit.

Even yet the entertainment was not concluded. On October 9th 1897 'INTERESTED' informed the Editor of the NDM that:

... Three years ago the worthy Ald (J) Horsley) himself elicited from Mr Watson the statement that the Blue Anchor, then as now offered in exchange for the new license, was to be closed on condition that he purchased from the owner (Colonel Cameron) as much beer as the Blue Anchor had been selling. This was certainly parting with some of the freedom, and as the value of licenses has since gone up greatly, the conclusion must now be at least as onerous, probably much more so...
... the public will naturally infer that one 'tied house' is to be replaced with another...

On October 12th, 1897 the NDM reported the end of the affair. Messrs Watson and Latimer resumed the dialogue: the same question about the arrangement with the Blue Anchor, and the same answer, that it would not be explained. Watson now admitted that he had formerly agreed to buy the same quantity of beer as the Blue Anchor from Camerons. 'INTERESTED' was well informed. The Mayor intervened and repeated the questions. Watson replied that the owner (but not the tenant) agreed that he could close the Blue Anchor and that there was no tie. Latimer continued to argue that it was a removal rather than a grant of license, that a license did not differentiate between free and tied houses, and that he was not satisfied because he represented property owners on the Estate who considered that the value of their houses would depreciate. He presented yet another petition, this time of 270 residents, and still another from employers. Watson countered with 544 residents in favour. The population of the Estate must have been expanding very fast.

Thus after five years of uncertainty, real or pretended, C. T. Watson won and "this announcement was received with some considerable applause in the body of the Court, which, however, was promptly suppressed". His persistence was well rewarded. In that very same year of 1897 there was a gold rush at Klondyke in the Yukon Territory in Alaska, and some time later the Central Hotel was nicknamed 'The Klondyke'. I never heard it otherwise named and am confident that the nickname was not ironic. It flourished until it was demolished in 1981 (Plate 20 p. 58).

It was not only as a resident, builder and innkeeper on the Central Estate that C. T. Watson was celebrated. In 1895 he became President of the 5th Hartlepool Model Building Society and in 1897 his civic worthiness was marked by appointment to the Hart Road School Board and in 1898 he acted as a leading citizen. The NDM headline of September 8th read:

A BLOCKED FOOTPATH

A deputation, headed by Mr C. T. Watson waited upon the Council in reference to the footpath leading from the Central Estate to the Central Marine Engine Works which was some time ago blocked up by the Railway Company. Mr Watson, who was spokesman of the deputation said the property owners and residents on the C. E. wished to ask the council to assist them in asserting their rights in the matter. The blocking up of the footpath had made it easier for people to come from West Hartlepool to Hartlepool to the different works than from the Central Estate which in reality was in the closest proximity to those works. The footpath, too, had been in existence for more than 50 years past. Of this fact they had proof from the recollection of people still living in the place, and furthermore the footpath was shown a properly delineated footpath on the Ordnance Maps of the last 53 years. Mr Watson said that no party could, as they knew, close a road that had been in use for 50 years, without first posting notices all along that road to the effect that it would be closed. The Railway Company had not seen fit to do this, but had taken the matter into their own hands. As a proof that they knew they were in the wrong the Railway Company would not, Mr Watson proceeded, take action and prosecute anyone for trespassing. Mr Watson further added that one old gentleman had died very suddenly from the exertion of getting over the fence that had been put up. Mr Watson, urging again that the assistance of the Town Council might be given on their side, said there were surely means of giving ready access to the Central Estate. It was a growing part of the borough - the only way in which the borough could grow.

A footbridge was suggested and a committee appointed.

Charles Thomas Watson, who had come to Hartlepool in 1889 from Musselburgh near Edinburgh, went on to become a Councillor in 1905 and Mayor 1917-1919. He died at the age of 91 in 1941 and his NDM obituary says that he was an early builder on the Central Estate when "few people had faith in the possibilities there". I regret not having known him: he had ceased to live in Cleveland Road before my time: and although my grandfather was a habitué (13 pints a night, it was said) I was reared teetotal.

In addition to local amenities, there were notable improvements in both neighbouring towns. From 1889 Central Estaters could stroll on the newly completed Hartlepool Promenade (Plate 23 p. 60), opened on Sept 28th by Lord Londonderry, and, from 1891, enjoy concerts and other entertainments at the bandstand on the amphitheatre (Plate 24 p. 60) below the Town Moor. The bandstand was the gift of the Hartlepools' new MP Christopher Furness, who had just defeated Sir William Gray at the polls. At the opening Mr Furness hoped that the spirit of harmony would henceforth prevail between the two towns! Whether Sunday concerts should be of sacred music only was controversial for a time. The verse about Hartlepool printed by the South Durham and Cleveland Mercury on February 14 1891 was witty and might have been prompted by the collapse into the sea of the Elephant Rock (Plate 25 p. 61), Hartlepool's only natural landmark, which the Borough Council had failed to save. Otherwise it was ironic to say:

> *"There is nothing striking in this dreary place*
> *Except the smacks upon the ocean's face".*

Smacks were fishing boats and were visible at any time, but Wombwell and Bailey's Circus and Murphy's steam roundabout visited Hartlepool in 1891 and the Hartlepool Regatta was revived after 17 years in 1892. From 1896 Estaters could travel to Hartlepool or West on electric trams: the steam trams had ceased in 1891. The improvement in public transport must have been palpable indeed. To travel to West Hartlepool by public transport it was no longer necessary to walk down to Hartlepool Station first. In 1900 the Tram Sheds, also a power-station, at Greenland were built, almost on the West Hartlepool boundary.

In 1894 Central Estaters could have seen cinema films on at least one occasion and, from 1898, have worshipped at the new St Oswald's Church, walked in the new Burn Valley Gardens and, from 1899, dined in the Grand Hotel, also by James Garry (Plate 11 p. 24) and enjoyed more concerts (probably by the same brass bands) at the new bandstand in Ward Jackson Park, all in West Hartlepool. Perhaps even better, from April 2nd 1894 Primitive Methodists could worship in their own Hart Road ('Little') Chapel which celebrated its Sunday School Anniversary as early as April 22nd in the same year and acquired a new harmonium two years later. From February 3rd 1896 Protestant children could be taught in their own Hart Road School (Plate 26 p. 61), built to accommodate 250 boys, girls and infants. The savings in shoe leather and legwear both on weekdays and Sundays for adults and children must have been considerable.

There was also a myriad of societies they could join, witness the adverts and reports in the NDM. If soberly inclined they could join the Rechabites or Sons of Temperance, and if also prepared to forswear smoking, the Templars too. The Temperance

Hall offered Pleasant Saturday Evenings. The Foresters and Buffaloes and other Friendly Societies for mutual aid in sickness and unemployment, were presumably more convivial and for the more culturally ambitious there were University Extension Lectures as well as Amateur Orchestral, Philharmonic Societies and a Music Club. For gardeners there was a Chrysanthemum Society and for rabbit fanciers an annual show. In West Hartlepool the opening of the Empire in 1899 meant that there were no less than four theatres. There were churches and chapels of every denomination and it is interestingly curious that only the nonconformists advertised their services in the NDM.

The fact that the Liberal Sir Christopher Furness (a shipowner) defeated the sitting Unionist MP, Sir Thomas Richardson (a shipbuilder) in the Khaki Election of 1900 (Plate 32 p. 111), emphatically against the national trend of enthusiasm for the appearance of victory in the second year of the Boer War, presumably owed something to the Trades and Labour Councils, respectively of trade unionists and their political allies.

In 1899 the Borough Council decided that ten boys per year from elementary schools should have scholarships to the Henry Smith (Grammar) School "to ascend the educational ladder... to university". This was the modest beginning of which, as will be seen, many Central Estate children later took advantage (Plate 27 p. 62).

Before the end of the century two of the founding fathers of the Central Estate had died. The first, surprisingly, was Matthew Gray himself who died on June 16th 1896 at the age of only 41. His father Sir William survived him only until Sept 12th, 1898, but was 76. The Central Estate, now beginning to flourish as a community, was in some sense a memorial to both.

Plate 20 - Central Hotel ("Klondyke") after the Great Fire Jan 4 1922

Plate 21 - Hart Road Backlane c. 1970

Plate 22 - Funeral passing Warren Cement Works, Hart Road, 1915
Clyde Terrace and the Lord Clyde Hotel (arched) beyond the sheds.

Plate 23 - Hartlepool Promenade, 1930s

Cannon on the right is "A Trophy from Sebastopol" from the Crimean War 1854-6

Plate 24 - Ampitheatre and Bandstand, Hartlepool Promenade, 1904

Plate 25 - Elephant Rock, c1885
It collapsed during a storm on May 10 1891.
The remaining stump is opposite the bandstand.

Plate 26 - Hart Road School, 1923

Plate 27 - George Colley picture of Henry Smith School c. 1935

Chapter 4: Central Estate 1900-1904

From the 1902-03 edition of Ward's Directory we learn that the number of Central Estate households increased by 86 from 451 to 537, that is to say by a fifth in only two years, to over 2500 people. Of these 8 were retired men (cf.8), 28 were widows (cf.18) and 3 unmarried women (cf.5) (spinsters) The increase was helter-skelter. So, too, was the rate of changed occupancies. Of the 451 households of 1900 only 208 remained, a turnover of 40% in only two years. The rate of turnover, however, varied dramatically between streets. Clyde Street and Terrace had become remarkably stable with four fifths of the householders unchanged, whereas all but one had changed between 1891 and 1900. Lambton Street had three fifths, Watt St. two thirds, and Arch Street, Stephenson Street and Hart Road a half or near it. In sharp contrast, Bell Street and Union and Cleveland Roads retained only a third, and Pease Street a mere fifth of their 1900 inhabitants. Later comparisons may suggest reasons for turnover, other than cheaper rents or earlier completion. It is certainly not self-evident why Watt St, for instance, should have generated greater loyalty than Bell St. Visually there was very little, if any, difference (Households Table Appendix I p. 291).

Since 1900 Arch Street had almost doubled its number of houses to 48 and Beaumont Street now had all its four houses occupied. Bell Street had added 2 to its 25 houses, Cleveland Road 3 to its 74 and Hart Road 16 to its 53. Clyde Place and Clyde Street were full and stable at 19 each, as was Lambton Street with 10. Pease Street had 3 more added to its 9, Stephenson Street 7 to its 51, Union Road 6 to its 42, Watson Street 17 to its 85, and Watt Street 1 to its 36. All streets were fully numbered. Rokeby Street, tangential to Hart Road, began the projection of the Estate towards the railway embankment (Map 6 p. 140).

Some occupations had disappeared from the Estate. There were no longer in residence a cutter, a domestic servant or a waitress, an electrician, a farm servant, a grocer's asst., a hosier, a manageress, a marine engineer, a marker off, a platelayer, a printer or a tram conductor (Occupations Table Appendix I p. 291).

On the service side at the labouring level there were new occupations: a coke drawer, a horsekeeper, a laundress, a mooring man, a steward, a timekeeper and a weighman. More skilled services were newly represented by a compositor and a lithographer, an insurance superintendent, a newsagent, a tailor and 3 tramdrivers. An electrical engineer may have been of professional standing. There were still an assistant overseer, a caretaker, 2 cartmen, a cashier, a mate, a plumber, a policeman and a police sergeant, a post office(r), a secretary, 2 shunters, a vanman, a waterman; and 2 surgeons. There were 1 more barmen (2), 2 more clerks (7), 3 more managers (5), 1 more signalmen (2), 2 more storekeepers (5), 1 more teemer (2) There were 1 less cranemen (3), 1 less mariner (4) and 1 less watchmen (1).

There were still a beer retailer, a hairdresser, a hardwareman and a watchmaker; 1 more bootmakers (5), clothiers (2) and grocers (7); 2 more butchers (7) and 4 more shopkeepers (9); still 2 fried fish dealers, 2 fruiterers and 3 confectioners; but 1 less dressmakers, 2 less dairymen (1) and 3 less drapers.

In skilled labour, fitters were stable at 26, joiners at 11, blacksmiths at 10, engineers at 8, bricklayers at 4, shipsmiths, tinsmiths and wire rope makers at 1. Boilersmiths increased by a third (18 to 27), brass finishers rose from 3 to 5, coopers 1-2, coppersmiths 3-5, machinists 14-16, millwrights 1-3, moulders 16-26 (one brass), platers 13-16, rivetters 13-21, shipwrights 3-13, wiredrawers 4-5. There were 1 less boatbuilders (3), 2 less builders (2), 2 less carpenters (4-2), 3 less caulkers (6), 4 less foremen (8), 2 less patternmakers ((7) and 2 less turners (7).

Unskilled labourers rose from 66 to 89, from the one fifth of 1900 to one seventh. The Central Estate was becoming more and more skilled, with a wider range of occupations and a decreasing proportion of unskilled labour. The large increases of boilersmiths, moulders and shipwrights etc. emphasised the predominance of shipbuilding as an occupation and way of life. This homogeneity of employment must have promoted the senses of affinity and community, however disparate places of birth may have been. Experiences - and grievances - must have been exchanged in the walks to and from work and in street, shop and pub conversations.

After the Central Hotel licensing controversy, it was the rather more serious subject of housing on the Central Estate which next hit the local headlines. In March 1899 Hartlepool Corporation petitioned against a North-Eastern Railway (henceforward NER) Bill to acquire land between Hart and Cleveland Roads for timber ponds and timber stacks for pit props. Not only would the stagnant ponds be a health threat and the stacks harbour vermin: the one direction in which already overcrowded and unhealthy Hartlepool could expand would be blocked. On Thursday March 16th 1899 the NDM reported:

THE CENTRAL ESTATE
PUBLIC PROTEST AGAINST N.E.R. TIMBER PONDS

> *A public meeting was held last night in Arch Street, Central Estate, to protest against the N.E.R. Bill to turn that part of the Central Estate beyond Union-street (sic) into timber ponds. The meeting was well attended, Mr Dodsworth being in the chair. The following committee was elected to draw up a petition for signature to the Corporation: Councillors Gardiner and Davis, Messrs Marshall, C. T. Watson, C. Lund, Wray, G. Davison, Birch, W. Powell, Pennen, J. Davidson, W. Kydd, G. Satchell, T. N. Wilkinson, A. Matthieson, A.Clarke, W. Clitheroe, T. Smith, R.Unthank, J. W. Fana, H. Taylor and R. Grant.*

It can only have been an open air meeting in the twilight but Messrs Marshall and Watson, the two builders, are noticeably present as is the W. Clitheroe who organised the petition in favour of the Central Hotel. Councillors apart, most were local residents. Unfortunately the committee makes no further appearance in the NDM, although its aims were partially achieved.

The NER plea to the Committee of the House of Lords (on May 12,1899) was that existing timber accommodation was exhausted and that the land was marshy and unfit for building. The Mayor of Hartlepool, Ald. Horsley, who was accompanied and supported by the MP, Sir Thomas Richardson, repeating the case for housing, made an interesting revelation:

> *... The Corporation had already negotiated, first for the whole of the land proposed to be taken, and then for part. The negotiations were not completed, because a lady, who*

had a life interest in the estate would not sign the agreement. It was expected, however, that in a very short time she would give way...

The lady was presumably Mrs. Matthew Gray, who stood to gain in any case, but as with the Arch Street Committee she makes no further appearance in the press.

Social class prejudice was skilfully exploited by R.J. Marshall, the builder, whose popularity presumably profited. He said that he considered the land fit for building and that timber stocks on the land would be detrimental to the Central Estate.

Asked by Mr PEMBER (cross-examining for the NER)

... why he thought timber an objectionable thing to have near a house, he replied by asking learned Counsel whether he would like to have a stock of timber put in front of his windows.

Mr PEMBER said that personally he would not, but he thought that a working-man might not be so sensitive.

The Corporation's will to fight the NER in Parliament was not in vain, for on August 2 1899 the Town Clerk reported:

... the Company have withdrawn from their Bill three lots abutting on Hart-road... Instead of the footpath, now existing across the fields it is proposed that a road... should be made, extending from the railway arch with a slight curve to Cleveland-road on the deviated road... and a flagged footpath will be made at the expense of the Company... It may further be added that the inhabitants on the Central Estate will not be troubled by the close proximity to their dwellings of timber ponds, which was at first so greatly feared.

Party politics as well as land and law was also (not surprisingly) involved. A Mr Will Sherwood was applauded by the NDM leading article of May 28 1900 for emphasising that under Clause 3 of the Housing of the Working Classes Act the Council could purchase land and build houses cheaper than private enterprise, let them at lower rents because it could secure loans and buy materials cheaper, and then demolish slums.

The issue was not apparently urgent. It was almost a year (April 23 1901) before the Local Government Board, the responsible government department, asked the Council "what steps they were taking with regard to the housing of the working classes". Ald. Hunter replied that "the hands of the Committee for the Housing of the Working-Classes were to a very great extent tied by their inability to purchase land... but he was afraid they had been to a certain extent forestalled... " Questioned by Cllr. Leahy, the Town Clerk (Mr Bell) revealed that the land beyond Union Road had been sold to the NER. (Mrs. Matthew Gray apparently had made up her mind.)

... The Company were prohibited from taking certain plots marked blue on the plan in order that three streets might be made towards West Hartlepool from Union-road and three towards Hart-road from Cleveland-road... "

This would almost have doubled the Central Estate, presumably consolidating rather than diluting the emerging community, but on August 28 1901 the NDM reported that the Improvement Committee:

... recommended the Council to waive the agreement with the North-Eastern Railway Company... except so far as regards a strip of land 83 ft. wide from the north side of Arch-street along Union Road and 2?5 ft. along Hart-road from Union-road... to set back the fence in Union-road from the south side of Arch-street to Cleveland-road...

Thus, behind the scenes, had the western boundary of the Central Estate been permanently delimited. All that remained to be determined was by what means what came to be known as the "Propyard" should be marked. In the same month the Council contemplated purchasing 33 out of 100 acres offered by the NER between Hart Road and Workhouse lane but on March 5 1903 the land was reported as too dear at £440 per acre. Whose foot the boot was on was implied on April 3 1903 when Cllr Leahy was rebuked for opposing concessions to the NER because it proposed "to spend a quarter of a million of money in improving the docks". The directorships of William (son of Sir William) and Sir Joseph Pease in 1899 may have been relevant.

This was the essence of the matter. Earlier that year the mayor had said that Hartlepool was in existence before the NER and that it was the commercial men of the Hartlepools that had pushed the trade of the port forward. As we have seen, this was not entirely true in the 1830s, but by 1900 port, harbour, railway and industry were indissolubly locked together, with the Corporation pulled and pushed between them as economic interest or political conviction prevailed.

Meanwhile on April 2 the NDM reported the Medical Officer (Dr. Rawlings)'s view "that 169 houses in the borough are unfit for healthy human habitation" and editorially instructed, or reminded, working men "to bring pressure to bear at election times".

The rebuke may have been effective. On June 13 1903 the NDM reported:

... The North-Eastern Railway Company have just made a start with 25 new workmen's dwellings in Union and Hart-roads, which, when erected, will relieve the housing difficulty somewhat, though it is noticeable that the growth of housing accommodation on the Central Estate does not bring about any material decrease in the overcrowding in the older part of the town. This is probably due to the fact that the distance from here to the principal works is so great as to make it inconvenient as a place of residence for a good many workmen.

This last observation certainly became untrue if it was not untrue at the time. I myself, in the middle 1920s, daily saw the long parade of men striding the mile back to the Central - and back again - during the 12.00 noon to 1.00 p.m. dinner break. For the small minority with bicycles, the only problem was to find sufficient road space amongst the quick marchers.

The issue came to its political head at the Council meeting of July 1, 1903. The Housing of the Working Classes Committee recommended the leasing of the land in Union and Hart Roads for building by the Council.

Ald. Hunter moved the adoption... They did not want to cater for the slum dweller, and for dissolute people, but for the working man receiving from 20s(hillings) to 23s per week, and having a wife and four or five children... The committee submitted that houses could be built with money borrowed at 3 1/2% which could be let at rentals which would pay the Corporation 4%... He was not a Municipal trader by any means... and when it came to the bettering of the people without doing harm to the ratepayers in general they should do it...

Municipal improvement by local government had been pioneered in Birmingham in the 1870s by Joseph Chamberlain as mayor; the town was "parked, paved, assized, marketed, Gas-and-Watered, and improved", but in the 1880s the term "municipal socialism" had been coined for this process with predictable prejudicial consequences. Opposition, if not defeat, was inevitable:

Ald. Horsley said he hoped the Improvement Committee would continue to press their recommendation that the land should be let by contract to builders. Today there were more empty houses in Hartlepool than there had been for nine years... If they were to allow builders to put up houses on the land, they would erect just the class of property that would let, and he contended there was no occasion for the Council to rush itself into debt to provide houses... He did not see why the Council should become speculative builders...

The matter was referred back but on September 2 1903 the proposal was defeated in full council. On July 6 the NDM's editorial comment had been concise and penetrating in advance:

... the opponents of this form of municipal enterprise take up the position that in good times slums must not be closed because the closing would cause: First, other areas to be overcrowded... second, that in bad times the Council must not build because (1) there are plenty of empty houses to be had, (2) the private trader is ready to erect just the houses that would be let, and presumably make a profit on the transaction, (3) because the Council could not erect houses and let them without losing the ratepayers' money. This line of defence lifts the whole responsibility from the Council. It is difficult, however, to reconcile all these statements.

On October 8 1903 an alternative possibility was moved under the Small Dwellings Acquisition Act of 1899, which gave the Corporation power to borrow money and lend it to anyone desirous of becoming the owner of his own house subject to a limit of four fifths. A Committee was appointed but Ald. Hunter observed that building societies could be more liberal and Cllr. Hart was sure that the Act was not workable in Hartlepool, where men were constantly moving about. The Committee reported on November 4 but made no recommendation.

At the October meeting Ald. Horsley opposed "tooth and nail" a motion that the 9 unsold sites on Union Road be acquired under the Housing of the Working Classes Act but lost by one vote when the question was reconsidered on May 4 1904. Part of the debate is almost unbelievable:

... Councillor Foxton stated that it had been said - not correctly in his opinion - that there was a very large insanitary area (in Hartlepool), but he begged to join issue with the medical Officer, and say that in his opinion a very much larger number of houses were included than should have been...
Ald. Horsley said the Sanitary Committee went round to every house mentioned by Dr. Rawlings Medical officer), and the majority of the Committee would tell the

Council that not one tenth of the houses would they close as insanitary...

So much for professional, expert opinion! The issue might appear to be dead but it did not quite lie down. On Aug. 8 it had already been reported that the NER was letting property bought for demolition for dock extension, and in October 1904 when the NER was reported as "offering sites in Union-road on condition that they are only used for the erection of workmen's dwellings... 10s 6d per yard... too large a sum to pay... the matter was allowed to drop... " (!)

There were other serious issues. On Friday January 30 1903 the NDM leader commented:

Hartlepool... has a licensing problem to deal with. The total number of licenses in the town is 86, and of these 69 are for the sale of liquor on the premises. The population is 22,723, which gives an average of one license for every 264 inhabitants... The minority report of the Royal Commission on Licensing stated that one public-house was sufficient for a population of 750, so that, judged by this standard, Hartlepool is certainly well supplied.

With an estimated population of 2500 and only three licenses, including the Lord Clyde, the Central Estate would appear to have been well on the sober side. How did its behaviour, as reported, otherwise compare? In 5 years there were 13 cases, only 2 of which were obviously drink-related, whereas there were streets in old Hartlepool, notably Alfred, Sunniside and Cleveland, which positively proliferated drunks, brawlers and thieves. The point is worth making because later there was a street on the Estate which acquired a bad name.

In 1899 a 16-year old girl was criminally assaulted by three youths who had been standing against the Hart Road Board Schools. They were tried and punished at the Assizes: but the assailants were not local boys. The body of a newly born female child was found in a parcel in a field on the Estate, but there was no evidence of local responsibility. A drunken lodger in Clyde Street was fined for assaulting his landlady.

In 1901 there was a fight in Clyde Place, but the miscreant in an attempted theft of chickens ("LOOKING FOR HIS NEW YEAR'S BOX") from Low Warren cottage was again an outsider.

In 1903 a widow in Cleveland Road was robbed of money and food by a coloured seaman, a drunk was apprehended at the Lord Clyde Hotel and three youths (addresses unspecified) tried to hide stolen prop ends in a back yard in Beaumont Street. A Lambton Street drunk assaulted a tram conductor near Bell Street.

In 1904 two Hart Road labourers were fined for playing pitch and toss on Cleveland Road and a Bell Street rivetter was committed for trial for criminal assault on a woman from Arch Street. A labourer of Clifton-street was drunk and disorderly in Cleveland-road on Nov. 18th and assaulted a tramcar conductor, named Martin Philburn, of 16, Bell-street

... Prisoner pleaded guilty, adding that he was drunk, and knew nothing about the affair, and was very sorry...

On Sept 12th the 23rd appearance for drunken disorderliness of a Hart-road labourer was reported and there was another from the same street on Nov. 14.

P.C. Crowther, the first resident constable (who was also a Primitive Methodist Sunday School teacher and local preacher) had also to deal with the theft of a clock from C. T. Watson, which the Hartlepool thief tried but failed to pawn. P.C. Crowther was additionally assaulted by a drunk who interfered with young ladies on a tram. Sadly on Friday August 19 1904 there was a much more serious case:

HARTLEPOOL YOUTH'S TRAGIC DEATH
INQUEST TODAY
VERDICT OF MANSLAUGHTER

A lad named John William Wrightson, aged 15, and residing in Warren-terrace, Central Estate, met his death under tragic circumstances at Hartlepool last night.

Deceased, who was employed at Messrs Furness, Withy and Co's shipyard, was returning from work, with two other youths, named Thomas Turnbull - also residing at the Central Estate - and Short, both of whom are also apprentices at Furness Withy and Co's, when the deceased, it is alleged, playfully pricked Turnbull with a piece of steel.. According to the evidence of the youth Short, Turnbull then took out a clasp-knife and apparently made an attempt to retaliate by pricking Wrightson's hand. Deceased, however, drew his hand away, and the blade entered his left breast.

At Turnbull's suggestion, Short ran at once for assistance, and Mr Buckle, chemist, rendered firs aid, whilst Dr. De Jong was soon on the scene. The latter ordered the lad's immediate removal to the Hospital, but on arrival there he was found to be dead.

Turnbull was afterwards taken into custody by P.C. Crowther.

On Monday August 22 1904 NDM reported:

THE HARTLEPOOL TRAGEDY
TURNBULL BEFORE THE MAGISTRATES
PRISONER COMMITTED FOR TRIAL

... A very large number of persons of both sexes were present during the hearing, and followed the proceedings with evident interest...

John William Short, apprentice fitter, was first called. His evidence was similar to his statement at the inquest. He deposed that deceased and Turnbull started "larking" at the edge of the Fish Quay. At Throston Bridge Wrightson took a piece of steel (produced) from his pocket, and put it up to Turnbull's nostrils. Turnbull moved his head somehow, and the steel went up his nostril which bled. Prisoner then put his hand up to his waistcoat pocket and drew a knife (produced) which the witness identified. He did not see Turnbull open the knife. Wrightson saw prisoner going towards him, and moved further into the road. Turnbull rushed at deceased to prick his hand, which was on his left side, with the knife. Wrightson pulled his hand away, and the blade entered his side. He ran into the middle of the road and shouted, "Oh, I am bleeding". Then Turnbull began to cry and told witness to go for Mr Buckle. In later evidence Short stated that when on their way home Turnbull said, "Don't go and tell them anything about the knife; tell them that it was that bit of a saw-blade". Witness replied that he dare not.

Cross-examined: Wrightson had been pricking at Turnbull since leaving work. They were all three mates together. There did not seem to be any quarrel between the other two, nor did Turnbull appear to be in a passion. They still seemed to be "larking on"...

Mr Nicolson (solicitor representing Turnbull): He knew the two lads (prisoner and deceased) were mates; one was never seen without the other. He knew them through being in the brigade. They were well behaved...

P.C. Crowther... stated further that when charged at the police station Turnbull replied, "Well, all I can say , Mr Crowther, is I am very sorry for what I have done. He started "larking on" first with his instrument. I had no intention of doing any harm to my chum"...

Charity and mercy prevailed:

Nov. 25 ALLEGED MANSLAUGHTER AT HARTLEPOOL
TURNBULL ACQUITTED

... The Judge... said, "The jury have acquitted you, and in my judgement have acted rightly. It was not manslaughter, but at the same time it arose from you larking with some dangerous things. I hope this will be a lesson to you and others like you, not to go larking and indulging in rough horse play. It must be a regret to you for the rest of your life that what you did has resulted in the death of your friend...

The Central Estate could not have been immune to other accidents. There were only four reported and all but one were fatal. On June 30, 1899 the NDM reported:

... the sister of the deceased, Frances Rudd (of 3, Warren Terrace) was sent on Wednesday morning for a pennyworth of ammonia for washing purposes. On her return she put the bottle on the table, and whilst she was in the pantry her little brother picked it up and drank part of the contents. Dr. Gibb was at once sent for, but although everything possible was done, the poor little fellow died...

On Thursday May 31 1900 the NDM reported:

At the Central Hotel, Hartlepool, this morning, the Coroner... held an inquest upon the body of a child named Edw. Thompson, aged two years and four months, son of a signalman residing at North-Eastern Cottages, near to the Hartlepool Cemetery, who was killed on the line yesterday.

Edward Thompson, father of the deceased, said he lived in one of eight cottages facing the railway line near to the Hartlepool Cemetery. A fence separated the cottages from the line, and admission to the latter was gained by a wicket gate... a key for the wicket - an ordinary carriage key - was supplied to each of the cottages, all of which were occupied by employees of the Company. Everybody who made use of the gate was supposed to close it behind him, but it was frequently left open.

The jury returned a verdict of "Accidental death" and recommended that the Company should provide an automatic fastener to the gate in question.

On Thursday January 7 1904 the NDM reported another inquest at the Central Hotel:

FATAL FALL OUT OF BED
CHILD'S SINGULAR DEATH AT HARTLEPOOL

... James J. Crooks, labourer, 22 Bell-street, father of the deceased child (2 1/2) stated

that his two sons took the child to bed at 10.0 p.m. on New Year's Eve…

About 1-30 a.m. on New Year's Day witness and his wife were sitting waiting for the "first foot" when he heard deceased crying on the landing. Jane Tuck, witnesses stepdaughter, went to the landing and brought her down… She shortly afterwards went to bed with the eldest daughter. Next morning about 10 o'clock one of the girls brought the child downstairs, and when asked if she wanted any breakfast, she replied, "No, I feel sick." Witnesses's wife then saw a small scratch on the head, and asked the child if she had fallen. She said, "Yes, I fell out of bed". Mrs. Crooks bathed the girl, and then put a white bread poultice on its head. Deceased had not been well previous to the accident, having had, witness thought, the whooping cough.. The bed from which the child fell was only two feet from the floor. They could find nothing on the floor that might cause the wound on the head.

Dr. Gibb said… (he) found that the skin covering the right half of the head was inflamed. There was a wound on the scalp about a quarter of an inch long, and a black eye. The child was in a very bad condition, and was suffering from whooping cough. In his opinion death was due to sceptic (sic) poisoning. The injury could have been caused by the fall, but something very poisonous must have entered the wound to cause such rapid inflammation.

The jury returned a verdict that death was due to the child accidentally falling out of bed.

"First footing" meant awaiting the first person to knock on the door in the New Year. By arrangement, and to ensure good luck, it was usually a dark-haired male who brought something black - normally a piece of coal - as a gift and who was rewarded with cake (a piece) and wine (a glass, usually ginger). In retrospect it appears strange that there was no reproach for parental neglect, if for nothing more.

The non-fatal accident was bizarre. The NDM of Monday June 26 1899 reported:

TRAM ACCIDENT
MR C. T. Watson INJURED

On Saturday, a singular and rather serious accident occurred at Hartlepool. Mr C. T. Watson was on the top of a tramcar travelling in the direction of West Hartlepool. He had joined the car near Trinity Church, and the seats at the end of the car being occupied, had remained standing at the top of the steps. When the car reached the double line on the Hartlepool side of Throston Bridge it stopped, and several more people got on. One of these passed Mr Watson in order to go to a seat at the front of the car, and as Mr Watson was leaning back to allow him to pass, another car from the direction of West Hartlepool came along the other line. The upright, to which the trolley arm of the latter car was attached, struck Mr Watson on the back of the head and knocked him off into the road… Fortunately no bones had been broken. Mr Watson recovered consciousness about ten minutes after the accident, and was conveyed home in a cab.

The quality of the NDM reporting is generally worthy of praise. In this example it vividly combines intricate technical information with evocative power and unobtrusive sympathy.

Mr Watson eventually recovered his career as well as his consciousness. His Central Hotel ran a yearly club which in November 1900 paid a dividend to its members, with Dr. Gibb chairing a smoking (i.e. men only) concert. In May 1901 Mr Watson complained to the Council about the large number of children who congregated on the seat, and who spread their washing to dry, in front of his house *on the Town Moor* (My italic). He had moved "up" from the Central Estate. Councillor Foxton commented:

> *I can say that I have sweethearted my present wife on that very seat thirty years ago... I object that the town should be ruled by individuals, and the Moor belong to a few and not to the whole of the inhabitants.*
> *The RECORDER: If Councillor Foxton sweet-hearted on that seat thirty years ago, is it at all surprising that there should be a number of children playing there? (Loud laughter).*

The NDM's editorial comment on Monday May 6 1901 was irreverent and slightly revealing:

> *The Hartlepool Town Council was in jocular mood on Wednesday night. The Council has always been noted for its short meetings, and occasionally for the joviality of its proceedings. But the hilarity was so great on Wednesday that the meeting lasted nearly three-quarters of an hour...*
> *Business of course is really done in committee.*

This can only have surprised those readers of the NDM who had not already reached the same conclusion themselves. Meanwhile there was an equally serious matter in hand. In January 1901 the Council allowed Mr Watson to enclose land at the junction of Hart and Cleveland Roads without having sought Improvement Committee authorisation, provided he extended the footpaths and paved the frontages. In May Cllr. Foxton revealed that this was for no less than six houses and commented that if these concessions were allowed to go on they might as well do away with the building bye-laws altogether. The Mayor and Town Clerk explained the procedural error involved, which was not Mr Watson's, and the matter was referred back; and apparently dropped. On April 3 1902, however, the NDM reported from Improvement Committee proceedings that:

> *... Mr C. T. Watson, having encroached on the Back-street leading from Watson-street to Pease-street, thus lessening the width of the street, he be requested to move the fence back in accordance with the estate plan passed, and that the original owners of the land be informed of such encroachment.*

This was a separate issue and on May 8 1902 it was recommended:

> *That the Council adhere to the estate plan... and that Mr Watson his assigns have notice to remove and set back the wooden fence... and in default that the Council take such action as may be advised.*

However, on July 3 1902 it was recommended:

> *That the Town Clerk proceed no further with regard to the encroachment by Mr Watson on the back street on the Central Estate.*

Mr Watson, still the licensee of the Central Hotel, was still lucky, or well connected: or both.

The Town Council's apparent complacency was not unchallenged. There was discontent about under-representation on the Council of the Throston Ward, which included the Central Estate, and there were contested elections for its seats.

On August 6 1899 NDM reported that Alderman Hunter had suggested an alteration in the respective parish boundaries of Throston and Hartlepool and other councillors added that Throston should have increased representation and that unequal representation bred dissatisfaction. On October 4 1900 it further reported Cllr. Leahy as saying that the ward was now represented by only one member instead of three, one having been absent for six months. Ald. Hunter said that the people of Throston had the remedy in their own hand. The only thing they could do was to ask Councillor Davies to either attend to his duties or resign his position.

The matter was delayed for no less than two years because of the 1901 Census but by June 1903 it was numerically established that with similar populations Throston had only three to Hartlepool's six councillors and that Middleton, with only a seventh of the population, also had three. On July 1 1903 the size of the Special Committee was increased but one of the added members, Ald. Horsley, said that the wards could not be equalized until the parishes were unified. On April 7 1904, nine months later, the same alderman pointed out that wards were created by Acts of Parliament and that he would stand by the status quo. It looked like an impasse.

The widening of the (male) franchise in 1867 and 1885 meant that sooner or later working class men would be elected to town councils as well as to Parliament. As far as the latter was concerned, from 1880 10 1900 the Member for the Hartlepools had alternated between Thomas Richardson, Liberal and then Liberal Unionist, and Christopher Furness, Liberal, both ship or engine builders, who defeated Sir William Gray, another Liberal Unionist and shipbuilder, in 1891. The Central Estate was not important enough to have a committee room although after 1895 Hart Road School was available as a polling both - doubtless to the delight of the children who would have had an extra day's holiday in consequence.

With Throston Ward, which included the Central Estate, it was different and in 1899 James Kilburn claimed to be the first working man elected councillor. In 1900 there were two vacancies, and John Moir who was elected unopposed in place of Cllr. M'Donald, recently deceased, was a shipyard plater of Tyneside origins and Scottish descent, 20 years a Hartlepudlian, who lived at 6 Arch Street. For the other vacancy there were three candidates, the William Sherwood commended by NDM for his interest in housing, Dr. William Scott Gibb (Plate 34 p. 112) who had a surgery in Cleveland Road, and R.J. Marshall the builder and contractor who had testified for the Corporation in the House of Lords.

Sherwood was a trade union delegate, Anglican chorister, Sunday School Superintendent and Boys' Brigadier, and therefore pre-eminently respectable. Yet on October 26 1900 he was rebuked by R.J. Marshall's chairman for mudslinging:

> *... Mr Sherwood had made use of what, to put it mildly, was a most objectionable expression, regarding not only Mr Marshall, but regarding Dr. Gibb as well... Mr Sherwood was reported to have said, "If the workers realised the power which the Municipalities possessed they would stand together, and they would not find trades-*

unionists canvassing against trade unionists either for jerry-builders or doctors" ... it was quite an edifying idea that a member of the working-class (Sherwood)... should have turned his thoughts in that direction (housing)... But Mr Sherwood had not the practical experience that Mr Marshall had, and that was where they claimed Mr Marshall to be superior to the other two candidates in the field...

R.J. Marshall was rebuked in turn by Dr. Gibb, whose meeting was much better attended, on October 29 1900, not for jerry-building (he was "quite ready to believe that Mr Marshall could build a good house") but for having claimed to be "first in the field" and for suggesting that medical duties would not permit the doctor to fulfil his council duties. He could manage the necessary 84 meetings per annum and had partners in any case. Mr Sherwood was even more severely rebuked for arguing that a working man should be elected because an injured "poor fellow" had had his outdoor-relief from the Board of Guardians withdrawn because his workmates had collected a handsome subscription for him. He was further rebuked for suggesting that he (Sherwood) was better informed, as an occasional distributor of relief than a doctor, on insanitary conditions and housing shortages. In eight years he had done more for the working classes than Mr Sherwood would ever do in his life.

In short, the contest was conducted solely on a "holier-than-thou" basis, As Dr. Gibb said:

... he had studied the addresses of the various candidates, and the very first thing that struck him... was their similarity rather than any difference. In the three principal things they had before them - the purchase of the Gas and Water Company, the under-representation of Throston and the better housing of the working classes -they were practically unanimous.... They had not to go to the poll on Thursday to vote between men of different principles, but for the man they thought could really carry out in the best manner those principles, and he made bold to say that he was that man...

Dr. Gibb also spoke about another issue which had reappeared:

... Dr. Gibb then went on to refer to the Mayor's remarks at the banquet the other night with regard to the amalgamation of Hartlepool and West Hartlepool, and said that he sincerely trusted that it would come to pass... and the boroughs would gradually get more and more friendly to each other, till the time came that Hartlepool and West Hartlepool would find out that it would be to their joint benefit to become one town (Hear, Hear and loud applause.)

He was victorious, polling 493 votes to R.J. Marshall's 408, with W. J. Sherwood a poor third with 182 (Plate 34 p. 112).

It was Ald. Horsley, retiring from his record-making seventh successive mayoralty, who had revived the amalgamation issue on Oct. 26 1900 to mark the approaching new century. (No nonsense about celebrating it in 1900!). The NDM was positively lyrical:

... the new Hartlepool... - a great town of one hundred thousand people... no temptation for the North-eastern Railway Company to play off the interests of one town against the interests of the other... Gas and Water... the tramways... a municipal

telephone exchange... The roots of civic life in Hartlepool lie deep in a historic past. For many centuries she has borne her part well in the civic and ecclesiastical and maritime history of the North of England. It is now suggested that her long years of accumulated experience should be united with the throbbing life of her daughter on this side of the docks and that the two should march hand-in-hand with the spirit of the times, and enable them to meet the pressing problems of the future. Floreat Hartlepool!

Alas! When, after sixteen months, the Borough Council at last on February 5 1902 voted merely on the appointing of a committee of inquiry into the proposal, it was lost by one vote: 12 to 11. But whose vote was it?

Ald. Rowe... said he was not one of those who would go cap in hand to West Hartlepool and ask them to take Hartlepool in... Hartlepool had everything to lose and nothing to gain from the amalgamation...

Councillor HART... Ninety-five per cent of the people of Hartlepool were against amalgamation... If such a step were to be taken, West Hartlepool ought to come to them, not they go to West Hartlepool.

Councillor LEAHY... There was nothing that West Hartlepool could give them but what they had already got, and it seemed to him that those who favoured the idea of amalgamation were those gentlemen who had a large share in West Hartlepool also...

Councillor MOIR, as a representative of the people, intimated his intention to vote against the resolution because he had found the feeling in his ward much against the amalgamation of the boroughs.

Councillor KILBURN... As one of the representatives of the Throston Ward, he could not vote for the motion until he had consulted those who had returned him.

At last, therefore, a Central Estate councillor and other working class representatives or sympathisers had spoken. It is, however, impossible to say that it was John Moir's vote which vetoed the union and endorsed old Hartlepool's conservative way. Little doubt, though, that the Central Estate colony identified with the Hartlepool mother-country.

Working class representatives remained a small minority, despite the change from trade union to Labour backing. Cllr. Moir retired in 1903 and was replaced by Cllr Withers but Sherwood was unsuccessful both in 1901 and 1903. At the end of Ald. Horsley's seven year reign, the mayoralty passed in succession to Cllrs. Harrison and Butterwick, both grocers. R.J. Marshall did not run again for councillor but continued to prosper as builder of the Destructor, the Public Library and (on the Central Estate) St Barnabas' Church as well as of many more houses and backstreets.

In November, however, TO-DAY, perhaps rather grudgingly, observed:

We have to congratulate Mr W. Sherwood on his victory in the North Ward of Hartlepool... . we must all admit that he does not go to the Council under false colours... he is President of the Hartlepools Trade and Labour Council, Chairman of the Hartlepools Housing Committee, and an Executive Member of the Gas Workers' and General Labourers' Union... He is also a member of the I.L.P... and, what probably is not generally known, of the Trades Union Officials' Total Abstinence League... he has kept the housing question well to the front at Hartlepool, and it remains to be seen whether he will be able to induce the Council to make any move in this matter now that he is in a position to argue with the members across the table...

He was soon in action: on December 8, 1904...

Councillor Sherwood... moved "That a Special Committee be formed to forthwith consider what work can be found for the unemployed... the improvements to the cliff ... might be brought before the Local Government Board... Also, the levelling of the old cemetery was work upon which unskilled labour might be employed... There were many streets which would do with repairing...
Councillor Hart thought the suggestion... was ridiculous...
Councillor Kilburn... could not understand his bringing this motion forward...
Councillor Withers was of opinion that no harm would be done...
Councillor Merryweather... was opposed to increasing the rates...
Councillor Foxton said he could not admit that there were any more people out of work... than was usual at this time of the year... What were the various societies Councillor Sherwood represented doing in the matter? Was it not the function of the various societies to find work for their members?... It was every man's business to provide himself with profitable employment...
Councillor Gibb said... they should first find out the extent of the poverty. Statistics might be made to prove anything, but if they had a register of those out of work... then the Council would have something to go on...
The motion... was lost...

It was scarcely surprising. The working class representatives were not themselves in agreement and Councillor Foxton did not hesitate to emphasise the class barrier. On the other hand Councillor Gibb was characteristically temperate, perhaps illustrating the community spirit. In any case the councillors needed to watch their steps. At the end of each year the NDM recorded possible council attendances, including committees: e.g. (1904) Gibb 98/132 (74%); Kilburn 72/82 (88%); Withers 83/117 (71%).

The NDM was an impressive newspaper, reporting national and international as well as local events. The Dreyfus Case, the Spanish American War, the Boxer Rebellion and the Russo-Japanese War were all covered between 1899 and 1904 but most attention naturally focused on the Boer War (1899-1902) because Britain was fighting the Boers in South Africa, and soldiers from the Hartlepools (including Private Crawford of Watson Street) were involved. The NDM was not only patriotic: very little local pro-Boer activity was reported, although, following the lead of Lloyd George on the issue, there must have been some.

The overlap between national and local events was copiously reported and commended, perhaps not always with critical detachment. On Monday March 5 1900 "Local Jottings" remarked:

To say that the Hartlepools were enthusiastic over the news of the relief of Ladysmith on Thursday would give but a faint idea of the actual reception of the news. The place went mad with joy. There was not a street or alley in the town that did not proclaim its satisfaction. Handshaking was the chief form of mutual congratulation... Business gave place to buzzers, bells and bunting - some say even to beer, but there were no cases at the police courts next morning...

Perhaps the police were celebrating too! It was a most unusual circumstance. The relief of Mafeking, which immortalised Sir Robert Baden-Powell, later founder of the Boy Scouts, supplied the new word "mafficking" to the language, meaning unbridled, not to say unseemly, rejoicing. On Tuesday May 22 1900 the NDM reported (in two page-length columns):

> *... The day was not an ideal one for the occasion. Rain fell more or less heavily practically all the time, but notwithstanding this we can fairly say that never have the streets been more thronged with people, and never has a scene of such patriotic fervour seized the inhabitants of the two towns...*

The editorial comment of Monday May 28 was wry and sophisticated, not to say sardonic:

> *Patriotic sentiment has during the past week exhibited itself in many guises - and disguises. It would, indeed, form an interesting psychological study to analyse the various methods in which public enthusiasm found vent. I noticed that in the cases of many people patriotism and thirst seemed very nearly allied...*
> *Moreover, South Africa did not have a monopoly of the fighting that took place on Monday, for on the evening of that day I myself witnessed a pretty little impromptu exhibition under Queensberry rules. An elderly woman interfered, however, and herself received the concluding few blows that were struck on either side.*

Self-evidently this could not have occurred on the Central Estate because the reporter could have had no reason to be there; and because the Estate was so comparatively respectable. On the other hand the Estate immortalised the Boer War by conferring (or having conferred) on the coastal boundary area with Hartlepool, which had housed the ironworks and the glass works (which became the site of the Destructor, opened on August 23 1900) the name "Spion Kop" (Map 7 p. 142). Unlike Ladysmith and Mafeking, Spion Kop was a defeat, not a victory. A "hill" no less than 4,800 feet high (1463 metres), "on the edge of a plateau five or six miles long", it was reported occupied on Jan. 25 1900 but abandoned on Jan. 26. The nickname may therefore very well have been ironic, unlike the "Klondyke" which was, as noted above, indeed a gold-mine. It is pertinent to recall that comparable foreign labels had been bestowed on earlier areas of expansion in both the Hartlepools in the previous century: "Egypt" in Hartlepool and "California" in West Hartlepool. It may have been the same sort of impulse which produced "Bunkers' Hills" in both Blackburn and Dover, etc., after Britain's "victorious" defeat in 1776 at the beginning of the American War of Independence.

Queen Victoria died on Jan. 22 1901 but the Coronation of Edward VII was postponed from June 26 to Aug. 9 1902 because of illness. Mrs. J. R, a Central Estate stalwart whose recollections I recorded in the early 1970s, proudly recalled that whilst Hart Road School children were marching around the playground practising for the forthcoming parade on the Promenade to celebrate the coronation, her uncle, caretaker of the Borough Buildings next door to the police station, shouted the news through the railings to the teacher that the King had appendicitis and that the ceremonial was therefore postponed.

The Town Council had what Ald. Hunter called the "good sense" to interrupt its celebration of the failure to unite the Hartlepools to send a telegram of sympathy to Queen Alexandra. On Coronation Day the NDM reported (with a characteristic prelude):

> *... The morning broke dull and cold, and the threatened rain descended at about 8 o'clock in a smart shower. In a few minutes, however, this had ceased, and an hour or so later the sun shone forth brilliantly over the gaily bedecked town...*
> *Mustering at their respective schools (despite the summer holiday) the youngsters - in all there must have been considerably over 5,000 of them - marched in procession to the Moor, and with commendable promptitude took up their positions in the phalanx in front of the raised platform reserved for the Mayor and Corporation... Practically every child carried a large flag, and each on his or her breast proudly wore the Coronation medal. The fine weather, too, enabled the little ones to don their prettiest garb...*

The NDM did not merely inform its readers. It entertained and amused them as well. Patent medicines, including "Pink Pills for Pale People" and "Sulphur Hair Restorer" abounded and in addition to poems (not all doggerel: Kipling and Hardy were included), short stories and serialised novels (on Fridays) it also offered "Hints for Housewives", "Clippings From The Comics", "Mirthful Mixtures" and "Jaunty Jocosities", in addition to "Stop Press" titbits - all for a halfpenny per day.

The advertisements inadvertently reveal instructive social as well as cultural information, such as performances of plays by Ibsen and Oscar Wilde. The contents of a house in Union Road, for sale by auction on January 30 1899, included:

> *SITTING-ROOM. - Carpet, Hearthrug, Mantel Mirror, Chest of Drawers, Gipsy Table, Musical Box, Plant Stand, Oilcloth, pair of Shades, Chairs, Coal Vase (sic) &c.*
> *BEDROOMS Nos 1 and 2. - Bedsteads, Wool Mattresses, Two Chairs, Chest of Drawers, Oilcloth, Gas Fittings, Cornice Pole, Shades, Brass Rail bedstead, Spring Mattress, Duchess Dressing Table and Washstand (marble top), Chamber Set, Clock, Chandelier, Bamboo Table, &c.*
> *KITCHENS. - Easy Chair, Leather Seated Chairs, Rocking Chair, Hearthrug, Tidy, Good Chest of Drawers, Square Table, Looking Glass, Wringer, Pair of Shades, and other Useful Utensils.*
> *HALL, STAIRS, AND PASSAGE. - Oilcloth, Hat Rack, Pneumatic Bicycle (Gent's), Wringer...*

The vendor, Mr Ferguson (who was leaving for London), was reasonably well-furnished by the respectable working class standards of the later 1920s. Comparison with a middle class household (10, Cliff Terrace, Hartlepool), advertised on the same day, is revealing. There was also a piano, there were watercolours and engravings, brass fenders, a clock and writing tables, in a drawing room, a dining room and a study, but other than probable differences of quality the furnishings were very similar.

It was well that the sinking of new collieries at Easington (1899) and Horden (1901) which would eventually export coal and increase power for purchases in the nearby Hartlepools by generating employment, were economic advantages to the Hartlepools. The obvious rail linkages were to be supplied by the NER which, in January and February 1899 respectively, proposed new lines linking West Hartlepool with Seaham, and Hartlepool with Sunderland. The June 1899 amalgamation of Furness, Richardson and Westgarth, ship and ships' engine builders, provoked the contented comment: "trade is flourishing", although Hartlepool complained that the NER refused to run excursion trains through from West Hartlepool to Hartlepool and that passengers might have to wait half-an-hour for the necessary connection. It was not until 1904 that autocars replaced the local linkage of two-carriage trains with the engine in the middle.

Although the NDM's annual end-of-year reviews 1899 -1901 were eloquently silent on the subject, on Wednesday Dec. 31 1902 it commented:

> *This has not been a prosperous year in the Hartlepools. The shipbuilding trade has been bad, and as the kindred industries were necessarily affected, employment has been scarce in several branches of trade...*

Exactly a year later the comment was identical:

> *The year 1903 has not been a very eventful one in the Hartlepools. Trade has been quiet... With the experience of two years of acute depression... 1903 will stand out as one of the worst years experienced in the shipping trade...*

Timber imports and coal exports had both increased, but the NDM opinion on the shipbuilding decline was ominous:

> *The principal cause of this is over-production, but it is also due to some extent to the increasing competition of foreigners... seventy per cent of the vessels trading to this port are foreigners...*

At the end of 1904 the comment was similar. On Nov 30 the editorial remarked:

> *... Yesterday morning brought the welcome news that the labourers had come to terms with the employers. The settlement was in the nature of a compromise... the men earning the lowest wages will not have to suffer a reduction. So far as the skilled workmen are concerned, the employers stood out for a reduction of 1s.6d per week on time and five per cent on piece rates...*
> *Commercially, the year does not differ in any marked manner from its predecessor... output (of ships) is slightly better than the average of the last ten years, but of course it suffers by comparison with the "boom" years 1899-1901... The coal exports are the most satisfactory feature...*

For this the credit went to Horden Colliery.

On Dec. 30 the REVIEW OF THE YEAR observed that there was war in the Far East but that England and France were on good terms. This was despite the fact that France's ally, Russia, was at war with England's ally, Japan. Consequently when Russian warships fired on British trawlers on the Dogger Bank, believing them to be Japanese destroyers, Russia apologised and paid compensation. But there was no prospect of decreased armaments expenditure. NDM commented:

> *"... The feeling that international disputes ought to be settled by arbitration is growing, but side by side with this sentiment is a strong opinion that the best guarantee that a nation can have of peace is to be prepared for war. The nations have not yet*

learned to trust each other… . when the pent up forces do break loose the struggles will be more severe… "

This was prophetically depressing in international terms but as to local amenities, on October 13 1904 the Hartlepool Free (Carnegie) Library (Plate 28 p. 81) opening attracted a large crowd of spectators, if not of borrowers, and on Nov 23 the new St Barnabas Church (Plate 29 p. 81) on Hart Road , Central Estate was dedicated. In Hartlepool the inauguration of electric light installation had been the chief event of the year, although the world-famous American "Buffalo Bill" (William Frederick Cody) had performed in person and Gilbert and Sullivan's "Gondoliers" had been performed by amateurs.

Plate 28 - Public Library Hartlepool 1905

Plate 29- St Barnabas Church

Damaged in the bombardment Dec 16 1914

Chapter 5: Central Estate 1905-09

Like Wards Directories, the Northern Daily Mail was not infallible. What was and what was not published on both events and opinions depended in part on the whims of editor and subeditors, the availability and competence of reporters and the haphazards of voluntary amateur contributions.

It is clear that many court cases were not reported. How otherwise can one account for the first news of defendants whose 25th or 45th previous appearance for similar offences has not been reported? Items of tantalising interest are not followed up, much less completed, and tact is evident much more for some who are reported than for others. Obituaries are endlessly beneficent, as one senses of those whose doings and sayings have previously been reported. As for the microfilms of the original papers, July to December 1905 and January to June 1910 are missing. Although the proprietorial and editorial liberal-nonconformist stance emerges over the years, the NDM needed to please as many of its readers as possible. For that reason alone it may have been as reasonably neutral and reliable as possible. It was invariably well-written and remarkably accurately proofread.

By the end of the first decade of the 20th century all the entertainments and pastimes noted at the end of 19th century persisted: brass and silver "prize" band concerts in the parks and on the Promenade, amateur orchestras and professional theatres, the occasional circus and funfair, and, for the more seriously inclined, university extension lectures, a Parliamentary Debating Society, friendly societies and temperance organisations. By 1910 the occasional motion picture display ("animated pictures") had become the regular twice-nightly cinema, some in converted and some in purpose-built premises. The former included the Hartlepool Town Hall (Plate 30 p. 110) and the Empress Theatre (later Palladium)(Plate 31 p. 110), the latter Black's Picture Hall in Lynn Street, West Hartlepool. The new craze for roller-skating also spread from old halls to new rinks.

> *Mar 4 1909:... Roller skating is just now becoming a craze all over the country, and Hartlepool is to be provided with a rink. The covered market ought to make an excellent place...*

The Central Estate must have provided some of the enthusiasts, although presumably not at 6.00 a.m.: on May 11 1909 NDM reported:

> *OLYMPIA SKATING RINK*
>
> *The Olympia Roller Skating Rink, Hartlepool, has taken its place among local amusements, and judging from the large attendances at each session, rinking is more popular than ever... Learners who are anxious to appear at the carnival are obtaining the maximum amount of practice by taking advantage of the first session, which commences at six o'clock in the morning...*

There were Amateur Operatic, Choral, Literary and Philosophical Societies, fur and feather fanciers (including pigeons) as well as flower shows, clubs for model aeroplanes and model yachts and for every sport from bowls to billiards, cricket to cycling, association and rugby football, from flying to motoring, from golfers to harriers, from marksmen to photographers: and for quoits.

Sport was copiously reported. Both Rugby Union and Association codes (but not Rugby League) and cricket were reported in the NDM. Apr. 9 1906 the "second annual victorious Rovers' (Rugby Union) return versus West Hartlepool" was almost a routine matter but on May 8 1908 something even more momentous appeared:

Last night the proposal to form a professional Association Football team in West Hartlepool, was discussed by a representative gathering of local gentlemen interested in sport. The new team will be known as Hartlepools United...

The "local gentlemen", presumably from both Hartlepool and West Hartlepool, were sixty years ahead of the politicians in perceiving that unity made more sense than competition.

The two Hartlepools did not merge until 1967. Be that as it may, all three clubs survived into the Third Millennium.

Railway excursions also flourished. On June 14 1907 the NDM reported:

... at Hartlepool the (Whitsuntide) bookings were also largely in excess of the previous year's returns, namely 6,695 as against 4,806. The heaviest excursion was that on Monday to Saltburn and Redcar... Barnard Castle was also largely patronised by local holiday-makers... The charming countryside in the neighbourhood of Castle Eden and Blackhall Rocks has probably never been more in favour with picnicking parties... "

Occasional musical offerings featured such exotics as the Berlin Philharmonic Trio, or Sousa's Band from the United States. Mendelssohn's" Elijah", Handel's "Messiah" or Stainer's "Crucifixion" were more regular fare. Church and chapel vied in linking worship with wholesome entertainment, and it is noteworthy that although the Central Estate Primitive Methodist Chapel (unlike Brougham Street) only occasionally, and St. Barnabas' Church never, paid for advertisements of their services, the NDM was generous with editorial space. It is highly unlikely that reporters were present, so that the regular reports of Sunday School Anniversaries, Harvest Festivals, American Evenings, Christian Endeavour, Central Brotherhood etc. etc. must have been contributed by church members and either handed in at, or posted to, the Mail Office. For a penny stamp, according to time of posting, same or next-day delivery was guaranteed(!).

Nov. 9 1906 *CENTRAL ESTATE P.M. CHURCH*
AN AMERICAN EVENING
... a recently introduced manner of raising funds... and the proceeds are for the New Church Fund... A capital musical programme...
After the programme the Rev. C. Humble... invited those who had been working for the American Evening to come forward with the money and state to the audience how it had been earned. This occupied nearly an hour... (Itemised in detail)... £76.0s.1d...
Crowthers, Spences, Wrays & Ringwoods...

These testimonies, which included tales of money-raising from home-made butter, herb beer, scrap iron, Sunday laid eggs, old clothes and custards etc. etc. may have been what distinguished an American from a native Evening. The recitations and songs (including the Hart-road Quintette Party) otherwise sound conventional.

Dec. 10 1906: Referring to the recent "American evening"... the editor of the "Home Messenger" writes: "If ever a church had providential help and guidance this church has it. We dare not but push ahead arrangements for the new church, and all points pretty clearly and distinctly to a start being made next year".

This is tantalising. The brick chapel of the early 1890s was as solid as a rock in the 1920s, so that this must be the first foreshadowing of the new chapel which was completed only in 1938, the year before the outbreak of the Second World War.

June 23 1908 SUNDAY SCHOOL ANNIVERSARIES
The Sunday school anniversary services in connection with the Central Estate P.M. Church were continued on Sunday, when Mr. Youden preached an excellent sermon in the morning, and gave a short address to parents and teachers in the evening. In the afternoon a children's service was held, presided over by Mr. Youden, when the children recited their pieces and dialogues, and sang special hymns and anthems... All the services were well attended...

The German-Jewish name Youden (Juden) is unexpected. Otherwise, apart from the fact that the special hymns were also sung in the evening, I can testify that the form of the anniversary persisted into the 20s and 30s. The "Central Brotherhood", on the other hand, did not.

Jan. 1909 CENTRAL BROTHERHOOD
The members of the above brotherhood sat down to dinner last night in the Central Estate Primitive Church. The proceedings opened with selections by the Brotherhood Band. At the dinner the company numbered over 70 members and visitors...

One wonders if the number was accurate, for the St. Barnabas Church of England (Plate 29 p. 81) as well as for the Methodist Chapel.

Nov. 6 1908 ST. BARNABAS CHURCH HOUSE
A new venture in connection with St. Barnabas Mission in the shape of a church house, was opened on Tuesday by the Vicar... A most substantial supper had been provided, thanks to the kindness of Col. Burdon, of Castle Eden, and several friends on the Central Estate, about 90 people partaking... It is intended to use the house for a youths' recreation and reading club, mothers' meetings, Bible classes, meetings and debates, sewing, teas, etc., until such time as a convenient hall can be built...

Col. Burdon was the owner of Horden Colliery, as will appear below. Bearing in mind the bad industrial relations at the colliery it was perhaps surprising patronage. Assuming impartial reportage, however, St. Barnabas' was a success story, despite the allegation of "nuisance".

Aug. 2 1906 PROPERTY COMMITTEE
... the Borough Engineer reported correspondence from the priest-in-charge (Rev. C. Leslie-Suggitt) of St. Barnabas' Mission Church, relative to the wooden erection on land near the church, and that the same had been set back to the building line.
That the Committee approve, and saw no reason to interfere , as the same was not a nuisance, as alleged.
May 8 1908: It was expected that when the Mission Church of St. Barnabas was

opened on the Central Estate, and the Sunday School commenced, it would bring relief to the school attached to the Parish Church of Holy Trinity, which for a considerable time has been overcrowded. The old school has, however, been very little effected (sic), as the new one is, I understand, filled with additional scholars, which shows that St. Barnabas's is indeed filling a long felt want...

The Temperance movement provided alternative entertainment to the consumption of alcohol at their weekly meetings: like churches and chapels they offered solos, recitations and the occasional lantern lecture, bazaar or sale of work but, again like churches and chapels, could not have whist drives or dances, elsewhere popular. The Old Boys' Institute offered the best of both worlds, offering Bible Classes in addition to football, billiards, and whist drives as well as Xmas Dinner to 100 poor children (AGM Report Oct. 13, 1906).

Jan. 26 1906: Hartlepool Education Cttee: A communication from the St. Hilda's Tent of the I(ndependent). O(rder of) Rechabites stating it was desired to open a juvenile branch for the Central Estate, and asking the terms of the committee for the use of a room in Hart-road School, was read.
It was resolved to grant the use of a room for £1 a year and a similar amount each for the caretaker and for gas.

It cannot have been an immediately direct result, but on Feb. 6 1906 the NDM reported that cases of drunkenness in the last year had decreased to 150 and that this was the lowest for the last eight years. Hence, perhaps, the headlines:

HARTLEPOOL CRIME STATISTICS
DECREASE OF DRUNKENNESS

As well as Tents of Rechabites and Juvenile Rechabites there were, in addition to Sons of Temperance (who met in the Central Estate Primitive Methodist Chapel) and Good Templars Lodges, there were also the (Primitive Methodist) Band of Hope, the North Eastern Railway Temperance Union, the Church of England Temperance Society, and the Young Abstainers.

Boy Scouts, Girl Guides and Boys Brigade(s), all closely bonded to one church or another, catered for more secular outdoor pursuits with a patriotic emphasis, witness this report of June 28 1909:

The wet weather of last week interfered with a great many engagements...
Nevertheless... the members of the 1st Hartlepool Company of the Boys' Brigade... inspection, manoeuvres, drill and physical exercises had all to be performed in the open air... it is to be hoped that Colonel Doughty's advice will be taken, and at the expiration of their service in the brigade... these smart, well-trained youths will be found swelling the ranks of the Territorials.

The Primrose League (which could raise funds by whist drives) and the Imperial Lads' Brigade were even more overtly party-political and colonialist.

There was also, as there had long been, horse-racing, reported daily in the NDM Stop Press. Gambling, however, was legally tolerated only on the race course and, if newspaper column inches are representative, betting was even more condemned and persecuted than intemperance.

On March 2 1905 a headline to the report on the Town Council meeting read:

BETTING IN THE STREETS AND ON THE SANDS...
PROPOSED BETTING BYLAW

A petition was read from the Brougham-street Methodist Church calling attention to the manifest increase of gambling in Hartlepool since the passing of the new betting bylaw at West Hartlepool, and earnestly beseeching the council, in consideration of the moral welfare of the townspeople, and especially of their young people, to put a similar bylaw into operation at Hartlepool.
Similar petitions were presented by... six churches, the Salvation Army and the Central Estate Primitive Methodist Church...

The debate oscillated between very high morals and principles and very low social class and party political peevishness.

Ald. Horsley... could fully bear out... what those people had said... He had no wish to interfere with the liberty of the subject... but he protested against others coming from different boroughs into Hartlepool for the purpose of bookmaking... Hartlepool was the happy hunting ground for all kinds of fellows to go there and take money out of the pockets, not only of men, but of boys...
Councillor Hart did not agree... He believed in the liberty of the subject. He thought every man had a right to do what he liked with his money... a working man had the right to bet, so long as it was with his own money...
Councillor Sherwood, speaking in support of a betting bylaw, said he had a direct mandate from 4000 working men... to vote for any bylaw which tended to suppress betting... The better class of working men did not want any facilities for betting.
Councillor Hart said he noticed that Councillor Sherwood's election address contained no reference to his opinions on this matter, else he was certain he would not have been returned to the Council...
Councillor Foxton said... there was... no need to interfere with the liberty of the individual. Referring to the petitions, Councillor Foxton sad those people would not only prevent betting in the streets, but would like to punish them if they did not attend their places of worship twice on a Sunday. They called that freedom. Their freedom was to compel everyone to do as they (the petitioners) liked. So long as they did not interfere with him and the welfare of the community, he thought that men of full age should have the liberty allowed them of exercising their rights as free born citizens...
Councillor Withers said he was glad... the time had arrived when they should take steps to put down the betting in the streets... One could hardly get to and from work for the people who loitered about reading racing and betting news. It was high time the young people should be protected from this diabolical evil...
Eventually the mayor's resolution... that the Town Clerk be authorised to draw up a draft bylaw prohibiting betting in the streets... was carried by 11 votes to 5...

Thus did respectability, with working class support, defeat liberal (or conservative) individual freedom. When at the next Council meeting a month later the bylaw was adopted with a similar two-to-one majority, the NDM reported that "the general public had turned up in great force and frequently applauded the speeches". We are not told how applause was divided but may well assume that the supporters of the bylaw outnumbered its opponents.

A long petition, stated to have been signed by 884 working-men of Hartlepool, against the proposed bylaw, was put in, together with a letter which informed the council that six lists, containing more than 4,000 signature had been stolen. The writer also asked where Councillor Sherwood had got his 4,000 signatures from, and state whether they were all of working men or whether they included the signatures of women and children.
Ald. Horsley inquired if the 884 signatures had been got in public-houses... .
Councillor Kilburn contended that men had a right to sign a petition in a public house as well as in the churches or chapels.
A petition... was also read from the officers and congregation of Holy Trinity Church... expressing the belief that the evil accruing from betting had much to do with the poverty prevailing in the parish...
Councillor Hart, repeating his earlier defence of the liberty of the subject, added... If they passed bylaw they would drive the bookmakers into obscure places where neither police nor anybody else could see them, and it would be much worse for the town (Applause)...
Councillor Kilburn... never backed a horse in his life, but... (s)o long as it was lawful for the upper or middle classes to bet, he claimed the same right for the poorer classes He had made enquiries, but could not find one trade or labour union branch in Hartlepool who had passed any resolution condemning betting...
Councillor Withers, as a working man and a labour representative, also spoke in support of the bylaw...
Councillor Marshall, also speaking as a representative of the working- men, claimed that if he desired to back a horse, he had a right to do so...
Councillor Gibb said he supported the motion at the last meeting... but although he had taken particular notice last week, he had not seen anything like the amount of betting as had taken place at West Hartlepool... For the present he could not see his way to support the bylaw...

The division was, by accident or design, much less clear-cut in class and party terms. Both were divided, and it is interesting again to note how Dr. Gibb, intentionally or by instinct, bridged the gap.

Despite the bylaw the Central Estate was not blameless. Cleveland Road had (at least) two bookmakers and Arch Street a gambler. Were they wickeder than the furtive police? On July 10, 1907:

Betting Prosecution. - John Thomas Stevenson (39), residing in Cleveland-road, and described as a bookmaker, pleaded guilty to a charge of frequenting and using Procter's-passage for the purpose of betting on June 10th and 20th... - Defendant: Have you any of the men here I was betting with? - Witness (P.C. Brown) No... I can give you the names of a few of them, if you like... - The Magistrates Clerk... Do you wish to ask any further questions: - Defendant: I think the least said the soonest done. (Laughter)... fine of £5 and 10s costs...

And on Nov. 4: *ALLEGED BETTING HOUSE*
HAIRDRESSER ARRESTED AT HARTLEPOOL
At the Hartlepool Police-court, this morning... Wm. Brownless, (24), a hairdresser of 47, Cleveland-road, was charged that he, being the occupier of No. 47 Cleveland-road, did use the same as a house for the purpose of betting with persons resorting

thereto on the 2nd November…
Inspector Peart said that, in accordance with the warrant handed over to him, he searched the premises of the defendant at 12-45 p.m. on Saturday. It was a barber's shop and was in the occupation of the prisoner. He there found the betting papers (produced), a racing guide book, and football coupons. He charged the defendant with keeping the house for the purpose of betting, but he made no reply…
Defendant said he had been in custody since Saturday dinner-time, and there was no one to look after the shop.
The Chief Constable said he had no objection to substantial bail…
Bail was allowed in the defendant's own recognisance of £20.

On Nov. 12: *KEEPING A BETTING HOUSE*
WHAT A DISGUISED POLICEMAN SAW
HARTLEPOOL HAIRDRESSER FINED
… The first witness, P.C. Freegard, of the West Hartlepool force, stated that at half past 12 o'clock on Thursday Oct. 31st he was in the defendant's barber's shop in company with P.C. Bell. He sat down and asked defendant to cut his hair, and P.C. Bell sat down on a seat opposite. During the time he was getting his hair cut he saw several men come into the shop and slips of paper and money to the defendant. He heard two men say "Sixpence each way" and "A shilling each way". Defendant took the slips and put them away in his trousers pocket… On the following day he visited the barber's shop at 1.35 p.m. with P.C. Bell. The latter had a shave, during which time several men came into the shop and handed slips of paper and money to the defendant. After Bell had been shaved he handed defendant two slips and put 2s. in respect of each slip on Electric Rose, in the name of John Spence. The horse was running in the Queensberry Handicap. Defendant replied, "We pay at seven," They didn't go at that time as the horse lost. (Laughter.)
Mr. Geipel (defending): How were you dressed? Witness: I was dressed in a blue smock, can, dinner basket, and a pair of old trousers.
The Chairman (Alderman Hunter): You wouldn't be dressed in a dinner can. (Laughter)

… Brownless was a single man living in lodgings in Arch-street… He was fined £5 and the costs.

On June 23 1908: *BETTING ON THE DOCKS*
TWO HARTLEPOOL MEN FINED
… P.C. Wilkinson stated, that… at 1-10 p.m., he was on duty in plain clothes, in company with P.C. White of the N.E.R. Police. They were concealed near the ballast cranes. At 1.10 p.m. the defendant came,. Between then and 1.55 p.m. he saw 48 men go up to him, including a clerk and an assistant schoolmaster. They each handed him slips of paper and money…
John Thos. Stephenson (42), a bookmaker, of 37 Cleveland-road was charged with a similar offence on the docks. - Defendant pleaded guilty… There was a previous conviction… for betting.- He was now fined £5 and the costs, or in default a month's imprisonment.

On Sept. 9, 190?: *RELIEF RECIPIENT CHARGED WITH BETTING*
Charles King, coal hawker, Clyde-place, Hartlepool, was charged… with betting. P.C. Farrand stated that whilst in concealment at noon… he saw the defendant in

Clyde-place. He saw King take three bets... The slips related to horses which ran yesterday
- The Magistrates' Clerk: Did they pull it off?- Witness: I have not looked at the results.
- Defendant said he had been out of work for some time., and had been "next door to starvation"... he had tried to do all he could to earn a shilling.
- The Chief Constable said the defendant was in receipt of two shillings a week from the mayor's Distress Fund during last winter. - A fine of 10s. and costs was imposed.

It was not only in respect of betting that there was entertainment in court, although one may conclude that there was a plentiful lack of wit, and wonder on what principle truth was separated from falsehood. Physical appearance presumably carried weight: and justice may not always have been done. On May 24 1906 NDM reported:

PROSECUTION FOLLOWS "JOLLIFICATION"
Elizabeth Clark, a married woman living in Clyde-street, and who appeared in court with a young child on her arm, was charged with being drunk in charge of the child on Saturday night.
- P.C. Crowther stated that he saw the woman in Hart-road. She was drunk and quite incapable of taking charge of the child, whose uncovered head was hanging over its mother's arm.
- Defendant admitted the offence, which was brought about, she explained, by a little "jollification", in which she took part on the occasion of the return from sea of her husband's brother. She had only two or three bottles of stout, and remembered nothing more.
- Chief Constable Winterbottom said the same thing had occurred before.
- Defendant: Yes, sir, it was when he came home last time, three months ago... a fine of 5s. and 7s. costs was (sic) imposed.

There was theft, not without ingenuity. On May 16 1906 the NDM reported:

"Adding Insult to Injury" - John Brown (29) labourer, Rokeby-street, West Hartlepool, was remanded on a charge of stealing two shirts, value 4s., the property of Jennie Bloom, pawnbroker, Northgate-street. - Ernest Bloom stated that on Saturday night he missed two shirts from the doorway of his shop. Half-an-hour later prisoner offered one of the shirts in pledge at the shop and witness recognised it.
- The Magistrate's Clerk (Mr. S. H. Belk): Adding insult to injury. (Laughter.)
- On this evidence a remand was granted for inquiries to be made.

There was unladylike behaviour, though all the fault may not have been on one side, as the magistrates clearly suspected. On that same May 16 the NDM also reported:

Sequel to a Courtship.
- An elderly woman named Mary Ann Dawkins was charged with assaulting Maud Beatrice Dunaway on May 11. Complainant said that Mrs. Dawkins came to her house in Bell-street, Central Estate, about 9.0 p.m., and after using obscene language, struck her twice in the face...
Defendant said that her son, aged 18, was to be married to the complainant very shortly. "In fact" she said, "everything is ready".
- Ald. Rowe: Is the cake made?

- Defendant: Yes, sir.
- Ald. Rowe; Are the guests invited?
- Defendant: Yes, sir, everybody is invited.
- Ald. Rowe: I'm not yet (Laughter).
- Defendant: In fact she has been with the boy to get him measured for his suit and he is only 18 years old and she is four or five years older. As to the assault, defendant said she spoke to complainant about her son visiting her (complainant's) house, and she replied by striking her... The case was dismissed.
- A cross-summons for assault was withdrawn.

Female assaulting female was one thing but husband assaulting wife was another, although, again, the fault may have been two-sided.. On April 16, 1907 the NDM reported:

HARTLEPOOL PETTY SESSIONS

...Thomas McHugh, of 6, Clyde Place, was summoned for having assaulted his wife, Alice McHugh.
- Complainant said that her husband had behaved cruelly to her for 12 years. On Saturday, April 13th, he gave her a black eye. He came home at night and threw a boot at her. This missed her and she ran into the street for protection. Defendant followed her and ill used her in the street, striking her in the face and kicking her in the stomach.
- Defendant said complainant was getting him into debt all over. He had just got a bill for a new hat she had bought
- Mr. S. Belk (Magistrate's Clerk): Hold your noise! She is entitled to a new hat.
- Complainant: It is two years since I had one, sir. (Laughter)
- Defendant further said that his wife had insured him for a shilling a week, but she had not insured herself for one farthing. (Laughter)
- Complainant said she gave up the insurance long ago.
- A fine of 10s. and costs was imposed.

On May 28 1909 someone else tried to diddle a pawnbroker. Perhaps she was un lucky. It may have been common practice, but required more than persuasiveness with an ultimately sharp-eyed shop assistant.

PAWNBROKER COMPLIMENTED

At the Hartlepool Police Court this morning... a married woman named Elizabeth Jenkinson, 22, Vincent-street, Hartlepool, was charged with stealing by means of a trick two skirts, value 6s 6d, the property of Edward Thompson...
- Ada Colley, an assistant employed by the prosecutors, said that prisoner went to the shop in Northgate-street and asked to be shown some skirts. Witness allowed her to take the two skirts produced on approval upon her promising to return that which she did not want to buy.
- Egbert Hancock, pawnbroker... stated that prisoner offered one of the skirts in pledge with him. She gave the name of Mary Johnson... Witness advanced her 2s 6d upon it. Later prisoner returned and offered the other skirt in pledge. This time she gave the name of Mary White... Becoming suspicious witness called a police officer and she was locked up... In reply to the charge she said: "I didn't steal them. I had had some drink.".
- The Chief Constable said there were 22 convictions against Jenkinson.

- Prisoner was committed to gaol for one month with hard labour...

Some cases were far from amusing, and much more lamentable. The "Klondike" was not merely a place of entertainment. On May 4 1905:

BURNING FATALITY AT HARTLEPOOL
DANGER OF FLANNELETTE CLOTHING

At the Central Hotel, Central Estate, today, Mr. Coroner Bell and a jury inquired into the circumstances of the death of Margaret Marshall (7), daughter of John Thomas Marshall, a moulder, residing at 6, Vincent-street... ' The father of the child stated that she was the eldest of three, and had been epileptic since birth. He was at work when the accident took place.

The Coroner drew attention to the great number of children who had lost their lives through mishaps of a similar character - an open fire and flannelette clothing. Flannelette was a most dangerous material, and as to the question of fire, he had through efforts of his own, induced manufactures to produce a fireguard at the small cost of 1s., which was a perfect safeguard to young children...

The mother, who was next called, said the child got up at about 9-40 yesterday morning, after the witness had had a very bad night with her. Whilst at breakfast her daughter was seized with a fit, and she was laid on the sofa where she slept. Between 11.15 and 11.30 witness went out to purchase something for her husband's dinner and returning about a quarter of an hour later, found the room filled with smoke, and the child laying on the floor, quite dead. Her flannelette clothing was burnt off her...

The Coroner said no one attached any blame to the parents...

Inspector Watson of the N.S.P.C.C., said... (s)he had received every medical and parental attention, and had one of the best of mothers...

On May 6 1906: *INFANT'S SHOCKING DEATH*

The shocking death of an infant... was the subject of an inquiry held at the Central Hotel, Central Estate, today... The child, along with another, was being wheeled by its mother beneath a railway bridge under which runs a siding leading from the No. 2 Gasworks, when a truck, which was being towed by two horses, came suddenly round a curve, and crushed the perambulator against the brickwork of the bridge. The mother and one of the children escaped injury, but the deceased child was thrown beneath the wheel of the waggons, and killed instantly...

Patrick Phillips, riveter, of 47, Watson-street, Central Estate, identified the body as that of his infant son, James Phillips (14 months).

The inquiry was adjourned...

Even sadder was the case reported on Apr. 3 1906:

SUICIDE IN THE SEA
MYSTERIOUS AFFAIR AT HARTLEPOOL
YOUNG GIRL'S TRAGIC DEATH

Mr. J. Hyslop Bell, Coroner, held an inquest at the Central Hotel, Central Estate, Hartlepool today, upon the body of Elsie Hall, 16, who resided with her widowed mother at 4, Bell-street, and whose body was recovered from the sea last night. The girl was seen at the water's edge at about noon yesterday. Shortly afterwards she disappeared. Several men ran to the spot, and one entered the water, but she was seen no more until the body was brought ashore by the returning tide.

... testimony... showed... that (witnesses) were on the North Sands, and their attention was drawn to a young woman who appeared to be "plodging". All of a sudden she disappeared... one of the witnesses remarking to his friend he believed a wave had knocked her over... ran to the spot three quarters of a mile away, and went about 12 yards into the water. He was a swimmer but did not go out into the water, the current being too strong...

P.C. Byrom... carefully examined deceased's pocket but there was nothing in it... The girl's mother said she had not seen her since 9.30 a.m, that she was all right then, and that there had been no trouble... the deceased's aunt knew of no reason why the girl should have drowned herself. Witness found no marks on the body... the girl was always of a cheery nature...

The Coroner: Had she any acquaintances that she might have gone wrong with? - No, she was far different to that.

Had she any religious melancholy? - No, sir...

A young girl named Cecilia McMahon, living at 12, Cleveland-road, said she met deceased at a quarter to 11 o'clock yesterday morning, and asked her what was the matter, as she was looking very sad. She started to cry, and said she felt poorly, and had a pain across her chest. Witness asked her to go to her grandmother's and see if she could give her anything to take, but deceased would not. Deceased had appeared the night before to have a slight cold and cough.

The Coroner, in summing up the evidence, described the affair as an insoluble mystery, and the jury found that deceased committed suicide whilst of unsound mind.

Unfortunate girl! It is almost certain that the shame of unwed pregnancy drove her to suicide and almost as equally certain that everyone knew it: hence the verdict. Presumably the Coroner was being charitably tactful and that may have been why he did not require a postmortem. The little girl's evidence was indeed clinching.

The sands adjoining the Central Estate could be a dangerous playground. On July 24 1906:

BATHING FATALITY AT HARTLEPOOL
BOY'S SAD DEATH
AN EXCITING RESCUE

A sad drowning fatality and a sensational rescue occurred on the North Sands, at Hartlepool, near the Cemetery, last night.

... The sands here, it is said, are of a treacherous character, and consequently dangerous for bathers, and the lads, having apparently got out of their depth, were seen to be in difficulties.

An apprentice carpenter... and Ivison Ridley, a blacksmith, of 62, Stephenson-street, were near by, and, observing the boys' danger, stripped and entered the water. They succeeded with difficulty in saving Fleetham, but were then too exhausted to make any further attempt at rescue. A joiner... also entered the water, however, and made a plucky and determined essay to save Stonehouse, but though he succeeded in bringing him to within a short distance of the shore, the drowning lad's struggles were so violent that he was compelled to release him. The boy then sank and was seen no more...

Seventeen months later accident struck again, this time wretchedly involving the postmaster who had unsuccessfully sought an off-license in 1896. Police-Sgt. Crowther had some unpleasant tasks. On Dec. 2 1907:

KILLED BY A TRAM
SHOCKING ACCIDENT AT HARTLEPOOL

A shocking fatality occurred on Saturday night at Hartlepool. It appears that Wilfrid Robinson... two year old... was visiting its grandparent, Mr. John Hayes, grocer, Cleveland-road, and at about 5.15 the child was observed playing in front of the shop. At that time the electric tramcar, No 24, was approaching the town from West Hartlepool, and when it had reached the loop-line opposite Pease-street, the driver... noticed the child was about to leave the footpath, evidently with the intention of crossing the road in front of the car. He instantly rang his bell, and applied the brake. The child seemed to hesitate, and than attempted to run across in front of the car, which knocked it down. The driver immediately brought the tram to a standstill, and Police-Sergeant Crowther, who happened to be a passenger, proceeded to release the child, whose right foot was held fast between the brake and the tram lines. Having liberated the child, he discovered it was suffering from a serious fracture of the left leg, while the flesh had been torn away between the knee and the upper portion of the thigh. The right leg was also fractured, and the child had sustained several bruises about the body.

The little sufferer was conveyed with all haste to the grandparents' house, where it was attended by Dr. Gibb until death ensued one hour later.

Towards the end of March 1908 there was a grotesquely gruesome death at the eastern end of the Central Estate seashore. The "Tips" (on Spion Kop) was a slag bank from the long-closed iron works of the 1860s which was nevertheless still smouldering and emitting poisonous fumes. The body of a penniless man who had been refused a bed in a lodging house was found. On June 4 908 Councillor Gibb raised the matter in Council. His concern was not entirely representative:

COUNCILLOR GIBB'S FEARS

... Cllr Gibb remarked it was by no means a small matter. There were underground fires all over these slag banks. "I am," he added, "perfectly certain if you don't make the South Durham Steel and Iron Co. understand it is a serious matter you will have a very serious accident occurring there". Councillor Gibb also reminded the Council a man was suffocated on those banks a couple of months ago.

Councillor Gardner said the place had been on fire more or less for 30 years...

Ald. Horsley remarked that it cost the Corporation about £300 to put out the fire amongst the tips at Middleton...

Councillor Sherwood said steps could surely be taken to put out the fire...

... the matter was again referred to the sanitary Committee...

A week later there was another death from "skylarking":

DEATH FROM COMPRESSED AIR...
POLICE COURT PROCEEDINGS
TWO YOUTHS COMMITTED FOR TRIAL

Wm. Harrison Woodward... and David Magnus Johnson... apprentice die-sinkers, employed at the Central Marine Engine Works, appeared on remand at the Hartlepool Police Court, charged with causing the death of Harold Wilkinson (18), Watt-street, Central Estate, another apprentice at the works on Saturday...

John Francis Burton, die sinker, Bell-street, Hartlepool repeated the evidence he gave at the inquest... The pneumatic pipe from which the deceased received a blast of compressed air was produced, and witness explained that when Wilkinson cried out the nozzle of the pipe was lying on the floor, about two feet away from him...
John Guthrie, foreman in the forge department... said Woodward, Johnson... and the deceased were under his supervision. When witness saw the deceased after the occurrence, he applied hot bricks and hot plates, believing that he was suffering from cramp. He asked Wilkinson... if he had lifted anything or if he had fallen, or if he had injured himself in any way. The deceased answered "No," He spoke to Woodward, who told him that he was about to blowdown the bench with compressed air when the pipe end flew up and caught the deceased in between the legs.... He had not had any complaints about the youths "skylarking". They were all very friendly indeed... Thomas Leech, an electrician... said... (i)t would not have had any effect unless it were held to the body...
Dr. Gibb gave evidence as to the condition of the boy.
Mr Geipel, in cross-examining, suggested to witness that if the pipe struck deceased it would cause a tightening of the muscles, which might result in the nozzle being held fast.
Dr. Gibb: I am afraid I cannot agree with that.
Dr. Robertson, house surgeon at the Hospital... stated it as his opinion that the nozzle of the pipe must have been held in close contact with the body...
The magistrates... decided to send prisoners for trial at the Assizes...

Dr. Gibb was right to have reservations. It is not clear who was lying most. The nozzle must have been in Harold Wilkinson's anus and it is unlikely that he himself put it there. The ongoing practice was described to me in the early 1930s by a shipyard engineering works apprentice.

On Dec. 7 1909 another inquest was reported. It is again reasonably clear that it was not the truth, the whole truth and nothing but the truth that was told.

THE WRONG BOTTLE
HARTLEPOOL MAN'S SAD DEATH

An inquest was held... on the body of Joseph Smith (31), millwright, 12, Pease-street... whose death occurred early this morning from poisoning.
The deceased returned home from work on Saturday afternoon, and went to bed. He was heard coughing, and when asked what was wrong he stated that he had drunk out of the wrong bottle. Dr. Milne... ascertained that the deceased was suffering from the effects of poison, composed of ammonia and turpentine, made up as a liniment...
Alice Smith, the wife of the deceased,, stated that her husband returned home and seemed as if he had had something to drink. He went to bed with his clothes on shortly after entering the house. About two hours later she heard him make a noise but did not think anything serious was the matter...
... Mrs. Smith said that there was a bottle of water in the room when the deceased went to bed...
A verdict was returned to the effect that death was due to misadventure.

Accidents also made good watching, as reported on Jan. 9 1908. The sea front was less than half-a-mile from the Central Estate, which was also the housing area nearest to Spencer's Farm. The Workhouse was little further away.

THE GALE
STEAMER ASHORE NEAR HARTLEPOOL

The terrific force of yesterday's gale was fully experienced in the Hartlepools from early noon until late in the evening... During the evening some thousands of persons congregated in sheltered positions along the sea front, to witness the tremendous fury of the sea...
... The disabled steamer.. the Nellie Wise, and the towing steamer the Henry Morton... were gradually driven back towards Hartlepool, and it was eventually found necessary for the disabled steamer to drop anchor and cast off from the other vessel. She dragged her anchor, however, and eventually a heavy sea struck her, and her anchor chain parted...
The vessel finally drove ashore not far distant from what is known as Spencer's farm. As soon as the information was received by the authorities at Hartlepool, large numbers of sightseers wended their way along the North sands and the golf links to the vicinity of the vessel...

May 11 1909 BIG BLAZE NEAR THE WORKHOUSE
A large straw stack situated near the Workhouse caught fire about 9 o'clock last night, and was soon burning fiercely. The blaze was plainly visible from both Hartlepool and West Hartlepool, and hundreds of people quickly thronged the roads leading to the workhouse... About an hour after the fire commenced... a man of the labouring class gave himself up...

Trade unions and trade associations had social as well as economic functions. In January 1906, for instance, the Hartlepool Trimmers and the Passenger Clerks ("including guards and porters") each had formal Dinners, as did also "a large number of members of the Hartlepools(!) Grocers' Association and, in 1910, the Fish Workers. In May 1906:

DRILLERS' SECRETARY HONOURED
Last night a successful smoker, arranged by members of the Hartlepool branch of the Amalgamated Society of Drillers and Hole Cutters was held at the Central Hotel, Central Estate... The remainder of the evening was spent in harmony...

"Harmony", of course, meant not the absence of fisticuffs but solo songs, invariably reported as well sung and well accompanied by a pianist. Moreover, like the Hartlepools Shipwrights' Benevolent Society, many, if not all, trade union branches held their meetings in public houses. One can see them as a more attractive venue for tired working men than cold halls. The abstainers could always drink lemonade.

More seriously, trade unions also offered sympathy and support in times of bereavement. Workmates made collections for deceased members and attended funerals as bearers and mourners. On Dec. 20 1909 notices of Deaths included:

VICKERS - On the 19th, at 78, Watson-street, Central Estate, John Watson Vickers, late of Stockton-on-Tees, aged 70. - Cortege to leave Wednesday at 2.30. - Friends please accept this (the only) intimation. - A(malgamised). S(ociety). of E(ngineers). members please note.

Public houses were naturally pleased to accommodate other social functions, one of which was the making of presentations:

Mar 10 1908 PRESENTATION
A good company assembled at the Lord Clyde Hotel, last night, to do honour to Mr and Mrs Davies who are leaving after a period of 18 years... In conclusion he wished the new landlord -Mr Spence, who was present-every success. The remainder of the evening was spent in harmony...

For the more productively inclined, the provision of land for allotments on which fruit and vegetables might be grown and chickens, rabbits and pigeons housed, was important but financially contentious:

Dec. 5 1907 THE ALLOTMENTS QUESTION
Councillor Sherwood asked whether... the matter was to be dropped, or whether they were going to ask any other landowner to give a price at which he was prepared to let his land. There was a great desire for allotments on the Central Estate... At the prices which had been asked, it was said to be impossible to make the allotments payable and he, therefore, thought they might try other landowners, or take some steps to bring their powers under the Act into force to compel the owners to provide land at a reasonable price.
The mayor said that no doubt the committee would be prepared to consider the matter if Councillor Sherwood would suggest where they could get land satisfactorily...

The issue was rapidly and happily concluded and the Warren Road allotments survived into the late 1930s:

Jan. 8 1908 IMPROVEMENTS COMMITTEE
... A letter having been read from Messrs Martin and Fenwick as to the proposed rentals of the land in Workhouse-lane for allotments, it was resolved that they be offered £4 per acre for the land...

Public functions such as Empire Day (May 24th: Queen Victoria's birthday) and Mayor's Sunday were always reported as well supported:

Nov 11 1907 ECHOES OF THE WEEK
A finer day than yesterday (Sunday) could not have been desired, and Hartlepool yesterday morning was en fete, the townspeople turning out in great force to do honour to their Mayor...

Issues affecting both primary and secondary education were reported.

Feb. 23 1906 HARTLEPOOL EDUCATION COMMITTEE
ALLEGED UNDUE PUNISHMENT OF A SCHOLAR
Amongst the correspondence submitted was a letter from a parent complaining of undue punishment of her boy at Hart-road School.
Councillor Withers said he saw the boy, and found that his back was black and blue. His (Councillor Withers') son had attended the same school, and had come home one day very much discoloured.
Councillor Gibb stated that the boy in question had a very nasty bruise across the chest - in fact right over the heart, and the skin was slightly broken. He moved that the matter be referred to the School Management Committee to take such action as might be deemed necessary.

Mr Purves urged the committee to use caution in whatever action they took, pointing out that if they attempted to deal with the masters they would never keep order among the boys.
Councillor Gibb thought there was nothing which justified a teacher hitting a boy across the chest, especially over the region of the heart. It might have been a very serious matter.
Eventually the matter was referred to committee.

No names were named and the outcome was not reported. The savagery was exemplary even by early 19th century public school standards and the boy was fortunate in having such champions as Dr. Gibb, whose patient he probably was, and Cllr. Withers. In the mid-20s there was still brutality at the school. In the mid-20s I myself witnessed regular caning of the backs of two quiet and harmless simpletons. It was, however, exceptional and at least did not draw blood.

In August 1907 the headmaster's request to establish a class for Standard 5 was refused for undisclosed reasons but his, or his successor's, application for an increase of salary in the following year succeeded despite opposition.
... The School management Committee further reported- That a letter from the headmaster of Hart-road Boys' School asking for increase of salary.. it was resolved that his salary be increased by £25 per annum...
Councillor Marshall... did not think the present an opportune time to increase salaries... Mr Purves... said that when Mr Coulson was appointed to Hart-road School he was receiving a salary of £200 a year at Prissick School... for 20 years he had been a headmaster in the town...
Councillor Marshall.:. When this headmaster took up this position he knew exactly the conditions-that his salary would start at £150...
The Chairman:... why the Committee recommend this £25 is on account of the services of this man, and of his leaving £200 a year in order to keep under this Board.
Mrs Kearsley: He is better off than the mistress of the Girls' School...
The amendment was... lost.

April 2 1908: A HEADMASTER'S SALARY
... the Town Clerk stated that he had received a letter from the Ratepayers' and Property Owners' Association protesting against the suggested increase.
Councillor Marshall... moved that the matter be sent back to the Education Committee... Councillor Sherwood... seconded the motion... Personally he could not understand why one certain individual was cited for an increase of 10s. a week, when they had men who had been in the employ of the Council for years, and who were only getting a little over 30s. a week, who had been refused an increase of 2s. 6d...
Councillor Gibb remarked that the increase was suggested with a view to bringing Mr Coulson's salary nearer to the amount he previously received... He hoped the Council would show their appreciation of Mr Coulson's past (21 years) services...
...Councillor Withers protested that the present was not an opportune time to increase anyone's salary...
Councillor Marshall's motion was lost, only five voting for it, and the Education Committee's decision to grant Mr Coulson an advance of £25 was confirmed.

It is unlikely that this article reported an exceptional occurrence; politics both local and national were, and remain, ever thus. Councillors Sherwood and Withers were socially partisan whereas Dr. Gibb, though probably no less socially partisan, appeared fair-minded. Mr Coulson, who retired only in 1928, probably deserved the increment. As I have good personal reason to know, he was good as headmasters go, doing his utmost to increase his school's score of grammar-school scholarships (Plate 62 p. 212).

On Sept 5 1901 the NDM had reported that J. H. Laverty of Hart Road (School) Plate 26 p. 61) had won a scholarship to the Henry Smith School which, although endowed by a 17th century charity, had previously been fee-paying only. In 1907 it was proposed that Durham County Council, under the 1902 Education Act, take it over, although Cllr. C. T. Watson objected that "this was a Hartlepool charity" and Ald Hunter that "the school should never have be been built because it could not be self-supporting". However, in 1910 Durham County Council offered new scholarships and although Ald. Hunter continued to object that "scholars or pupils from other schools in the county" might get scholarships, the gateway to secondary education for, amongst others, the children of Central Estate was widening.

Meanwhile, Hartlepool children were not perfectly well behaved. On Nov 2 1908 the leader writer of the NDM observed:

> *I was glad to notice last week that Chief Constable Winterbottom had called attention to the nuisance caused by marking buildings with chalk... The children seem to have a perfect mania... Nothing is sacred from them... "I mildly remonstrated with them... What they (two girls) said would pain me to repeat"...*

Substitute graffiti for chalk and it might be 1998.

The NDM files from July to December 1905 are missing so that we are deprived of the leader writer's comments on the state of the economy at the end of the year, but on July 18 1906 he noted that the official returns for June 1906 bore evidence of the steady improvement in trade especially in the iron and steel and engineering trades. On Christmas Eve 1906 he said that the year had been a remarkably good one for the local shipbuilding trade: in fact the number and tonnage of vessels built at the Hartlepools during 1906 constituted a record for the port, despite the recent two months strike. The local coal trade was expected to exceed 2,000,000 tons - a figure that had not been approached since the palmy days of the early seventies. This had been rendered possible principally by the development of Horden Collieries. On March 21 1906 he had already said that the opening of the new coast line would bring the Hartlepools into closer touch with the important towns to the North and South. It did.

The strike theme recurred in the following year, 1907. In August a general shipbuilding strike in support of Tyneside caulkers (who sealed the gaps between the iron plates of hulls) on the demarcation line between them and their apprentices was countered by a lockout and ended by a compromise. So also, in November, did a railway strike. On December 30 "Echoes Of The Week" attempted to balance the pluses and minuses. The year could certainly not be described as one of great prosperity but had not been devoid of favourable features. On the one hand, people engaged in the shipbuilding and engineering trades experienced a reaction from the exceptional activity which characterised those industries in the previous year, but on the other hand the coal, iron, and import and export trades had shown considerable vitality. But the boom had proved of short duration, the outlook for 1908 being most depressing. It was, said the author of "Echoes Of The Week", apparently due to overproduction in shipbuilding.

It is, consequently, not surprising that on March 1908 the NDM should have reported that Hartlepool people were feeling the effects of the bad times. About 1300 men were walking the streets and nearly 1,000 of them were receiving no strike or out of work pay. Assuming there were, on an average, four people per family, some 4,000 Hartlepool people did not at present know where their next meal was coming from. When it was remembered that the population of Hartlepool was about 23,000, the fact was brought home that about one sixth (17%) of the people were in a very sad plight.

The Central Estate was presumably proportionately affected. The response of the Town Council mingled generosity with peevishness. It sent a deputation to William Cresswell Gray, Matthew's surviving brother now in charge of the Central Marine Engineering Works and shipyard, to urge the NER to start with a promised dock enlargement scheme. Alderman Horsley, however, protested against men causing strikes to the detriment of their poorer fellows, and then not contributing to their assistance. This was politically and socially frank if not a little uncharitable. It was not for the first time.

Despite the boom of 1906, on Dec. 10 1906 the NDM leader had observed that at this time of the year there were always a large number of people who felt the pinch of want, and, on Dec. 20 it was reported that a special meeting of the Town Council had been held to discuss distress. The responsible government department, the Local Government Board, had refused to authorise the formation of a Distress committee under the Unemployed Workmen' Act but...

> *The Mayor explained... (t)hey had about £8 in hand as a surplus from an old fund, and it was proposed to hand over £5 to the Salvation Army for the purpose of providing free breakfasts to the poor persons of the town.*
> *Councillor C. T. Watson thought the Council might hand over the whole £8... (and) suggested that some further enquiries should be made... "for whatever monies the County Council had procured for the alleviation of distress"...*
> *Ald. Horsley reminded the meeting that it should not be forgotten the present dispute was caused by one class of men who, when their helpers were becoming poverty-stricken, should put their hands into their pockets and assist them. It was because of the attitude of the platers in the whole matter that they would not get the sympathy of the public during the present strike, which was doing a great amount of mischief...*
>
> *Dec. 21* *DISTRESS AT HARTLEPOOL*
> *£50 FROM THE RATES*
> *A FUND TO BE RAISED*
> *... The Town Clerk announced... that the County Council had no funds applicable... Councillor Sherwood... move(d) that the Council issue an appeal to the charitably-inclined public in order that the deserving poor should be able to tide over the Christmas season... (He) favoured the relief being given in kind, and upon the ticket or token principle, by which means the persons could go into a grocer's or butcher's shop and obtain goods to the value of the coupons...*

The Mayor said he would move that £25 be granted... out of the rates, and that he would personally supplement the amount...
Councillor Sherwood intimated he would withdraw his proposition if the mayor would kindly increase the amount to £50. (Laughter.)
The Mayor said he would move that the amount be £50... and that subscription lists be placed at the banks...

The Christmas spirit was evidently at work; £50 was not ungenerous and it was to be in cash rather than in stigmatising coupons, to be produced in the presence of cash-paying customers, which the radical Councillor Sherwood had nevertheless suggested. The distinction between the deserving and undeserving poor, already established in the reign of Queen Elizabeth I (1558-1603), obviously persisted.

In that same December of 1906 "Echoes Of The Week" further commented:

If anyone had doubted that the distress... was acute, he, or she, need only have visited the Throston Board School, Hartlepool, yesterday, when the Trades Council, out of the Sunday Free Breakfast Fund, provided a breakfast... There were altogether 500 children, necessitating two sittings... It is to be hoped sufficient funds may be forthcoming to carry on these breakfasts until work improves in the district.

The round-figure estimate may have been generous and not all the children, quite possibly including some from the Central Estate, were necessarily needy; young appetites might accommodate a second breakfast. The reality of the distress is, notwithstanding, unquestionable. Two years later, on Nov 2 1908 "Echoes Of The Week" observed:

During the past five or six years, whenever distress has prevailed in the Hartlepools, the Trade and Labour Council... have provided breakfasts on Sunday mornings for the needy children... Breakfasts were provided from last December right up the beginning of July, and as the distress is still very acute in the district it was decided that a start should be made this winter much earlier than usual. On Sunday, October 10th, a breakfast was provided in Throston School, Hartlepool, at which 500 children were fed.

Two years later still, on Nov 16 1910:

SOUP FOR THE POOR

Soup was yesterday kindly distributed to about 150 poor children... "What's the matter with the kids?" said a portly constable who saw school children run along High-street, Hartlepool, this morning. On hearing a poor little mite about six years of age, without any boots and stockings on, and with his legs blue with the cold, saying "Please missus I've fallen down and broken my basin, and I can't get any soup," interest was aroused, and on visiting Daniel's Band Mission-room, the officer saw there about 200 children, their little faces expectant of good things to come. A few minutes later, basins of soup and thick slices of home-made bread were served out by the host and hostess...

The succession of rival local shipbuilding or ships' engine-building MPs (Plate 32 p. 111) for the Hartlepools began with Ralph Ward Jackson in 1868 and continued, with only one short break, to alternate between Richardsons and Furnesses until

1900. In the "Khaki" election of that year - "khaki" because of the continuing Boer war "pro-Boer" Liberal Sir Christopher Furness, who survived as Member until the second election of 1910, surprisingly defeated "pro-war" Conservative Thomas Richardson, whose party was victorious. Like the Richardsons, father and son, and Sir William Gray who was defeated as candidate in the by-election of 1891, Furness sought the reputation of a good employer. In December 1909 the NDM commented that shipbuilding "overproduction began to tell its tale" and that consequently the employers on the North-East Coast demanded a reduction in wages, which was stubbornly resisted until Sir Christopher Furness proposed his co-partnery (sic) scheme, lauded as "a silver streak visible in the dark cloud". The year had been a better one, with 6 more ships built than the 13 of 1908; the comparison, however, with 1906 which had produced no less than 43, was still dismal.

> *... The following figures show the fluctuations in shipbuilding in the Hartlepools during the last ten years:*
>
> ***Dec. 20 1909***

Year	Vessels	Gross Tonnage
1900	39	138,542
1901	30	115,251
1902	21	84,717
1903	28	87,053
1904	32	101,318
1905	35	169,282
1906	43	163,865
1907	29	111,040
1908	13	41,383
1909	19	72,592

Table 2 - Shipbuilding 1909

The figures for coal and coke exports told a rather better story:

Year	Tons
1900	1,208,755
1901	1,917,411
1902	1,270,108
1903	1,418,288
1904	1,652,000
1905	1,611,065
1906	1,794,425
1907	1,906,526
1908	2,154,218
1909	2,325,464

Table 3 - Coal & Coke 1909

Nevertheless distress prevailed.

Earlier, in March 1908, Sir Christopher, contributing £50 for the relief of distress, told the Mayor of Hartlepool that the depression would continue until such times as the trade of the world overtook the present steamship-carrying capacity of this and other countries, and that unless concessions were made by employers and workmen the bad times would continue. In June 1908 Sir Christopher recorded his opposition to strikes as political weapons and, deploring the consequential loss of orders and citing instances of the friendly resolution of employer-employee disputes, advocated cooperation, arbitration and profit-sharing as preferable to class war. His "copartnery" scheme was thus directly aimed against current syndicalist theories, which saw the general strike as the workers' ultimate economic and political weapon against the ruling class.

On Oct. 24 1908 NDM reported that what was now renamed "co-partnership" would be tried and on April 23 1909 that Sir Christopher was rewarded with the Freedom of the Borough of Hartlepool. In his speech of thanks he was frank: co-partnership was patriotic as well as beneficial. He proposed a National Conference: of leading employers.

"THE TREATY OF THE HARTLEPOOLS"

... "the ending of the strife in our local industries by the introduction of the principal and practice of Co-partnership into the ship-building yards... in the vitally important work of safe-guarding and extending the gravely threatened position of England as the world's greatest industrial power - the task of re-fortifying and rendering impregnable the citadel of British industry, trade and commerce... we may not have to fight the German nation - God forbid! -... but who can deny... that in industry, in trade, in commerce, they are competitors no longer to be despised...

At the end of the following year, Dec. 30 1909, NDM rejoiced that the scheme had been entirely successful in a period of acute industrial depression. The workmen who had invested a part of their weekly wages in the firm had received a 9% dividend which, according to Sir Christopher, was two thirds higher than could have been obtained from the Post Office Savings Bank.

The other suggestion he made on the occasion of his presentation, reverting to an earlier possibility, was less successful. No one took any notice.

THE UNION OF THE BOROUGHS

... "their interests are identical and not antagonistic and I would have you consider how greatly unity of purpose, acting in concert with unity of interest, may influence the near destiny of these two important communities to their lasting well being...

A possible alternative or supplement to Hartlepool's dependence on shipbuilding was to revive its pre-industrial function as a health and holiday resort and on Nov 8 1906 a special committee was appointed by the Town Council. Its remit, however, was limited to persuading the NER to advertise Hartlepool equally with other places round the coast, on the same footing as Scarborough. It was to cost the Council (and the ratepayers) £50 per annum and by January 1908 Cllr. Sherwood queried the investment and suggested that slum clearance would make Hartlepool healthier and wealthier without advertisement. The Council also (in 1906) discussed the improvement of bathing facilities and only two years later (June 1908) it had been decided to buy no less than a dozen portable bathing tents. A bathing pool, however, had to wait until 1924.

As to party politics, the NDM observed on Oct. 23 1906 that there was not much excitement or interest manifested in the municipal elections. The only contest was taking place in Throston Ward where shipwright Cllr. Withers of Watson Street was successfully challenged by Mr A. H. Lightfoot, clothier and outfitter with shops in both the Hartlepools. At the poll declaration ex-Cllr Withers said he had done his best for three years and remarked that if Mr Lightfoot would do the same for the electors as he had done, they would be very thankful, and then they would kick him out. (Laughter.)

In fact they did so at a by-election in less than eighteen months. In March 1908, having been declared bankrupt, Cllr Lightfoot was challenged by two Central Estate residents, Frederick Emmerson, insurance agent of Watson Street who enjoyed Labour and trade union backing, and John Turner of Arch Street, joiner and undertaker "with Conservative leanings", who won, with ex-Cllr Lightfoot bottom of the poll. In 1909, nominated by dairyman Charles Chambers and hairdresser Tom Newton, he won again against the same Frederick Emmerson.

The impasse on the comparative under-representation of Throston ward on the Town Council continued despite the protests of Cllrs Gibb and Kilburn. As in 1904, so in 1907, the idea of representation according to population was rejected on the same grounds of the cost of an Act of Parliament and the 1882 undertaking to Middleton, when it came in with Hartlepool rather than West Hartlepool, that it should have three councillors and an alderman. A repeat of the earlier proposals for a union of the two Hartlepools, despite the additional support of the member, Sir Christopher Furness, was also defeated.

Despite the protests of Cllrs. Kilburn, Sherwood and Withers, the Tramway Company, doubled its workmens' fares from a halfpenny to a penny per stage in 1906. Cllr Withers said that there was a tremendous number of people living now at the Central Estate, and instead of going over to West Hartlepool they now came into Hartlepool, and it would be an even greater inducement for them to come if the halfpenny fares were reintroduced. They were not reduced, of course, and Cllr. Withers should scarcely have been surprised.

It was the question of the marking of the boundary of the Central Estate between Union Road and the NER's propyard (without timber ponds) which re-inserted the Central Estate into the headlines. The agreement with the North Eastern Railway Company of 1901 had been for a six feet high wooden fence, but on Feb. 8 1906 the NDM report on the Improvement and Property Committee revealed that the Company wished to raise it to nine feet. As so many prosecutions revealed, prop ends, saleable as firewood, were constantly stolen. The Committee recommended refusal but:

> *... .Ald. Hunter submitted an amendment that the Company be allowed to raise the fence to the height of 9 feet. He remarked that the Company's request seemed to be reasonable, for they asked merely for this concession in order to protect the property*

of gentlemen who brought a considerable amount of trade to the port, and the Council should put no obstacle in the way of such provision. They had granted a similar privilege in regard to the fence erected in Cleveland-road...

Cllr. Sherwood argued that three feet of open fencing, wire-work, metalwork or something of the kind should be placed above the six-foot fence. It would be unfair to the tenants of the houses in the district, and to people who had built property there on the understanding that there was to be a six-foot fence only. Cllr. Gibb agreed. The thoroughfare was one of the few in the town which had one side as an open space, but, owing to the hoarding, that was to be interfered with. Cllr. Lightfoot added that it was detrimental to the value of working men's property. The matter was referred back to committee.

It became apparent that the company had had its way despite the agreement. By July 4 1907 Mr and Mrs G. E Fowler of Arch Street, Mr T. Billsborrow of Union Road and Cllr. Lightfoot had been informed that the nine feet fence had been erected according to agreement. They were offered the comfort that it might not be used as a bill-posting station but heard within a month that the Company's offer to set back the fence if the Corporation paid for the flagging and paving had not been accepted.

It is not easy to see what the improvement of six feet rather than nine would have been. The Company had bought the land for timber storage, not open space and the lower fence would merely have revealed a little more of the monotonous 30 feet high stacks of pit props which were packed as close together as fire precautions (such as they were) permitted. The Propyard was the permanent backdrop to the Central Estate. The Borough Engineer reported that the N.E.R. might consider an application to set back the fence in Union-road, subject to the Corporation paying the cost of flagging the footpath. It was reported "that the committee do not recommend the Council to approve of the same at present...

The other boundary of the Central Estate on the opposite side of the propyard, was dedicated as Montague Road on Aug. 4 1909 by the NER. It had been paved and kerbed by the Corporation.

The Central Estate had expanded into the area between Hart Road and the railway embankment with the addition of Hutton, Vincent and Rokeby Streets which were sufficiently advanced to pay streetage by January 1905. It was not that existing streets were full but that the economic depression had not yet become visible. The pressure for new housing to replace slum-clearance continued, despite Cllr. C. T. Watson's protest in June 1906, against the expert opinion of the Medical Officer, of the Borough Engineer, of the Sanitary Inspector and of the County Medical Officer. "They must have a certain class of houses for a certain class of people in Hartlepool". Had he retired as a builder? As will appear, he was by now a paid-up member of the ratepayers association.

Union Road (Map 7 p. 142), which belonged to the Corporation, was failing to attract purchasers and in August 1906 it was resolved that the sites be offered for public competition by auction. When Cllrs. Sherwood and Hart suggested that the land be used according to the Housing of the Working Classes Act, Ald. Horsley went immediately to the social heart of the matter. Why did not the bodies who had the interests of the working-men so much at heart - the trades unions which spent thousands of pounds every year on strikes - step in and build cottages for the men? They were the men to do that, and not a Corporation.

Dr. Gibb supported Cllr Sherwood's allegation that many of the better working-class men had left Hartlepool because they could obtain better houses in West Hartlepool. Unsurprisingly, Ald. Horsley's view prevailed.

Only a month later the nine sites were leased by the Corporation to a builder, who had attended the auction but failed to bid, at 5d per square yard. As Cllr. Sherwood pointed out, the Council had failed to sell the sites. So, too, did the leaseholder. Seventeen months later, having in the meanwhile vainly tried to buy the freehold of the land from the Corporation, in May 1908 he explained that he was unable to carry out the terms of his lease, and asked the committee to relieve him of seven of the sites. The committee complied.

The NDM continued to keep its readers reasonably well-informed on matters of national and international concern. Fortunately the writer of "Echoes of the Week" had a sense of humour. On May 21 1906 he celebrated an improvement in local train services:

> *We shall begin next week with a service of auto-cars between the Hartlepools. True there may be "many a slip between the cup and the lip"... all one's forecasts about auto-cars are apt to be treated as jokes, and the fact that All Fool's Day has been chosen for the opening of the new service is apt to make a sceptical generation more doubtful about the accuracy of the news...*
> *Then the opening of the new coast line will bring the Hartlepools into closer touch with the important towns to the North and South... Crimdon Dene Viaduct has also ten arches... The maximum height from the ground to rail level is 96 feet and the length 687 feet. The brickwork measures about 11,000 cubic yards and contains 4,000,000 bricks. The total number of bricks used in the construction of these four principal viaducts is 12,000,000 and if they were placed end to end they would stretch to a distance of 1,775 miles. I may add that I have not worked this sum. I give you the statement as it was made to me...*

On Sept 9 1907 he made a revealing statement: he may not have been quite so liberal as he wished to appear:

> *It is not often that I disagree with Councillor C. T. Watson, but when he comes to describe the attendance of members of the Council at the promenade concerts on Sunday as a public duty, I certainly cannot follow him...*

It will be recalled that in his struggle for a license for the Central Hotel - C. T. Watson, as well as having friends in high places, had become a popular figure and that in 1897 he had appeared as a champion of the common man in the matter of a blocked footpath. His protests in 1901 against the display of washing and the misuse of a seat, both near his property on the Town Moor, were, on the other hand, unashamedly self-centred as well as snobbish, and although unsuccessful in these, he still got away with defiance of planning regulations in 1901-2. In 1905 he became a town councillor, soon well-known for outspokenness. What do his words, independent of his deeds, reveal?

In 1906 he continued his defence of the Town Moor by (successfully) opposing the construction there of a quoit alley for working men. There was, he said, a quoit club in Hartlepool of which he had been a member for 12 years, and others could be formed so that working men could have their own.

Later in he same year it seemed that his attitude towards housing had changed from that of a builder to that of a slum landlord. The debate was a rerun of the 1903 contest between council officers who were professionally qualified on sanitary matters and town councillors who were not. The Sanitary Committee chaired by Cllr. Gibb had recommended the closing of insanitary properties. Cllr. Watson suggested that before the Council took such a drastic step that:

> *... a small committee of practical men of the Council should ascertain whether the properties could be put in order or not. The proposal... would mean... depopulating the town, and thus interfering with the business of tradesmen... They could not expect houses rented at something like 1s.6d., 2s., and 2s 6d. per week, with landlords paying rates amounting to 10s 2d in the £ to be like palaces with marble halls. They must have a certain class of houses for a certain class of people in Hartlepool... It was possible there would be nothing left for the owners but to go to the Workhouse...*
>
> *Councillor Hart said he could not understand what the mover of the amendment meant by "practical men". They had had the opinion of the Medical Officer, of the Borough Engineer, of the Sanitary Inspector and of the County Medical Officer...*

He might have added Cllr. Dr. Gibb himself as another expert. As in 1903, the majority of the Council accepted the officers' expertise.

His stance in August 1907 on the transfer of Hartlepool's electricity supply from one company to another certainly sounds reactionary although entertainingly expressed in an otherwise dull meeting.

> *... Councillor C. T. Watson said he desired to move an amendment... what they did object to was the proposal to hand over their birthright... Another matter... was a number of persons in the town tired of the present electric lighting. (Hear, hear.) If some members of that Council had the light in front of their houses they would soon form a similar opinion. Those who opposed the motion... did not desire to apply the principle of the dog in the manger: but he added, "We don't want to be the fly for the spider every time" (Hear, hear.) The net had been spread several times, and they had walked into it. (Hear, hear.)... He objected to the present system of lighting in the town. They could get a far better light with the incandescent system...*

By "incandescent" he meant gaslight. Never were metaphors, of dogs, spiders and fishing, more colourfully mixed. Certainly, at least in retrospect, a preference for gaslight over electric light sounds eccentric, even if it might be, as he argued, cheaper. If gaslight was so much better, would he have wanted it outside his own house? He went on, however, to move no more than that the decision be deferred. Perhaps, like Gladstone in Disraeli's opinion, he was "carried away by the exuberance of his own verbosity".

He could certainly sound as intemperate as any self-righteous radical, though the subject was the reduction of rates. At a special meeting of the Council, to consider a rise of a halfpence in the pound, he was reported as follows on Oct. 18 1907:

COUNCILLOR C. T. Watson'S PROTEST

... Councillor C. T. Watson:... I beg to move there be a reduction of the rates by 6d. ... I am going to move we reduce our estimated expenditure by something like £1500... I only want to keep myself in order. I don't know whether this is the proper method. I shall move that every member of the Corporation be dismissed. (Laughter.)... there was very severe depression looming over Hartlepool for the coming six months. He thought it was most ungentlemanly - he would put it in another way - it was most reckless and most disgraceful the way in which the different committees were raising their expenses. "I will begin with Ald. Rowe", he continued. "I will take you all round". (Laughter). Don't laugh. I mean what I say... You (Ald Rowe and Ald. Harrison) told me lies... You both said the rates would come down."

The Mayor: I think that is rather objectionable.

Councillor C. T. Watson: Who says it is?

The Mayor: I say so.

Councillor C. T. Watson: I speak the truth. I don't care, Mr Mayor, with all respect to you... The only way to get at this is to move that the Surveyor's salary be reduced by £100 per annum...

Ald. Rowe: I said I hoped it would be so.

Councillor C. T. Watson (excitedly): I am prepared to give you a £10 note now and retire. I am disgusted with it. ("No, No")...

Councillor C. T. Watson: I will move that the estimates go back for reconstruction and withdraw my previous motion...

Ald. Horsley (indignantly): I protest.

Councillor C. T. Watson: If you object hold your hand up.

Ald Horsley: You should attend to your committees, sir, and see that the expenditure is kept down.

Councillor C. T. Watson (heatedly): A subcommittee was appointed, and you are chairman of it, but you never called us together. You have got too much of your own way here...

He carried the day - or the night. The amendment that the estimates be referred back to the various committees was then put to the meeting and carried. The relief, however, if any, was only temporary. Rates continued to rise.

Before the end of the first decade of the 20th century there was, nevertheless good news on part of the fiscal front. On Sept 9 1908 NDM reminded its readers that on and after January 1 1909 old age pensions would be payable to qualified persons who had attained the age of 70 years. It was an advanced age at that time and the weekly payment of five shillings (now 25p) was scarcely generous. It was nevertheless a distinct social improvement which must have generated some smiles on the Central Estate.

It was not the only socially good news at the time. Though less spectacular than the pension, it confirmed a beneficent long term national improvement.

Jun. 5 1909 *TO-DAY...*

... in recent years there has been a decline in the birth rate... But the death rate has also declined the result being to increase the average age of the population Here is a

table giving the figures. Per 1,000 of population

Period	annual birth rates	annual death rates	annual natural increase
1881-1885	33.5	19.4	14.1
1886-1889	31.4	18.9	12.5
1891-1895	30.5	18.7	11.8
1896-1900	29.3	17.7	11.6
1901-1905	28.1	16.00	12.1
1906	27.1	15.4	11.7
1907	26.3	15.0	11.3

Table 4 - Births & deaths 1881-1907

... the most striking decline has taken place... in the years... since 1899, and is due... to the increased attention which has been given... to the subject of infantile mortality... As to the causes of death, it is apparent that the mortality from nearly all the principal diseases has decreased materially in the last 30 years. The most important exceptions are pneumonia, diphtheria and cancer. Typhoid fever has greatly declined, and typhus fever has almost completely died out.

Tuberculosis should have been added to the list of persistent killers, but the Medical Officers and Sanitary Inspectors were winning despite rate-saving councillors.

Patent medicines continued to flourish. Pink Pills for Pale People persisted, and to them were added, for example, Doan's Backache and Kidney Pills; Peps - a Pine Forest in Every Home; Swamp Root, the Great Kidney, Liver and Bladder Cure; and Zam-Buk for Hurts and Sores. Not all (if any) were quack remedies. Scott's (cod liver oil) Emulsion and its competitors, though unpopular with children, unquestionably contributed to health improvement.

Plate 30 - Old Town Hall (Queens Cinema), Hartlepool, 1966

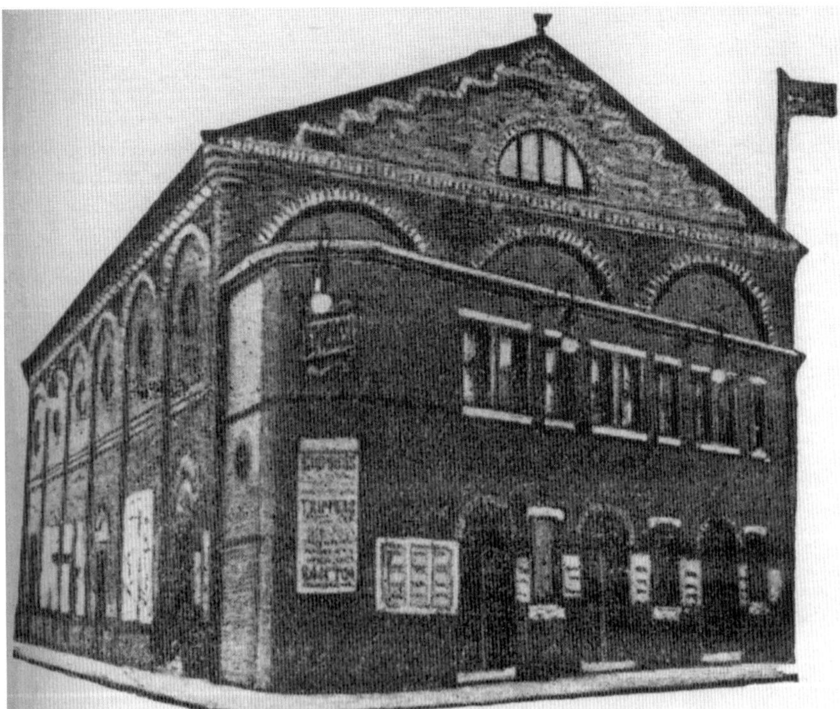

Plate 31 - Salvation Army Citadel /Empress Theatre/Palladium Cinema/ Bingo Hall, Hartlepool

Plate 32 - MPs 1868 to 1922

Plate 33- Parade, Cleveland Road, Coronation of King George V, June 22 1911

Close and highly piled pit props, later responsible for the Great Fire of Jan 1922

Plate 34 - Dr W. S. Gibb (circled), 1924

Chapter 6: 1910-1914

By 1912-13, according to Ward's Directory, there were some interesting differences of development. Physically the Estate had expanded. There were three new streets to the north of the original triangle between Hart Road and the railway embankment. Hutton Street had 7 occupied houses, Rokeby Street had 39 and Vincent Street 12, a substantial addition of 58 to the housing stock. Moreover, Hart Road had exploded to 110 households from 79 and now had its Anglican Church, St Barnabas. Strangely, however, the increase in the total number of households was a mere 11, from 511 to 522, and although there were still some stable streets - Arch, Beaumont, Lambton and Pease - Cleveland Road and Clyde Place/Street had each lost 3, Bell Street 4, Watt Street 5, Stephenson Street 13, Union Road 17 and Watson Street no less than 38! The total number of households lost was 83 and assuming that Ward's Directory had not been merely careless, the reason must be sought. (Households Table - Appendix I p. 291)

As earlier observed, the birth and early rapid growth of the Central Estate were the offspring of boom conditions. Unfortunately booms are followed by slumps and at a time when foreign manufacturing competition was increasing, long and large strikes in the coalfields, the railways and the shipyards greatly increased unemployment between 1907 and 1912. Housing and the ability to rent or buy it was an obvious casualty.

Dr. Gibb in Cleveland Road no longer had a partner, there were 3 less insurance agents and there were less barmen, bootmakers, butchers, clothiers, confectioners, dressmakers, fruiterers, grocers and tailors. There were one manager, one wagon inspector, one watchman and one waterman less and 9 less in road, rail and sea transport: some 37 in total. (Occupations Table - Appendix J p. 292)

There were, however, more bricklayers, a slater and a second sculptor, more cartmen, clerks, coal merchants, drapers, fish curers, fishermen, fishmongers, fried fish dealers, assistant grocers, hairdressers, milk sellers, plumbers, police sergeants, secretaries, shopkeepers and weighmen, plus a compositor, a farm manager, a manageress, a shop assistant, a slater and a timekeeper and 17 more in transport: some 65 in total. With stability in other service employments, and newly resident curates, customs watchers, dock gatemen, dockmasters's assistants, dredgermen, gangers, gas meter inspectors, motormen, packers and a retired police inspector, adding a further 29 to the total, the losses, therefore, were not in service employment. On the contrary, the proportion of service employment was increasing. If we add the 17 retired men, the 22 widows and the one unmarried lady householder, the respectability of the Central Estate was ascending even higher.

In skilled labour there were (in total) 46 less boilermakers, coopers, coppersmiths, diesinkers, draughtsmen, forgemen, furnacemen, machinists, millwrights, patternmakers, rivetters and shipwrights but 47 more boatbuilders, blacksmiths, trimmers, drillers, engineers, foremen, joiners, moulders, teemers and turners as well as 10 newly resident diecutters, iron dressers, painters, ropers, sawyers and a steam gauge maker. With another 15 in stable employment, builders, caulkers, cement millers, tinsmiths, toolmakers, wire rope makers and wire drawers, the losses must therefore have mainly been of unskilled labourers and in fact their number was halved, from 72 to 37.

The residence of a curate confirms the building of St Barnabas Church on Hart Road and the employment of sawyers confirms the establishment of the propyard (where timber used in coalmines to support the roof of workings were sawn to length and seasoned) on the Old Boys' Field, immediately to the west of Union Road. Surrounded by a high wooden fence topped with barbed wire it was a very abrupt and blank boundary.

The turnover of households had reverted to its earlier level. Only Arch, Beaumont and Pease Streets had as many as a quarter of their 1902 inhabitants, Clyde and Lambton had a fifth and the rest varied from a sixth (Bell, Cleveland, Hart, Stephenson and Watt) to a 12th (Union). Parts of the entries for Bell St and Cleveland Rd. are illegible but the conclusion that four fifths of the population were newcomers - apart from the few who had moved house within the Estate - re-establishes the phenomenal mobility of early 20th century labour and presumably diluted and delayed community development.

On the other hand there is interesting evidence for the stability of particular streets witness the survival from 1900 of individuals and families from 1900 and earlier. From 1891 5 men surnamed Black, Cox, Grant, Spence, Thompson and perhaps a 6th, Ward still lived in the same streets in 1912. From 1902 Arch St had 9; Bell St had a dairyman from Arch St; Cleveland Rd. had 11 including a fitter from Arch St, the widow of a foreman whose sons were bricklayers, another widow who changed the 'i' in her name to a 'y' and C. T. Watson (who had swapped a manager for a manageress at the 'Klondyke'); the landlord of the "Lord Clyde" was now a Spence in place of a Davies; the Clyde streets had 4 (not including the landlord of the 'Lord Clyde'); Hart Rd. also had 10 including the Cement Works analyst and the Ropery manager, secretary and foreman. Lambton had 2, Stephenson 7 together with the police sergeant late of Watson St; Union had 5 and Watson 9. Only Beaumont and Pease had none. Fifty eight is a small proportion of 522 but a stable 10% minority may be of considerable social importance. One may suppose that the trouble and cost of removal was not lightly undertaken: presumably, people stayed if they could.

Two more social trends may be noted. The first was upward social mobility. A plater had become a shipwright, a fitter had become a marine engineer, a moulder had become a shopkeeper, one labourer had become a craneman and another a fitter. One fitter had become a foreman and another foreman had reverted to being a blacksmith (unless he had a son with the same initial) but these were promotions in skill or status or both.

The second trend was the importance of shopkeepers amongst those who stayed as residents, perhaps naturally because demand for their services was bound to persist. From 1900 to 1912 (and well beyond in many cases) Arch St had grocer R. H. Rowe (Alderman), beer retailer Mrs Middleton, fish-shop keeper G. H. Heal, hairdresser Tommy Newton, as well as a cobbler and, from 1901, the Cooperative grocery and butchery. Cleveland Road had the same monumental sculptor (whose work must still be visible in the two local cemeteries) W. Bradbury from 1902-25, Dr. Gibbs' surgery from 1900-35 and J. Hayes the grocer (and would-be beer retailer) 1900-22.

There was a confectioner on the Bell St corner from 1900 to 1935 (Cockburn's, politely pronounced "Co'burn", from before 1912), C. T. Watson's Central Hotel 1900-35 and there was a shop at No. 60 which housed bootmakers 1900-2, a pawnbroker in 1912, dining rooms in 1921 and then Davison the butcher 1924-36.

The Lord Clyde Hotel was, of course, a fixture and Hart Road had the Twedell coal depot 1900-12, but the shops of Mrs Dando, Mr Mitchell, Mrs Palmer (fancy draper) and Charles Chambers the milkman dated only from 1912. Stephenson St had Wade the butcher 1900-1913 and Davison, another butcher 1900-36. Watson St had a fish shop managed by a succession of married women 1900-36, a draper run by a succession of Redshaws 1900-36 and Mr Banks and then his son ran a grocery for the same period. The Banks also owned a number of houses on the Estate including 54 Stephenson St for which, 1922-26, the rent was 6s 3d per week.

Some interesting individuals begin to emerge in addition to Alderman Rowe, (who now, as already reported, lived in Hartlepool). J. Hayes, and C. T. Watson, already named and noted in the story of the licensing of the Central Hotel. R.J. Marshall was another prolific builder from the earliest days and like C. T. Watson was more than a mere business man. In 1900 he converted the house on the corner of Stephenson Street/Hart Road, which he had offered to Mrs Jenny Robson's shipwright father, but who then died, into a shop for his widow. In 1903-04 on Hart Road he built the Railway Cottages (which were terraced houses) and the farm labourers' cottages as well as St Barnabas' Church (Plate 29 p. 81) to which he donated the lectern. That he should have been recalled as "a canny feller" by Mrs Frances Kettlewell in 1979 was praise indeed.

The church, which survived until 1998, daughter church to Holy Trinity, Hartlepool, was built on 'Scotty's Field'. Mrs J. R recalled that the ground was consecrated by the planting of a Processional Cross in November 1903 "before a brick was laid". It was carried through a hailstorm by Sunday School children from Trinity. The foundation stone was laid in April and the church opened on November 23rd 1904. The deficit outstanding from the funds raised by penny cards savings and bazaars was met by Lady Gray, the benefactress of St Oswald's. It was named as 'St Barnabas' by its first incumbent, Parson Powell, who came from a similarly named church in Darwen Lancs. In 1909 it became High Church because (according to Mrs Robson) its new incumbent, Father Cobb, who taught history at Henry Smith's School, had married a Roman Catholic.

Mrs J. R. on Empire Day, May 24th 1908 (another cold day), took part in a school pageant on 'Britain and the Colonies' on the Town Moor. Children from various schools represented different colonies with their various products and welcomed 'Britannia' who was towed on a gun-carriage. Later there were Morris dancers on the Friarage Field and "every child had something to take back. It was glorious. We never had a show like it"!

John Metcalf turned himself from boat-builder to joiner and undertaker and throve as such into the 1940s. Tommy Newton, who added confectionery and newspapers to barbering, was something of an intellectual as well as a shopkeeper. Tom Pailor rose from labourer to garage proprietor and later to cinema manager. George Fowler moved from shipyard worker to compositor. Jack Lumsdon was a lepidopterist as well as a patternmaker and made a chest of drawers for his butterflies wit all the skills of a cabinet maker. Will Burton the rivetter was a photographer (with his Thornton Pickard reflex camera and the tiny coal house in his backyard transformed into a darkroom) of professional standards. Tom Crowther moved from labourer to trimmer and became the Sunday School Superintendent of the Primitive Methodist Chapel. His brother Joe, the Central Estate's first resident policeman, was promoted sergeant, taught in the Sunday School, was a local preacher and by 1938 had succeeded in financing the construction of a new Hart Road Chapel, by which time he had retired and become an ironmonger. Tom was a rotund, rubicund man with a warm voice and smiling manner. Joe was tall and thin with a bony face and a superficially grim manner. Both were family men with daughters who all married active chapel workers.

By 1912 my grandfather George Woolford had emigrated from Darwen, Lancs. (in reply to an advert in a local paper) as a tap and die maker and had established his family in Hart Rd. He contributed generously to C. T. Watson's profits. Mrs Dando, in whose house the local football club first met, organised picnics for schoolchildren on half-holidays and brought tins of sweets which she produced at sensible moments. Charles ("Chuckie") Chambers, the milkman with his horse and cart, was a Good Templar, which is to say total abstainer from tobacco and alcohol. He organised concert parties for church socials and later became a town councillor and mayor. Mr R. S. Boswell, who came from Sunderland as a plater, was a self-educated working class intellectual, a socialist, a trade union official (Boilermakers), an allotment gardener and a male voice chorister, also later became both councillor and mayor. Jack Edmundson, a remarkably quietly spoken Geordie blacksmith, was one of the first local wireless (radio) constructors. Tom Billsborrow, who certainly classed himself as an intellectual, who had made a lathe as his proof of craftsmanship and was the only man to use the back step for mounting his bicycle, was promoted from fitter to foreman. Mr Banks, the grocer's son, was kind. Whenever I went with my mother to pay the rent he invariably folded a small sheet of paper into a cone and filled it with sweets for me. His sister, similarly kind, was addressed as "Lady"! Whether she approved or not she had been christened "Ladysmith" in (or after) 1900 to commemorate the Relief of Ladysmith in the Boer War.

Headline status for the Central Estate, which had been slightly improved by the N.E.R's cession of Montague Road on the boundary with West Hartlepool, was somewhat surprisingly re-achieved on June 8 1911:

ST. BARNABAS' BELL

...attention was drawn to the complaint made in respect to the ringing of the bell of St Barnabas' bell... (which)... prevented railwaymen from obtaining their ordinary rest after returning home from work on Sunday morning...

The Town Clerk read the following letter from the Rev. Cobb... anent the complaint... "the bell is only rung at the usual times and for the usual length of time... the whole thing emanates from one man who considers his Sunday rest is disturbed. The bell does not ring on Sunday earlier than eight. It seems to me that what he wants is not a Council, who will see that he sustains no injustice, but a grandmother to see him tucked in. If, however, he manages to find cause of complaint on this matter and induces others to give their signatures, he is taking, as I need not inform you, quite

the wrong course. His only method is to secure an injunction from the High Court... which he would not stand the remotest chance of obtaining. Did I consider the matter really entailed any hardship I would gladly consider it, but I am convinced it is not...
Cllr. Sherwood spoke in support of the complaint.
Ald Hunter expressed his surprise at a letter of that kind being written by a Church of England minister... contemptible to treat the Corporation in such a way. They should remember that 36 men, residents on the Central Estate, had signed the petition, and that they were asked by the man who caused the complaint to treat it with contempt. It was scarcely dignified on his part. He moved that it be referred to the Improvement Committee.
Cllr. Sherwood seconded... the men who complained were not averse to going to church. They were not atheists but ordinary God-fearing men. It was, he said, not an ordinary church bell, but an old shipyard bell, which was formerly used for calling the men to work and dismissing them. The bell was now rung by boys swinging on the rope...
(N)othing but insult came from this Christian gentleman. There was indeed great room for education in Christian charity...

The Rev. Cobb's back was palpably up and the unnamed protester may not have had much difficulty in mustering 36 signatures. That Cllr. Sherwood should have supported them is not surprising, although his knowledge of residents outside his own ward is rather striking, and the relevance of the origins of the bell and of its ringers is not self-evident. He might better have pointed out that the summoning bell was only a street's width from the row of railway houses. Much more surprising is the unusual support from Ald. Hunter, normally very much a supporter of the 'Establishment' whose back was also clearly up. The matter continued reverberating until and after Christmas. On Dec. 7 1911 it was reported that the Improvement Committee had deferred the matter for a petition to be submitted at a later date, and on Jan. 3 1912 that the men were petitioning the Bishop of Durham (Plate 29 p. 81).

They asked that the ringing should be discontinued on week-day mornings, and that on Sundays it should only be rung for morning, afternoon and evening services... they had approached the vicar, but he resolutely declined to consider the matter.
The Mayor observed that the petition was a very temperate one, and it was agreed that... the Council should give... their support.

The immediate result is not reported. The bell continued to ring for years after both the 1914-18 and 1939-45 Wars but was silenced during the first precisely because it disturbed sleeping workers, and during the second because, except in case of invasion, church bells were silenced.

Meanwhile, and perhaps more praiseworthily, both Church and Chapel continued their social as well as their religious services, always including Anniversaries and Harvest Festivals, with teas, American Evenings and cricket clubs: they may have played each other but it is not reported. St Barnabas' had whist drives and a football club as well. In March 1914, in the new St Barnabas' Hall, reprieved from Improvement Committee refusal in Aug. 1913, a Unionist political meeting was held. The Hall must have been for hire. The Rev. Cobb's political views, as will appear, were very different.

The Central Estate Primitive Methodist Church could, comparatively, perhaps fortunately, only figure in "The Hartlepools Day By Day". In September 1910:

A very interesting ceremony took place on Saturday afternoon, when over 50 bricks were laid by the scholars attending the above Sunday school, each brick representing a contribution of 5s. towards the cost of the new building... an address... a goodly number sat down to tea...

The children's names (and numbers of bricks) were published, many of which continued into the 20s and 30s and beyond: Yeal, Crowther, Close, Billsborrow, Shepherd, Weatherhead, Lumley, Palmers, Grimmer, Elwine and Wray. That improvements rather than a new building were the objective is shown by mention on Jan. 11 1911 of the opening (by the Mayoress, Cllr. Gibb's wife) of vestries, with heating and electric light. As with the church, this was a community within the Central Estate but also, like the school, which taught all children who were not Catholic, of it. The other component of this crisscrossing duality of rivalry and community was street loyalty Union-roaders and Stephenson-streeter etc., boys sometimes fought each other in gangs, but could be friends at school or Sunday school and would presumably have stood together against outsiders, had there been any.

The Sons (and Daughters) of Temperance continued to flourish in their Primitive Methodist lodgings, with rabbit pie suppers, whist drives and dances(!), and outings to Hesleden at which bags of sweets and nuts were distributed. The names of the leaders and their wives continue to be Edmundsons and Fowlers, but what is to be understood from Bro. W. A.. Noble's address reported on Oct. 25 1910 on "Alcohol and its effect on the human body", the lecture being illustrated by practical tests and experiments... "! A month later the, presumably safer, subject was: "The child as a national asset. An interesting discussion ensued".

Presentations continued to be made to retiring landlords and prospective emigrants at the Central Hotel, but not without sober competition from St Barnabas' Hall. Hart Road school was available for Liberal Party socials whist the Corporation itself organised children's sports:

June 2 1914: CHILDREN'S SPORTS AT HARTLEPOOL

For the fourth year in succession the children's sports and pleasure carnival was held on the North Sands, Hartlepool. The welcome bright sun and the favourable state of the tide helped materially in gathering together a record crowd... The streets leading to the sands were bedecked with bunting, the Hartlepools Military Band... discoursed all the latest popular music, and coconut shies, football ranges, shooting galleries, roundabouts, hoop-las, donkey rides, swing boats, dart boards and all the rest of the popular amusements were provided in plenty...

A start was made with the sports programme at 11 a.m., when the Boy Scouts commenced their walking match, the route from the Ann Crooke's school being via Cleveland- road, Brougham- terrace, the Workhouse, Hart-road and back to the Coastguard Station.

The chief event of the afternoon was, of course, the men's tug-of-war, in which there were 17 entries... The greasy-pole climbing, the bun and treacle eating competition, and the flour and marble contest created endless laughter, and everybody seemed in happy holiday humour throughout.

... The principal subscribers were Sir Stephen Furness... Mr Wm. C. Gray... Coun. C. Toshack Watson...
The ascent of an air balloon at 2 o'clock signalised the start of the various contests.

Greasy poles, buns and treacle, etc, are self-explanatory but how flour and marble(s?) were combined puzzles the imagination. There were doubtless tears as well as laughter, but assuming that the reporter caught the spirit of the occasion, it was, especially in retrospect, a goodly day. Brief and cheap entertainment for the workers sponsored by the employers it may have been, but it must have been freely given, gave pleasure and may have fostered social cohesion. It was incomparably better than the deadly sequel of war.

On Feb. 13 1914 Chief Constable Winterbottom in his sixteenth annual report stated a decrease of 26 indictable offences in 1913 from the 72 of 1912. In 1912 there were no committals to Assizes and only one in 1913 which was very satisfactory considering the large floating population during the fishing season. This appeared under the congratulatory headlines:

HARTLEPOOL'S GOOD RECORD
FREE FROM SERIOUS CRIME

The Central Estate was in step. Between 1905 and 1909 there had been reported 3 assaults, 5 betting offences, 2 thefts and 1 drunk. Between 1910 and 1914 (to the outbreak of war) there were reported only 3 assaults, 1 betting offence and 5 thefts. Some of the incidents were nevertheless noteworthy.

Sept 21 1910 *ASSAULT WITH A SHOVEL*
E...... . J...... . (50), 30, Vincent-street, Hartlepool, was fined 12s 6d. with costs, with the alternative of one month's imprisonment, at the Hartlepool Sessions today, for assaulting Catherine June Wilmot, on the 14th inst. - Complainant said she had no peace at all with the defendant, who was a neighbour of hers. On the date named she met her in the street, and defendant struck her with a shovel. Since then she had been very ill.
- P.C. Farrand said he was called to complainant's house after the assault had been committed. - Chief Constable Winterbottom remarked that J...... .., against whom there were 25 convictions, was one of the worst characters in the town.

Mar 12 1913 *A NEIGHBOURS' QUARREL*
... Complainant said that she lived at 38 Cleveland-road, and that defendant lived next door... on Saturday night at 11-45, she was awakened by a knocking at her door. She went downstairs and asked three times who was there before she received an answer. On going to window she saw that it was defendant, her husband and son. (She) told them to go away as she did not want to have any bother with them, and after a while they went away. At 2 o'clock in the afternoon of the 3rd, Mrs H. came into her (complainant's) backyard, followed her upstairs and dared her throw a bucket of water upon her. She also called her "a nasty expression" and said she was carrying on with the lodgers, and threatened to "tear her to pieces"... Defendant stated that at 11.30 on Saturday night, she was in her house, and her husband and son were also present. She heard a knocking at the wall, from the room occupied by Mrs P..... next door... They accordingly went downstairs and knocked at Mrs P's front door... (who) said she was knocking because the piano was being played. Defendant replied that it

was not her piano at all, but… belonging to a party who occupied the tenement below them. Complainant then called her a "dirty bad hussey" and said that she would throw a pail of water over her if she did not go away. On the Monday she again saw Mrs P., and had simply tried to convince her that it was not her piano… She emphatically denied using the foul name alleged and that she had never said that she would "tear complainant to pieces"…

With or without the wisdom of Solomon the Bench dismissed the case and advised the women to keep apart, but revealed which of two they disbelieved less by charging costs to the defendant. They were also surprisingly clement in a more serious case of assault:

Dec. 27 1912: SCENE IN A HARTLEPOOL HOTEL
… a man… living at 152 Hart-road… was charged with assaulting PC Ferrand… called into the Central Hotel to arrest prisoner who, the barman said, had been using very bad language. Witness asked him to leave the premises quietly, and… then picked up a pint glass, emptied it of its contents, and threw it at the barman.. The glass struck the barman in the face… then turned round and struck witness in the mouth with his fist and butted him with his head. He was about to rush at him again, and witness had to draw his truncheon to protect himself.

The miscreant got off with fines only. The Bench took a more serious view of domestic crime:

Aug. 21 1912: WIFE'S STORY OF ILL TREATMENT
…J. S… of 91 Union-road, Central Estate, was summoned by his wife who alleged persistent cruelty… On Aug 10th her husband came into the house, complained of the fire being out, and struck her about the head with his belt.. Owing to his conduct she was compelled to leave the house. About eight weeks previous he was sitting reading a Sunday paper, and she was nursing the baby. Reading from the paper, he said, "A man with his throat cut and the wife dead," and then got up and struck her with his fist, almost stunning her. He had a poker in his hand and he threatened to "do for" her… On another occasion he threw his boots at her, striking her on the head. He was addicted to drink, and had lost work as a consequence… M. H. stated she was in defendant's house on August 10th when he threatened to throw his wife through the window. He subsequently got… (her)… into a corner and struck her several times with his fist… On another occasion he threw a pair of scissors at her. Defendant denied the accusations, and stated that his wife struck her head on a chest of drawers as he was pushing her away from him. Every time he was out of work she led him a dog's life, and every time they had a few words she left him and went to her mother's. The Bench granted a separation order, defendant to pay his wife 2s. per week, and the woman to have the custody of the children.

There were also a drunk and a gambler, and a dairyman fined for watering his milk. One of the thefts involved another lady from Union Road, and some thefts were more petty than others.

Oct. 19 1910 BOYS AND TURNIPS
Six boys were ordered to pay 5s. 6d costs at the Hartlepool Police-court this morning for doing damage to turnips in a field belonging to Thomas Snowden, Warren Farm, Hartlepool.

Nov 8 1910 *A PROMPT ARREST*

About ten o'clock this morning Mr George Briggs, carrier, Central Estate, Hartlepool, reported to the Hartlepool police that his horse had been taken from its stable. Chief Constable Winterbottom at once had the police of the various neighbouring towns communicated with by telephone, and as a result of this prompt measure, the Sunderland police apprehended two men with the horse on the highway near that town.

Nov 9 1910 *ALLEGED THEFT OF A MARE*

Two Sunderland labourers... were remanded... When charged with stealing the mare prisoners replied, "That's right."

Nov 16 1910 *ALLEGED THEFT OF A MARE*

... at the stable in back Watson-street... bay mare and head collar, valued £18... they offered to sell it for £4.10s... committed for trial at the next Quarter Sessions.

May 6 1912 *COAL STOLEN FROM ROLLEY*

..on Saturday last he (coal dealer) left his rolley, containing 23 bags of coal, at the back of the Central Hotel. He later missed two bags of coal. A boy... stated... Scott remarked, "Don't say anything, will you, because we want a drink of beer," and took a bag of coal from the rolley and put it in the Central Hotel yard. The other prisoner also took a bag... removed the coal into an adjoining yard. Margaret A... , 73, Watson-street spoke to Scott bringing a bag of coal to her door, and offering it for sale. She refused to buy it. Someone shouted that a policeman was coming, and prisoner dropped the coal, and ran through her house and out of the front door. Another witness... of 81 Watson-street... stated that... came to his door, and offered a bag of coal for sale. Witness gave him 9d for it... .Later Sergt Crowther came to his house... charged prisoners... previously convicted five times whilst... had appeared twice... prison for one month...

The Central Estate was also the scene of other thefts. On Feb. 2 1914 three men from Hermit Street, Hartlepool, were fined for theft of scrap-iron from the NER's new timber storage grounds at the Central Estate, an offence repeated by four named but unlocated labourers a week later and, a month later, by two unusually persistent lodging house residents. One of these latter was fined and the other, previously convicted, imprisoned:

... PC Branham (N.E.R.) said that at 11.15 yesterday morning he was on duty at the timber sidings at the Old Boys' Football Field, when he saw the defendants searching among the ballast for scrap-iron. Upon seeing witness defendants went behind a timber truck, where witness found them examining two bags of scrap iron. He cautioned defendants, and let them go, at the same time taking scrap to a stable-yard on the Central Estate for safety. Fifteen minutes later witness saw defendants leaving the stable yard carrying the bags of scrap iron...

The novelties in this sparse record of crime on the Central Estate or by its denizens were an offence against the Sunday Observances Act, two cases of cruelty to animals, and an offence against the Shops Act. It is interesting to note that ice-cream making was still an Italian occupation, that the RSPCA was so active, and that shop workers were at last entitled to a half day's holiday per week. It is also worthy of remark that some policemen and other officials were kindly disposed.

May 15 1912 *SUNDAY OBSERVANCE ACT*

... an Italian... was charged... P.C. Ferrand stated that at 3.45 p.m. on Sunday he was on duty in Hart-road, near the second arch. He there saw defendant with his barrow, selling ice-cream... About two hours later witness again saw defendant selling ice-cream. This time at the junction of Hart and Union-roads... a fine... and costs...

Feb. 5 1913 *ONLY FIT TO BE SLAUGHTERED*

a... labourer, of 57 Watson-street, was charged with working a pony whilst in an unfit condition. P.C. Walker... saw defendant leading a pony at a trot along Watt-street... exceedingly lame, and the defendant was flicking it with a whip. Witness overtook defendant in back Rokeby-street, where he saw the pony standing on three legs, the near head limb being raised about a foot from the ground. Witness examined the foot and found that there was no shoe upon it... The foot as swollen and hot about the fetlock, and practically only the shell of the hoof remained, the inside having been eaten away by canker... Inspector Hughes (RSPCA.)... In witness's opinion the animal was only fit to be slaughtered... He knew defendant was a poor man... He asked that only a small penalty might be imposed... he (accused) was fined only 2s. 6d and 10s. costs.

March 11 1914 *THE SHOPS ACT*

The first prosecutions at Hartlepool under the Shops Act were taken this morning when Henry E. Leeming, a grocer, of 10 Pease-street, and Sarah Watt, grocer, of 104 Hart Road, pleaded guilty to having kept their premises open for the sale of groceries on Wednesday afternoon, Feb. 25th last... The Chief Constable said that he had received many complaints from tradesmen... he did not ask for a penalty, but just the payment of costs.... .

April 21 1914 *FLOGGED A PONY*

... coal hawker, of Hart-road, Central Estate, was charged today at the instance of the R.S.P.C.A... P.C. Johnson said he saw defendant backing the pony... He was mercilessly flogging the pony across the neck and shoulders with the whip-stock. Witness could not discern any cause of the flogging. —Defendant denied kicking the pony. He "just tipped it on the side with his foot", he said. The pony, he added, was very stupid when backed. — A fine... with costs...

The number of fatal accidents fell from 8 in 1905-09 to 6 in 1910-14 and although there were more suicides there were no more deaths from "skylarking". Some of the verdicts were more self-evident than others: scalding is reasonably obviously an accident, but suicide by a woman's grave could have been motivated by more than unemployment. In none of the cases was independent witness reported. Reading between the lines suggests pity rather than rebuke.

Oct. 25 1910 *THE SCALDING FATALITY*

An inquest was held at the Lord Clyde Hotel on the body of John Joseph Taylor (3), 1 Clyde Place: mother... prepared a hot bath for the child, and while her back was turned he fell into it and was scalded. The child was taken to a chemist and treated with oils.

Later a doctor was sent for but the child died... Accidental death.

June 2 1911 THE TRAGEDY IN HARTLEPOOL CEMETERY
... inquest... on the body of Frederick Dawson Bonner (52) of 69 Cleveland- road... who was found lying at the Hartlepool Cemetery yesterday with his throat cut. He died later at the Hartlepools Hospital... at five minutes past one o'clock yesterday he found deceased lying face downwards on the ground near the grave of the late Mrs Rawlings... A razor was found near the deceased... a steady man. During the past five or six weeks he had been out of employment... previously he acted as coachman to the late Mrs Rawlings... The jury... verdict... a self-inflicted wound... being of unsound mind... owing to being out of employment.

July 22 1911 BATHING FATALITIES AT HARTLEPOOL
William John Wheatley (10) of 32, Bell-street... school holidays yesterday... a bathe in the sea from the North Sands... Wheatley entered the sea with a companion named Davison... With great courage Davison swam out and succeeded in bringing Wheatley towards the shore. He, however, became exhausted and had to release his hold... and had to be assisted out of the water by a man named Palmer.

There was an inquest in the Lord Clyde Hotel in August 1912 on a lady from West Hartlepool who died from heart failure ("probably accelerated by alcoholism") on a visit to Clyde Street, but it was more than a year later that another Central Estater, a shipyard worker from Union Road, died from accidental (work-related) causes. He was said to have fallen from a ladder which he had climbed "to get his dinner".

Mar 1912 DEATH FROM HEART FAILURE
An inquest was held in the P.M. Church Buildings, Central Estate... into... the death of Jas. Curley, (58), a single man... The Deputy Coroner... informed the jury that Curley was in the Workhouse Hospital in September last. He was then suffering severely from bronchitis, and it was realised that he might die at any time. — John Boyle, of 36 Watson-street, said deceased, who lodged with him was a shipyard labourer. For many years he had been ailing, and would be off work for three or four weeks at a time... He had been off work very nearly ever since he came out of the Workhouse, but got started on Friday... and worked all Friday night and up to noon on Saturday. He worked part of Monday also, but had to lay off and was unable to return to work any more. Witness advised him to see a doctor, but he said, "I know what's the matter with me; I'll be all right in a day or two"... A verdict of "Death from heart failure due to bronchitis" was recorded.

There was "another case of smallpox... a man about 50 years of age", and the case was from the Central Estate. On May 10 1912 the Hartlepool Medical Officer of Health advised people to keep away from the vicinity of the smallpox hospital. Many people, he said, frequented the sand dunes belonging to the N.E.R., and also stroll along the wall and fences bounding the Port Sanitary Hospital. He was right. It was a convenience for children at play as well as for young lovers in search of a little privacy.

Otherwise the rest of 1912 and the whole of 1913 were mercifully clear of accidental fatalities. The worst thing that happened was the burst of a water main in Union Road on Mar 21 1912 which deprived all the inhabitants of Hartlepool of their water supply. Many people obtained supplies from the railway station and a number of water carts were sent around the town.

Less fortunately, on July 1 1914 NDM reported:

THE TIMBER POND MYSTERY

... the inquest on the man found drowned in the timber pond at Greenland failed to establish the identity of the deceased. Later, however, a local bootmaker, who had given the man employment identified his body. He said the man gave his name as James Dunningham, aged 35, of 39, Buchan Street, Glasgow. He worked up to 7.0 p.m. on the 25th, and when he left the shop he remarked: "I am tired of my life". He was told not to talk so foolish, but to come to work next day, and he replied, "I will if I come, and if not I will be somewhere else". He did not put in an appearance the next day, and subsequently his body was found.

Free entertainment of varied sorts continued to be available. Fairy Cove was only a half mile from the Central Estate.

June 6 1912 *BIG VESSEL WRECKED OFF HARTLEPOOL*

ASHORE ON ROCKS IN DENSE FOG

CREW RESCUED

The firing of rockets last evening created considerable excitement among the residents, hundreds of whom rushed to the promenade, to find their first fears of a ship ashore fully confirmed.

... Within a mile of the promenade, nearly opposite what was Fairy Cove Battery, it was found that the Norwegian full-rigged three-masted ship Otra was hard and fast on the rocks... the rocket apparatus... from the sands... but four efforts failed owing to the distance...

No time was lost in launching the lifeboat... towed to the vessel by the tug William Gray... managed... to rescue the skipper and the remaining members of the crew... six... had been able, by means of their own boat, to get on board the tug Eddystone... (which)... had the ship in tow when she went aground...

... it is considered to be impossible to refloat her... Hopes are entertained, however, that the greater part of her cargo (pit props) might be saved. When the fog cleared thousands of people flocked to the promenade to get a glimpse of the wrecked vessel...

Less than six weeks later, on July 15 1912, there was a repeat performance:

STEAMER ASHORE

FOG CASUALTY AT HARTLEPOOL

ATTEMPTS TO REFLOAT THE VESSEL FAIL

There was considerable excitement at Hartlepool yesterday afternoon when it became known that owing to the density of the fog a steamer had run ashore on the North Sands, close to where the Otra stranded some time ago... the SS Braemount... of Glasgow... a rocket was fired... The vessel being in perfectly smooth water, there was no danger, and the pilot boat was sent from the ship to say that no assistance was needed...

There was no reported sequel, so that subsequent efforts at refloating the vessel must have succeeded. It was otherwise with the Otra, perhaps because she had no engines. On Aug 13 1912 the strong swell split her sides:

THE BREAKING UP OF THE OTRA

Exciting scenes have attended the breaking up of the iron sailing ship Otra... now only a tangled mass of iron marks the spot where she went ashore. Sea View-terrace and the adjoining banks this morning resemble a small timber yard, there being numerous stacks of props which have been salved (sic). These are being sold by auction and are being speedily carted away.

Last night's scene on the beach was one which will not be easily be forgotten. The news that the vessel was breaking up quickly spread and hundreds of men, women and children hurried to the beach... Many persons waded waist deep in the sea... and in consequence of the strong tide which was running... there were several narrow escapes...

Many of the boys made quite a harvest out of the wreck, being paid 1d and 1 1/2d for each prop secured and brought to the bank...

A pit prop was a metre and a half long and about 20 cm in diameter, so that strength as well as foolhardiness was needed to land one. They were of good quality softwood. Legally they were flotsam, but NDM does not reveal on whose behalf the auctioneer worked. (Plates 35-36 p. 132)

On Apr. 14 1914 pit props were in the news again. A stack of them caught fire in the timber yard near Greenland. Prompt and successful measures were taken to prevent the spread of the flames to surrounding stacks of timber. Presumably crowds had no time to gather.

Unique free entertainment was provided on May 14 1914 by the Army which flew in no less than 12 aeroplanes onto the seashore off Seaton Carew (Plate 37 p. 133). The NDM was lyrical in a leading article:

TO-DAY

The visit of the airmen created a great stir in the Hartlepools... It was a very orderly crowd that visited Seaton Carew yesterday, and all the interesting events of the day passed off without mishap... Everybody seemed delighted with the fine view obtained of the flights, and the descents on to the sands were particularly thrilling.

The aeroplanes were naturally objects of much interest, and it is impossible to estimate how many thousands of people examined them during the day. The tram service was working at great pressure during the day...

From the Central Estate to Seaton Carew was two tram rides away or a good hour's walk. On May 6 at the Hartlepool Town Council there had been characteristically comic previous publicity:

VISIT OF THE AEROPLANES

The Town Clerk read a series of letters that had passed between himself and the authorities on the subject of the visit of the Army aeroplanes. From these it appeared that an interview had been arranged, but that it did not take place, and that later a letter was received intimating that arrangements had been made with West Hartlepool...

[We may add that it would appear that the misapprehension that the aeroplanes were to visit to Hartlepool had arisen in consequence of the omission of the word "West" in the addressing of the preliminary correspondence respecting the matter]...

Twelve aeroplanes, wind permitting, might have landed on the North Sands at spring low tide, for a short time. Otherwise there was no room. One may further infer that no progress had been made on the Union of the Hartlepools. As the NDM's "Echoes of the Week" reflected on Jan. 20 1914, it would send up the rates in West Hartlepool, whatever the Local Government Board might want. The more downright opponents of amalgamation would urge "that it were well, at all events, to postpone the evil day as long as possible"...

Hartlepool's own amenities continued to increase. The Old Pier was extended in 1909 and to cinema shows at the Town Hall in 1910 (Plate 30 p. 110) were added the conversion of the Empress Theatre into the Palladium Cinema in 1912 (Plate 31 p. 110), and although there was, naturally, nonconformist opposition, in 1911 boxing matches were permitted at the Skating Rink.

Cllrs. Sherwood and C. T. Watson continued to hit the municipal political headlines, sometimes in conflict, sometimes not. Councillor Watson continued as a builder, witness his description as such for the elections of 1912, although not on the Central Estate, and continued as an ebullient spokesman for his causes, though some of them changed. The 1907 champion of gas against electricity for street lighting had changed sides by Jan. 1911 when he seconded the motion in favour of the latter.

Councillor Sherwood, as usual, was in opposition but they nevertheless combined in Oct. 1911 remarkably to enforce the resignation of the Borough Engineer for alleged overcharging for fireplaces for houses in Warren Street, neglectful administration and failure to obey committee instructions. "I knew the town was being had", said, Cllr. Watson, "and I set myself to solve the thing... As for driving him (the Borough Surveyor) out of the town, what about him driving the poor, struggling ratepayers out of the town?".

Although no longer a resident. Cllr. Watson continued to champion Central Estate causes:

> *Mar 2 1911* *QUESTION OF A RIGHT OF WAY*
> *Councillor Watson moved: "That the Council take immediate steps to have the footpath leading on to Cleveland-road, opposite the Post office, Central Estate, reopened as a public footpath, and that the claim of the N.E.R. Company to such footpath be contested... If the NER Co get their Bill through the town would definitely lose this footpath, which was a very great convenience to workmen and to children taking their fathers' dinners... It had come to this, either they would have to fight, or they would have to surrender... We burnish our armour, and it gets very bright and brilliant. Then we let it lie dormant until one cannot tell whether it is armour or a sack...*

Oratory and the support of both Cllrs. Sherwood and Turner were not enough and Cllr. Watson's motion was defeated, although by only one vote. The individual calculations of votes, party interests, and personal principles (or prestige) defy analysis. It is, however, perhaps surprising that it was Cllr. McDonald and not Cllr C. T. Watson who waved the flag in Feb. 1911 when the Board of Trade, relative to the forthcoming International Exhibition at Turin, suggested that the Hartlepool corporation should have a silk banner on view there, emblazoned with the borough coat of arms. Cllr. Sherwood thought it would be a waste of money. Cllr. Mcdonald, possibly tongue-in-cheek, supported the suggestion to spend the money.

We shall stand high in the councils of the nation and be a prominent figure on the Continent, he added, amidst laughter. "People will be astonished to find there is such a place on the face of the earth, and representatives of every race will be wanting to know what is the meaning of 'Hartlepool'". (Laughter)

Ultimately it was decided to adopt the suggestion. No repercussions, national or international, were reported.

On Feb. 14 1912 at a Town Council meeting at which the leasing of the Town Hall as a cinema was sanctioned, Cllr. Watson, again the people's champion, submitted that Hartlepool people should have an opportunity of seeing picture shows without having to go to West Hartlepool. He nevertheless supported Cllr Sherwood in insisting that the otherwise deprived Choral Union should have the Town Hall for an evening. They also agreed in March 1912 that the local Excelsior Male Voice Choir should have a £20 grant to make possible a performance in Paris. Unfortunately, on April 8 1912 the NDM leader had to report that:

The Hartlepool Town Council achieved a somewhat hurried "volte-face" at their meeting he other night over that grant of £20 to the Excelsior Choir. Their excuse, I suppose, is that they had no idea that the grant would meet with the popular opposition that has been evidenced... I learn, however, that.. the Council... will not allow the choir to suffer... Indeed, I am told, that the suggestion... that the members of the Council should themselves make up the amount is already being acted upon.

This was not ungenerous and no doubt both Cllrs. Sherwood and Watson contributed. They continued, however, mainly to disagree until the last moment. On May 2 1912 Cllr. Watson moved that rates be reduced because they had been reduced in West Hartlepool. Cllr. Sherwood, who won on this occasion, said that the gap should be filled by government grant. A month later it was reported that the Mayor had expressed regret that Cllr. Sherwood was leaving the town. He was sure he was voicing the feelings of all the members of the council when he said that, although they had not agreed on every point, they all felt he had been a very able member of the Corporation. He trusted that at Sunderland he would have health to carry out the work that lay so near to his hand. (Hear, hear.). In fact Cllr. Sherwood, who had gone so far as to say in April 1911 that he didn't care whether the Coronation of George V was celebrated or not, and whose council attendances had fallen to 47% as compared with C. T. Watson's 76% and Dr. Gibb's 66%, had been selected to fight a parliamentary seat in the trade union-labour interest (in which he was not successful).

Despite Cllr. Sherwood, the Coronation of King George V was duly celebrated (Plate 33 p. 112). On April 6 1911 the Town Council asked:

that households and businesses be asked to decorate their houses and places of business, and prizes to be offered for same... That householders be asked to illuminate their houses at night with candles and night-lights. Procession on the morning of 22nd of June to St. Hilda's Church. Singing by school children and choirs on Promenade of patriotic hymns etc... That the school children be presented with a box of chocolates each. That a tea be given to the old people of the borough. That a bonfire on the Moor be lighted at night...

On June 23 1911 NDM reported that the Moor and Promenade were thronged with people last night, and that the concluding items in the Coronation festivities were marked by great enthusiasm. The five prizewinners on the Central Estate were, amongst others, named.

In Aug 1912 the Council proposed to buy a vacant plot of land adjacent to the promenade for a park. Throston Ward Cllr. Turner, of Arch St, opposed:

> *... the Throston Ward had a prior claim... At the south end of the town they had the promenade, the Moor and the Cliff, whilst in the Throston Ward they simply had a rubbish heap... and it had been like that for 20 years.*

He was right. The "rubbish heap" was the Tip of the old iron works, next to the Destructor on Spion Kop. Cllr. C. T. Watson, rates or no rates, opposed him and won, although Cllr. Turner was assured that the necessary promenade extension would be built. Indeed it was: but not until 1930.

In addition to Alderman T. W. Watson and Cllr. C. T. Watson, another Cllr. C. T. Watson was elected in Feb. 1913. He was Charles Toshack Watson, a butcher, and after a debate on how the two C.T.W's should be distinguished, it was suggested that they might be known as "Senior" and "Junior". Charles Thomas Watson objected: if so described they might be taken for father and son and he "was not quite old enough to be the new councillor's father". (Laughter.) The agreed solution was that the new member should be known as "C. Toshack Watson".

In addition to his new Presidency of the Hartlepool Rovers' Rugby Club, Cllr. Gibb continued his good offices, being elected Mayor for the third year in succession in Nov 1912, although he said that it was not in the best interests of the town, or of the Mayor himself:

> *One is apt, after presiding over the Council for two years, to begin to fancy one's self. I trust that if you find during the coming year that my conduct in the chair is a little more arbitrary... you will put the blame on the right shoulders - your own. (Laughter.)*

Commenting on the fact that West Hartlepool Corporation now owned all the trams, he again lamented the disunion of the Hartlepools. It was in vain. Municipal socialism was not to the taste of the Hartlepool Town Council. Nor was a contribution to the cost of a new road from Easington. As for boys playing football on waste ground on the Central Estate when there was a recreation ground a quarter of a mile away, there were fines, although one of the magistrates dissented. Windows, it was said, had been broken and passers-by struck with the (full-sized) ball. Law and order must be upheld.

Educationally the Central Estate had something to celebrate. The J. H. Laverty of Union Road who had won a scholarship to the Henry Smith School in Sept 1901 had returned to Hart Road School as a pupil teacher:

> *Sept. 3 1910* *PRESENTATION*
> *Yesterday afternoon, at the Hart-road Council School, Hartlepool, Mr James Laverty, who is leaving the school to enter the Battersea Training College, London, was the recipient of a handsome attache case for correspondence, and a fitted leather dressing*

case, subscribed for by the scholars and teachers of the school. In making the presentation the hadmaster spoke of the many excellent qualities of Mr Laverty as a teacher, and wished him every success for the future. Mr Laverty suitably responded.

He may have been the first Central Estate child to ascend the social and educational ladder to proceed to professional status via the grammar school (Plate 27 p. 62), an ascent which many more were later to follow. Their chances were obviously much improved by the opening in October 1911 of the extension which more than doubled the size of the school. James Garry, the planner of the Central Estate, was present but is not named as the architect.

The other noteworthy educational event was the opening of an elementary school for Hartlepool's working-class Roman Catholic children in Hart Road on April 1 1913. Predominantly from the poorer quarters of the town, they may well have seemed to intimidate some of the more "respectable" children on the Central Estate. They certainly did in the 1920s, as I myself vividly recall.

Hartlepool naturally participated in the 1911 Census. On Nov 2 1911 "To-Day" observed that:

... The last census showed us that Hartlepool has to deplore a reduced population and it is definitely stated that people are leaving the town because of the inconvenience they have to submit to in living there. So acutely do the members of the Council feel the necessity of something being done... that it is possible questions may be asked on the subject in the House of Commons.

In fact, the subjects currently under discussion by the Council were railway and post-office facilities, but if anything was done it was not in the House of Commons. On Feb. 8 1912 the Medical Officer of Health reported that the infantile mortality rate was very high, brought about in part by inclement weather, and dark and unhealthy surroundings. This, clearly, was not a reference to the Central Estate which had little or no slum property Ignorance on the part of the mother, contaminated feeding utensils, and food infections by dust and flies, however, could (he said) occur even in otherwise sanitary surroundings. He added that it was to the good water supply that the practical nonexistence of typhoid fever and the good condition of children's teeth was due. He might have added that the prime cause of local depopulation was probably slum clearance in old Hartlepool rather than nationally falling birth and death rates.

The fluctuations of the local economy continued to be recorded. Whereas on July 7th 1910 a Labour Exchange for Hartlepool was reported ("in association with the West Hartlepool establishment") and on Dec. 8 the Town Council applied for a govern ment grant for the unemployed, on Dec. 14 1911 "To-Day" noted "a very prosperous year. The opening out of the coalfield to the north has increased the importance of Hartlepool as a coal exporting centre, and the additional facilities provided by the North Eastern Railway Company have been thoroughly tested... .the fish trade is developing, and there is a prospect of more trawlers being attached to the port". On Dec. 23 "To-Day" remarked that the shipping and shipbuilding trades had almost reached the bumper figures of 1905 and 1906. In 1910, 21 ships had been launched and in 1911, 34.

The article went on to observe that but for "the coal strike and minor labour troubles" shipbuilding output would have been even larger. There had, additionally, been boilermakers' lockouts in 1911 and 1912... (NDM missing AUG-DEC 1913)... but both 1913 and 1914 appear to have been quiet. Perhaps the shipbuilding copartnership was still working.

The NDM was not a paper of record and it was not bound to report every dispute and disturbance which occurred. Whether by chance or intention, its readers may not have appreciated, what is very clear in retrospect, that they were surrounded by social, political, economic, imperial and international volcanoes. The new political flavour was syndicalism, the theory that as workers had little prospect of amelioration from party politics, the revolutionary remedy was the general strike by trade unionists against which mere governments would be powerless. In 1907 a general railway strike was threatened and, as in 1908 with the NE shipbuilding strike, necessitated government intervention. In 1910 the army intervened in the S. Wales coal strike and in 1911 in Liverpool dock strikes, in both of which there were fatalities. In 1912 miners successfully struck for a minimum wage and by 1914 a Triple Alliance of railway, docker, and miners' unions threatened the victory of syndicalism.

During the same years suffragists fighting for votes for women turned militant with suicide and arson, were force-fed against hunger strikes, and then released to be re-arrested under the "Cat and Mouse" Act. The House of Lords was only just defeated from striking against the Budget of 1909 and in 1914 a part of the army itself went on strike to prevent Home Rule in Ireland where rival Catholic Nationalists and Protestant Ulster Unionists, respectively backed by Liberals and Conservatives, armed for war. Civil war in Britain itself seemed as near as at any time since 1660.

As to national politics, the Liberal shipbuilder and shipowner Christopher Furness, who had defeated Liberal Unionist Sir William Gray in 1891, but had been ousted by his Liberal Unionist opponent Thomas Richardson in 1895, returned victorious against the conservative trend of the 1900 Khaki election, and, now Sir Christopher, was not even opposed in the Liberal landslide of 1906 and, victorious again in the first election of 1910 on the issue of the House of Lords' rejection of the 1909 budget. Unfortunately the files of Jan-Jul 1910 are missing so that there is only a hint of electoral impropriety in Cllr. Sherwood's reference to an election petition in July 1910. There had, however, been a by-election in June 1910, presumably arising from an alleged electoral gaffe, at which Sir Christopher's (Lord Furness in 1910; death 1912) nephew Stephen was (nevertheless) returned, a choice that was confirmed in the December 1910 General Election (Plate 32 p. 111).

Past, present and future national political leaders, including Edward Carson, Herbert Samuel, Philip Snowden and Sydney Webb, continued to woo the voters of the Hartlepools at public meetings. Such national and international events as the death of Captain Scott at the South Pole, the sinking of the Titanic, the launching of the Mauritania and the Balkan Wars were amply reported. In 1914 Hartlepudlians could sign the Ulster Petition against Home Rule for Ireland.

The NDM continued to advertise additional delights. If readers did not respond to advertisements for the Stockton Hippodrome, in West Hartlepool there were new cinemas, The Royal Electric, the Northern and the West End; the newly formed branch of the Workers Educational Association offered University Tutorial Classes in History and Economics as well as "lecture rambles under the guidance of a geological scholar"; Hartlepudlians could witness "the Coast of Death" on roller skates at the Queen's Rink, or Bostock and Wombwell's Circus; be taught how to make lantern slides or model aeroplanes; visit the new Transporter Bridge across the Tees at Port Clarence, the new Fish Quay in Hartlepool or the newly consecrated New Cemetery.

There were Gramophone Concerts, Spiritualist Meetings, Fish Workers' Dinners, a Turnip Competition, the Hartlepool Rovers (Rugby Football) Debating(!) Society, performances of "Elijah" (Mendelssohn), "The Crucifixion" (Stainer) and "The Messiah" (Handel). Charities, both offering and soliciting support, included the Hartlepool's Hospital Ladies Linen League, the Indigent Sick Society, the Life-Saving Society, the Children's Society, and the Crippled Children's Guild, as well as political, trade union and religious associations by the score. Those interested in fashion were told (on Mar 13 1911) that the "hobble" skirt had been totally eclipsed by the "harem" skirt - which had, perhaps not ineptly been called "the latest Turkish atrocity". Since the reference was to Bulgarian Atrocities, Armenian Massacres and the current excesses of Sultan Abdul Hamid II, it was not in the best of taste.

There was an Automobile Association for local motorists, a Golf Club for local golfers, and a new promenade at West Hartlepool's Seaton Carew. Baden-Powell's Boy Scout movement of 1906 was rapidly and enthusiastically taken up.

Meanwhile the larger world was changing, with wireless telegraphy, X-rays, radium and relativity as well as the conquest of the air (and of the English Channel by Blériot in 1909) and the discoveries (or inventions) of Freud and Jung which conspired together to undermine traditional beliefs. With the addition of Unemployment and Health Insurance in 1912 to the Old Age Pension of 1908, however, the lot of the poor was being improved. This cannot have been merely providential: or entirely unconnected with the new nationwide popularity of striking and striking hard. At the same time the Victorian tradition of improvement continued with better roads, cleaner streets, ampler lighting, better systems of sewerage & drainage, more numerous parks, better equipped free libraries, and more efficient inspection under the Adulteration Acts & the Weights & Measures Acts. These occurred despite Britain's loss of industrial supremacy, witness relative falls in iron and steel production and in inventiveness: oil technology, the internal combustion engine, the motor car, the airship and the aeroplane were all successfully pioneered abroad.

Plate 35 - "Otra" Ashore, Jun 5 1912

Plate 36 - Otra's Jettisoned Cargo Rescued

Plate 37 - Aeroplanes at Seaton Carew May 14th 1914

The Mayor-Elect of Hartlepool (Councillor C. T. Watson) and Mrs. Watson.

Plate 38 - Councillor and Mrs C T Watson, 1917

Plate 39 - Central Marine Engineering Works Crane, 1914

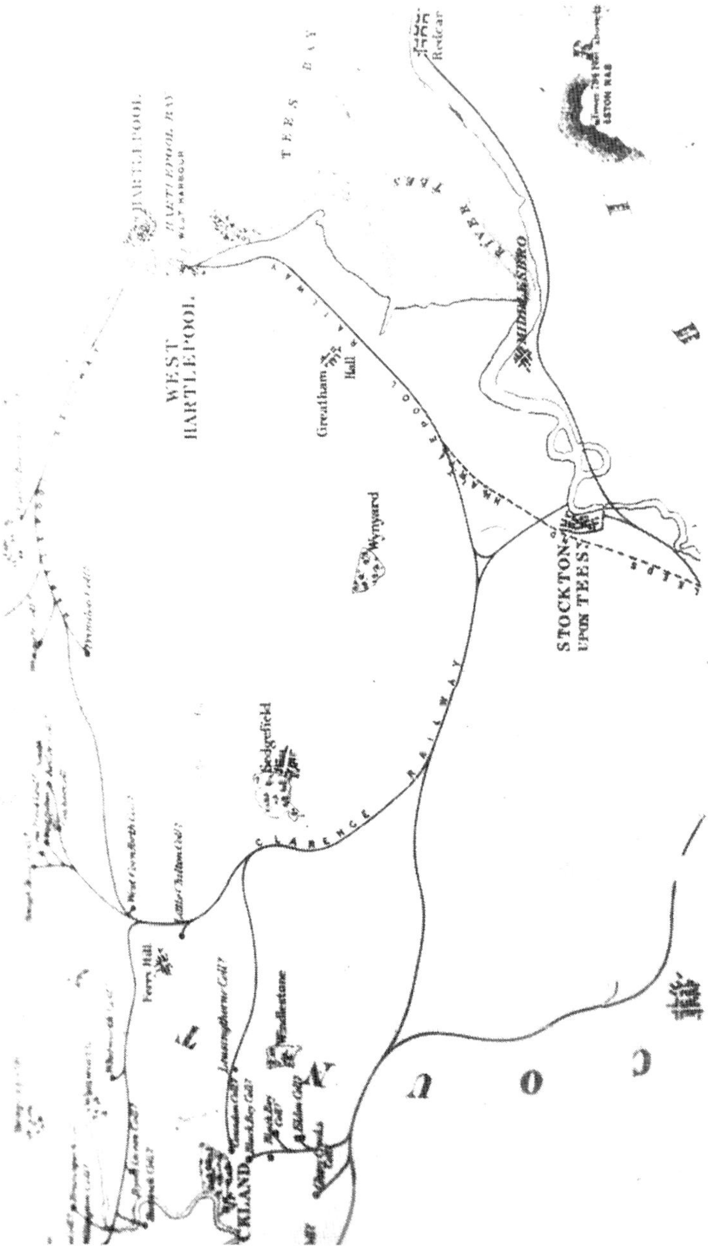

Map 1 - Coal Railways 1848

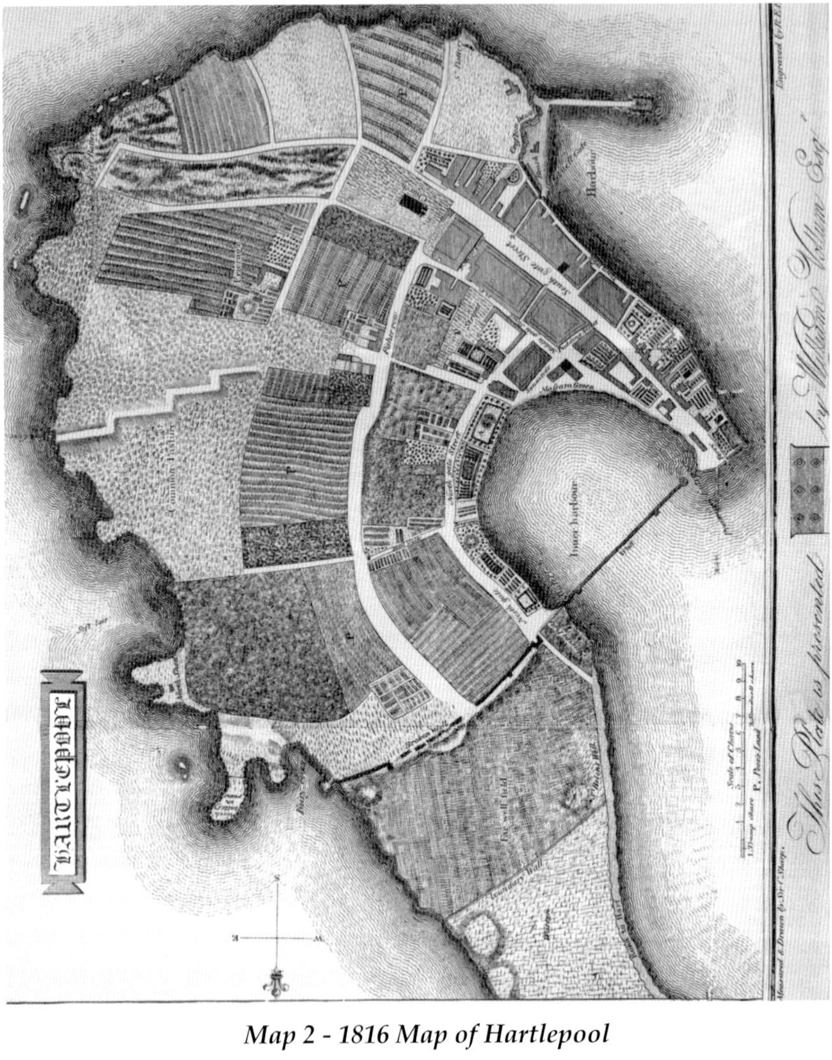

Map 2 - 1816 Map of Hartlepool

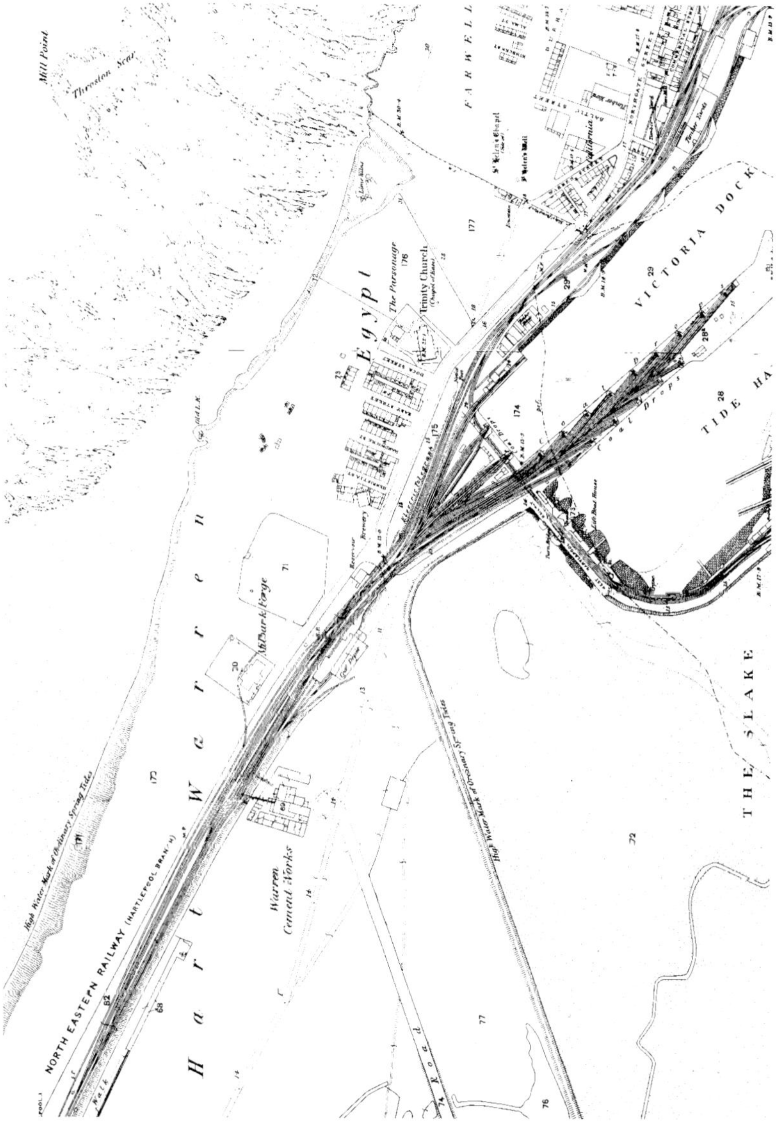

Map 3 - County Durham 1857 Ordnance Survey Map

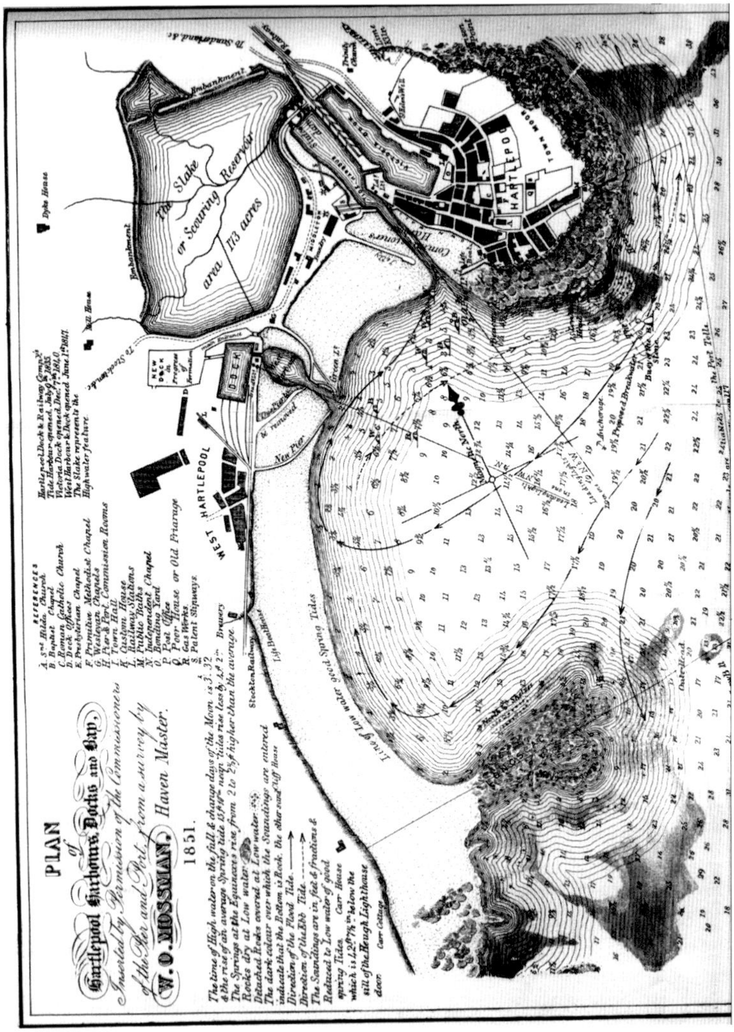

Map 4 - 1851 Map of Docks and Bay

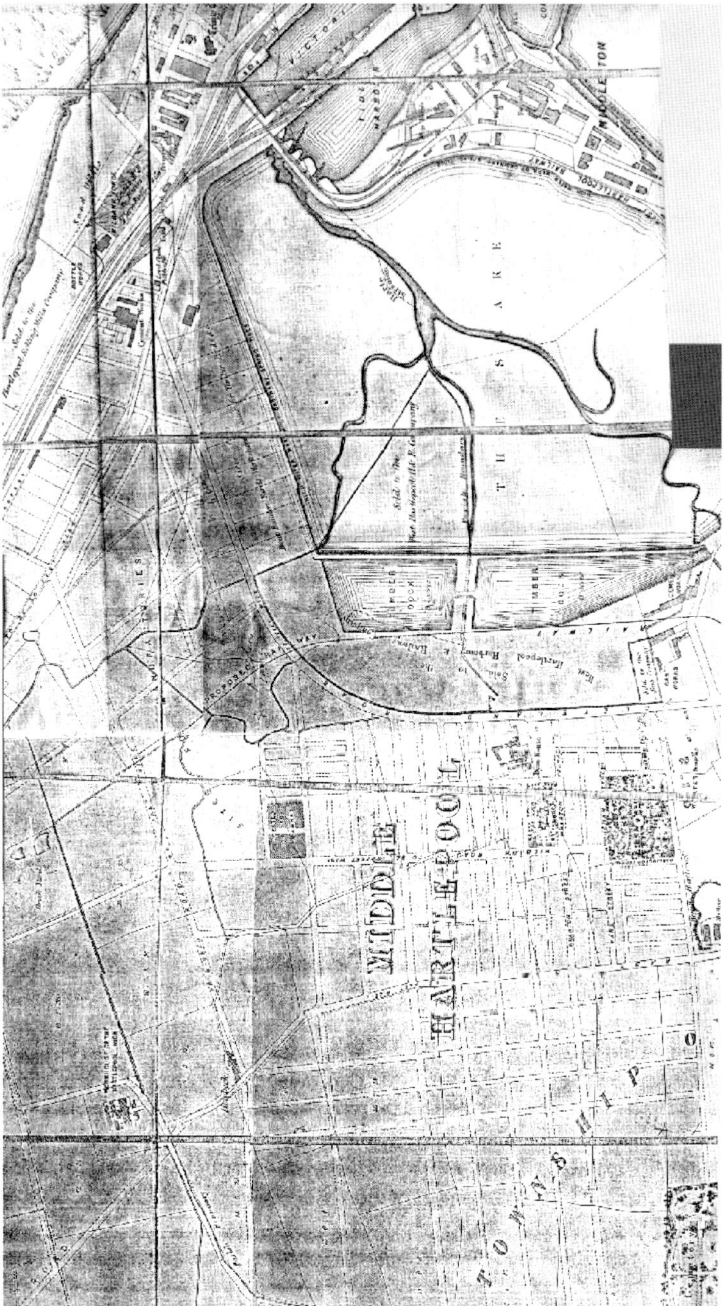

Map 5 - Undated Plan for Middle Hartlepool

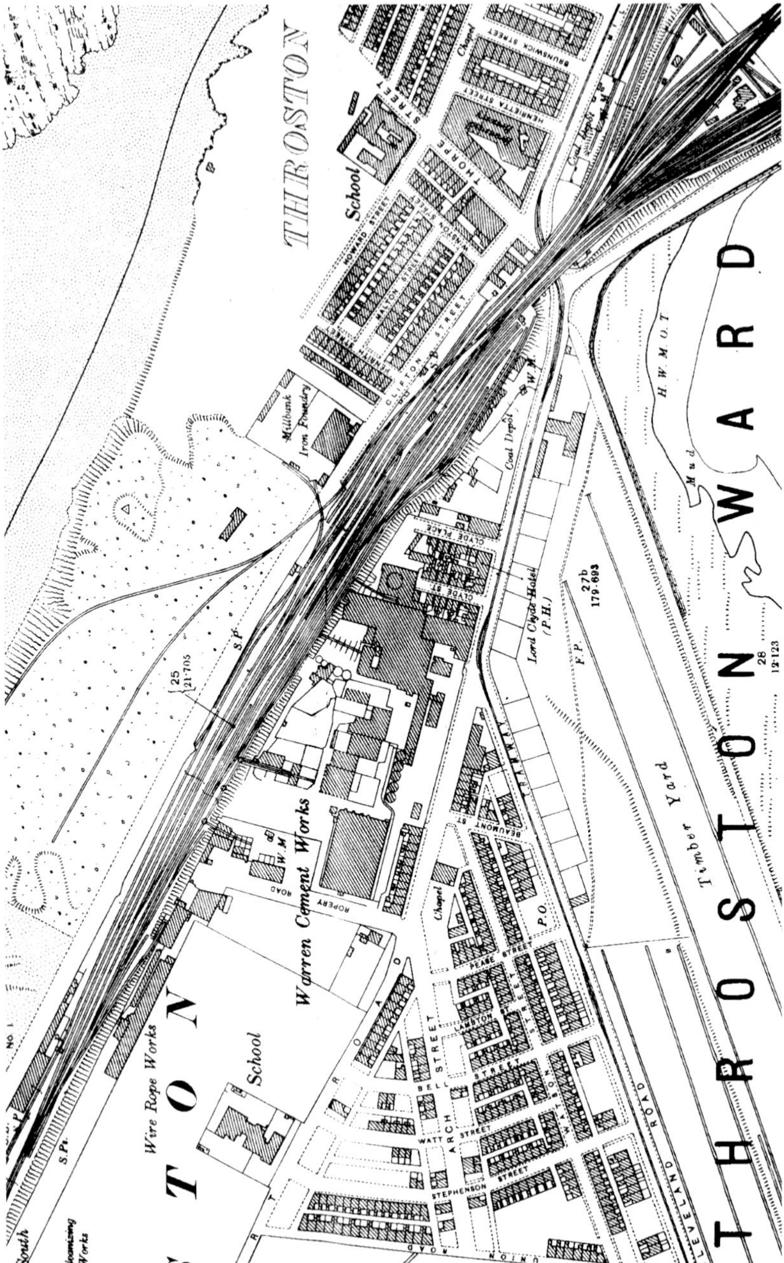

Map 6 - The Central Estate 1897

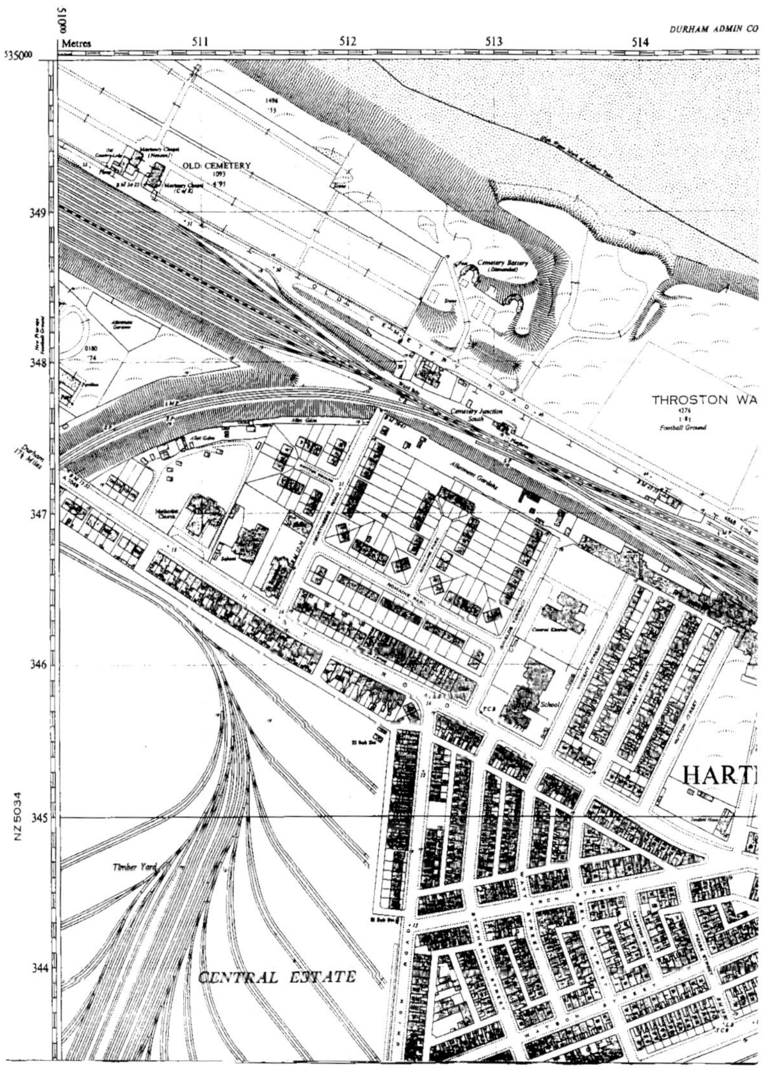

Map 7 - Hart Ward 1930's

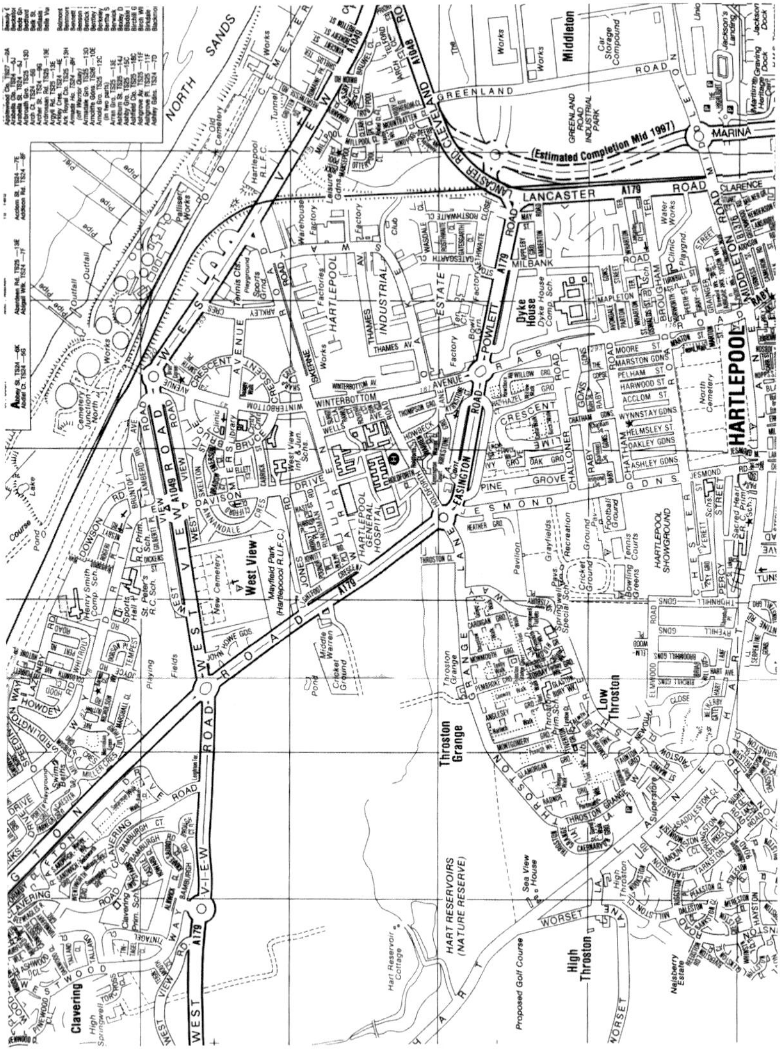

Map 8 - Hartlepool 2001

Chapter 7: 1914-18

Britain's declaration of war on Germany on Aug 4 1914, at the beginning of what was later named the "First World War" came to almost everyone as a surprise, despite the alarms and excursions of the previous decade. Hartlepool had not been physically involved in battle since Tudor times and the only successful invasion of England since 1066 had been by invitation in 1688. Although from the turn of the century the NDM had informed its readers of worsening relations with Germany, notably in terms of naval rivalry, as "Echoes of the Week" observed on Aug 3 1914, "most of us, in our inmost hearts, although we feared the storm, expected that it would not burst. We felt that the results of a war between half a dozen powerful nations would be so terrible that the statesmen of Europe would, in the interests of our common humanity, somehow manage to avert it. But this was not to be… "

Although on August 6 the Mayor of Hartlepool, Ald. T. W. (not C. T.) Watson was reported as saying that it was his duty "to use every endeavour to impress upon the people of this ancient borough that there is no need for them to have any fear of suffering from a shortage of provisions or a lack of adequate protection", the phlegmatic Town Council, characteristically, went on to debate the condition of the tramways and to agonise on the flagging or asphalting of footpaths. Whilst Belgian neutrality was being violated and the British Expeditionary Force was marching to glory and death on the retreat from Mons and the Battle of the Marne, NDM (Aug 13) reported that the well known Hartlepool schoolmistresses, the Misses Hunter, hurriedly returned from holiday in Germany, said that "the Germans did not want to fight… men (waiters) actually cried when they had to cease work and go to fight". The journey "was accomplished under most serious difficulties… I sat on a portmanteau in a corridor for seven hours… everyone having to carry his or her own luggage… ".

This, with hindsight, was pitiful in more senses than one, but, perhaps more seriously, on Aug 21 it was reported that the Mayor of Hartlepool had started a War Fund and that public houses and clubs were to close at 10 p.m. and open at 8 a.m. (sic). On Aug 21 a page-wide notice publicised Lord Kitchener's appeal for a New Expeditionary Force ("Your King and Country Need You!"), with a recruiting office at West Hartlepool. Meanwhile an echo of the war came to the Central Estate. On the same day it was reported that a boy bathing on the north sands was rescued from drowning by Robert Snowdon:

> *… Meantime, two Territorials, who were stationed at the Battery on the sandbanks near to the Cemetery, ran down and by their united efforts, managed, after a considerable time in resuscitating the youth by means of artificial respiration. The incident is being reported to the Mayor of Hartlepool with a view to Snowdon receiving due recognition for his brave rescue.*

Perfect justice may not have been done: the Territorials, who must have been local lads, may have deserved equal praise. By Nov 10, however, the Central Estate was indeed involved in the war. Two former Hartlepool police constables had already been wounded at the front but on Nov 22 1914:

KILLED IN FRANCE

News has been received that Private James Matthews, who was in the 2nd Durham Light Infantry, was killed at the front on October 23rd. Matthews, who before the beginning of the war, was a labourer in the timber yards here, resided at 30 Rokeby-street. He was 24 years of age, was married, and leaves a widow and two young children. A message conveying the sympathy of the King and Queen and signed "Kitchener" has been received by the widow.

One may hope that the widow was comforted. Matthews, whose age may have been misreported, could only have been a reservist recalled to the colours. He got only two lines more than William Pearson (38), an iron moulder of 13 Watson-street, whose body was found on the railway between the Hartlepools near the Cemetery West Bridge. It may have been more gruesome.

... Deceased had apparently been run over by a train, and the head was completely severed from the body. The remains were removed to the mortuary.

None of this, however, could have prepared the Hartlepools for the experiences of Wednesday December 16th, 1914, which were, almost incredibly, chronicled on that very day in the NDM:

PROCLAMATION.
NAVAL BOMBARDMENT.

The civil population are requested, as far as possible, to keep to their houses for the present. The situation is now secure. The Group Leaders of each Ward will advise in case of further danger.
Any unexploded shell must not be touched, but information as to the position thereof given to the nearest Policeman or to the Police Station...
GOD SAVE THE KING

On the next page:

THE BOMBARDMENT.
HARTLEPOOLS AND SCARBOROUGH SHELLED
OFFICIAL STATEMENT

Germans Engaged by Our Ships
The Press Bureau this morning issued the following:
The Secretary to the Admiralty makes the following announcement:
German movements of some importance are taking place this morning in the North Sea Scarborough and Hartlepool have been shelled, and our flotillas have at various points been engaged.
The situation is developing.

On the following day, Thursday Dec 17 (Plates 38-39 pp. 134-135):

THE BOMBARDMENT
OFFICIAL STATEMENTS
ADMIRALTY MESSAGE

... Yesterday morning a German cruiser force made a demonstration upon the Yorkshire coast, in the course of which they shelled Hartlepool, Whitby, and Scarborough...
As soon as the presence of the enemy was reported a British patrolling squadron

endeavoured to cut them off...
The losses on both sides are small, but full reports have not yet been received.

Thus did the Hartlepools became front page news of both national and international significance, Winston Churchill, First Lord of the Admiralty, did not get it quite right. Hartlepool was not, of course, upon the Yorkshire coast, and whether the losses were small is a matter for debate. NDM reported 40 killed, including J. Cook of 28. Rokeby Street and Mary Elizabeth Watson of 162 Hart Road, killed in Union Road.

On Dec 18 an unsurprising panic was reported:

Apparently through an unfortunate misunderstanding there was a considerable amount of excitement... this morning, the possibility of another bombardment gaining more or less general credence...
The origin of the scare appears to have been a misreading of an official message to the effect that hostile airships were to be looked out for... the message added that the rumours might be false, but everyone was to be prepared.

On Dec 21 NDM reported that George Redshaw identified the body of his wife, Margaret Ann Redshaw,. They resided at 51 Watson-street, Hartlepool...

In fact, the Hartlepool total killed was 63, the West Hartlepool total 56 and the Central Estate total five:

Cook, James *28 Rokeby Street*
Hodgson John *58 Stephenson Street*
Houston William Stephenson *75 Union Road*
Redshaw Margaret Ann *50 Watson Street*
Watson Mary Elizabeth *164 Hart Road*

It was more than enough: the Central Estate was in the front line (Plates 40-41 p. 161).

In apparent contradiction to Kitchener's army recruiting message that "Your King and country Need You", on Dec 28 NDM carried an advertisement from the Admiralty and William Doxford & Sons Ltd., ships' engine builders of Sunderland:

WORKERS! YOUR COUNTRY NEEDS YOU!
HURRY UP WITH THE SHIPS AND GUNS!...
The man in overalls is fighting his country's battles as truly as the man in uniform...
The Bench is important as the Trench. You can hit the enemy as hard with hammer and rivet as with rifle and bullet...

Some Hartlepool men (and women) may have been confused by the conflict for their services. On Jan 7 1915, however, the Hartlepool Town Clerk appeared to be more concerned with the question of compensation for the bombardment:

Councillor C. T. Watson: Does that mean you will help the property owners to rebuild?
The Mayor: No, no. We are ascertaining the amount of the damage in order to be in a position to certify it when the owners put in their claims to the Government...

On Mar 15 1915 Cllr. Watson was again, consistently it must be said, on his feet:

> *... .with a view to relieving the pressure on the rates consequent upon the bombardment, (he) moved that steps should be taken with the object of deferring the repayment of instalments of loans this year, paying only the interest...*

He was neither seconded nor supported and... "The matter was dropped".

Meanwhile on Jan 14 1915 NDM reported:

> *INQUEST ON A VICTIM OF THE BOMBARDMENT*
> *The inquest on the body of John Hodgson (62) of 58, Stephenson-street, Central Estate, Hartlepool, whose death was the 112th which has occurred through the bombardment of the Hartlepools, was held by the Coroner, Mr J. Hyslop Bell, in the Central Hotel, Central Estate, today...*

On Jan 22 1915 NDM reported the death of the 116th victim of the Bombardment and the loss of Hartlepool trawler "Doris Burton", whose mate Absolom Cave, one of the five lost, lived in Cleveland Road.

On Feb. 8 1915 there was a Public Notice:

> *GUN PRACTICE*
> *Will take place from Heugh Battery and Old Pier, Hartlepool, between the hours of 11 a.m. and 3 p.m. on Thursday, Feb. 11, 1915.*
> *BY ORDER*

It is ironic though unfair, because of the hindsight involved, to recall previous responses to gun practice. It will be recalled that on December 8th, 1892 the NDM reported that "The new battery about to be erected by the War Office on the south side of the cemetery raises a question of right of way in which the Town Council is interested". In 1896 six-inch guns were installed and, on January 7th 1897, fired, and caused enough damage to require compensation.

More than ten years elapsed before the problem was reported to have recurred. On Aug 18 1908

> *GUN-FIRING NUISANCE*
> *... a petition... had been received concerning the damage to property and injury to health caused by the Territorial forces practising at the Heugh Battery... The General Officer asked for the views of the Corporation on the matter, bearing in mind the fact that in the event of Hartlepool having to be defended, these guns would have to be fired.*
> *... The petitioners added that they were not unpatriotic... and they pointed out that it could be prevented by practice being held elsewhere, and at no great distance from the town. Many of them, who were large employers of labour, desired to live there, but if the gun-firing was continued as at present, they would have to seriously consider the necessity of leaving the town...*
> *... Ald. Hunter said that... (h)is own feeling was that the firing could be carried on near to the Cemetery. It would be no great inconvenience to the Volunteers to go there. He claimed to be as patriotic as anybody... but their highest rateable value was in the district where these guns were fired...*

Councillor Turner hoped that the gun-firing would not be taken to a spot near the cemetery. The damage to property on the Central Estate would in that case be just as great...
Ald. Horsley said that they ought to think about the rateable value that was being damaged. He lived only a few yards from these guns... That (Hartlepool) was a sea-side town, and if they had no guns and no batteries, a man-of-war would never come near them. They only went to armed towns... When the firing was carried out at the Cemetery Battery, they never had a complaint, from the very fact that they were a long way from any houses. Now they had dismantled that battery and come to the Moor...
Councillor Turner recognised that the firing was a nuisance, and reiterated his statement that it would be just as bad near the Cemetery.
The mayor moved that a petition be sent to the War Office similar to that prepared by various prominent townspeople... the motion was carried.

No public response was reported to the information, on Sept 28 1908:

FLEET TO PASS HARTLEPOOL
MESSAGE FROM LORD CHARLES BERESFORD
"The Battle Fleet Squadron will pass Hartlepool about 1 1/2 miles off at noon to one o'clock on Tuesday the 29. It may interest you and the inhabitants to know this beforehand. Hope it will be a good clear day and a good view."

Reassurance came from no less than the Prime Minister himself, Mr Asquith, on Mar 23 1909:

TO-DAY...
... the Premier yesterday said that "Old women of both sexes whose slumbers have been disturbed by fantastic visions of German Dreadnoughts landing an invading army upon our shores, can dream in peace for the next twelve months"... The simple proposition is, "Will our position be reasonably secure in five or six years"?...

On the same day To-Day commented:

We are told that a "Zeppelin" of the present-day type could reach this country in ten hours and do enormous damage in a short space of time... but there is still no harm in noting the facts that point to the possibilities of such a conflict.

Three months later, on June 22 1909, there was reported:

GUN-FIRING AT HARTLEPOOL
DAMAGE THROUGH CONCUSSION
The monthly meeting of the Port and Harbour Commissioners was held this morning... on the 9th instant gun firing practice was carried out at the Lighthouse Battery. Although only three shots... were fired, a considerable amount of damage was done. Eleven panes of glass were smashed... and some of the slates... were blown off and loosened. The concussion, however, did not appear to have had any adverse effect on the structure of the lighthouse itself...
The Chairman (Ald. Horsley): With respect to that gun-firing business, I think we ought to take action to stop it if we can do so... It is smashing everything up... It is terrible. They are Tynemouth people who come to Hartlepool to try this battery. Let

them stop at home and fire there... Let the Government make proper places for them...
... there was the cemetery battery, but they came and dismantled it... They say it is not in the right spot... (I)n a case of war a ship to damage that gun would have to blow the lighthouse down.
Ald. Wilson: The lighthouse is between the devil and the deep blue sea. (Laughter.)...

Less than two months later, still, on Aug 5 1909:

DAMAGE BY GUN-FIRING

... Councillor Sherwood moved that... if... compensation was not granted that the Town Clerk be instructed to lay the whole question in the hands of the Borough Member and ask him to raise it in the House of Commons... the motion was agreed to...

Aug 20 1909 *TESTING THE DEFENCES*
The manoeuvres taking place in the Hartlepool Bay... are testing the efficiency of the local coast defences...
Three cruisers are taking part in the attack, whilst the defending force consists of the... Heugh and Lighthouse batteries at Hartlepool... this morning the attacking party... opened fire...
The response from the batteries was immediate... Lieut-Colonel Robson... is in charge... there is little likelihood of the cruisers taking the defenders unawares...

Almost five years elapsed before the matter again became urgent. On Jan 8 1914:

THE GUN FIRING

The Mayor... It was all right talking about patriotism, but they had to suffer and to pay...
Cllr. J. T. Graham remarked that there was already a battery site which was not being used near the cemetery. Perhaps the War office had forgotten they had it...

Feb. 5 1914: *GUN FIRING:*
The reply from the War office was to the effect that the Army Council could not accept liability for the damage...
"I don't think we should leave it there" exclaimed Councillor C. T. Watson; and Councillor Gibb moved that the Council ask the Borough Member (Sir Stephen Furness) to see if he could do anything in the matter...
The Mayor: We have to be disturbed in time of peace and shot at in time of war: so we ought to be paid for the damage we sustain in peace time.

He was congratulated by an NDM leader on Feb. 9 for "refreshing terseness" and on Mar 5 1914 the MP, Stephen Furness, replied that he would raise the question in the House if he got no satisfaction.

Whatever the outcome, the Hartlepools were bombarded on Dec 16 1914, but the feared invasion did not take place although trenches were dug and manned on Spion Kop. It was not, in fact, part of the German plan to invade and conquer, but to tempt out the Grand Fleet into the arms of the German High Seas fleet. NDM does not reveal why the guns had been removed from the Cemetery Battery. It was presumably not because of Central Estate protests. Furthermore it is perhaps retrospectively regrettable because, whilst the lighthouse masked one of the Hartlepool batteries

(Plates 42-43 pp. 162-163), the Central Estate, including the gunless Cemetery Battery, had a ringside seat.

On March 5 1915 the attempt to open a second front to relieve pressure on Russia by the attack on the Dardanelles, in which there were Hartlepool casualties, was reported as was also, less surprisingly, on April 6 1915, that "holiday traffic was down". On April 9 1915 it was revealed that the St. Barnabas whist drive, which was to have been held on the day of the Bombardment itself, had been held in the Church Hall because the church itself had been wrecked. Another whist drive in which about 40 took part, followed a tea at which "about 112 sat down" on June 2 1915.

On June 2 1915 there was, perhaps, more timely news.

> *CENTRAL ESTATE TIPPERARY CLUB*
>
> *The old Club House in Union-road, Central Estate, has, thanks to the generosity of Mr A. B. Horsley and the labours of the Ladies' Sewing Meeting been reopened and is much appreciated by the men. Recreation, billiards, etc, music, light refreshments (at very moderate charges) are provided. We are asked to state that gifts of books, periodicals, games (draughts, cards, chess, etc.), would be very acceptable and may be sent to the Rev. R. L. Lane, 84, Hart-road, or Miss Cartwright, Hart-road Infants' School.*

On June 17 1915 the Tipperary Club, at 24 Union-road, was formally opened with a parade and the hoisting of the Union Jack (Plate 48 p. 165):

> *... Col. Rivers... assured the audience that those clubs were very much appreciated by the military authorities because they kept the en together and acted as a sort of counter attraction to places less desirable... a good effect on recruiting. A great many mothers thought that when men joined the services they got bullied and knocked about and no one cared much about them... When they came there and saw much interest the inhabitants, and especially the ladies, took in the men's welfare, comfort, and recreation, and went back home and told other women, that would cause a good many of the waverers to come in. A good many men would join the services if only they had a little persuasion, and that came better from women than men... If only they got hold of the mothers they would easily get hold of the boys...*

Col. Rivers was disarmingly frank and astonishingly naive about both bullies and mothers, although the Central Estate lady volunteers deserved great thanks. No less than 41 of them are named, nearly all recognisable for prewar good works with church or chapel connections.

As was predictable, casualties from the war fronts came in. Sgt Arthur Elwin of 11 Hutton-street was reported killed at the Dardanelles on July 5 1915, J. Stevenson of 10, Watson-street wounded in France on Oct. 6, Fred Ridsdale wounded and missing at the Dardanelles on Nov 1, Jack McMahon of 69 Cleveland-road killed on Nov 11 1915.

No more Central Estate casualties - though some may have been unreported; the chances of publication are not recorded - appeared until July 24 1916 when Mr and Mrs J. Barker of 6 Bell-street received word that their son, Gunner James Barker was dangerously ill in hospital at Rouen, suffering from wounds in the left thigh and knee received on July 14. His brother, Joseph was wounded in February and had just come out of hospital. On July 27 1916 Pte. George Gough of 35 Rokeby Street was posted as missing in France. On Aug 1 the same was reported of Bert Hall of 47 Arch Street, and on Aug 5 of Pte. Parr of 45 Stephenson Street. On Aug 29 the death of Bert Hall, whose parents lived in Watson Street, was confirmed. On Sep 12 the second wounding of a soldier from 24 Warren Terrace was reported and on Oct. 16 the death of J. P Hoey of 9 Cleveland Road. On Oct. 24 George Vasey of Cemetery Lodge was reported missing and G. W. Carter of 5, Stephenson Street killed. On Nov 1 the death of William Spence of 3 Bell Street was reported. On Nov 7 Gunner George of 2, Pease Street was awarded the Military Medal but Mrs Laverty, of 102 Hart Road learned that her brother was wounded. On Nov 29 Pte. Henry Jackson of 8 Watt Street was reported killed and, on Dec 18, that Arthur Carrigan of 16, Stephenson Street had died of wounds.

Most, if not all, of these must be attributable to the Battle of the Somme of July 1st 1916 onwards, when the volunteers of 1914 were slaughtered. The Hartlepool and West Hartlepool casualties obviously outnumbered those of the Central Estate but, although statistically difficult to verify, the Estate at least took its share, and perhaps more. Since each street was in itself a neighbourhood, few inhabitants can have failed to feel involved and to grieve.

April 22 1917: Pte. George Gough (aged 20) of 35 Rokeby St, was reported missing believed killed, and on May 10 Cpl. Gilmartin of 26 Union Road, killed. In the same month Pte. James Outhwaite of 19 Bell Street was reported killed and Gunner Charles Sanderson of 10 Rokeby Street... "now the Lord, who loves him, has taken him away from the suffering and has him in His own safe keeping". His parents may have been comforted. On June 27 1917 Gunner H. Tyson of 47 Union Road was reported as suffering from severe gas poisoning. On July 18 1917 Sgt Edward Gissing of 83 Watson Street received the Military Medal for gallant and soldierly conduct. On the previous day Sapper G. Rowland of 10 Watt Street had died of wounds and by Jul 30 Pte. Robert Hancox of 7 Clyde Terrace had been admitted to hospital wounded by gas and burns. On Aug 9 Pte. John Blackett of 11 Clyde Street was reported killed. On Sep 24 Sapper Briggs of 38 Hart Road was reported gassed and on Oct. 10 Sgt Livingstone of 27 Watt Street reported killed. On Oct. 23 Sgt Jones of 37 Rokeby Street, on Nov 19 Sgt Cartwright of 10 Bell Street, and on Nov 25 Pte. James Medley of 81 Watson Street were reported seriously injured. Pte. George Clark of 37 Arch Street by Dec 15 had been awarded the Military Medal.

On Mar 19 1918 Samuel Gray of 25 Rokeby Street was reported dead whilst a prisoner of war in Turkish hands, and on March 23 Pte. Haswell of 34 Arch Street wounded with gas shell. On April 22 Gunner Bartholomew of 42 Rokeby Street was reported wounded and Cpl. Wm Medley of 5 Lambton Street in hospital for shell shock. On April 23 Joseph Tolson of 15 Hart Road was reported gassed and on April 25 Lance Cpl. James Lobb of 51 Union Road and on April 29 William Ainsley of 170 Hart Road were reported wounded for a second time. The Central Estate received its third Military Medal, as reported on May 2, through Corporal Joseph Crowther, son of ex-Sgt J. J. Crowther.

HONOURED BY FELLOW TRADE UNIONISTS

At a meeting of patternmakers... Corpl. J. Crowther... was the recipient of a silver tea service... Corpl Crowther risked his own life by going out to bring in wounded under very heavy enemy fire... In handing the gift to Bro. Crowther. Mr Storrow added "That you may long be spared to enjoy the fruits of your share in the great victory which is sure to come to us and our brave Allies if we hold fast...

Another gas victim, Sapper Ernest Braid of 5 Bell Street, was reported on May 13. On June 10 Signaller Hastings of 46 Stephenson Street was reported wounded and on July 4 Wilfred Roberts of 56 Stephenson Street, Sgt Kenneth Hardy of 119 Hart Road and Signaller Kydd of 42 Cleveland Road were reported missing. In the same month Pte. Stephenson of 10 Watson Street was reported wounded for the third time and Sgt Haigh of 31 Rokeby Street as prisoner of war. On Aug 5 Pte. Wetherell of 10 Greenland Cottages was presumed dead.

On Sep 20 1918 Lance Corporal William Wolfe, of 168 Hart Road, was reported wounded in hospital, and on Sep 23 Pte. Connelly of 37 Rokeby Street killed. On Oct. 22 Pte. Andrew Hay of 8 Union Road, and Corpl. J. R. Vasey of 26 Warren Terrace were reported wounded for the second time. On the same day Able Seaman Peverell (20) of 43 Rokeby Street was reported killed. The "In Memoriam" columns constantly witness the anniversaries of the slain.

As will appear, casualties continued to be recorded long after the Armistice of Nov 11 1918. Meanwhile, it is interesting to speculate, why so large a proportion of casualties should have come from Rokeby Street.

In other respects, understandably and reasonably, life appeared to go on as usual. One of the Throston seats on the Council was contested by Richard Barraclough of 14 Watt Street, iron turner, in Nov 1914. He was unsuccessful. St Barnabas' whist drive, postponed from Dec 16 1914, the day of the Bombardment, was held in the (undamaged) church hall on April 7 1915 and on June 1 the annual congregational tea and entertainment with another whist drive. On April 17 (Saturday!) the Central Estate Primitive Methodist Church Band of Hope entertained children in the cause of temperance and went on to celebrate yet another anniversary on Aug 15.

On Oct. 13 the brother of a resident of 77 Union Road was convicted of the theft of £6, most of which he gave away, from his brother in law. On Nov 25 it was announced that Dr. Gibb, now Medical Officer, ordered Hart Road Infants' School to be closed for a month because of insufficient heating. The infants' response, presumably not hostile, is not recorded.

On Dec 28 1915 for "obvious reasons" it was impossible to make the usual survey of the state of trade, of which there had been a great deal but "it had not all followed the usual channels... Indeed for the shipowner the past twelve months have been unprecedentedly prosperous. The rise in freights... has been phenomenal... The timber trade has necessarily suffered... (and)... there is a considerable falling off in the quantity of coal and coke exported... in the second six months there was a remarkable revival...

With the sinkings of merchant ships by gunboats and battleships and then by submarines, the war must also have been unprecedently prosperous for ship- and engine-builders and their workers. The Central Marine Engine Works giant cantilevered hammerhead crane had just been completed in time and although just beyond the

Central Estate, was as native and familiar to its skyline as the propyards, witness Reg. Smythe's cartoons of "Andy Capp". (p 289)

In 1916 on Feb. 27 the Primitive Methodist Church distributed Sunday School prizes and on Mar 2 the Town Council debated whether or not allotments within the New Cemetery a mile (1.6 km) from the Central Estate) were too far away for use. The allotment holders would have had to walk or cycle the distance, as, in fact, later they did as I can testify. What the Council decided is so obscurely worded as to be unfathomable. Land in Workhouse-lane (Warren Road) would obviously have been preferred.

On June 5 a bicycle stolen from Miss Dora Heslop from outside Holy Trinity Church was spotted by a boy in Hart Road. Defendant's wife said he was always drunk. On July 26 a man from Hart Road confessed to Sunday gambling on the north sands, whereas on Aug 7th sports were to be had there. The Primitive Methodist Chapel went on from anniversary to harvest festival as regularly as St. Barnabas' held its teas and whist drives. Its bell, however, which had rung so controversially in 1912 had been at least partially silenced. On Oct. 25 1916 NDM reported:

AFTER THE PARTY

... Sergeant Holmes said that 12.55 on Sunday morning last he was in Hart-road when he heard the sound of a melodeon and singing. He came across a group of youths congregated near Throston Bridge... Defendants said they had been to a party, a soldier friend being home from the front. They had had a good time, and were setting one of the company home. It was stated that there had been many complaints about noises in the streets at night.

Alderman Hunter observed that men who had been working hard all day wanted sleep at night... church bells were not even allowed to be rung in the evenings.

The defendant youths were let off with a caution and 5s. costs.

The war returned visibly to Hartlepool on Nov 27 1916. (Plate 49 p. 166) On Nov 28:

THE END OF THE EAST COAST RAIDER

... A Zeppelin, which approached the North-East Coast at about 11.30 last night was brought down in flames by the anti-aircraft defences and destroyed. The airship approached from a southerly direction and was immediately picked up by searchlights, whilst anti-aircraft guns came into action. The vessel manoeuvred to escape the rays of the searchlights, but without avail, and within a few minutes crowds of spectators observed that she had been hit. From the nose of the ship flames were seen to travel rapidly along the envelope and the whole of the giant airship was soon a burning mass. The Zeppelin gradually tilted to a perpendicular position and slowly fell into the sea.

The whole of the district was brilliantly illuminated by the glare of flames and large crowds of people witnessed the end of another of the enemy's airships... The people cheered wildly.

Over a hundred bombs were reported to have been dropped but the reporting was much more circumspect than for the Bombardment: censorship had, unsurprisingly, increased since 1914.

The war interfered, or influenced, in other ways. On the second anniversary of the

Bombardment (Dec 16 1916) the Central Estate War Savings Association was mentioned in the NDM and on Apr. 2 1917 holiday makers were banned for a week from the North Sands. On Aug 21 1918 was announced:

> *HARTLEPOOL'S THIRD NATIONAL KITCHEN*
> *The Hartlepool Corporation have shown great enterprise in the matter of national kitchens, the third of which was opened yesterday, this being situated on the Central Estate, at the corner of Hart-road and Stephenson-street... Mr K... addressed the gathering, and also referred to the advantages of such institutions throughout the country. The kitchens were the means of conserving food, and also of bringing about economy in light and fuel...*

Assuming that the communal kitchen, perhaps with a refrigerator, was not installed in Mrs Dando's shop, it must have been in the (presumably) unoccupied house opposite. In the absence of further details, one can only wonder about the economic and social dimensions of the experiment.

It was presumably a consequence of the submarine war against shipping, and the consequential food shortage, that the following headline and article appeared.

> *Sep 11 1917HARTLEPOOL ALLOTMENT HOLDERS' ASSOCIATION*
> *On the Central Estate, Hartlepool, at the beginning of this year the N.E.R. Co. laid out in garden allotment plots the field which was formerly used as a football field by the "Old Boys". These plots were quickly taken up, and by the diligent work of the holders, today they are a very pretty sight... An association has been formed with the title of the Hartlepool Allotment Holders' Association, and has now a membership of 120.*
> *The Association has during the season purchased a spraying machine which has been in use, and the crops have derived great benefit from the result of the spraying... It is the intention of the Association to make arrangements for the purchase of seeds, manures, etc., for the ensuing season for the benefit of the members...*

On Feb. 13 1917 "Local Amusements" included notice of... "the introduction on the British front at the Battle of the Ancre of those huge, weird looking landships, the Tanks, and it is small wonder, therefore, that the Royal Electric Theatre... was last night packed to the utmost... " The attractions of the Grand and Palace Theatres and of Northern Pictures, the Palladium and the Hartlepool Town Hall were palpably pale in comparison.

On Mar 3 1917 the Central Estate Tipperary Club (Plate 48 p. 165) reported another Concert and Supper. Five days later the long-postponed inevitable occurred. The price of the Northern Daily Mail doubled from a half to a whole penny The cost of paper, doubtless truly, was said to have trebled. The war may also have been the reason for this item from the Town Council proceedings:

> *... Coun. Turner... intimated that for the present the destructor was not in operation, and that refuse was being tipped on "Spion Kop". He added that for a long while it had been thought that much material that was going into the destructor need not be burnt, and at present objectionable material was being buried. Ald. Gibb described the closing of the destructor as one of the most retrograde steps Hartlepool could possibly take. At this time of the year there was necessarily a good deal of fish*

refuse, and there was also tradesmens' refuse and vegetable refuse... They were laying themselves open to a great deal of disease...

There was another Central Estate Primitive Methodist Church American Evening on April 11 1917 with details of individual contributions from sales of teacakes, jamjars, rags and bones etc, public teas, concerts and social evenings etc. By July 30 Tom Crowther, the trimmer, was noted as Sunday School Superintendent and soon afterwards Charles Chambers, the Hart Road milkman, was Chief Templar. Central Estate Boy Scouts continued to parade: Oct. 4 1918 Monday parade; Tues. Band practice; Wed. Wolf Cubs; Thurs. band practice; Fri. first aid, signalling etc. It was a whole way of life and, being church based was presumably organised by the St Barnabas' incumbent.

On June 7 1917 speaking for the Town Council, Ald. Gibb congratulated William Gray, "a large employer of labour", on the award of a baronetcy, instancing his generosity to a housing scheme and to local hospitals. No opposition was reported. On June 14 1917 the Royal Visit of King George V. and Queen Mary, greeted with bunting and patriotic songs, to the shipyards and engine works was detailed in three breathless columns (Plate 50 p. 167). On August 2 1917 there was testimony indeed to the wartime party political truce. Trade unionist Albert C. Lund of 122 Hart Rd. was co-opted as a Council member. On August 17 1917 record holiday railway bookings were recorded, "an excellent barometer of the present prosperity at present prevailing in the Hartlepools". Thanks to German submarines the demand for ships and engines was insatiable.

On November 7 1917 a headline announced:

THE MAYOR-ELECT OF HARTLEPOOL (COUNCILLOR C. T. Watson...)

Below a portrait of the Councillor and his wife was written (Plate 38 p. 133):

The Mayor-elect of Hartlepool, Coun. Chas. T. Watson, is a Scotchman by birth, and claims Perth as his native place. In his early days he came to Hartlepool where, as a builder and contractor, he has been well known for many years. His excellent business abilities and own genial personality have rendered his election to the chair a most popular one. It was in 1905 that Coun. Watson was first elected to the Council and from that date he has devoted much time and energy to the work of the Corporation. He is a most active man, and in addition to managing his own private business, and taking part in the work of the Council he has also devoted much time to educational matters. He was a member of the old School Board, and continues his work in this direction on the Hartlepool Education Committee. He is a Churchman, and a member of St. Hilda's Church... Mrs Watson... is a native of Hartlepool, and a member of an old and esteemed Hartlepool family - the Richardsons...

It may be commented that Cllr. Watson married wisely as well as well. The report of his installation as Mayor - in succession to Ald. T. W. Watson - on No 9 1917 said that: "He was the pioneer in developing the Central Estate, and much of the prosperity of this district was due to his energy and enterprise". The same report added the information that the Council had co-opted three working men to its membership, with which, said Cllr. Carter, the Mayor-elect sympathised.

At his Central Hotel on November 17 1917 there was an inquest on a Hutton Street rivetter, injured at work in Gray's shipyard, attended by Dr. Gibb but found dying outside the Cement Works. The jury found that death was due to heart disease, accelerated by the accidental injury to the hand whilst deceased was following his employment.

In January of 1918 - after three and a half years of war - the submarine war imposed the rationing of butter and margarine and more land for allotments was consequentially wanted. Farmer Snowdon of Low Warren Farm on Hart Road could supply. In March there was another air raid and, although the bombs fell on West Hartlepool, they generated a new offence:

> *Mar 20 1918   UNSCREENED LIGHT: A HARTLEPOOL SCENE*
> *... Sergt. Marshall... said that at ten minutes to eleven o'clock on the night of the 12th inst, he noticed a light coming from a bay window of the defendant's house (15, Cleveland Road). He knocked at the door and a woman shouted: "I won't put the light out. Go home and mind your own business."*
> *- PC Fishburn said the blinds were drawn but they were ill-fitting. There was a large hostile crowd outside the house, threatening to break the door and the window.*
> *- Inspector Carr said he received no reply to his knocking. A crowbar was obtained and the door burst in. He went upstairs and saw the defendant. He ordered her to put out the light. She said "I won't: I want the light and I am going to have one". Witness turned out the gas, and the woman said, "I shall light it again". Some pliers were obtained and the meter turned off. Many of the crowd outside were armed with stones, and were threatening to break the windows.*
> *- Defendant said thee was a small light in the bedroom in consequence of her husband's illness. She denied that she refused to put out the light. People were knocking at the door, annoying her, she said, because she would not associate with them.*
> *- Inspector Carr said he threatened the woman with arrest. If she had been fully dressed she would have been arrested   in August 1916 the defendant was fined for a similar offence. - the Chairman said they had decided to fine her £5 or 28 days' imprisonment. It was only the fact that her husband was ill that had caused them to give her the option of a fine. They considered her conduct very reprehensible...*

The fine was indeed heavy and, because of the reasonable fear of more air raids, understandable. The crowd, however, must have been mainly of neighbours, and the defendant's plea that it was because she would not associate with them may well have been accurate, whether justified or not. Assuming that NDM is trustworthy, it was an uncharacteristic occurrence on the Central Estate.

So was the offence reported on Aug 11 1918, although the named youths may not have been immediately local:

> *Aug 14 1918   YOUNG GIRL MOLESTED BY BOYS*
> *... Complainant stated that she had been on an errand to the Central Estate and was returning when F... P... took hold of her and pulled her up a passage., B... going and helping him. They then pulled her down and when she shouted they ran away. C... she alleged had previously received some fish and chips which B... had taken from her... Complainant showed the coat which she was wearing at the time, and which had been torn in two places in the scuffle. P... , in defence, said that when they worked in the shipyard with complainant they used to do the same sort of thing, and*

she took it all in fun... Both P... and B... said the coat had been torn previously by some wire at the place where complainant had been working...

Although complainant's father said that B... had said he "didn't know why he had done it and P... "that it wasn't only him" it is impossible to be certain who was spinning more truths than lies. The magistrates, however, were not in doubt that the assault had been committed and the pair each were handsomely fined £3, or 28 days. Their choice of sentence is not recorded.

On Nov 9 1918 Cllr. C. T. Watson was re-elected Mayor of Hartlepool with the usual encomia. Replying, anticipating the Armistice of Nov. 11, he said, doubtless with unintentional irony:

... They were met today... under very much brighter circumstances than had been the case for the past four years, during which time they had had many sad and anxious moments. The clouds had looked very black at times. Now these clouds were being displaced, he hoped for ever, and he trusted that future generations would never have to endure the agony of suspense that they had had to bear... the enemy could be made to pay dearly for the losses sustained by this country... a suitable monument should be placed in their little park...

This was eventually done... In at least one way, however, war of a sort went on. So much manpower had been diverted to the armed forces that for civilian employees prosperity strikes rather than desperation strikes had been successful for several years, and the assumption was apparently that the end of the fighting would make no difference. On Jan 7 1919 NDM reported:

IDLE SHIPYARDS...

Over 5,000 Men Now On Strike

... on the subject of the 47-hours' week...

... boilermakers, shipwrights, blacksmiths, engineers, enginemen and cranemen, general labourers, painters, smiths and strikers, forgemen and machinists...

Anniversaries of the 1914 Bombardment naturally stimulated reminiscence.

"More or less people couldn't make out really what it was!", recalled Mrs Kettlewell sixty five years later. Mrs Jenny Robson (née Jones) recalled that she met her mother-in-law-to-be (in Stephenson/Watt Street backlane) who said that if the Germans came her husband couldn't get up because of his asthma. People (said Mrs Robson) gathered in the street, which was wrong, but they didn't know what to do. The Germans could have landed on the sand banks. The top of Nellie Nichol's house (on the Stephenson Street/Hart Road corner) was blown off and William Houston was killed in Union Road. Mrs Edmundson and Mrs Watt ran with their children along Cleveland Road towards West Hartlepool and a shell hitting the railway bridge blew off Norman Edmundson's foot and Ralph Watt's arm. The Jones family, whose canary was singing above it all, were calmed by Mrs Middleton, the off-license beer retailer in Arch Street, who took them into the cellar and opened a bottle of port wine. The East Window of St Barnabas, on the day of its Annual Tea, was shattered during a communion service and the incumbent was shell-shocked.

The Bombardment was the earliest recollection of Bob Tyson of 5 Vincent Street, then aged five. He heard a big bang, was covered with soot from their damaged chimney and then carried down Union Road on his uncle's shoulders towards Cleveland Road where people were making their terrified way towards Greenland and West Hartlepool. Bob's house, like every one else's, was left wide open, with his grandma's Xmas cakes on the table. Hart Road School, he said, was hit.

A similar observation occurs on p. 15 of John Ward's "Dawn Raid: The Bombardment of the Hartlepools" (Printability Publishing, Wolviston: ISBN 1 872239 01 3: 1989). On Cleveland Road: "One house had been almost entirely demolished but the upstairs fireplace was still attached to the wall. There was no floor or front wall but the teapot was still on the hob where the occupants had left it when their breakfast was interrupted".

The Northern Daily Mail reprinted many recollections on the 50th anniversary in 1964. Alderman Chambers, already mentioned in Chapter 4 and always known as "Chuckie" because his name was "Charles", recalled (Plate 69 p. 216):

" On Dec 16th, 1914 I was coming out of Richardson Westgarth offices after leaving the milk shortly after 8.0 a.m. when if my memory serves me rightly, three shots were fired seawards and someone passing by said that they were practising. Then in the twinkling of an eye shells started falling around and it was really frightening. I was driving along Sea Terrace Middleton with my milk float when my pony was hit by a piece of shrapnel which made a hole in its jaw one could put one's hand through. When I got out to see what had happened several women in their night clothes got into the float. With shrapnel falling all around I told them the only sensible thing to do was to go and get their clothes on. I hadn't got much further when more people were hit and I was asked if it would be possible for me to take some of the wounded to the hospital. I well remember saying I did not think it would be possible for the pony to undertake the journey but I was willing to try. I took all the milk out of the float and as you can well imagine I was most relieved when at last I reached the hospital. I was unable to get anything there to bind up my pony but someone gave me a pillowcase and with that we managed to dress it. I returned to Middleton to pick up my milk and set off for home. At that time we lived at Middle Warren Farm and I decided to take the short cut by the gasworks at Greenland. When I was about ten yards away the gasometer was hit so I had to turn back, unyoke my pony and with the rein under my arm had to take shelter in the propyard. It was no safer there either. Several times I had to move from one stack of props to the other. Eventually I reached home worn out by such an ordeal. Somehow my pony managed to survive but the vet's fees were much more than the compensation I received."

The Bombardment lasted forty minutes and in that time Ald. Chambers's wounded pony galloped three good miles, a very marathon of a performance.

T. M. Temple, a Central Estate resident wrote: "On the Bombardment day I was 16 years old and worked at Gray Peverells, now Binns. My mother came in and told my sister and me that there was a naval battle in the North Sea. I still set off to work as usual, walking from Cleveland Road on the Central Estate to "West". When passing the propyard at Union Road I saw pit props dancing out of the waggons and I thought it was the vibration.

By now the noise was terrific and when I reached Greenland Bridge there were great bursts of shrapnel in the sky so I decided to turn back but soon changed my mind when I saw that the Tram offices, which I had just passed, were now strewn across the road, so I ran on. The gasometer in Montague Road was blazing and in front of me a tramcar was throwing off coloured lights. It was really frightening. I saw the Middleton Road gasometer blazing and all the workmen were running up Middleton Road from the shipyards. Outside the wrecked Scandinavian Church a poor workman lay with his arm blown off. I eventually got to Ward Jackson Park and was there until a man on horseback said to the hundreds who were there that it was now safe to go home. When I got back to Cleveland Road it was to find that two huge pieces of shrapnel had come through our roof and the debris was all on the bed where my sister and I had been sleeping. We had an improvised bed in the kitchen for weeks after with no window anywhere and no gas. This was in December. Yet looking back what strikes me most is that I must have had a charmed life." - a becomingly modest comment!

The train to which an unnamed lady refers must have stopped in view of the Central Estate. "I was a 13-year-old schoolgirl at the time of the bombardment. I attended Henry Smith Grammar School and came into Hartlepool each day from Wellfield station where I lived. That morning the school train was packed with children from the colliery places, Thornley, Wingate, Wheatley Hill, Shotton, Castle Eden, Hesleden and Hart. The guns were firing before we left Wellfield but we thought it was a heavy thunderstorm. No instructions had been sent to station masters and my father, who was Station Master at Wellfield, allowed the train to leave. It was the same at Castle Eden, Hesleden and Hart, even though from Hart Station there was a very good view of the three warships firing. The train moved on, children leaning from all the windows, watching what they thought was a naval battle. About midway between Hart Station and Hartlepool the train came to stop on an embankment where the sea came closer to the railway. The ships were firing on one side and the gasometer blazing on the other. We children did not connect the two, until the guard came running along the train saying that shells were passing over and we were to get down on the floor. The fact remains that a train load of children were there on the railway embankment, stationary and a sitting target until the firing ceased and the ships departed... "

There was no enemy landing, of course, not because of the trenches on Spion Kop but, as already remarked, because it was no part of the German plan. A tablet on the Hartlepool promenade (Plate 44 p. 165) still "marks the place where the first shell from the leading German battle cruiser struck at 8.10 on the 16th of December 1914 and also records the place where (during the Bombardment) the first soldier was killed on British soil by enemy action in the Great War 1914-1918". The NDM recorded on the 75th Anniversary, Dec 16th 1989, that "an unnamed local woman aged 90 says: 'A young territorial called Houston was the first army casualty. He came from the Central Estate and was engaged to a girl called Alice Shepherd". This confirms Mrs Robson's recollection that this was the above-mentioned William Houston of Union Road who was a soldier in the Territorial Army. According to John Ward, Mrs Redshaw of Watson Street was killed as she crossed the road from a sick neighbour's, with whom she had spent the night, to her house (also a shop) to get her children ready for school.

Edith Crosby, aged 97 in 1994, told me that the brilliant window-dresser who was her boss at Gray Peverell's shop in Hartlepool was a German, Fritz Niehaus, but as soon as the war broke out he disappeared. This was why the Germans knew that the Heugh battery was partially blinded by the lighthouse (which was actually true) and therefore attacked Hartlepool, which "proved" that Fritz Niehaus was a German spy!

Mrs Robson's recollections of the panic which spread on the rumour of a second bombardment on Friday Dec. 16 1914 had a characteristically humorous gloss. Mr Wade the Arch St butcher got his black cart out to take people to West Hartlepool. Mrs L. had a collar and tie in her hand which prompted someone to laugh. Someone picked up in Union Road had a bottle of whisky in his pocket, so someone said: "What about pianos?" and someone else quipped that they couldn't get those on their backs.

The routines of war disturbed and changed the routines of peace. The Infant School was transferred to St Barnabas' Hall so that Hart Road School could become a billet for soldiers, who did bayonet practice and other trench warfare routines on Hart Road west of St Barnabas' Church beneath the shadow of the railway embankment. "Kiddies", said Bob Tyson, "used to stand in front of the (schoolyard) railings and the soldiers used to say :'Go and get us a packet o' Woodbines (cigarettes) at Mrs Watts'. They was kept in, you see. They used to give us the canes, the little sticks they used to carry; we thought it great wi' one o' them". At the end of training, they marched, headed with a regimental (West Yorks) band, from Hart Road to Cleveland Road via Union Road to the railway station. As Harry Elliott, who saw them, recalls, "For many it was little more than a death march". He also recalls the flights of the blimps, small, non-rigid dirigible airships, which patrolled the coast on U-boat (submarine) patrol.

The downing of the German Zeppelin L34 on the night of November 27th 1916 (Plate 49 p. 166) was also recollected. It flew in over Blackhall Rocks and dropped 16 bombs, killing four people. It was caught in searchlights, barraged by anti-aircraft guns and set on fire by aeroplanes from Seaton Carew. A Lieutenant Ian V. Pyott is credited with the kill. In fact the zeppelin came down over Teesmouth but it was watched by crowds in Hartlepool and West Hartlepool. Mrs Robson saw it from Stephenson Street and heard Mrs A, Mrs E, Mrs L. and Mrs W. (all respectable ladies whom I myself later knew) sing, ironically indeed, a current sentimental ditty for troops serving overseas: "Keep the Home Fires Burning". Mrs Robson herself cried, went home and said to her mother that they were somebody's children even if they were Germans.

Bob Tyson's father woke him and carried him outside into Vincent Street where he saw " like a big ballpoint pen lit by the searchlights with a small flame just at the front end. It was covered in no time at all. Everyone in the street was cheering and shouting. I am told by a lady from West Hartlepool that the shout in her street was: "Burn!, you buggers, burn!"

On March 13th 1918 Zeppelin L42 dropped 21 bombs on West Hartlepool, killing 8 and injuring 28. Returning from a Confirmation service at Trinity Church, Hartlepool, Mrs Robson sheltered near the Cement Works, then bought fish and chips for supper and went home. When the thuds came she had to get under the bed with a crucifix to please her mother. Bob Tyson's father used to look out of the bedroom window at the (railway) signal cabin. "That was our warning. If the lights were low they were expecting a raid. We used to go under the stairs and the people next door - her husband was in the forces - used to crowd in underneath the stairs".

Two days after my own birth, on June 12th 1917 in Arch Street, King George V and Queen Mary visited the Hartlepools and toured the shipyards (Plate 50 p. 167). Less than a month later, Hartlepool's most notable son Reg Smyth (later Smythe), the creator of the world-famous cartoon lay-about "Andy Capp" was born in adjoining Union Road on July 10. (See Appendix H, p. 288)

Plate 40 - Bombardment Damage, Dec 16 1914: Baptist Chapel

Plate 41 - Bombardment Damage Moor Terrace 16 Dec 1914

Plate 42 - The Bombardment of the Hartlepools December 16th 1914 (from a painting by James Clark R.I.)

Plate 43 - Bombardment Damage to Central Estate 16 Dec 1914

Plate 44 - Bombardment Memorial

Plate 45 - Lighthouse Battery, 1914

Plate 46 - Replacement Lighthouse, Town Moor, 1915
A gaslit lantern from the demolished lighthouse was transferred to a temporary site. Bell-shaped bonfire 1918.

Plate 47 - Rebuilt Lighthouse, 1926

Plate 48 - Tipperary Club

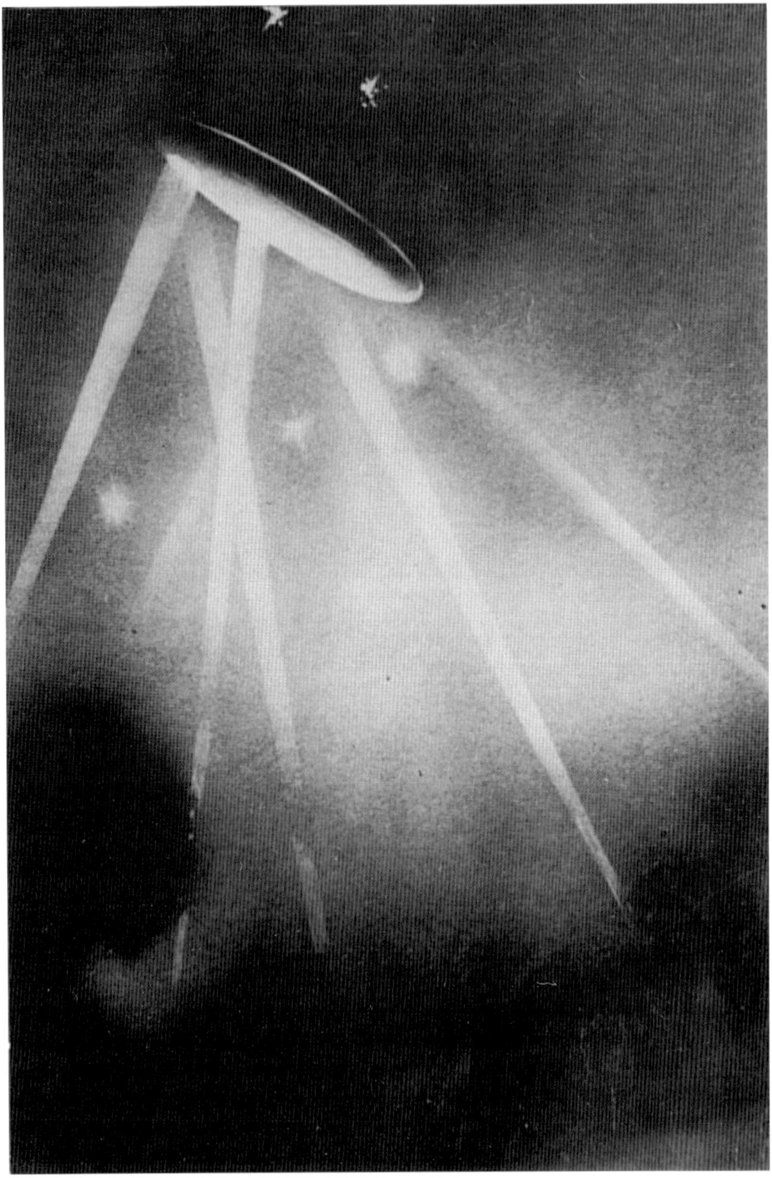

Plate 49 - Zeppelin over Hartlepool, Monday Nov 27 1916

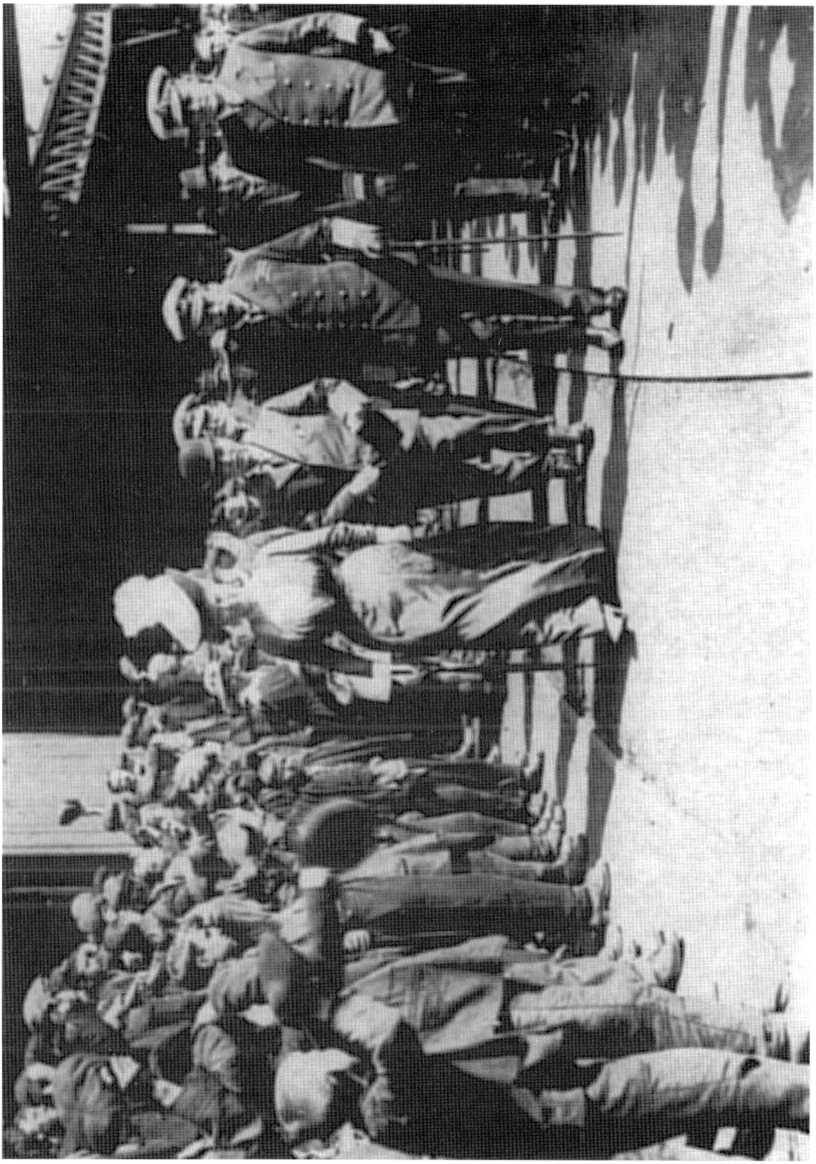

Plate 50 - King George V & Queen Mary visiting Grays, Jun 14 1917

Chapter 8: 1919-23

Although the "Great War" of 1914-18, later renamed World War I, was a national and international watershed, despite the casualties and the damage, Ward's Directory for 1921 of the Central Estate barely registers it.

The caretakers, cranemen, firemen, fish curers, fishmongers, forgemen, fruiterers, galvanisers, gangers, hardwaremen, horsekeepers, manageresses, ropers and shipsmiths, shunters, signal fitters, slaters, spar makers, tool makers watch makers and wire rope makers were eliminated. All these together had, in 1912, numbered 33.

Bricklayers, butchers, cement workers, clerks, drillers, foremen, hairdressers machinists, packers, secretaries, stonemasons, storekeepers and teemers were halved: total 51 less than 1912.

Coal merchants, coal trimmers, engineers, fishermen, joiners, marine engineers, moulders, platers, sawyers and turners were reduced by a third: total 35 less than in 1912.

Cartmen, drapers, weighmen and wiredrawers quartered (11 less); plumbers halved (3 less); dressmakers (10 less) and labourers (34 less) cut to a tenth. The sum total of reduction from 1912 was 177.

On the other hand, analysts (1), beer retailers (1), bicycle dealers (1), blacksmiths (11), boatbuilders (9), boilermakers (21), boot repairers (2), brass finishers (4), builders (2), compositors (1), confectioners (1), coppersmiths (3), dairymen (1), diecutters (1), electricians (1), engine drivers (1), fried fish dealers (3), furnacemen (1), gas meter inspectors (1), grocers and their assistants (9), innkeepers (2), insurance agents (1), iron dressers (1), managers (4), pattern makers (6), policemen and sergeants (3), rivetters (10), shipwrights (9), strikers (1), tinsmiths (1) and vanmen (1) were stable. The respective totals were, almost unbelievably, in 1912 105 and in 1921 104

Mates, newsagents and surgeons doubled; fitters, signalmen and timekeepers increased by a third, and shopkeepers almost trebled. Respective totals were 46 and 79.

There were 13 newcomers: a bookbinder, a dining room keeper, two delegates, a dock pilot, a picture framer, a rent collector, a sanitary inspector, a seaman, a schoolteacher, two stampers and a wireman.

The sum totals were in 1912 548 and in 1921 383, a shrinkage of almost a third. So great a decrease is not attributable to war casualties and presumably evidences postwar depression. The upward economic and social trends were confirmed: the increases were skilled and professional, not labouring.

In Arch Street there were 13 survivors (or people of the same name, widows or sons) from 1912 (33%) and 4 from 1900 (10%). Beaumont Street was not recorded in 1921 but in 1924 there were 2 survivors from 1912 (50%). In Bell Street there were at least 6 from 1912 (26%) and 2 from 1900 (9%). In Cleveland Road there were 23 from 1912 (44%) and 9 from 1900 (17%). In Hart Road (including Clyde Terrace) there were 47

(43%) from 1912 and 10 (20%) from 1900. Hutton Street is not recorded for 1921 but in 1933 there were 3 survivors from 1912 (42%). Lambton Street is not recorded for 1912 but in 1933 there was one survivor from 1912 (10%) and 2 from 1900 (20%). In 1921 there were 5 survivors from 1912 (44%) and 1 from 1900 (11%). Rokeby Street is not recorded for 1921 but in 1933 there were 10 survivors from 1912 (25%). In Stephenson Street there were 16 from 1912 (35%) but only 1 (2%) from 1900. Union Road had 11 survivors from 1912 (35%) and 4 from 1900 (10%). Vincent Street was not recorded in 1921 and in 1933 had no survivors from 1912 but Watson Street had 19 (30%) from 1912 and 11 (11%) from 1900. Watt Street had 9 (28%) from 1912 and 3 (8%) from 1900.

The evidence of continuity, averaging 35% from 1912 and 9% from 1900, is, whatever the multiplicity of family circumstances and desires, strong. Despite or because of wartime boom and peacetime slump, the Central Estate remained a desirable residential area in the 1920s. It was, indeed, expanding, although it is true that there was nowhere else for Hartlepool to expand.

NDM reported a special meeting of the Hartlepool Town Council on June 18 1919. In addition to the approval of new housing in the old town, Ald. Gibb proposed the building of 86 rather than 20 houses (facing south and west) on Hart Road "between the railway bride and the second arch. It runs parallel with the railway, which is on the east side of the road". This was the beginning of West View, a geographical as well as a housing expansion of the Central Estate (Plate 51 p. 190). The proposal was not for an extension of the terraced housing norm but a more modern concept of squares and semidetached houses, not only with a view over farmland and countryside but each with both a front and back garden. The cost of the site was £1,550 and Low Warren Farm shrank by 8 1/2 acres.

It was a breathtaking change in scale and scope, without any of the pre-war sniping by builders and ratepayers, against subsidised housing for the working classes. Councillor C. T. Watson, now Mayor and presiding over the meeting, raised no objections. What had changed? Neither the Council nor the Government had been captured by the Labour Party but the "climate of opinion" had changed and the postwar boom had not ended. The Coalition Govt. under Lloyd George, with its sweeping 1918 majority, had passed Addison's Housing and Town Planning Act which gave open-ended subsidies to local authorities for housing.

Eighteen months later (Dec 18 1920) the climate had changed - or reverted to normal. To a deputation of unemployed asking for work to be provided by the Corporation Ald C. T. Watson (no longer Mayor) moved:

> *"That all resolutions passed by the Council on the 1st December relative to the laying out of bowling greens and tennis courts on the Town Moor, the erection of a pavilion and the enclosure of a portion of the Moor... be rescinded... the time was inopportune... widespread opposition from ratepayers... The work... was, however, not a work of public utility...*

After long debate he was defeated and Ald. Gibb's motion "that application should be made that Hartlepool be classed as a distress area was carried". Throston Cllrs. Turner (undertaker) and Vasey (boilersmith) were on the majority side.

Unemployment in the Hartlepools had already been in the news for a month, the figure quoted on Nov 18 1920 being 1500. Two days later the Trades' Union Council sent a deputation to the Town Council asking for the provision of work and on Dec 7 1920 the Town Council sent a deputation to the Port Commissioners to ask for a "work of public utility", namely a northward extension of the Promenade. On behalf of the Commissioners Mr T. H. Tilly replied that it would take 12 months. On Dec 15 1920 a Joint Committee of Masters and Men was proposed and on Dec 20 an Employment Committee deputation urged action under the Ministry of Transport's Development Commission or the National Relief Fund. The new Mayor (Ald. J. T. Graham) was sympathetic but on Dec 30 NDM's leader was consciously pessimistic and unconsciously prophetic.

Twelve months ago... it was evident that the abnormally high cost of building ships would sooner or later check the demand for new tonnage, and we are now visibly nearer to what threatens to be a very serious slump in shipbuilding... the world's shortage of tonnage has been overtaken... fluctuations in local shipbuilding...

Ships	
1900	39
1914	20
1918	28
1919	20
1920	16

Table 5 - Shipbuilding 1900 - 1920

It was only the beginning of a long sad story. The wartime prosperity strikes of dockers, miners, railway men and shipyard workers had continued in 1919 (for such things as "breakfast intervals") but demobilisation from the armed forces had re-flooded the labour market and wartime boom was predictably succeeded by peacetime slump. Furness's co-partnership scheme of 1908 had not survived but in March 1919 Gray's shipyard and engineering works offered a profit-sharing scheme to employees who did not take part in local strikes and who fulfilled other conditions. In May 1920 the average payout was £19 (the equivalent of some two months pay) for each of the 2,830 employees, and although 27% were disqualified for one reason or another, these were the lucky ones.

On Nov 18 NDM reported that the unemployment felt in October "was not due mainly to the strike of miners. There was another factor as well - the slackness of work in the ship repairing yards... shipbuilding orders have been lost owing to inability to guarantee time of delivery, and there is considerable under quoting by Rotterdam and other Continental ship-repairing firms... " A forecast to N. E Engineering and Shipbuilders in May 1920 that in three or four years the greatest depression ever experienced in shipbuilding would be experienced was wrong only in being too optimistic. The "greatest depression", which lasted on and off until 1940, had already begun.

So had the endless procession of deputations of the Trades Union Council to the Town Council asking for public works to relieve unemployment and of the Town Council to the Port and Harbour Commissioners asking them to help. There were Joint Committees of Employers and Employed in 1920, and in 1921 Distress Funds, Joint (Hartlepool and West Hartlepool) Mayors' Funds, (for which the Hartlepool Regatta was revived), concerts for the unemployed, free cinema tickets for the unemployed and unemployed Demonstrations when the Hartlepool total reached 1525 and the NDM leader of Dec 30 admitted that "our worst fears have been realised".

The census of 1921 revealed that the percentage national increase of population, which had been 11.65 in 1891 and 12.17 in 1901, had dropped from 10.89 in 1911 to 4.93, although the figure for County Durham was 7.9. War casualties were only a relatively small part of the answer: longer term social and economic trends were operating. More immediately significant was the fact that West Hartlepool (68,689) had nevertheless increased by 5000 in population whereas Hartlepool's total (20,961) had increased by only 346.

In twelve days of February 1922 the Hartlepool Soup Kitchen dispensed soup, bread and dumplings to 2,940 people and in May the unemployed total reached 2740. By Sept 1922 public works to relieve unemployment were promised by the Town Council, including the widening of Warren Road, a bowling green and more tennis courts for West View, quoit alleys and a miniature golf course. The quoit alleys did not materialise and the miniature golf course was no more than a putting green. Nevertheless Lord Londonderry opened them all, together with an open-air sea-bathing pool on the Promenade, on Aug 25 1923. The Town Council was doing its best, not only to provide employment but also to develop Hartlepool as a seaside resort. Which of the two was the less effective is a matter for debate.

At the end of the year the NDM's economic verdict was that little more than marking time had been achieved: 5 ships had been built as against the 4 of 1922 (and the 43 of 1906) and whilst timber imports were slightly up, coal exports were slightly down.

Mutual recriminations abounded. On Mar 7 1921 NDM reported that at a demonstration of unemployed Coun. Carter had said:

> *... in my humble opinion there is only one reason for unemployment, and that is that it is the result of the system under which we have to live - a system that is breaking hearts and homes every day... The present industrial system... produced a condition of strife that "undermines confidence, damns religion, and makes us take part in a battle in which all of us are losers"...*

He was backed by the Rev. H. G. Cobb (High Anglican) curate/vicar of St Holy Trinity) who denounced the dole (unemployment benefit) as degrading because it was payment for doing nothing and compared it unfavourably with the Elizabethan Poor Law of 1603 which stipulated that work must be provided for the unemployed. The government could have done it, but:

> *... it would have been dangerously near to nationalisation - it would have been dangerously near to coming into competition with the Capitalist...*

Father Cobb may have sounded like a Marxist, but could scarcely have been. Mr

Robert Smillie, President of the Miners' Federation may have been. On Oct. 1, 1921 he was reported as saying that the blame should be placed "on the shoulders of those who had locked the miners out...

> *... It did not begin in March. It was plotted months before March. The British Industries Federation and organisations of capital in this country recognised that the miners would have to be broken before they could attack other trade unions... The Prime Minister was now preaching class war more than any of the Labour agitators, and he was inviting the land-owning class and the capitalists, the manufacturers and the wealthy to close their ranks and unite in order to fight the Labour Party...*
> *... The Government... ought to settle men and women on the land and maintain them until they could earn a proper livelihood instead of paying out doles...*

On Feb. 3 1922 another trade unionist, A. A. Gregg (of the National Alliance of Employers and Employed) put it differently:

> *... he could not agree with the theory that the only way to cure unemployment was to expropriate owners and rebuild the social system anew with units of an entirely new sort. It was impossible suddenly to create new classes of men, and it was impossible to scrap the present system simply because it was reeling from the shock of a set of circumstances that no other system could have faced without breaking altogether... the policy of the Alliance... was a better way because it tended towards the introduction of the "human touch", the removing of suspicion, and the creating of goodwill and understanding between employer and employed.*

Mr Gregg seems to have anticipated what would later become the national consensus. The equal and opposite view, as expressed by Dr. Murray Butler of Columbia University, New York, was quoted by NDM on Aug 8 1923:

> THE FALLACY OF SOCIALISM
> *... The word Socialism has an attractive sound, and much of its appeal is due to the sentiment which has become attached to it. The doctrine itself, however, rests upon a series of historical, economic and psychological fallacies...*
> *... Socialists are fond of asserting that all wealth is the product of labour, As a matter of fact, however, labour alone never has and never could create any wealth worth speaking of. Labour alone is barely able to earn subsistence, and that only of the rudest and crudest kind. Wealth is the creation of brains, of skill, of character. It is trained labour, skilled labour, righteous labour, which creates wealth, and it is the training, the skill and the righteousness which do the creating and not the labour... The higher and more effective types of brains, of skill and of character are entitled to their rewards, and society has provided for these rewards through the system of private property.*

There was no shortage of self-righteousness on all sides of the economic and social divisions and there was no shortage of local evidence that prolonged mass unemployment was a poor substitute for the promises of victory and of post-war elections. There were, at the same time, efforts to bridge the gap. The image of the "good employer" was cultivated. In January 1920 the freedom of both the Hartlepools was presented to Sir William Cresswell Gray, son of the founding Sir William, and his benefactions, as well as his profit-sharing scheme, were enumerated (Plate 73 p. 234).

... In 1898, in memory of his father, he paid off the debts on all the churches in the two towns... He has been a generous contributor to the Durham College of Science, the Missions to Seamen, the Bishop of Durham's Church Extension Scheme, the Leysian Missions to the Victoria Alms Houses. He presented swimming baths to West Hartlepool... and started the Hartlepools Hospital Trust... Recently he gave to the West Hartlepool Memorial Fund... and is giving the town a museum and art gallery and among the projects he has in hand is one for making splendid recreation grounds... and a convalescent home.

The recreation grounds, "Grayfields", contained: "(f)ootball, cricket and hockey grounds, tennis courts, bowling greens, quoit alleys and a running track... the Institute... will contain a reading room and library, a billiard room, gymnasium, club and committee rooms, a large canteen, changing rooms and baths. The convalescent home, endowed with £10,000, provided for 30 patients for "employees who have been sick, or who may have met with an accident". As NDM observed in a leader:

During the war we heard a great deal of the new England that was to arise on the foundations of the old one, but the good intentions that were so freely expressed and the promises that were so lavishly made have, in many instances, evaporated in words... (but) Sir William is obviously anxious to do all in his power to assist in creating improved conditions of work and social life...

In the same month of January 1920 there was reported:

An interesting ceremony took place yesterday at the offices of the Warren Cement Works Ltd., where Mr David Cox was the recipient of a present on the occasion of his marriage... directors of the company were present, together with the officials and staff. Mr McBride, the works manager, also spoke and referred to the happy relationship existing between the principals and staff.

Presumably this was easier in a small than in a large firm but nothing similar was reported for years. Under prevailing conditions of deepening slump and increasing mass unemployment it would, in any case, have been surprising. However, the annual cricket match at Warren Farm between the Police and the Corporation reported on Jul 21 1921 in aid of the Unemployment Fund which attracted "a good number of unemployed workmen", was at least a gesture in the same direction. Characteristically, Ald. Gibb was the captain of the Corporation and although his team was defeated, his bowling, perhaps ironically, was said to be one of the "outstanding features of the game".

Another long sad story, at least temporarily, dwindled, although it could not die. In 1919 another name, the youngest son of Mr and Mrs Armitage of Hart Road, was added to the list of Central Estate soldiers who died in the war, whereas Mrs Kydd of Cleveland Road's son came home from a prisoner-of-war camp. The army restored Hart Road School to its teachers and scholars, the Golf Links & Pavilion to the golfers (although only to the immediate extent of 9 holes) and a hall for dances, roller skating, boxing and concerts. The Primitive Methodist Church organised an "At Home" for returning soldiers and St Barnabas' a concert to fund a war memorial. "Peace" was celebrated with speeches, bonfires and fireworks and the Town Council, after agonising between a hospital extension and cottage homes opted, after a public meeting chaired by Mayor C. T. Watson, for a war memorial on the Promenade in the already existing garden at Redheugh Close (Plate 52 p. 192). On Dec 17 1921 the bronze statue of "Triumphant Youth" on a stone pillar, with an accompanying screen naming 351 serving men killed and 52 men, women and children killed in the Bombardment, was unveiled.

The St Barnabas' War Memorial, containing 32 names, was dedicated in January 1920 by the Rev. H. G. Cobb, the Henry Smith School Memorial, containing 36 names (out of the 250 who served: i.e. 14%) in October of the same year. Regrettably, however, by December 1920 the post-war slump was so severe that the sixth anniversary of the December 16 1914 Bombardment was "not suitable to existing conditions". Post-war euphoria had already reverted to pre-war parsimony. On Mar 21 1919 NDM reported:

WEST HARTLEPOOL WINS THE TANK

"Egbert", the tank offered in competition by the National War Savings Committee, has been offered to the borough of West Hartlepool, the sum raised... representing an average of £31.9s.11d per head of the borough's population...

The implication is that no other borough in the country surpassed this average, however attained, and on April 29th "Egbert" was ceremonially installed on Stranton Green where it remained for many years (Plate 53 p. 191). Yet on Mar 29 1919 Hartlepool, also, was offered a tank. A year later, on Mar 4 1920 NDM reported on the Council meeting:

THE GIFT OF A TANK

... Coun. Sample asked if they could not "stop it", adding, "It would soon simply be so much scrap iron".

"You know what the upkeep will be", remarked the Mayor.

"If we can possibly get out of it —" suggested Coun. Turner, and Coun Sample, pursuing his argument, interpolated, "It will just be a nuisance to the town, like the old guns and one thing and another",

"We can reply that we cannot find a site suitable", suggested Ald. Hunter. Ald. Watson (apparently referring to the damage recently done to seats, etc., on the promenade: "Put it on a site near the Coastguard Station: it will soon disappear.

Coun. Williamson: Let Mr Howkins have it for a breakwater.

Coun. Turner amplified his previous observation by definitely proposing that the Town Clerk should see if they could possibly get out of accepting the gift, and it was understood that the Town Clerk would write declining it...

Nevertheless extracts from the German Admiral (von Scheer)'s version of the 1914 Bombardment were quoted on Mar 15 1920, notably:

... the Seydlitz opened fire on the Cemetery Battery, and scored several hits, so that at last the fire was only returned by one 15 cm gun and one light gun from the battery...

The rebuttal in the same article was immediate:

... As a matter of fact there were no guns at all on the Cemetery Battery, which was dismantled years before the war...

This confirmed the confident statement later made by a councillor, but the situation might, in the meanwhile, have been changed and there was always the "fog of war" which could have twisted the truth. However on Oct. 26 1922 "F. M", commenting on the German report, conclusively observed:

> *... A saving bit of humour comes when we read that the shells from the Cemetery Battery fell one to two hundred yards short (of the German cruiser), and that the guns were soon silenced. We know that this battery had been dismantled of its guns, and instead of being silenced was never noisy...*

Anyone in a position to contradict - and there must have been many continuing Central Estate residents - who could, and might, have done so. None did.

Long after the war - indeed until the early 70s - buildings known as "The Battery" survived as a playground for children, with a "Mess Room" and two or three other rooms half filled with sand and inclined to be smelly: tramps had presumably improvised sanitary facilities there. Above, on top of the sandbanks, there was a circular concrete gun emplacement, six feet high, with a huge iron cogged wheel some two or three metres in diameter as its base, on which, presumably, had been mounted an anti-aircraft gun able to swivel in any direction. There were also two concrete circular pillars six feet in diameter and four feet high, with short iron pivots in the centre, on which machine guns had presumably been mounted (Map 7 p. 141).

Col. Robson who was in command of the defences at the time of the Bombardment, writing in Jan 1922, added a fascinating precedent. It had happened before:

> *... It is an interesting fact that this is the second recorded artillery action at Hartlepool... In 1650 an Irish frigate boarded a Newcastle ship near Hartlepool, which, the Governor seeing, caused some of his guns to be so planted that they shot the Irish frigate through and through and caused her to hasten away and leave her prize, which came safe into Hartlepool...*

It was not an exact parallel: on that occasion, during the Cromwellian conquest of Ireland, the bombarding boot was on Hartlepool's foot, not vice versa. Col Robson was quoting from a publication by the Surtees Society, but went on himself to observe:

> *... The artillery defences at Hartlepool can be traced back for over 300 years, and the present Durham R.G.A. are the lineal descendants of those ancient gunners who manned the local batteries...*
> *... The personnel, officers and men of the manning details... in 1914 belonged to the Hartlepools, many of them living close to the batteries. As fire commander, owing to interrupted communications, I had little to do during the action, but had the satisfaction of having trained the fire command... The telephones, fixed on poles were put out of action by the first 11.2 inch shell from the Von der Tan, which struck the right hand front corner of the battery...*

In July 1922 claims for 1914 Bombardment damage had still not been settled but the Member for the Hartlepools, W. Howard Gritten (Plate 32 p. 111), who was complaining about it, was, perhaps not surprisingly, informed by the Secretary of the Royal Commission on Compensation for Suffering and Damage by Enemy Action that:

... there must be a certain amount of necessity felt through the delay of these cases, as they have been outstanding for such a long time; but it is impossible for the Royal Commission to give undue priority to any particular case, unless, as I have pointed out before, absolute necessity is shown...
... with the thousands of claims which we have to deal with, it is rather a difficult matter to pick and choose, and I trust you will appreciate this...
... The Royal Commission has no funds at its disposal, and can only make recommendations to the Treasury...

One must hope that he was not joking and, indeed, that all the claims were genuine. Thus did the war appear to have petered out.

On January 4 1922 not only Hartlepool but the Central Estate itself achieved national headlines for the first time since the 1914 Bombardment (Plates 54-57 pp. 191-193):

ACRES OF FIRE...
HUNDREDS OF STACKS OF PITWOOD DESTROYED
A fire that has already consumed hundreds of stacks of pitwood and that has most ominous possibilities is at present raging at the timber storage ground of Messrs George Horsley and Son at Greenlands.
It broke out somewhere in the neighbourhood of 1 o'clock this afternoon and with half-a-gale blowing from the north-west, it quickly assumed proportions of a huge, unmanageable conflagration...
... The gale, driving diagonally across the storage ground, the fire tended in the direction of the point where Union-road enters the Hartlepool road, and before 4 o'clock several of the houses in Union-road were involved...

The NDM leader of January 5 was even more descriptively eloquent:

... Viewed in the evening from the high ground in the west of the town, the spectacle was most awe-inspiring. For a distance of half a mile there was what looked like a sea of roaring fiery billows... The worst feature of the fire was the destruction of a large number of tenement houses on the Central Estate... At the moment from eighty to one hundred families are homeless...

The unnamed reporter added more details:

... On the Union-road grounds are the contorted skeletons of what were railway trucks. The scene of devastation was intensified by the empty gaping shells of the houses and shops... Partly fallen and tottering walls were all that remained of the row of double tenemented houses in Union-road, and the same remark applies to the three end blocks of buildings in Cleveland-road... and the Central Hotel... houses are also affected in Arch-st and Watson-st...
... The Cooperative Society's stables in Arch-st... collapsed in the course of the fire, but the horses had been removed earlier in the afternoon...

SCENES AND INCIDENTS...
"There's two of the drawers missing"; "No, that's not our wringer"; "Ay, and the sideboard's all cracked"."
These and many like expressions were to be heard this morning at the Hart Rd. schools, the market, and other places, where last night the furniture and effects of

many of the threatened houses were stored...

One tenant has lost his piano, but he found his wringing-machine in a side street...

... In all, over 80 families are homeless, and these, last night, were given shelter by kind-hearted neighbours...

On that same Thursday, Jan 5 1922, the Mayor, Ald. J. Turner, appealed for donations to a relief fund, and the first to respond was Sir Wm Gray & Co., Ltd, with £100, accommodation in his Convalescent Home, in unoccupied houses at his new suburban shipyard at "Graythorp" or in the "Gray, Peverell and Co" shop in Hartlepool. The Mayor of West Hartlepool contributed and there were collections at Durham Cathedral, at the Empire Theatre in West Hartlepool and from the hundreds of spectators of the ruins. The Middlesbrough Church Army opened soup kitchens. NDM recorded subscriptions by the hundred and the total topped £1300 in two or three days. NDM also reported:

NO CLUE TO ORIGIN OF FIRE

... So far as we can glean, the only facts that are known are that whilst a number of employees on the Messrs Horsley timber ground were having their dinner in a cabin on the ground a boy rushed in crying that the timber was on fire. The men at once did their best to cope with the blaze, but their efforts were defeated by the gale.

On Jan 9 1922 two possible causes were named:

... a spark from a locomotive, which just before the outbreak was performing shunting operations... may have lodged in one of the stacks of timber. The second theory is that the fire may have been caused by the fusing of one of the electric cables that conveyed power to the saw benches in the yard...

It may have been a big spark or the insulation of the cables was so rotted as to be useless. It may have been carelessness or vindictiveness...

Other details emerged on Jan 9:

Hundreds of rats and many rabbits perished in the fire.

Regarding the pig which was seen scampering towards the height of the fire, the worst has not happened. It appears that the animal first refused to leave the sty, although the flames were uncomfortably near and it was not until a fireman turned the hose upon the pig that it was persuaded to quit. It promptly bolted but was headed off...

By Jan 10 1922 the Relief Fund, including £150 from King George and Queen Mary, had reached over £6500, according to the Mayor Ald. Turner. On Jan 22 there was a Grand Concert at the Grand Theatre to raise funds, on Feb. 2 £326 from the Lord Mayor of Newcastle was reported.

By Feb. 22 1922 recriminations about the respective contributions of the Hartlepool, West Hartlepool, Stockton and Middlesbrough Fire Brigades started with the last-named independently reporting on them to the Home Office. By Mar 2 the Town Council was reminding West Hartlepool that the services of its Fire Brigade, for which it was allegedly charging excessively, had not been officially requested. In July of the following year, 1923, the winding up of the Fire Fund and who should carry out the necessary audit of admittedly unprofessional accounts was also contentious. In Sept 1923 the precautions taken by the North Eastern Railway Company to prevent a recurrence of the Fire were criticised: more hydrants on the Central Estate were acceptable although still invisible, but the ten feet of clear space between timber stacks and roadside fences was insufficient. Moreover, the stacks were now even higher.

The accounts were reported closed on Sep 13 1923. The total raised had been £11,447 and there was a net balance of £1200. No more claims were eligible, the auditor was satisfied and the accounts open, after long disputation, for inspection - by councillors only - but the quibbling continued. It was locally commented that every house in Union and Cleveland Roads now had a piano. Who was on oath?

There were other forms of fallout from the Fire. On Jan 11 1922 a man was fined for theft from furniture when it was removed from a house on Cleveland Road during the fire:

> *...the Mayor (Ald. Turner) remarking that it was a most despicable action to steal from a fellow-workman, particularly under such circumstances. The Chief Constable said that there was still a quantity of furniture, etc, missing and he hoped this would act as a warning to others who might be withholding goods.*

On Aug 8 1922 a lady on the Central Estate was fined five shillings because smoke, flames and burning soot issued from her chimney near the timber yards. Under pressure she admitted her chimney had not been swept for a year.

It was not until Aug 25 1923 that public rejoicing was reported, although it was heavily qualified (Plate 70 p. 219):

> *HARTLEPOOL'S GALA DAY*
>
> *Today Hartlepool is en fete, the occasion being the opening of the recently constructed bathing pool, tennis courts, bowling greens, promenade... by the Marquess and Marchioness of Londonderry. Right royally have the inhabitants... responded to the appeal of the Town Council to decorate their premises... even the humblest buildings contributing their quota. Today marks a new epoch in the history of the town. Today sees the consummation of two years of thoughtful debate, hard work and wise action...* (Plate 58-59 pp. 193-194).

The Marquess improved the occasion by expounding the "European Situation", endorsing the government's policy of sympathising with French insecurity but criticising French methods of exacting reparations from Germany. He was less guarded on the question of unemployment:

> *... the question of unemployment is one which not only requires sympathetic but also scientific handling. The principle of the "dole" is one which no one can regard with any degree of satisfaction, and least of all, the working man, but in the present abnormal state of unemployment the necessity of maintaining the working population who are forced out of employment through no fault of their own is one which no Government can possibly neglect. It seems to me therefore, incumbent on all those who are in a position of employing labour, whether they be individuals or Corporations, should lose no opportunity... to do whatever lies in their power to provide work.*

It was grudging, and what the alternative to the "dole" (unemployment benefit) was he did not specify. Cllr. Robson regretted that unemployment had been responsible for the work being done, but rejoiced in the fact that it had been done. In other words it was "public works", funded, like the Poor Law, by the ratepayer or taxpayer, presumably as an insurance against public unrest. As NDM observed in its leader of the night before (Plate 23 p. 60):

> *... The extension of the South Promenade and the other improvements... have altered Hartlepool almost beyond recognition... A great deal of labour that would otherwise have been unemployed was utilised in making these improvements... For very many years the town was neglected, but recently there has been an awakening of public spirit, and it is producing excellent results.*

Not that municipal politics had become a love-feast. According to R. Robson (JP) in Oct. 1919:

> *... "Business men" and "practical men" and "the workmen's friend", as they had described themselves at all elections, had dominated the Council, "and", he added, you have not far to go to see what has really happened". Today, in Hartlepool, they owned everything that took money, and nothing that brought in money, and in this respect he referred to the private companies upon whom they were dependent for electricity and gas... he was certain there were no ideals in the minds of many members of the Council, nor were they gifted with outlook... "*

Nevertheless in that year's municipal elections the Labour vote against C. Toshack Watson in the North Ward was split between two Central Estate working class representatives: R. S. Boswell, boilermaker, and T Smith, trade union organiser. Neither, naturally, in such circumstances, succeeded. Ironically, in March 1919 the Durham Miners' Association had celebrated the achievement of a Labour majority on Durham County Council, with Peter Lee, commemorated in the naming of a post-World War II new town, as its Chairman. This was, indeed, a change and it had important implications, notably in educational policy.

A year later, in Nov 1920, Boilermakers' Secretary J. Vasey won the Throston Ward for Labour at his first attempt. The eloquent backing of the Rev. H. G Cobb, now promoted from the Curacy of St. Barnabas' to be Vicar of Holy Trinity Church, Hartlepool, may have helped. He invited the Trades Union Council to attend church on the following Sunday afternoon and "it was agreed unanimously to accept the invitation". Less than a fortnight later the Rev. Cobb supported another Labour candidate, R. H. Carter (publican), in a Throston by-election, and he, too, was successful. A year later still, in Nov 1921, however, the Labour challenge to the other (long-standing) Throston shopkeeping councillor was defeated, and there is no traceable or necessary connection between the election of the Rev. Cobb to the Presidency of the Labour Party in February 1922 and the repeated Labour victories of R. H. Carter and J. Vasey against Thornton Bulmer, (draper and Primitive Methodist local preacher), in 1922 and 1923 respectively. Thornton Bulmer, who had already stood for another ward, predicted that "third time would be catchy time", and in 1924 he succeeded (Plate 61 p. 195).

It is interesting to note how long the apprenticeship to Council membership and the determination to win could be. In 1922 Mr R. S. Boswell of the Central Estate, future

Mayor, was again bottom of the poll against C. Toshack Watson, as, in 1923, was future Mayor Charles Chambers (Plate 69 p. 216). Both were nonresidents of the wards they proposed to represent.

The question of the amalgamation of the two Hartlepools, not surprisingly, arose again and was discussed and negotiated in April 1919, in June, October and November 1920 and in November 1921 but, unsurprisingly, not in 1922 or 1923 or 1924 despite the "WONDERFUL LOCAL PAGEANT In 10 Brilliant Scenes, portraying by Art, Music and Costumes, over 1000 years' History of the Ancient Borough... HARTLEPOOL'S PAST IS THE HISTORY OF BOTH TOWNS... in the Town Hall, Hartlepool on Dec 9 and 10 of 1920. In November 1921 NDM published G. W. Sivewrights's "Hartlepool's Assets"...

> *... Amalgamation. - Why this craze for amalgamation?... Hartlepool people have kindly feelings towards West Hartlepool, and have never said an unkind word to their disparagement... We have passed through too much suffering to be anything else than friends...*

G. W. Sivewright was, patently, not on oath, but his opinion continued to prevail. As the Borough Treasurers jointly reported (on Oct. 7 1920) rates in Hartlepool were 5d (2.4p) in the pound higher than in West Hartlepool. West Hartlepool was also ahead in public transport. Its trams served Hartlepool as well as West and in 1922 it introduced "railless trams" (trackless trolley buses) on the Foggy Furze route (Plate 67 p. 214).

At the national level it was not until the post-war election of December 1918 that the Liberal Party's monopoly of the Hartlepool seat in Parliament since 1900 was interrupted by Conservative Howard Gritten, the Coalition candidate. Gritten was novel in another way. He was a professional politician. With at most two exceptions, all his predecessors as MP since 1868 had been local ship owners or shipbuilders, from Ralph Ward Jackson through Thomas Richardson to the Furnesses. The first Sir William Gray had also been a candidate. To have had a "local" representative had presumably seemed advantageous and the change may have been regrettable. When the wartime Coalition broke up in 1922 Gritten was defeated by Liberal William Jowitt who held the seat against Gritten in 1923, the election which produced the first Labour government. It was also in 1918 that a Labour candidate (W. J. Sherwood) first stood, winning 19% of the vote, a proportion which did not subsequently diminish although it was not until 1945 that Labour won the seat (Plate 32 p. 111).

Although there was, fortunately, nothing to compare with the Fire in scale there were other post-war mishaps, not to say tragedies. Tramcars collided in fog at Greenland Bridge on Feb. 24 1920, though no one was injured, and there was a dog fight followed by an assault and cruelty to one of the dogs by one of their owners on Spion Kop just before Christmas. Much more regrettable were the deaths of an Arch Street boilersmith's 18 year old son by drowning on the Block Sands in June 1921, and, in February 1922 of a 48 year old unemployed fitter who had slept out for a week in one of the dugouts at the Old Cemetery Battery and was found by the Matron of the Fever Hospital (alerted by a boy) lying on the sand behind the Cemetery wall. Death from pleurisy accelerated by the cold was the coroner's verdict.

Even worse was the earliest of this sad sequence. The NDM headline on Dec 18 1919 was:

MURDER AT HARTLEPOOL
MISSING GIRL'S BODY FOUND

Buried in the North Sands

... About 9 o'clock two men... who were passing along the sands, had their attention attracted by a neatly-heaped pile of sand, beneath which, on further investigation, the dead body of the child was found. There were evidences that the child had been outraged and then murdered, a piece of string being tied tightly round the throat.

On Tuesday afternoon, the little girl, who attends the Throston Infants' School, went home at about 4.30, but, her tea not being quite ready, went out to play. That was the last that her parents saw of her. It is stated that about 5 o'clock a little girl... a child of four, and a little boy saw deceased going in the direction of the sands in the company of a soldier.

The place where the body was found is only some 200 yards from Howard-street... about 15 yards above high-water mark, the little girl was buried, a depth of about three inches of sand covering her...... There had been no attempt to dig a hole in the sand, the body having simply been laid on the beach and covered...

... P.C. Rawson... (said)... At present there were neap tides. If there had been spring tides the body would have been covered...

... Whoever had done it... had been very deliberate... and had taken great pains to smooth down the sand. It was just like a grave...

The site was just eastward of the Central Estate. On Dec 19 1919 the Coroner's jury returned a verdict of "Wilful murder" against some person or persons unknown and suggested the offering of a substantial reward for information. On Jan 21 1920 the headline was:

ACCUSED MAN'S CONFESSION

... dated 8th January... in which Holmes said that... he walked along the beach at Hartlepool and about teatime the same day he saw two children playing at a street corner. He gave one of them a penny to get some sweets and she got the sweets at a corner shop... She came back to him and he picked her up and carried her in his arms to the sands. "I just touched her on the leg", he said "with my hand and she shouted out. I put my hand over her mouth. I thought she was dead. I carried her to the midden and covered her with straw... he slept on the midden that night... He walked about the town that day, and when it got dark he took the child from the straw... and carried her to the sands. He laid her down and covered her with sand.

"I didn't intend to kill her", he said, "and that is the truth".

As we now know, in the 2000s, confessions are suspect, but the accused, a 31 year old local "labourer or miner" (not "a soldier") with "a vacant expression" and "no trace of emotion" was identified three weeks after the murder by a little boy, recollected by several lady fish-shop customers from five weeks previously as apparently shell-shocked and "childishly" saying that he was going to see his mother in Easington the following day. He was, more convincingly, further identified by the man who stabled his horse in the yard with the midden in which the accused was found. His accent was "different to what is heard in the district". It was he himself who led the police to the stable yard. He was further identified as a docker by his former employer but claimed that he had seen another man buying sweets for a child and then carrying her to the sands and burying her. Questioned by his father-in-law he had then confessed and signed. Confession apart the evidence is circumstantial.

"Dishevelled" at his trial at Durham Assizes, reported on July 6 1920, Thomas Holmes, now described as a miner, pleaded "Not guilty". Two doctors claimed that tests had shown that he was sane. Defence counsel and another doctor contended that he was imbecile. The judge said that it was either manslaughter or murder. The verdict was not reported but must have been "guilty" of the one or the other. Who could say? In any case, the parents of Throston children, which included the Central Estate, were reported as unwilling to let their children play out-of-doors.

There were other mishaps, some more serious than others. In March 1919 two Central Estate women were fined for sending children under the age of 14 for beer from the Arch Street off-license and in May a tram inspector was assaulted at Throston Bridge. In July 1920 a Norwegian seaman was accused of feigning drunkenness when caught on the roof a house in Romaine Terrace attempting to get through a window, and in December not only was there a dog fight on Spion Kop followed by an assault on the winning dog by the losing owner. Just before Christmas two householders from Bell Street and Wilster Terrace were fined for not registering the particulars and nationality of their lodgers under the Aliens Order. The NDM reporter observed that it was an unusual case but the "aliens" were Irish and the peace which created the Irish Free State had only just been signed. In March 1921 a Union Road mother was fined for not sending her daughter to school for six months and in June of the same year the 18 year old son of an Arch Street boilersmith was drowned off the Block Sands. In March 1922 two brothers were fined for stealing coal from the sidings near the North Cemetery and in May a man was sent to prison for three weeks with hard labour for starving seven pigs on the Central Estate. In January 1923 the two year old son of a West View labourer was killed stumbling in front of a horse which was being overtaken by a lorry. At the same time a Bell Street boat-builder died from septicaemia following an industrial accident. At the end of the year a Warren Terrace labourer was fined for keeping a gaming house which was open to women and children as well as men.

Whether by chance or policy NDM frequently printed only the names but not the addresses of minor offenders and the amount of petty crime on the Central Estate or by its inhabitants may have been under-recorded. This was, however, the post-war Britain of the so-called "gay young things" and of Eliot's "Waste Land". It could hardly have been more sober.

Apart from the Fire, free spectacle was limited to shipwrecks in Feb. 1921 and April 1922. The latter was spectacular indeed, coming to rest "broadside on the promenade wall, minus her rudder and propeller... a crowd of people (of which I, aged 4, was one) gathered on the promenade and watched the fish nets and the personal property of the crew being salved by means of travelling baskets. The crew had left by boat after - according to the captain - realising that they had been "beguiled by the light" (from the lighthouse) in thick fog.

There were, fortunately, some better things to report. The Primitive Methodist Church (Plate 71 p. 217) (always known locally as "The 'Little Chapel'") and St. Barnabas (Anglican) Church (Plate 29 p. 81) (always known locally as "Barny's") continued to proffer their "At Homes" and "Anniversaries" and "Teas", etc, with the addition (temporary in both cases) of a Cricket Club to the former and a Football Club and a Social Club to the latter. The former achieved 21 NDM reports 1919-23 as against the latter's 7. It may have been that the former advertised almost weekly, the latter seldom or never. It may have been that the former had a more assiduous press secretary, willing weekly to trek over to the NDM office in West Hartlepool. Perhaps the Editor of NDM was biased. It can scarcely have been that whereas the Vicar of St Barnabas was President of the Labour Party, the Chapel accommodated an electioneering meeting for Thornton Bulmer, one of its local preachers, who sought to sit as an "Independent" in the interest of rate cutting. Both chapel and church, with only differences of emphasis, strove to maintain the existing social structure, although in one respect the Chapel was more emancipated in employing a woman, "Sister Kathleen", as full-time evangelist.

In Sept 1921 a Hartlepool Councillor's daughter from the Henry Smith School won a rare State Scholarship and County Exhibition, each worth £80 per annum, and in the following month a former HSS scholar from Cleveland Road, Wilburt Nelson graduated MA at Glasgow. In June 1923 two old scholars, brother and sister Yeals from the Central Estate (and the Chapel), graduated from Durham University.

In March 1923 Mr M. Pickering of Cleveland Road achieved a so-far unique distinction by the grant of a patent "for an improvement in drawer and shell match boxes". The idea was "to prevent the drawer of the match box being drawn more than half way out by putting such an obstruction through the face of the shell as will come into contact with the ends of the drawer". Alas! Mr Pickering is not reported to have made a fortune.

Because of the food shortages caused by German submarines (U-boats) during the war, the pre-war demand for allotment gardens (by the descendants of peasants expelled from the land by 18th Century enclosures and industrialised into workers) received increased governmental support and on Sept 8 1919 NDM reported:

> *HARTLEPOOL ALLOTMENT HOLDERS' SHOW*
>
> *The President of the Association (Ald. W. Scott Gibb, JP) presided at the opening of the show held in St. Barnabas' Hall and St Mary's Schoolroom, adjoining. He was supported on the platform by Coun. J. T. Turner. Ald. Gibb in his opening remarks, said that the show was in many respects better than the Association's effort of last year… Incidentally the Alderman mentioned that in their new housing scheme… each house would be provided with a garden…*

Not only is this further evidence of middle- and working-class collaboration. The availability of both Anglican St Barnabas' and Catholic St Mary's School accommodation for the Show was an unusual local example of religious toleration and cooperation.

The Third Annual Show was advertised on Aug 13 1920 and reported on Sep 4. This time there were over 600 entries, a band in attendance and prizes for children's collections of wild flowers. In October the County Horticultural Adviser W. S. Sharp (who created a new early potato, "Sharp's Express") commenced a series of public lectures for allotment holders, and when in Nov 1920 the North Eastern Railway Co gave notice to holders to quit the Old Boys' Field, President Ald. Gibb himself, with Cllr. Turner's support, suggested a deputation to the Town Council to prolong the notice from three to twelve months and to provide alternative land . The deputation alleged that they had previously been driven by the NER in succession from the Slake, from land near the Old Cemetery and from land adjacent to the Old Boys' Field. It was not more land for pitprops which the Company needed but more railway wagons. Perhaps some allotment holders would be in worse places if they were not on the allotments (Laughter).

The Council, which in June 1920 had already agreed that there should be more allotments in the New Cemetery, expressed sympathy and a year later, in Nov 1921, the compulsory lease of land in Warren Road from the local farmer, himself the tenant of the Milbank Estate, was reported, and although the purchase was not completed until June 1923, a theft of beetroots from an allotment there had already occurred in September 1921. In April 1922 fourteen more plots from the same farm on land near the Horse Shoe Arch were also reported, and on Aug 21:

HARTLEPOOL ALLOTMENT HOLDERS

In the unavoidable absence of the President, Alderman W. Scott Gibb, the Chairman (Mr R. S. Boswell) introduced the Mayor (Alderman J. T. Turner), who declared the show open.

... The Mayor... had, in fact, been an allotment holder himself, although not a very successful one. Proceeding, his Worship pointed to the advantages accruing to the allotment holders and the community generally by the efforts of the Society...

It was trite but true. It was also true that Mr Boswell and Ald. Turner, who were brothers-in-law of strongly opposed personal and political views, publicly collaborated in this good cause. In June 1923 some of the allotments were flooded but rents were not remitted because the Allotment Holders themselves had recommended purchase of the land in question. In that year the show, now including pigeons as well as rabbits, was held at the Rink in Hartlepool on Sep 1, but the issue of flooding remained unresolved. Using clinker supplied by the Borough Engineer and sand from the sandbanks, some allotment holders had built up the land 18 inches and one (in fact Mr Boswell) no less than three feet. Petty point-scoring was inevitable. Coun. Lightfoot said that these huge tasks could not have been accomplished had the men not been out of work and that the Council was exploiting the unemployed. Coun. Parkinson frankly acknowledged the work put in, but added, perhaps uncharitably: "They could now derive the benefit from their work".

Both the "Klondyke" (Central Hotel) and the "Lord Clyde" (pub) continued to offer more than mere alcohol. Perhaps in competition with the Allotment Holders, now including rabbits (and shortly to include pigeons) in their Show, the Hartlepools and District Fanciers held their quarterly (rabbit and guinea pig) show in the Central Hotel in June 1923. In October the Lord Clyde accommodated the "successful" "smoker" (men only) for the Winding and General Engineers' Society which proceeded from talk of "the depression" to (vocal) "harmony".

For those willing to travel as far as Middlesbrough - and transport in chars-a-bancs (single-deck coaches: "sharras") was available to subscribers - music of the highest quality was available from such world-class performers as Cortot, Mcormack

Thibaud, Suggia and Rubinstein. For those content with more local offerings the churches and choral societies offered an endless supply of concerts, cantatas and oratorios.

Wireless (radio) broadcasting for entertainment had existed from 1920 and the British Broadcasting Company from 1922. In April of that year NDM forecast "wireless for all" and successively reported demonstrations of morse, the construction of "crystal" and "one-valve" sets and the information that broadcasts from Newcastle were within range. In January 1923 the Wireless Society heard Newcastle on a loudspeaker driven by no less than three "valves" and broadcasts from London were heard in the following month. In December 1923 NDM reported a lecture and demonstration on the subject to the Foremen's Mutual Benefit Society and began printing advertisements for wireless sets. It must have been about this time that 20m long wires, strung between poles 10m high ("outdoor aerials"), began to appear on the Central Estate. How many "indoor aerials", 20m long wires invisibly strung in a horizontal V-pattern in the lofts of houses there were, is unknowable. There was a ten shilling (50p) license to pay from 1922.

This was a novel form of entertainment, the more so because it was home-based unlike theatre, or cinema. These continued to exist in competition, with the latter now an essential component of the national way of life. Not only was it considerably cheaper per seat. It was beginning to compete with the architectural splendours and decorative luxury of its older rival. Just before Christmas 1920 the new "Picture House" in West Hartlepool was illustrated (still unusual) as well as extravagantly described in the NDM (Plate 60 p. 194). It had an arcade with shops, tea and waiting rooms, ample accommodation under cover for those awaiting admission, 2,100 comfortable tip-up seats raked for uninterrupted viewing of the screen, a balcony, decorative panels, Axminster carpets, controlled central heating and fan-driven ventilation and lighting that prevented eye strain by increasing or diminishing rather than flashing on and off between films. It was said to have the largest auditorium and to have been the first wholly reinforced concrete theatre in the country. Strange, perhaps that it should have been so unimaginatively named as compared with the "Palladium" which preceded it and the "Majestic" and "Odeon" which later followed. Tom Mix, Charlie Chaplin, Mary Pickford, Harold Lloyd and Rudolph Valentino etc, etc, all "stars" in America, were as well known in Hartlepool as in Hollywood.

Amateur rugby and professional cricket (with leading articles on Test Matches) and football continued to flourish and occupied much reporting space in addition to the weekly "Football Mail" on Saturdays. In June 1920 it was hoped that Hartlepools' United would enter the Third Division (North) of the Football Association next season, although funds were needed for players' wages and ground improvement. They succeeded, but in August 1922 their finances were "not so cosy as they would have been under normal industrial conditions". Nevertheless gates numbered up to a thousand and chars-à-banc were available for away matches.

My personal recollections date back to 1922 and the earliest and most vivid is the Fire of Jan 1922 . I saw the smoke in the middle of the afternoon but it was not until after 6 p.m. that my parents and I watched the mile-long billows of flame sweeping towards us from the junction of Union and Cleveland Roads and grasped that if the wind did not change our own house in Stephenson Street would be threatened. Fortunately we had relatives in newly-built West View and there we spent an uncomfortable night on the sitting room floor. Fortunately the wind changed and our house was spared, unlike those of some of our neighbours in Union Road. I also recall the stacks of furniture in Hart Road School playground, notably a massive and forlorn wringing machine.

It was in late August of 1922 that I started school at Hart Road Infants and, after a rebellious first day, almost uniformly enjoyed it. By this time, although my immediate family was wholly Lancastrian in origin and dialect, I had played in the streets long enough to become a working class Hartlepudlian child in accent and attitudes. The street culture was intense, not to say fierce, and I learned to play, fight, swear (without knowing the meaning of some of the words) and many of the "facts of life" (without understanding them) with gusto.

We were fortunate children, despite the fact that our fathers were often unemployed. In addition to the streets and back-lanes, which were safe playgrounds, we had the sandbanks, the seashore and the countryside within half a mile, not to mention the urban delights of both Hartlepool and West Hartlepool. Our first loyalties were to "our street", though these were soon extended and enriched by "our class", "our school" and "our Chapel" or "our Church". It pleases me in retrospect that "our street" included Catholics and Anglicans as well as Nonconformists and that although we continuously quarrelled, religious sectarianism was never the cause of more than badinage.

Back lanes (Plate 21 p. 58) were right enough for football ("footer"), the opposing walls acting as goalposts. Goal posts could also be chalked on the walls of houses adjacent to empty corner sites, on which chalked wickets served for cricket. Empty sites could also be used for marbles (which needed small holes in the ground), and for ball-bouncing games. There were never enough of us for teams so that football could only be "shotty-in", in which the reward was to become goalkeeper for defeating the existing custodian three times. Cricket could be played by as few as two boys. Back lanes also hosted quoits, because the peg could be driven between the cobble stones, and more furtive games like "Mill On Fire" (see Appendix E p. 275) and tying two back doors together and kicking them both, or kicking only one, and running away as soon as voluble wrath was aroused.

Front streets, with pavements and gutters and the road in between (along which the passage of a car or a lorry was a rare event indeed) were superb playgrounds. Pavements were ideal for tops and whips in due season, and gutters for the game of marbles called "Follow" ("Foller"). The varieties of "tag" ("tiggy") were numerous. In most of them he who was "on" stood on the roadside edge of the pavement whilst his opponent(s) stood with their backs to the wall, and he tried to tag ("tig") anyone who passed the necessary test as he (and they) tore across the road to the safety of the opposite pavement. For two players the favourite was "Guessies" which required a sweet shop window from which he who was "on" gave the initial letter of a confection which the other had to guess. For small groups the variations were in the rituals preceding the chase: "Three Jolly Sailor Boys", "Golden Things", "Tippy Finger", "Tug o' Bay", "Illy Illy Arky", "Fly Jack and Be Gone" (see Appendix E p. 275). For larger groups (preferably at night in the dark) there were "Leavo", "Spy Sheep" and "Jack Show The Light" (see Appendix). Other non-tag games were "Throw Out Your

Luggage" and "Judge" victimised small or ingenuous boys at whom dirt was thrown at the climax of the "game". "Mill On Fire" was even cruder.

For larger games a base was needed, a "bay" as it was called. In "our" half of Stephenson Street, below Arch Street, there was a solitary gas-lit lamp post which threw a small pool of light into otherwise almost total darkness. It was known as "Kings' Lamp" because it stood outside Mrs King's house, and although she chased us off from time to time, justifiably angered by our noise, we always drifted back. It was also unique by daylight, offering a pole to climb and cross bars on which to swing (Plate 26 p. 61: note typical lamp post).

Deciding who was "on" was decided by counting ("Twenty one's on!") or by reciting, one word per person in succession until only two were left:

> *"Icketty picketty, i-solicketty, bombadairy jig.*
> *Every man that has no hair ought to wear a wig,*
> *Pig's snout, all out: I am IN and you are OUT!"*

Either pavement or road could be chalked for "Hopscotch" and either pavement or road be used for all the many varieties of "Leapfrog" - "Hop, Skip and Jump", "Nigger", and "Fly". A wall was needed for "Montykitty".

Paper aeroplanes and zeppelins were usually "flown" in the street, which was also a suitable arena for ball-bouncing and catching games ("Ceps"), and skipping, although this was something normally left to the girls. Very occasionally, lead by the older boys, we would include the girls in "Ring a Ring a Roses", "Polly Polly Wallflowers" or "Statues". Otherwise the girls skipped, played "diabolo" or performed elaborate hand and leg rituals whilst bouncing balls against the walls of houses by themselves.

The "country" began with Low Warren Farm between the railway arches, with its duck pond and cattle, and beyond the arches with fields and a "beck" in which tadpoles and tiddlers could (occasionally) be caught. On Easter Mondays and Whit Mondays there was morning exodus, by consensus of children and adults alike, for picnics with sandwiches and teacans (or lemonade bottles) to the "denes", wooded valleys running down towards the sea at Hart or Crimdon. Towards evening the crowds would return, furbished with huge bunches of primroses, cowslips or bluebells according to season.

A side road, later Heortnesse Road, from Hart Road, led under the railway embankment round a bend and up a slope to Cemetery Road, the sandbanks, the Battery, Spion Kop, the Tips and - fifty feet below - to the seashore (Map 7 p. 141). The sea might be anything from twenty metres to a kilometre from the bottom of the banks, according to tides and seasons. Whatever the tides and seasons, high watermark was always clearly defined by the detritus of wood, pieces of bark, candle ends, cinders, sea-coal and the occasional dead bird. Towards Hartlepool the rocks began, with pools of seaweed, starfish and the occasional crab or periwinkle. Three miles north the sandbanks turned into caves at Blackhall Rocks, another picnic favourite. In summer when the sea had warmed we paddled ("plodged") either along the breaking waves or in the large shallow pools left in the sand by the retreating tide. As children we made sand castles (with underground tunnels). Swimming was discouraged: the coast was treacherous. In colder weather we "roly-poly-ed" (rolled) down the banks, "tracked" courting couples seeking quietude in grassy hollows, made fires in tins salvaged from the Tips, flew kites, tried to hit birds with stones from slings and (later) played golf with one club and one ball.

In the Old Cemetery there was the occasional funeral to watch. In the Jewish Cemetery alongside, always locked, we could see by climbing the walls a strangely different fashion of gravestone. Then came the Fever Tent and beyond it "Sandy Park" which, by accident or design was an acre or so of flat and grassy land, ideal for football. The ground became hillier down to the Horseshoe Arch and the hollows were filled with nettles. Beyond the Arch was the golf links which remained a right of way as far as Dene Mouth. Finding lost golf balls in competition was lucrative as well exciting: they were saleable to golfers (for two or three pennies) if usable and a source of elastic for catapults, etc, if not, and the heavy core was a handy missile.

The Infant School was mixed although boys and girls sat apart. We were kindly and efficiently taught to read, write and count, to sing and play games, to sew and make rugs, and to pray, by three women teachers and a headmistress. The greatest punishment was a tap or two on the hand with a short, broad stick.

At age eight boys and girls were separated and the regime for boys was rougher and tougher, with older boys, men teachers and a headmaster to contend with. The bamboo cane was frequently used, much more by some than others, and the quality of the teaching varied from the sympathetic to the brutal. A great deal was learned by rote, from arithmetical tables to psalms and scriptural stories, including lists of rivers and mountains, and a certain amount of verse. There was a lot of singing but the only exercise was military style drill and the only craft, apart from drawing, rolling out lumps of Plasticine into sausages. Seating was in order of scholastic merit, measured by sums and essays, from the top to the bottom of the class. Hart Road School was "Church of England" but only Catholics were excluded. They had their own school, also in Hart Road.

Nearly all children went to Sunday School. At the Primitive Methodist Chapel the intonation of prayers was very different from the chanting mode of the day school. After afternoon Sunday School, respectable working class children went for walks with their parents. The Promenade was a favourite resort, especially when brass bands played in the Bandstand in the amphitheatre. Street games were not played, and shops were shut (Plate 24 p. 60).

Plate 51 - West View, Central Estate, mid 1920s

Plate 52 - Hartlepool War Memorial, 1921

Plate 53 - "Egbert" the Tank: West Hartlepool

Plate 54 - Great Fire: Central Estate, Jan 4 1922

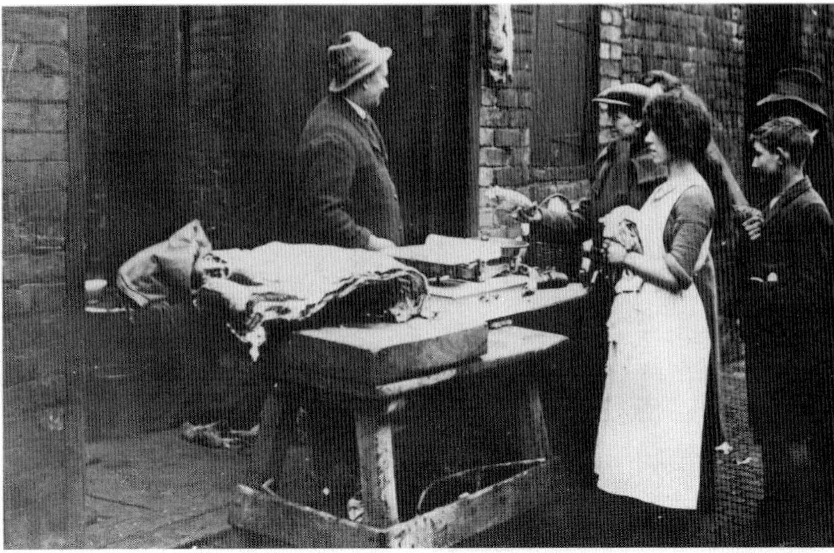

Plate 55 - Great Fire: Davidson the Backlane Butcher

Plate 56 - Great Fire: Emergency Soup Kitchen

Plate 57 - Great Fire: Puzzled Postman

Plate 58 - Bathing Pool 1923

Plate 59- Bowling Green 1923

Plate 60 - Picture House, West Hartlepool, 1920

Plate 61 - Councillor Thornton Bulmer (ringed)

Chapter 9: 1924-29

Despite the prevailing economic recession, Wards Directory for 1924 (Appendix I) adds an architect, a pharmacist, a professional golfer, a town clerk and two teachers to the 1921 professionals, an analyst, a curate, a school teacher and two surgeons. The ranks of the skilled were augmented by a baker, a boatbuilder (2), three more brass finishers (8), three more bricklayers (5), four more butchers (6), two more caulkers (40), ten more clerks (14), six more trimmers (17), three more drapers (6), five more drillers (9), four more electricians (5), two more engineers (3), seven more fitters (43), two more foremen (10), two french polishers (2), six more grocers (14), three more guards (5), two more insurance agents (3), three more joiners (14),five more machinists (9), another manager (5), two more marine engineers (7), three more moulders (19), one more newsagent (3), two more painters (3), a piano maker, another plumber (3), four more policemen (5), a stocktaker and a supervisor. The "bridgeman" presumably worked the swingbridge across the dock gate at Middleton.

More or less stable were blacksmiths (-3), boilersmiths (-1), book binders, boot repairers, builders, cartmen (+1), cement workers (+3), coppersmiths (-1). cranemen, dairymen (+1), fish curers, fishermen (+1), fried fish dealers (+1), furnacemen (+1), hairdressers, innkeepers, mates (+1), millwrights (-1), packer (+1), patternmakers (-1), platers, post officers, rent collectors, rivetters, sanitary inspectors, sawyers (-1), secretaries, shipwrights (-1), signalmen (-1), steam gauge makers, stampers, storekeepers, strikers, surgeons, teemers (+1), timekeepers, tinsmiths (+1), turners (+1), single men or widowers (+2), widows (-3), spinsters (+1), vanmen, weighmen, wiredrawers (+1) and wiremen.

Even the labourers had increased (+8). The Central Estate was less unfortunate than many areas, even during the depression. It continued to offer more attractive housing to the skilled survivors from mass unemployment. Whereas in 1921 Arch Street, Cleveland Road, Hart Road, Union Road, Watson Street and Watt Street all registered falls from 10%-20% in occupation, presumably the cumulative result of war casualties and depression, in 1924 recoveries to 1912 levels or better were general. In addition there were 86 new houses in West View (Plate 51 p. 190), superior in size, amenities and outlook to all its streetbound and gardenless predecessors, which attracted working class "aristocrats" and lower- to middle-class professionals. The 1921 drop in the number of households from 522 to 469 was succeeded by a rise to 617. Despite the continuing fall in the national birth rate and the continuance of economic depression the Central Estate was expanding and improving.

Five years later, in 1929, the 16 additional households in West View and Hart Road virtually equalled the unoccupied houses in other streets: there was a net decrease of only 4. As to occupations, middle class professionals like the architect, the brewer, the curate, the piano maker, the rent collector, the town clerk and the sanitary inspector of 1924 had gone, almost all from West View. The Central Estate had also lost a bicycle dealer, a boot repairer, a builder, 8 fitters, a grocer, an insurance agent, a manager, a newsagent, a rolleyman, a tinsmith and a turner, not to mention two schoolmasters. On the other hand, accountants and analysts, blacksmiths and boilersmiths, boatbuilders and butchers, electricians and engineers, foremen and french polishers, guards and innkeepers, joiners, millwrights and patternmakers, rivetters and shipwrights, pharmacists and golf professionals, etc, etc. were stable and there were more agents and bank clerks, barmen and chargehands, cranemen and firemen, gas workers, hairdressers and hardwaremen, hauliers and inspectors, moulders and platelayers, platers and plumbers, policemen and sawyers, shopkeepers and timekeepers, shunters and signalmen, superintendents and supervisors. Additionally there were a felter, a funeral furnisher, a gateman and a garage proprietor, a dripping refiner, a grave digger, two pipe fitters and a traveller - and two ship's captains: a trawlermaster and a tugmaster. The number of labourers had doubled but on balance the Central Estate continued occupationally and socially to climb, according to current standards, despite the depression which in 1929 plunged the national economy to new depths.

Arch St had 26/47 (55%) survivors from 1924: in the meanwhile J. J. Crowther had ceased to be a police sergeant and had become a hardwareman; that is to say a small shopkeeper selling pots, pans, kettles, pokers, coal tongs and scuttles, etc, etc., From 1900 H. Hutchinson survived as dairyman, and T. Newton who had added hairdressing to newsagency. J. Edmundson, blacksmith, survived from 1902 and the labourer T. Pailor had become a garage proprietor. J. Metcalf had transmuted from boatbuilder to funeral furnisher. The widow of T. Angus also survived from 1902 as did J. Thomas and T. Walker, still fitters, J. Cassidy still moulder, and Miss Frain, daughter of widowed Mrs Frain. From 1912 there were 10 survivors (20%).

Beaumont Street (4 houses) had two survivors from 1924 (50%) and one from 1912 (25%). Cleveland Road had 34/58 (59%) from 1924, 11 from 1912 (16%) and 3 from 1902. Hart Road had 71/117 (61%) from 1924, 27 from 1912 (25%) and 10 from 1902: as always, some were obviously widows or daughters. Pease Street had 6 from 1924 (60%), 3 from 1912 (27%) and 1 from 1902. Stephenson Street had 28/44 (63%) from 1924, 15 from 1912 and 4 from 1903. Union Road had 23/44 (52%) from 1924, 9 from 1912 (20%) and 7 from 1902. Watson Street had 43/67 (64%) from 1924, 15 from 1912 (23%) and 7 from 1902. Watt Street had 22/31 (71%) from 1924, 8 from 1912 (25%) and 0 from 1902. West View had 46/86 (53%) from 1924.

The average of personal or household stability over the 5 years was 60%. People who had moved within the Estate included the names Edmundson, T Crowther, J. J. Crowther, A. J. Woolford, B Hood, F Cox, R Boswell, J Lumsden and C Kettlewell. In fact there was a hierarchy of streets in terms of respectability. At the bottom was the top end of Union Road, all "up-and-downers", many of whose houswives stood with arms folded at their front doors, staring or glaring at passers-by. The parents frequently figured in court proceedings. The children were rougher, less well clad and nourished than the average: some went to school, even in winter, with bare feet. Next in the scale (as I recall it) were Watson, Vincent, Rokeby and Hutton Streets and then Stephenson, Watt and Bell Streets (both ends) and the lower end of Union Road, mainly respectable, as were Lambton and Pease Streets. The top end was Arch Street and Cleveland and Hart Roads. West View was in a class of its own.

I canvassed the views of Mrs K. and Mrs JR. as to the bad name of Union Road. The former thought that a few undesirables gave the street a bad name. The latter blamed it on lower rents to which families were driven by their taste for drink.

Nationally there was some economic improvement between 1924 and 1929 with falling levels of unemployment despite the General Strike of 1926. Locally, although rail and dock strikes against wage reductions continued, there were signs of improvement. In 1924 Grays opened a new shipyard at suitably-named Graythorp between West Hartlepool and Middlesbrough, and a mineshaft was sunk at the Cement Works to a bed of anhydrite below, not because it was used in making cement but because it could be profitably exported to Synthonia (later ICI) at Billingham (Plates 65-66 pp. 213-214). In the same year a fish meal factory, which manufactured manure from rotting fish, was established in Hart Road. All three created a few new jobs but unfortunately the latter, because it was "offensively smelly", contradicted the image - and the reality - of the Town Council's policy of sustaining and improving Hartlepool's claim to be a health resort. At Richardson Westgarths' an experimental double-acting two-stroke diesel ship's engine, which promised greatly increased fuel efficiency, was being pioneered and in 1928 an order was secured, a year before Grays' launched its 1000th ship. Unfortunately in that same 1929 the Wall St Crash precipitated a world slump of even greater depression than that of 1921, which plunged unemployment in Britain's staple industries, including shipbuilding and coal exports, to unparalleled depths. The North East Coast Trades and Industry Exhibition at Newcastle, in May 1929 (which I saw and at which I marvelled) was therefore unfortunately timed.

In contrast to rising unemployment, less relieved than pre-war by emigration, the Council financed public works: a promenade extension, a bowling green with the prospect of a tennis court and a putting green and an improvement in sewage disposal, a paddling pool, a yacht pond, and the conversion of the Skating Rink into a dance and concert hall. These were intended to reduce unemployment but could not be other than proportionately (or disproportionately) pathetic. The emphasis was on reduction of the rates, which in 1921 were reduced by a shilling in the pound: 5%. Free concerts for, and free admission to the Bathing Pool for the unemployed may have helped and they were congratulated by the Chief Constable in 1924 for not resorting to crime. More remarkable, if accurately reported, was " the exemplary conduct of the people of the borough" during the General Strike of 1926. Although on May 3rd NDM (which was obviously not on strike) reported local dock and steel strikes, and on May 4th that there were no trains, buses or trams, there was no reference to a "General Strike" despite the facts that an appeal to volunteers to maintain essential services and the proclamation of a state of emergency were published. I myself, then almost 9, recall rumours of riots in the adjacent collieries: the miners, who fought against more hours of work for less pay, were the spearhead of the General Strike and stayed out for five months more: but although for 10 days the country was said to be on the verge of political revolution, Hartlepool and the Central Estate were, rightly or wrongly, through apathy, intimidation or self-censorship on the part of the NDM, quiet. Riots, however, were reported from Newcastle, Gateshead and Middlesbrough as well as Glasgow.

At the national level, in January 1924, the Conservative government under Stanley Baldwin was succeeded by the first (minority) Labour government under Ramsay MacDonald. At the General Election of Sept 1924, the "Red Letter" election in which the government was (falsely but not entirely incredibly) accused of accepting bribes from Soviet Russia, Liberal Sir William Jowett was defeated by Conservative Wilfred

Sugden as the Member for the Hartlepools, a victory confirmed in the 1929, 1931 and 1935 elections, despite (or because of?) the Votes for Women Act of 1928, only contradicted in (and since) 1945.

At the County Council level, Labour regained control in 1925 from "Moderates" and "Independents". At the local level local prejudices (or principles) persisted. Public transport controversy continued between Hartlepool and West Hartlepool, the latter favouring first trams and than trackless (electric) trolley buses, the former motor buses. Trams, followed by trackless buses, survived on existing routes but motor buses were eventually permitted to serve West View, at the cost of rival Bills in Parliament. Consequently it is not surprising that the West Hartlepool invitation to amalgamate in 1925 was "declined with thanks" or that in 1927 Hartlepool should have rejoiced in retaining its own police force although far short of the qualifying level of 75,000 population.

In 1925 the Central Estate ceased to be a part of the Throston Ward and became Hart Ward in its own right (Map 7 p. 141), although the resident Labour candidate. R. S. Boswell was defeated in the election which followed in 1926, and he was defeated again, although this time by a resident from West View, an electrician, but also a Labour candidate. In 1926 Central Estate-born John Arkley was elected, although he was a self-employed plumber, later shopkeeper, not a "working class " man, defeating Thomas Pailor who ran the only garage on the Estate. In 1927 Thornton Bulmer, the Hartlepool draper and Primitive Methodist Local Preacher, who was also a Good Templar, retained his seat as a rigid ratepayers' champion, also defeating Thomas Pailor. In 1928 unidentified (by the NDM) Cllr. E. P. Sturgeon was elected, defeating Thomas Pailor for the third time, and Charles Chambers, the Hart Road milkman, Good Templar and concert-party organiser, at last became a councillor - for Middleton. The more it grew physically, the more the Central Estate politically became an integral part of Hartlepool.

Despite the prevailing economic climate the Estate continued to grow. Under the Labour government's Housing (Financial Provisions) Act of 1924, conservative Ald. Gibb in 1925 proposed not only 50-150 more houses for West View in aid of slum clearance but two tennis courts. In 1927 the Town Council, which had already purchased six fire-damaged houses from C. T. Watson in 1924, purchased land between the Old Cemetery Road and Vincent Street for 78 more houses and in consequence the allotment holders, some of them with pigeon lofts, were given notice to quit and were denied compensation. "Romaine Park", another new housing estate, was to be created on land cleared of allotments between Hart Road School and Heortnesse Road. Before construction began there was controversy about the allotment of houses to (allegedly) already well-housed people. Presumably local councillors had some influence in the allocation of council-owned property (Map 7 p. 141).

There was also controversy that Romaine Park dwellings were to be lit with electricity rather than gas, unlike West View. On the other hand, as Cllr. Vasey argued in 1925, if the Town Clerk could have a garage in West View, so should other tenants. West View also came to have other advantages; not only a shop, but a shop with an off-licence (in spite of Cllr. Bulmer's and the Sunday School Union's opposition), and a telephone kiosk in addition to two tennis courts ad a children's playground.

Inevitably there were fatal accidents on the Central Estate, averaging one per year. A body washed ashore, a child drowned, a scalded child prematurely discharged from hospital, a baby scalded to death, another child killed by a bus, a workman buried alive at the Cement Works, another found dead on a railway line: all these could have occurred at any time since 1889. The novelty was a road fatality - in West View on Friday March 6, 1925.

> *... .just after taking the curve at West View, opposite the Horse Shoe Arch, the car ran into a handcart. A tyre burst and the car skidded and overturned, colliding with one of the ornamental trees at the edge of the pavement and also with a lamp post. Both the occupants were flung out violently and Mr G... .. appears to have been killed almost instantaneously... The handcart, it seems, was standing outside one of the houses in West View and Mr F... and Mr W.... who were using it to convey soil, were near it at the time, but jumped clear as the car struck it. It is stated that a lamp was attached to the handcart, and that this was throwing a light in the direction from which the car approached. Moreover... the headlights of (the) car were burning brightly.*

At the inquest on March 9, one of the West View residents said that:

> *... .his next-door neighbour borrowed a flat handcart from the grocer's shop on the West View Estate and witness was assisting him to take bags of soil over to his garden.*
>
> *There was an oil lamp at the rear of the cart. This was alight and when at about 8.30 o'clock they had the cart pulled up to the pavement... , they shifted the lamp so that it was at the outer side of the cart and facing up the road towards Hart. They had taken four bags of soil on the cart from a field a little way down the road towards Hartlepool, and as they were lifting the third bag out of the cart they saw the headlights of a car coming round the bend. When they were carrying the bag up the garden path they heard a report as of a bursting tyre... Mr J. H. Miers, the Borough Engineer... said he thought it was quite possible after passing the first street lamp the driver of the car would not be able to see so well...*
>
> *The jury returned a verdict of "Accidental death" and stated that there was no negligence on the part of anybody.*

It was a comfortable, if not a comforting, conclusion. One may well, amongst other matters of lights and speeds, wonder if the soil carriers had Farmer Hall's consent to remove soil from his fields in the dark.

Even more sad was the suicide of Oscar, the adopted teenage son of Father Hatch, the Curate of St. Barnabas', recently married, who lived opposite the church on Hart Road.

As to crimes, some were more petty than others. There were unlicensed dogs, an unlicensed motor cycle and unlawful parking, thefts of potatoes, whisky and coke, assaults of men on men and women on women, and juvenile vandalism on allotments, again on an average of one per year. Less commonplace, on Aug 19 1924, were:

> *ROUNDABOUTS WHICH OBSTRUCTED*
>
> *At Hartlepool Police Court... H... S... was summoned for causing an obstruction in Bell Street... the defendant was in charge of a set of roundabouts, used by children,*

and which stood on a horse-drawn waggon. They stood in the middle of the thoroughfare and had a motor car turned into the street quickly there would probably have been a serious accident. Defendant made a charge of a penny a ride, and took 1s 9d in eight minutes...

Defendant, who was wearing the DCM and General Service medals, said that he usually took his roundabouts down back streets, but on Aug 19 he could not get down them because of the washing hanging out to dry...

This latter fact could not have been unusual. Although housewives tended to favour Mondays as washdays, there were always exceptions: but this was a Saturday, which would have been very unusual. Even on a Saturday a motor car turning into Bell Street would also have been unusual... P.C Johnson, though perhaps over-officious, was only doing his duty. There was, in my recollection, a Tom Buttery of the Central Estate who also had a horse-drawn roundabout. He did, however, stick to the backlanes, perhaps on weekdays only.

More spectacular, in Union Road, was a drunk who was alleged to have threatened to cut the throats of his wife and children and to have "stacked some mats and furniture in the middle of the floor... poured oil on the heap and... then set fire to it. He was (only) fined. In the same year 1928 a man was (only) fined for firing an unlicensed revolver on the Golf Links.

Declining drunkenness was, according to the Chief Constable in 1925, attributable to unemployment as well as to shorter licensing hours (which had been a wartime innovation in the interest of increased armaments production, prolonged into peacetime). On the other hand, according to the Medical Officer, the Carnival was blamed for an increase in the infant mortality rate: "children were found on the streets with parents till the small hours of the morning... The loss of infantile lives is vary largely due to ignorance and indifference on the part of parents". Yet in the same report the high incidence of disease was directly attributable "to the poverty-stricken condition of the town... The food of the people is remarkably deficient in vitamins... " The M.O. nevertheless ended by blaming the abolition of outdoor relief (in food) under the Poor Law in favour of an increase of "dole" (unemployment benefit in cash) which was "unwisely spent". In other words the poor were responsible for their own problems, although bad housing was admitted as partly to blame.

Other events deemed newsworthy record the existence of Central Estate Women Unionists (Conservative) and Hart Ward Unionists. The demolition of an ex-army hut on Hart Road, used as a dwelling and a shop and known as "Snowdon's", was ordered despite the housing shortage caused by the Great Fire, but must have been cancelled because it was later reported as having been burgled. The Primitive Methodist Chapel acquired a site adjacent to St Barnabas' Church for a new chapel (completed in 1938), ordained two of its Sunday school teachers as local preachers and replaced its harmonium with a pipe organ which needed the services of an organ blower. It held an unspecified "Love Feast" but the Sons of Temperance, which it normally housed, had to resort to St Barnabas' Hall for a whist drive to celebrate their 25th anniversary. Father Hatch of St Barnabas' attracted many boys to his church by the successful organisation of Boy Scouts and Cubs. Brownies and Girl Guides, if any, were not mentioned.

Allotment Holders continued to hold their annual exhibition, adding rabbits and pigeons to the lists, perhaps in competition with the Central Hotel which continued to host Fanciers' Shows. Their annual rent was now 12/6d per annum, more than an average day's pay, so that when they were flooded they were not pleased, in 1925, for a remission of (only) half the rental of the flooded portion and were further annoyed in 1927 by rats and by the Corporation's refusal to compensate them for expulsion from Vincent Street for new housing purposes. They went so far as to hire a room at the Central Hotel for a meeting which may or may not have helped the permission they secured for pigeon lofts, provided the pigeons were long-distance and three quarters of the plot was cultivated. The rats, for which they were initially advised to complain to Durham County Council, were later attributed to the tipping of butchers' refuse on Low Warren Farm which was ordered to move the site further away, and in 1928 a representative (my father!) was co-opted into membership of the relevant Council Committee.

The Central Hotel, still owned by C. T. Watson, still ran a Club which continued to pay dividends. In 1925 the dividend per member was 12s. 3d, a useful sum as mentioned above, but unlike the Cooperative Wholesale Society (with grocery and butchery in Arch Street), which could reasonably boast of paying dividend at 2s.0d in the £1 (i.e. 10% on purchases) a year earlier, the percentage was not revealed.

In July 1928 the Town Council decided that Mr Coulson, headmaster of Hart Road School (Plate 26 p. 61), would not be replaced on his impending retirement, and that boys would henceforth have to walk a mile or so to Galleys' Field (Plate 63 p. 212). Cllrs. Bulmer, Arkley and Sturgeon protested but Ald. Gibb did not think that children would be harmed by a little walking. Cllr Carter said that shoe leather would cost parents, mostly unemployed, £168 per annum but did not spell out how. The arrangement, said to be temporary, was permanent and Hart Road ceased to be an all-age school for boys. It continued to educate children and girls.

More Central Estate children had continued to win scholarships to the Henry Smith Grammar School and some of them, girls as well as boys, followed the example of Laverty in winning prizes and gaining college and university places. Moreover, in 1926, Roger Stead, of Arch Street, one of the Central's left-wing working-class intellectuals, was appointed caretaker with residence provided, and consequently resigned as Secretary of the Allotment Holders' Association. Party politics at the County Council level may have played some part in this appointment, as it was, allegedly, also, in the appointment of John Moor, MC, MA, BSc to the headmastership in 1925. Mr Moor's sporting, military and academic achievements were fortunately beyond cavil, and his headship was long and successful.

For those unable to pass the necessary eleven-plus examination and whose parents could afford it there was private provision in West Hartlepool at "Osborne" (boys) and the "Convent" (girls), services of which one or two Central Estate parents took advantage, to the disadvantage in street popularity of the children involved.

Natural events like storms provided the Central Estate with free spectacle. A (steam-driven fishing) drifter went ashore in fog off the bandstand on the Promenade in 1925 and in 1927 another, the Jessmar was beached, whole, undamaged and upright on the North Sands at high spring tide, immediately below Heortnesse Road. One could walk all round it at low tide and a ladder would have afforded easy access. Unscathed by theft it was safely refloated on a later high tide, but was small beer in comparison with another natural event, the total eclipse of the sun on June 29, 1927, long predicted and precisely on time.

Despite or because of the prevailing economic depression there was a major novelty in Hartlepool's man-made entertainment in September 1924 with the organisation of the first (municipal) Carnival (Plate 70 p. 217). On Sept 17 NDM reported:

> *... Northgate is a blaze of colour. Flags and bunting decorate nearly every shop. All kinds of flags are affixed to the tram standards, and every street lamp is covered with coloured paper... Generally speaking, the poorest streets are the most lavishly decorated...*
>
> *Over 1,000 children entered for the fancy dress parade... They made a wonderful display... the younger children were placed on decorated lorries, the elder children walked, and headed by the band of the R(oyal) G(arrison) A(rtillery), proceeded to the Friarage Field...*

Receiving King Carnival's petition to hand over the ancient town for revelry, the Mayor, wearing his chain of office, replied that the spirit of jollity was not to be denied for the space of four days, though no harmful proceedings must be permitted, though no thought of maintaining dignity should restrain the happy impulse which impelled his subjects to innocent enjoyment. There were no adverse reports and despite the prevailing economic gloom, with unemployment increasing, no less a sum than £1100 was raised for charities, mainly the Hospital. In fact the Carnival became a fixture for many years, always with processions and collecting boxes, and always with the Town Moor taken over by all the fun of the fair: swings, roundabouts, stalls for pies and peas, cocoanut shies, three card games, an albino "professor", the seventh son of a seventh son, who told fortunes, traction engines and the caravans in which the showmen lived, bright lights from flares and lamps, and the competing noises of steam engines and fairground organs.

This was the entertainment highlight of the year, but week by week, in addition to the more and more numerous cinemas, the numerous churches, chapels and choirs (including Gray's shipyard and Richardson Westgarth ships' engines), dances and brass band concerts, skating rinks and variety theatres, pubs and temperance organisations, there were occasional concerts of chamber music and of the Hartlepools Symphony Orchestra, ballets (starring none other then Pavlova herself), a "Pythagorean" class on comparative religion and a radio society or Esperanto classes for the few, and new broadcasting stations and talking pictures (in 1928 at the Picture House) for the many. The Picture House had already outstripped the other silent cinemas by the employment of an orchestra under the flamboyant, hair-tossing Senor Angel Blanco rather than the usual single piano accompanist. There were also new automatic dispensing machines to sell cigarettes in exchange for coins in the slot when the pubs and shops were closed, and machines that took and produced your picture while you waited.

In the rivalry between theatre and cinema on the one side and home entertainment on the other, the opening of new broadcasting stations (5XX and 5GB) in addition to the existing network of the former private British Broadcasting Company, by the

British Broadcasting Corporation under parliamentary control from 1926, together with continuously improving technology, gave the "wireless" (radio) as it was known, with its concerts, variety shows and educational programmes, an advantage. The disadvantage was that receiving licenses (10s. 0d: 50p) became compulsory but the diminishing need for large and expensive "outdoor" aerials on masts meant that "indoor" aerials in the lofts of houses proliferated. Not all their owners paid.

More permanent, in 1927, was the replacement of the lighthouse (Plate 47 p. 165), automatic and electric instead of hand-driven and gas-lit, which had obstructed the guns during the Bombardment of Dec 16 1914 but returned to its former site in 1926, and the consecration, in the same year of the new chancel of St Hilda's Church (Plate 74 p. 235), financed by the Gray family and organised by the Rev. F. T. Salter (locally known as "Sammy"), the Rector of Hartlepool who, since his advent in 1924, had made a great impression. In less than a year he had, as the "Window Cleaner", been allotted a Saturday night column in the NDM for "Sermons on Paper".

Even more permanent was the replacement, from 1926, of trams by "trackless" buses (Plate 67 p. 214) which took their power from two overhead cables rather than one, but which were as manoeuvrable as any motor bus and not confined to the centre of the road. At the same time, end product of more wrangling between the two towns, Hartlepool was allowed to run motor buses via West View from West to old Hartlepool, but not to the Central Marine Engineering Works, which would have saved a lot of sweat and leather. In 1928 West Hartlepool modestly decided not to have an aerodrome.

Ald. Gibb (Plate 34 p. 112), who continued service as general practitioner in Cleveland Road, was (rightly and reasonably) awarded the Freedom of the Borough of Hartlepool on April 26, 1927. He had practised as a doctor and served the community since 1892, as councillor since 1900 and as Mayor 1910-12, and who had consistently, as Chairman of Housing, sought housing improvement. As President of the Hartlepool Rovers Football Club (and of the Allotment Holders and Gardeners Association, etc, etc), he had given distinguished social and civic service. This was confirmed by his election to a fourth mayoralty in 1928.

Farmer Hall of Low Warren Farm, with whose name some mothers attempted to frighten their children into better behaviour, prosecuted two Hartlepool boys in 1924 for stealing potatoes, but relented when they admitted the theft, having previously denied it. In August 1925 he further complained of both potato and turnip thefts. "It is hard lines", he said, "A man puts his labour into the land and his little bit of capital, and when it is just coming to profit it is absolutely destroyed". In fact, though a strict but fair employer, he was, as I recall, a generous and kindly man, and he enjoyed some reward when in June 1928 he won both first and second prizes for fat bullocks at the Haswell Show.

Thomas Pailor, who had risen to the highest rank for a noncommissioned officer in the army (Regimental Sergeant Major) thrice defeated as would-be-councillor (but later successful) appears to have been cast in the C. T. Watson mould. His money, however, went into garages and chars-à-banc rather than pubs and speculative building, and he successfully diversified into leasing the old Town Hall for a cinema in 1927 (Plate 30 p. 110). Like C. T. Watson, he had a brush with the Improvement Committee in 1925 Aug 27. Having bought the premises from Mr Bradbury he had submitted a plan to the Borough Engineer to remove the paving, provide crossings in Hart Road and Cleveland Road in order that motor vehicles should have access, and storing petroleum on the site but without having submitted a plan and without Works and Watch Committee consents. Ald. Turner, although he approved what was being done, had stopped it and it was referred back for further consideration. This was the end of the matter and Pailor's Garage became a well-known landmark and its entrance a novel observation point for children, though less spectacular than the smithy nearer the old town where there was a forge and flying sparks when horses were shod and broken iron hoops ("boolers") mended for a penny ha'penny.

Inevitably there were obituaries. On Feb 22 1925 died Ald. R. H. Rowe, who had had a grocer's shop in Union Road in the early days of the Central Estate. He moved to Hartlepool from Yarm in Yorkshire in 1865 and qualifies, like C. T. Watson, as a father of the Central Estate.

On May 14 1927 the "Northern Daily Mail" celebrated its half-century, revealing its origin, on May 26 1866, as a Conservative rival ("South Durham Herald") to the Liberal "South Durham and Cleveland Mercury". Rowland Burdon and Ralph Ward Jackson were amongst its backers as a morning paper, but it was not until May 14 1877 that a companion "Northern Evening Mail" was published, and not until 1884 that, now the "Northern Daily Mail" but still an evening paper, recovered from bankruptcy under new management and with the (Liberal) Furness family amongst its shareholders.

Rehoused in 1900, still in West Hartlepool but always catering for readers and customers in both towns, it experienced and created, as well as recorded, national as well as local history:

THE BOMBARDMENT

The bombardment of the Hartlepools was a small incident in the Great War and what happened at the "Mail" Office was a small incident in the bombardment... Soon after 8 o'clock (December 16, 1914) there was a rumbling noise seawards. Rumbling noises were common in those days and at first no one took much notice. As the sound grew in volume and intensity a member of the staff looked from one of the front windows to see what was happening. At that a moment a telegraph pole on the other side of the road snapped like a matchstick and a shell whizzed past the end of the building. The observer communicated the intelligence to the rest of the staff who interpreted the message as a "notice to quit" and hurriedly left the building. It was well they did for a few moments later a second shell crashed through the roof of the readers' room, causing a great deal of structural damage...

"BUSINESS" BUT "NOT AS USUAL"

As soon as the bombardment was over the staff began to trickle back to the office, and soon everyone was ready to "carry on as usual". We did "carry on" but not as usual... The censor's message was to the effect that we had to publish nothing about the bombardment. This was not unsatisfactory, for at that moment publishing was at a discount.

In a short time the reporters had collected a great deal of information about what had occurred in various parts of the Hartlepools, and as the day wore on we overcame the mechanical difficulties, and thanks to a good deal of hand setting, were ready to issue a paper. Still the ban was not lifted

In his book on "The World Crisis" Mr Winston Churchill tells us "that telegraph and telephone were pouring the distress of Hartlepool and Scarborough to all parts of the kingdom and when the War Committee of the Cabinet met news, magnified by rumour, had produced excitement." Evidently Mr Churchill thought something should be done about it, and the following message was issued:

"German movements of some importance are taking place in the North Sea... Scarborough and Hartlepool have been shelled. The situation is developing".

We were at liberty to publish that, but it was not helpful, as most of us, perhaps because our nerves were on edge, thought the situation had already developed. Mr Samuel Storey, who had motored over from Southill, saw the absurdity of the situation - as we all did. He belonged to a generation that did not take kindly to the pert interferences of "Dora". He insisted that we should print the paper, censor or no censor, and no remonstrance would make him alter his decision. The order was given, but just as the wheels of the printing presses were beginning to turn, the ban was lifted, and those of us who had been conjuring up visions of being blown from the guns of the Heugh Battery by Colonel Robson... heaved a sigh of relief.

Mr Samuel Storey was the purchaser of the NDM in 1884, whose grandson of the same name was chairman in 1927. "Dora" was the "Defence of the Realm" Act, of August 1914 which imposed press censorship, and threatened prosecution for breach, if not the capital punishment as hinted above.

Anniversary articles pictured all the Hartlepools' MPs since 1868, many of the mayors of both towns and many of its great ship owners, summarised the history of the two ports and their shipbuilders, and of the civic rivalries still unresolved. It was not, reflected the Editor, a good time for stocktaking of the port which in the vision of Ralph Ward Jackson had been the future "Liverpool of the North-East Coast". It had ranked fourth in the kingdom for registered tonnage in 1890. In 1912 it had registered 245 owners of 713,087 registered tons, but in 1926 only 41 owned only 173,466 tons. It had played an important part in the development of the "Plimsoll line", which, in the interests of seafaring safety, had limited cargo weights to national and international levels of safety. As for the future, in addition to the coal mines to the north, there were promising developments to the south of zinc works, salt works and chemical (later ICI) works, although facilities for docking (and building) larger ships would be difficult to achieve.

Anniversary articles also usefully summarised the histories and rivalry of the Hartlepools. As to amalgamation "during the past 70 years", the editor opined that old Hartlepool's claims to an extended area were not pursued with sufficient vigour. "Years slipped away without Hartlepool taking any action, and meanwhile West Hartlepool grew in importance... In the early eighties an attempt was made, and a bill actually prepared to form a combined borough of Hartlepool, West Hartlepool, Throston, Middleton and Seaton Carew... The negotiations broke down... on four main points.

FOUR POINTS

In the first place Hartlepool thought that the Municipal Buildings should be the municipal buildings for the extended borough... At that time West Hartlepool had no municipal buildings. Looking back... it is difficult to resist the impression that the (West Hartlepool) Commissioners did not treat Hartlepool with the consideration it deserved. If they had yielded on the point... it is almost certain that in a few years some ***central site*** *(my emphasis) between the two towns would have been obtained... But the builders of West Hartlepool were impatient of restraint...*

Another of the terms insisted upon by the Hartlepool Council was that their officials should continue in office after the amalgamation... and a third term was that Hartlepool, Middleton and Throston combined should have equal representation with West Hartlepool... (and) differential rating for Throston and Middleton for a period of five years...

WEST HARTLEPOOL TAKES ACTION

Why these points, or some of them, could not have been settled by an independent referee it is difficult to understand. The negotiations broke down and the West Hartlepool Commissioners, with characteristic vigour, set out to obtain by other methods, what they had failed to gain by bargaining. At that time Throston and Middleton... were not part of Hartlepool. They were governed by local boards... and the West Hartlepool Commissioners... proposed to annex both districts as well as Seaton Carew. Feeling between the towns ran high and this action... added fuel... obviously West Hartlepool had a claim to Seaton Carew... but... seemed to have about as much right to annex the moon... as they had to take Throston...

In May 1883 the matter came before a Select Committee of the House of Commons the selection of which and/or of members of which the Member for the Hartlepools, Thomas Richardson MP. may have influenced, who was a Liberal supporter of the Liberal government. Certainly politics of some sort or other determined the outset as the continuation of the article suggests.

A MOVE BY "KING JOHN"

... To some extent the issue turned on the wishes of the inhabitants, and though neither Throston nor Middleton were anxious to surrender their independence they decided, when they saw they would be incorporated in one or other of the authorities, to throw in their lot with Hartlepool. At that time the late John Horsley was in the zenith of his power, and he managed a short time before the inquiry to get himself elected Chairman of the Local Throston Board. At the inquiry counsel for Hartlepool was able to point triumphantly to the fact that the Mayor of Hartlepool and the Chairman of the Throston Local Boar was one and the same person. That clinched Hartlepool's contention that there was a close connexion between the two places...

In fact the article (by "The Editor") goes on to reveal that although Thomas Richardson (of ships'-engine builders Thomas Richardson and Sons, later Richardson Westgarth) favoured the uniting of the five townships, the annexation of Throston and Middleton would forever prevent it.

AMALGAMATION - IN THEORY

... "I think", he said. "if Throston and Middleton were attached to West Hartlepool it would forever destroy the probability of an amalgamation of the whole. It would

divide the districts altogether and isolate Hartlepool... the animosity that now exists would exist for ever. That animosity is an old feeling that grew up with the growing up of West Hartlepool. There ought... to have been no West Hartlepool. It ought to have been all one Hartlepool. Mr Jackson, in creating West Hartlepool... created it not precisely in opposition to the people of Hartlepool, but in opposition to the docks at Hartlepool. A feeling of animosity between the two places grew up when those new docks were established, and the feeling has grown ever since.

Mr Richardson was an acute observer and, as MP for both places, able to be unusually frank. Another local shipbuilder, Edward Withy, equally frank, implied a more material motivation:

"The West Hartlepool scheme... really proposes to take the very vitals from Hartlepool. It would take the Marine Engineering works of Richardsons and Sons, the marine works now being erected by William Gray and Co., our own shipyard, the Cement Works, the Hartlepool Fish Quay, the rolling mills and the fish-curing place which is now being put up...

Only the amount levied in rates could have been affected, perhaps adversely. Whatever the reasons, parochialism prevailed (as it still does in English local government) and the Central Estate became an extension of Hartlepool rather than of West Hartlepool.

My own recollections continue with the Carnival Parade of 1924. Most memorable, apart from the innumerable floats with their scantily-clad little and less little girls, echoing and applauding the applause they attracted, was the perambulator with the man inside, dressed as a dummy-sucking infant, attended by a demonstrative male "mother", accompanied by howls of applause and numerous pennies for the collection boxes.

In the following annual Carnivals I recall the roundabouts, swings and organs on the Town Moor, all driven by electricity generated by magnificent steam-driven traction engines (themselves the greatest - and free - spectacles, with their delightful mixture of steam, hot oil, and whirring wheels). Free, too, for all the children of Hartlepool, were the arrival and erection of the roundabouts, cocoanut shies, pie-and pea stalls, etc, etc, and the caravans in which the showmen (and their wives and children) lived. We could watch but never afford the cake-walk (with its fan-blown revelation, with accompanying shrieking, of female underwear) or the Chairoplanes (Plate 70 p. 219) or bucking horses, but we could and did organise our own carnival in Stephenson Street. The currency was cigarette cards and those skilful enough to flick one from their fingers to knock over another, propped against the wall, from the edge of the pavement, were rewarded. So were those who could bounce a small, hard ball, steel ball-bearing or pottery, ("bulliker") to dislodge another, close to the wall from across the pavement. My own invention, a bootbox with an inch-square hole in the front and a small bell at the other end, which had to be rung by a marble from across the pavement, did not long survive. A frustrated customer, older and bigger than me, disintegrated the apparatus with one shrewd (and deserved) kick. We shouted our entertainments with the fairground jargon we had heard: "Sort 'em up, sort 'em up: a penny a go and a pr(o)ize every t(o)ime".

The total eclipse of the sun on June 29, 1927, was an experience of awesome contrast. In the dull morning light, long before 5.0 a.m, the Central Estate flocked en masse to the Battery, Spion Kop and the sands, as did others everywhere in the two towns and the county across the whole country to the NW coast. Unfortunately clouds obscured the sun during totality, but the predicted dawn and the awakening of the birds was duly interrupted by the return of night and the silencing of the birds before the second dawn and their second awakening. The clouds suddenly lifted as people turned for home and the partial eclipse was suddenly splendidly viewable through the smoked glasses everyone carried. There were the sun's corona and the moon's shadow in all their splendour. It was unbelievably, magnificently unforgettable. I was there. By 7.30 a.m, having breakfasted, I went into Stephenson Street to seek a playmate. Not only was it a beautiful day: it was an extra holiday. That night NDM reported:

> *...The Cemetery Siding at Hartlepool presented a lively appearance. On the seaside and the railway track stood excursion trains from London and elsewhere... specially constructed ladders were placed first at one carriage door, then at another to allow passengers to alight... a continual procession to a cafe in West View which was open for the occasion...*
> *The first-class "sleeping" train standing beside the less luxuriously appointed coaches was in complete darkness, the passengers sleeping until shortly before the time for the commencement of the eclipse. Among the passengers was Mr Geo. Bernard Shaw...*

The world-famous playwright's no-doubt distinguished impressions of the event, and its Central Estate setting, presumably acerbic, do not appear to have been recorded.

Maternal pressure ensured my attendance at the "ordination" of the two Central Estate Primitive Methodist Sunday School teachers. To my surprise (and dismay) it was a very emotional occasion. Both confessed to unplumbable depths of sin before they were "converted", and, knowing both of them well as earnest and virtuous young men, I could not imagine what these could be. Both wept as they acknowledged their debt to their mothers. In retrospect I perceived ritual and formula in what was supposed to be a spontaneous and improvised ceremonial. My mother's fervent approval was a warning of her ambitions for me.

Maternal pressure also took me to the revivalist and teetotalitarian meetings, at Brougham Street Methodist Church in Hartlepool, of the Lancashire evangelist Tom Holland and his family who re-enacted tearful conversions of drunkards into abstainers and of other sinners who repented and were "converted". My tears on the second annual occasion enforced premature withdrawal from these emotional orgies, a feeling subsequently reinforced by participation in Sunday School sessions with local hot (i.e. weeping) gospellers and annual emotional processions around the streets of the Central Estate with a banner, beseeching people to be "saved": with no visible response whatsoever.

The Chapel's replacement of a harmonium with a proper pipe organ was an occasion signalised by a recital by Mr. Pickersgill of St Oswald's Church, which filled the Chapel to overflowing; even my father attended. Organ blowers were needed to pump the bellows supplying the wind, and my progress from assistant to the Assistant's assistant to total responsibility for three Sunday services and weekly choir practices, not to mention practices for Sunday School Anniversaries etc, etc, was rapid indeed.

I was brought up to "shop at the Coop", and it was the dividends, which rose to 2s/6d in the £1 (12.5%) on purchases, never drawn but accumulated, which enabled my parents, in 1926, to purchase the house in Arch Street (which had a bathroom), paying a deposit of £150 and undertaking to repay the Amalgamated Engineering Association over a 20-year period for the remaining £250. My father was Treasurer of the Hartlepool Branch No 7 of the Amalgamated Engineering Union, Secretary of the Allotment Holders' Association and, for a time, their representative at Council meetings. As a trained nurse, my mother was consulted by neighbours on minor ailments and frequently nursed children with major illnesses.

From 1926 my father moved from Gray's to Richardson Westgarth and despite occasional short-time working ("week-and-week about") was well enough paid to be able to afford both electric lighting and radio from 1929. The lighting was an improvement on gas. The radio was a revelation which transformed our lives.

When Mr Coulson (Plate 62 p. 212) retired as headmaster of Hart Road Boys' School I was one of the children affected. I do not recall the agitation against the cost of shoe leather for the necessary mile walk to Galley's Field School in 1928. It was an enjoyable change, soon replaced by the rather longer journey to the Henry Smith School, which necessitated bus or bicycle for the short "dinner" (lunchtime) break.

"Passing the scholarship", a three-tiered ordeal (two written examinations and an interview) was a social turning point. Although I continued to play in the street for some time, the demands of homework and the pleasures of new interests and associations began the process of separating me from my original background, although there were sufficient Central Estatians - some fifty in seven years - who preceded, accompanied or followed me to the grammar school, to mitigate the process.

Plate 62 - Hart Road Scholarship Class 1923
Teachers: left James (Pat) Patrick, right Joseph (Joss) Wright,
centre William (Tip) Coulson, Headmaster

Plate 63 - Galleys' Field School 1960s

Plate 64 - The Promenade

Plate 65 - Cement Works 1920s

Plate 66 - Cement Works Pithead 1920s

Plate 67 - Trackless Trolley Bus

Plate 68 - Hartlepool Health Resort c. 1901

Plate 69 - Councillors Charles Chambers & Robert Boswell 1953 (ringed)

Plate 70 - Carnival Chairoplanes (Shuggyshoes?)

Plate 71 - Civic Restaurant

Former Hart Road Primitive Methodist (Little) Chapel Interior

Chapter 10: 1929-35

My personal recollections are naturally dominated by school (Plate 27 p. 62). The transition from "elementary" to "grammar" was dramatic. Different teachers, male and female, for different subjects, different classrooms for different subjects: chemistry and physics laboratories, an art room, a woodwork room, a gymnasium, and a playing field. Girls as well as boys in the class room, "intervals" instead of "playtime", a bell, wielded by a "prefect", to divide one class from the next, text books and notebooks galore, a field for sports and games instead of a tarmacked playground... These were agreeable changes. Less agreeable were the very unequal qualities of the teaching: one or two teachers were brilliant, and a few were competent. The rest were dismal. Many years later I asked the headmaster, John Moor, then retired, why this was. He explained that he had inherited the bad ones from his predecessor, although not all of the new appointees were good. Fortunately it did not matter: as one of the better teachers said to me: "A good pupil succeeds in spite of the teacher". The school atmosphere was highly competitive. Form placings at the end of each term were vital and there were prizes for the top three at the end of each summer term, presented in public at the annual Speech Day to the thundering applause of fellow pupils. For those who won teaching college places for two year courses or for those who won university places and went on to teacher-training after graduation the applause was long and generous. For those who won State Scholarships, for each of which there was a day added to the Summer holidays, it was tumultuous.

In long retrospect the school was a successful exam-passing machine because students were strongly motivated. Against the permanent background of the slump, and more particularly from the World Slump of 1929, the school offered not only the possibility of escape from unemployment, but that of advancement from the status of wage-earning worker to that of the comparatively well salaried, holidayed and pensioned professional. (There were, of course, others like trade union officialdom and nonconformist church ministry, which did not demand formal qualifications.) Most frequently the goal was the teaching profession, but there were occasional doctors and lawyers, musicians, parsons and the odd farmer. These derived from the children of professionals - headmasters, parsons, pilots and police inspectors - and shopkeepers who attended the school. The school bridged what was then the wide social gap between blue-collar and white-collar employment or, in class terms, the gap between the working and lower-middle classes. Although some children below the respectable working class level passed the entrance scholarship there was a high dropout rate from the poorer end. School uniforms, woodwork aprons and sports gear were not cheap. Only those who lived more than three miles from school were entitled to free or subsidised transport. School meals had to be provided or paid for by children whose homes were beyond reach of home in the dinner-break. In addition, the tiny wages of 2/6d per week which messenger boys could earn from shopkeepers as soon as they were 14 years old were necessary to balance poor household budgets. From the third year onwards the dropout rate accelerated, and of the seventy annual new entrants, less than a quarter survived beyond matriculation (Oxford School Certificate) at age 16 and entered the Sixth Form. Of those who did, three quarters opted for maths and science and only the residue for the arts. For this there were two convergent reasons. Maths, physics, chemistry and biology were better taught than English Literature and foreign languages, and at Billingham, less than 10 miles away, Synthonia, later Imperial Chemical Industries, had an apparently insatiable demand for laboratory technicians for which Higher School Certificates (now A-levels) were the essential qualification.

Joint membership of classes, shared experiences of victories and defeats at the hands or at the expense of teachers, and joint participation in games and sports welded into school loyalty Hartlepool children of differing social origins. The same processes worked similarly between the children of Hartlepool and those of the colliery villages within ten miles of the school because secondary education was a County Council responsibility and the more or less permanent Labour majority from 1919 onwards regarded equality of educational opportunity for boys and girls and for urban and rural dwellers alike as paramount. Children from the collieries spoke a different language (see Glossary) with a very different accent, and, because they were almost exclusively miner's sons and daughters, had shared from birth an even more concentrated community training. Inevitably there were misunderstandings, rivalries and fights. Many of the colliery children's fathers were deputies and overmen (i.e. "foremen": better paid) and they had pennies to spend every day at the school tuck shop, but shared their sweets with those who had not. Friendships and visits were exchanged across the gaps of dialect and distance. School pride and loyalty were intense bonding agents. As at Galley's Field elementary school there was a house system (Romans, Spartans, Trojans, Barbarians) but it had no expression beyond occasional rugby games and the annual Sports Day. Unlike Galley's Field, however, patriotic and public school songs were not sung.

The school was unusual for its time in admitting girls as well as boys: segregation beyond primary school was the general rule. The reason was economy rather than enthusiasm for equality. One grammar school was cheaper than two, especially after fee-paying had been abolished. The social consequences were considerable. In the first two years there was little contact. Girls sat on one side of the classroom and boys on the other. Boys were strapped for misbehaviour or poor performance and girls were not. Girls were addressed by their first names, boys by their surnames. In the earlier years girls were normally top of the class. The only occasion of sanctioned fraternisation was the Annual Form Xmas Party at which there were mixed games including the Grand Old Duke of York. Otherwise girls and boys were expected to walk to school separately. By the end of the third year, however, although the girls' gym slips and blouses attempted to conceal their developing charms, adolescence supervened and pairings, alleged or actual began. The pattern was that Fifth and Sixth Form boys competed for the favours of the prettier or more personable girls in the lower forms. They had "dates" which were walks or cinema visits and went as far as kisses and cuddles. There was said to have been one pregnancy before my time there, but in my seven years there was only one publicised case of expulsion for paternity. By 1935 dancing was permitted in the Hall after lunch-time on wet winter days, and pairs were known to drop out from the Grand Old Duke of York at Xmas parties into secluded corners. Old Scholars' Dances were very well attended and many school marriages were projected, some of which materialised. At least, the partners had acquaintances, friends, recollections and loyalties in common.

The Central Estate was well represented, especially in scholastic achievement. One of the first State Scholars, in the 1920s, was a girl from Stephenson Street and between 1934 and 1938 three boys also merited the same distinction. In addition to many teachers and at least one headmaster, there were several RAF aircraftsmen and NDM journalists, a sanitary inspector, a pharmacist, a nurse, a professor of agriculture, a distinguished wartime meteorologist and a naval officer. One scholar from Romaine Park fought on the government side in the Spanish Civil War and one from West View was lost on the aircraft carrier Ark Royal at the beginning of the 1939-45 war.

Although school homework more and more successfully competed for my evenings, I continued regular attendance at the Primitive Methodist Chapel and its many functions until the spring of 1933 when I rebelled. Consequently I took part in annual Sunday School Demonstrations when scholars wearing coloured ribbons ("nil green" for Hart Road) to indicate their particular church or chapel marched behind banners to the amphitheatre on the promenade and took part in a joint afternoon service in the presence of civic and church dignitaries to the accompaniment of the Salvation Army Band. It was not ecumenical: Catholics and some Anglicans (including St Barnabas) did not take part. The NDM invariably made Anglican abstentions clear, but did not explain the reason(s). There was great rivalry requiring adult intervention as to who should carry the tassels at the end of the ropes on the banner, together with disagreements as to who should walk in the first file.

Emotionalism - tearful confessions of sin and sobbing experiences of redemption - were even more the staple of Camp Meetings, also commemorative. Like the Demonstration, the Camp Meeting was held in the open air in summer but the venue was always St Barnabas' Field which surrounded St Barnabas Church. Presumably it was hired for the afternoon. Certainly it was on the same field that the new Primitive Methodist Chapel (primarily the achievement of ex-Police Sgt, later hardware man J. J. Crowther) opened in 1938, was built. The motivation behind both these transactions cannot have been merely commercial, although neither Anglicans nor Catholics supported the Methodists in opposing extended drinking hours for the Miners' Gala in Durham (1930) or for visitors, allotment holders or working men (1935). The Sons of Temperance, still housed weekly in the Chapel, had to hold their whist drives and dances in other premises, including both St. Barnabas' Hall and the Cooperative Hall.

Otherwise the annual round of Anniversaries and Harvest Festivals, Concerts, Bazaars, At Homes, American Evenings, Sales of Work, Teas and Garden Parties (without a garden) continued. In 1933 a Sale of Work was hosted by Dr. Margaret Gibb, Alderman Gibbs' daughter who, like him, combined medical services with public service. With or without tea and buns, chapel entertainment was vocal, usually of poor quality, with or without ALCMs (Associates of the London College of Music). In addition, in both 1929 and 1933, there were Negro Minstrel Troupes. I recall them with embarrassment, not because they were blacked up and red-lipped Sunday School teachers - racism was not a current issue - but because the accents, beneath a veneer of "American" disguise, were unmistakeably Hartlepudlian, and the "jokes" wretchedly feeble.

In retrospect, the most significant event of the period was the Union of 1931 when

Primitive, Wesleyan and other Methodist sects merged into unity. I do not recall even a mention of this momentous change. Nor do I recall any instruction, systematic or otherwise, in the meaning of Methodism, Primitive or otherwise. Through occasional attendance at Wesleyan Churches I concluded that the main difference was the social composition of the congregation: some were better off than others. From occasional attendance at St Barnabas and the occasional Catholic funeral of dead schoolmates I observed forms of worship fundamentally different from Methodist simplicity and informality. Anglican and Catholic services were colourful and dramatic, with robed choirboys, priests in skirts with fancy dress decorations, and swinging and scented censers. My personal reactions were negative although I made a censer from a cocoa tin and swung it to emit puffs of smoke from a smouldering newspaper.

It was otherwise with secular entertainment, although I was not one of the boys fined for singing on the Cliff at the 1929 Carnival. Pocket money of no more than sixpence per week did not permit rides on Murphy's Proud Peacocks, Flying Chairs or Jumping Horses. A meat pie and mushy peas was the limit. Cinemas at 4d or 6d per afternoon or evening, were another matter and a weekly visit, or more, became a matter of course. The Picture House led the way with talking pictures ("Show Boat") in 1929. All the other cinemas caught up in the next four years although in 1934 the Hippodrome tried to revive stage shows and in 1935 vainly offered Erny Paine and Violette Coote in direct competition with, in the same week, Clark Gable, Myrna Loy and Laurel and Hardy. It was an uneven contest. Senor Angel Blanco and his orchestra and the piano accompanists at the other cinemas simply disappeared.

Fortunately some of the amateurs nevertheless survived. Good local musicians including young people like R. S. Boswell (piano) and S. Corner (violin) and older singers like Daisy Teal drew crowds, especially when they teemed up with established groups like Charles Chambers' Good Templars. Under the leadership of George Pearson the Musgrave Street Wesleyan Church created the "People's Own" Orchestra which attracted the best local talent and performed often and everywhere from the Borough Hall to the Central Estate Primitive Methodist Church. Male voice choirs abounded. In addition to Grey's Shipyard and Engineering Works, Richardson Westgarths, the LNER and the Cooperative Wholesale society competed with the Excelsior and the Hartlepool Choral Society - though there may have been, and almost certainly were, overlapping memberships. These were in addition to church, chapel and school choirs, some of which were excellent. There was also a Hartlepools Symphony orchestra which gave concerts twice a year. The March concert in 1935 included a Beethoven overture and piano concerto, Mozart's "Eine Kleine Nachtmusik", Mendelssohn's "Italian" symphony and works by Grainger and Elgar. I warmly recall excellent performances of Beethoven's Eighth and Schubert's Fifth in 1938.

Part of the reason for any decline in local music making was the abundance and excellence of music on the radio, both from the BBC (including Sir Henry Wood's Promenade Concerts) and from abroad. Foreign station programmes were detailed in the NDM from 1929 onwards with a brief lapse in 1933. Several of them - Radio Luxembourg, Radio Normandie and Radio Toulouse - became very popular for endless broadcasts of very light music interrupted by advertising slots which presumably paid for them. Wireless sets could now be run without purchasing three different batteries because they plugged directly into the electricity mains. Consequently some people left them on with windows open even when they went out, to the discomfort of their neighbours.

There was still occasional free entertainment. Top of the list was Edward, Prince of Wales who, on July 3rd 1930 opened the new promenade extension (Plates 72-73 p. 234). It was indeed a gala occasion, with a half-holiday for the schools, particularly for HSS Form IIb which avoided unpopular lessons in Geography and Mechanics. We happened to have allotted places at the point where the Prince descended from his limousine and my distinct impression was that West Hartlepool, which had welcomed him first, had wined and dined him very well indeed. King George V's Silver Jubilee took place in 1935 and although it was not free, NDM celebrated with a suitably retrospective 32 pp supplement.

On two Saturday afternoons in July in successive years (1931 and 1932) I happened to be on the North Sands (with a golf club and ball) when the King's Cup Air Race for seaplanes flew past barely above sea level. One of them was scarlet from nose to tail and all were breathtakingly impressive with more than a hint of menace.

In the summer there was also free entertainment in the amphitheatre on the Promenade close to the Bandstand where "pierrots" in conical hats and comical costumes were allowed to perform. Such were, in 1931, the "Silver Squibs", who could pass round a collecting box for the odd penny from anyone thinking it worth the price. Even had we thought so - and we did not - we had no money. In 1934 the town Council withdrew its support from promenade Concert Parties: the venue "was not a good pitch". In 1933 there was a visit from HMS Warspite which could be seen if not visited. In 1933 there were traffic lights in operation for the first time - in West Hartlepool. In the same year a new cinema, the Majestic (in West Hartlepool) could be seen in course of construction, and in the following year Throston Bridge was widened.. Before the war there were two more new cinemas, also in West Hartlepool. A new cinema was built in Hartlepool just before the war but never opened...

Had we been interested we could have learned the new universal language, Esperanto, which its advocates naively thought would diminish the chances of war by removing linguistic misunderstandings. We could also, presumably, have attended the Jewish Literary or Zionist Societies. There were monthly Fanciers' (rabbits and pigeons) in St. Barnabas Hall. If eligible we could have attended numerous Women's Bright Hours or the British Women's Total Abstinence Union. We might even have joined the Warren Road Allotments Ratting Club which killed 360 rats between Sept 1930 and March 1931.

The Central Estate even produced, briefly, a national celebrity. In 1935 Harry Lee of Stephenson Street, boxing in his grandfather's name of "George Bunter", defeated the British welterweight champion. More local celebrities were, as before, Charles Chambers the milkman who was still the leading Good Templar and concert organiser, won and lost Town Council seats for the Middleton Ward, and T. H. Pailor, at last a councillor in 1930 who rivalled C. T. Watson himself as an entrepreneur. He owned the only commercial garage and petrol station on the Estate (at the junction of Cleveland and Hart Roads), ran the Queen's Cinema in the old Hartlepool Town

Hall, planned (but did not succeed) to establish a café, camping sites, bathing and toilet facilities at the Tunnel Arch on Heortnesse Road, but succeeded in purchasing land opposite West View for a large expansion of housing to accommodate former fishermen slum-dwellers on the Croft (sea-front near the harbour) which was being demolished.

In 1930 the death of William Little, a blacksmith's striker, at the age of 82, "one of the oldest and longest inhabitants of the Central Estate" was deemed worthy of mention in the NDM. So, too, was the death of Alfred Windross of Arch Street in 1934 for having served F. W. Mason (of the High Street) as a bookbinder for 43 years. Born and apprenticed in Stockton, it was he who had made the presentation books for the Prince of Wales and Princess Mary on their visits to Hartlepool.

If NDM were wholly trustworthy, only West Hartlepool Allotment Holders held shows in 1929 and 1935, but as the son of the Secretary of the Hartlepool Allotment Holders and Gardeners Association I recall that this was not the case. There was never a year during which my father did not wash and polish his round and kidney potatoes, carrots, parsnips and turnips, etc, for exhibition, although NDM recorded only that the Association did not welcome permission in 1933 for the keeping of poultry on all allotments and in 1935 did not want responsibility for collecting rents from a Poultry Centre for the unemployed and asserted that there was no demand for allotments from the unemployed. The 55 new allotments created in 1931 presumably catered for such demand as there was. NDM reported in 1935 that the Corporation wanted £2/2/- for the hire of the Borough Hall for a show, but not that the show was in fact held in the new Hartlepool Cooperative Hall. I recall it vividly, not only because my father took the chair and won most of the prizes but because Ald. Gibb, still President, congratulated me on my State Scholarship and, shortly afterwards, caused the Town Council to send a letter of condolence to my mother when she was suddenly widowed a month later.

I do not recall (and did not at the time read) the romantic serials in the NDM which were resumed in 1929, nor the "Quoit Notes" in 1931, the "Billiard Talk" or the bowls talk ("On the Green") any more than the endless football, rugby and cricket reports. I do recall the increasing incidence of "In Memoriam" verses. Whether "do-it-yourself" or chosen from a catalogue was never indicated. Examples from 1932:

Thy will be done seems hard to say,
When those we love are called away,
But perhaps some day we shall understand
When we meet again in a better land.

Sweetly they sleep, while others sigh,
Softly their peaceful heads doth lie,
United in heaven, God's glory to share,
Now they are free from sorrow and care.

As to the proceedings of the Town Council, I recall that the new houses built in Vincent and Hutton Streets carried on from where the building of Romaine Park had stopped in providing scaffolding for boys to play on. In 1929 boxing was added to roller skating at the Borough Hall, at first tentatively on Mondays and then regularly on Saturdays in 1931. Neither of these amenities attracted me. I recall the breakdown of the Cement Works dust extractor in 1930, which whitened the whole Central Estate, and remarking that if it wasn't cement it was sand from the shore, sawdust from the propyards, or kippers from the kipper houses according to the direction of the wind. I was not aware in 1930 that Mrs Scott-Cowell was the first lady councillor in Hartlepool, nor that in the same year there were to be no pedestrian crossings ("Belisha Beacons") despite the Minister of Transport Hore-Belisha (whose name positively invited - and got - ribald jokes.)

I was not aware that the Town Council got a new chamber, first mooted in 1913, in 1935 and did not dance on the Promenade, which the Town Council permitted although it involved closing a right of way. I did not note the application by Cameron's Brewery to build a new pub at the then end of West View (Plate 75 p. 235), although I recall patronising it just before the outbreak of war. With 154 new houses in prospect the Central Estate was perhaps in danger of losing its identity. All the housing sites, which stretched as far as the new Cemetery, were on what had been Hall's Farm. "Up the road", the shorthand for "the country", had been pushed a mile further from the town.

Having previously postponed the use of the Borough Hall for skating, it was only in 1929 that the Town Council grudgingly sanctioned boxing but it proved so popular that in 1931 it was promoted from Monday to Saturday nights. In 1933 tennis on Sunday on the municipal courts was defeated, but in 1935 it was agreed that there were so many holiday camps - tents and shacks on the beaches at Crimdon Dene - that regulation was needed. The fact, however, that trolley buses caused radio interference was not deemed to merit intervention.

In 1929 the possibility of a union of the Hartlepools was revived by the new Mayor of West Hartlepool, but only in his induction speech, and in 1933 West Hartlepool proudly celebrated the centenary of its first Improvement Act. In 1930 West Hartlepool sought to expand, although not at the cost of Hartlepool. It was to the south, and when Hartlepool sought to expand in 1934 it was to the north, against Easington Rural District Council. In April 1935 an ERDC spokesman appearing before a House of Commons Select Committee on its own Bill stated that in the matter of town planning Hartlepool "has slept in for seven years". A month later Cllr. Brownless admitted to the Town Council that its Joint Town planning had not reported for five years. Its chairman, Cllr Arkley, riposted:

"UNJUSTIFIED STATEMENT"

> *... I want to say definitely that that was an unjustified statement. I do think that when a responsible representative of a local authority makes such a statement he should be sure of his facts.*
>
> *Coun. Arkley went on to explain that it was difficult to make a report on town planning. In view of the technicalities of the subject his own view was that the Borough Engineer constituted 95% of the Town Planning Committee, the legal adviser about 3% and the council 2%.*

As a rebuttal it was somewhat less than entirely convincing, and in July a report was promised for September, although this was not reported (by NDM) in the account of that meeting. Cllr Arkley, however, did not forfeit the electors' confidence and he was re-elected for the Hart Ward in November. After the declaration of the poll he followed immemorial custom in complementing his (railwayman/Labour/trade unionist, Fred Windebank) opponent on a sporting fight. "We leave this balcony as friends", he said, having, as a jobbing plumber and shopkeeper, already obliquely reproved him:

> *... As a working lad I have fought this fight off my own bat without seeking the aid of political candidates - only the aid of working lads like myself who have rallied round me...*

The comparison was presumably between a non working working-class "lad" and a working-class "man".

In 1931 the charges for the assistance of the West Hartlepool to the Hartlepool Fire Brigade drove the latter to prefer help from Billingham, which, though further away, was cheaper. In 1933, however, a joint sewerage scheme, dependent upon government funding, forced the 'Pools into reluctant collaboration at the cost of some delay. In 1934 the West Hartlepool invitation to collaborate in the establishment of a civic airport was accepted. It materialised: in 1939. Nevertheless there was a joint Hartlepools Employment Committee:

> *... The Secretary's report for the period Sept 25 1934, to December 23, 1934, showed that there was an increase of 950 in the number of unemployed in the area as compared with the figures on Sept 24, 1934. There was, however, a decrease of 1,029 as compared with the figures a year ago.*

THE REGISTER				
	Men	Women	Boys	Girls
West Hartlepool	7,179	438	215	153
Hartlepool	2,621	107	197	146
Horden	1,012	35	—	—

Table 6 - The Unemployment Register 1934

There was also a Hartlepools Trades Council which in January 1935 protested against the Town Council's decision to ask the Minister of Health to approve building 18 rather than 12 houses to the acre, and to ask the Member (Howard Gritten) to support a resolution demanding the restoration of cuts in benefit inflicted by the 1932 Health Insurance Act. Neither was reported as having succeeded.

No one could be unaware of the economic plight of the town. In 1930 there were more than 10,000 unemployed in the Hartlepools of whom 3000 were in "Old" Hartlepool. The only orders for the shipyards were for repairs, hopper barges or the odd engine.

The post-war figures of ships built fell from 20 in 1919, through 16 (1920), 6 (1921), 4 (1922), 5 (1923), 14 (1924), 9 (1925), 8 (1926), 17 (1927), 14 (1928 and 29), to 10 (1930) and 0 in 1931. In 1906 the number had been 48.

There was a new match factory, four years from planning to production, in West Hartlepool in 1935, which mainly employed girls. In 1931 there appeared a possibility that Synthonia from Billingham, which was experimenting on the production of oil from coal, might build another factory in Hartlepool but it was presumably cheaper to import oil, of which there was more than a surplus. No new factory was built. In 1933 Hartlepool appropriately got a new Employment Exchange. In 1934 it was reported that employment was at its best since 1929 but that the unemployed total had nevertheless increased by 205. In 1935 it was first announced and then denied that there would be a Special Areas grant.

The irony in NDM's comment of Jan 5 1935 must have been unconscious:

> *The past year has been a notable one in the history of the Hartlepool Council. Ambitious improvement schemes have been formulated, some of which are not yet completed, and one - the joint sewerage scheme - not started, but quite definitely there have been sincere efforts to restore Hartlepool to a place in keeping with its traditions.*

In October 1935, however, the newly created North-Eastern Development Board proposed the creation of industrial estates with modern factory buildings, the formation of an organisation for financing new industries, the reduction of Public Assistance to lower rates to enable local authorities to undertake works they could not otherwise afford, increased expenditure on relief works and an increase of purchasing by Government Departments in the area. The special area should be increased to include Teesside, which could and later did include Hartlepool... More relevant to the solution of the unemployment problem, in retrospect, was a communication from the Town Clerk in July 1935.

> *A circular from the Home Office dealing with air raid precautions and bringing to the notice of local authorities the precautionary measures which would be necessary for safeguarding the civil population against the effects of air attack in those parts of the country which might be subject to attack by hostile aircraft...*

Despite the clear reference to war it attracted neither comment from councillors nor a headline in NDM, and was referred to the Chairman and Deputy-chairman of the Watch Committee with power to co-opt additional members. On the other hand, again with ironic hindsight, a complaint with precise precedents from the years before 1914 received full attention not from the Town Clerk and the Council but from the Member for the Hartlepools and the Secretary of State for War:

> *DAMAGE BY GUNFIRE AT HARTLEPOOL*
> *MINISTER AND QUESTION OF COMPENSATION*
>
> *Mr W. Howard Gritten has received the following letter from Lord Halifax, Secretary of State for War... You were good enough to bring to my notice... representations which have been made to you regarding damage sustained by houses near the battery at Hartlepool. Unfortunately it is not always possible to place coast defence batteries in isolated positions. Of necessity the choice of it is determined by military considerations.*
>
> *The amount of firing of batteries in or near towns is restricted to a minimum. For*

instance at Hartlepool no firing of heavy shells for purely training purposes has taken place for some years past. The necessity of periodical tests of the guns remains, but the interval between successive tests is usually considerable, often as much as two years. In fact I am informed that the only firing of heavy shells at Hartlepool this year took place on July 20 and was confined to the hour between 3. and 4. pm on that day. As regards the question of compensation, it has to be borne in mind, as I have explained, that such firing as takes place is a matter of military necessity. That being the case, it is not possible for my department to admit claims for compensation, provided that the firing is properly carried out and that there are no abnormal circumstances.

I have had a detailed report on the present case, and I am assured that the firing was not abnormal in amount and was properly executed, and that every precaution was taken to warn the residents in neighbouring houses. In these circumstances I am afraid that claims for compensation cannot be admitted.

Assuming that Lord Halifax was accurately informed and that the claims were genuine, residents in the Cliff area may have forgotten to open their windows, although that would not have protected their ceilings or their slates. Some may have been too young to recall the Bombardment of Dec 16 1914, although on the 21st anniversary of that calamity in 1935 NDM recorded:

The regimental flag of the Durham Heavy Brigade R.A. (TA.) is flying at the Heugh Battery today, and tonight the brigade is holding its annual "Bombardment" dance at the Armoury in commemoration of the part which the brigade took in the action against the German battle cruisers…

The main economic topic continued to be the relief of unemployment. In 1930 it was revealed that since 1921 £140,000 had been granted to the Hartlepools and that a further £5,000 (which would create no less than 22 *(sic)* new jobs) had just been donated by the Unemployment Grants Committee, plus another £10,000 (643 jobs) for a Necessitous Area. In 1931 the Corporation undertook to permit 29 houses to be built on the Headland (i.e. the old Hartlepool), 50 more in 1934, approaching a total of 400 since 1919. In 1935 employment on the joint sewerage scheme with West Hartlepool mentioned above, was limited to 10 weeks each although the necessary pipes were to be manufactured locally. More encouraging in 1935 was the sanction for 154 more houses at West View. The disparity between need on the one hand and assistance on the other needs no emphasis, but active protest was recorded only in a demonstration in 1933 against the Means Test of 1931 which denied relief to the unemployed until their own and their family resources were exhausted. A diet of herrings, sold on the streets for four a penny, could have relieved their hunger: like me, however, they may have had other preferences.

In 1929, to improve Hartlepool's prospects as a seaside resort, an Entertainments Manager was appointed - for £125 per annum - and in 1931 two tennis courts were converted into a miniature golf course, and in 1935 more sand was deposited on the Block Sands and the (unheated) bathing pool was improved by building its wall higher against the wind (Plate 58 p. 193). Any benefits from these efforts may have been negated by the refusal of the justices to permit an extension of hours to clubs and pubs from 10.00 to 10.30 pm. even for the summer period. On the other hand, in 1935, those councillors who objected to closing the promenade amphitheatre for dancing on Monday and Wednesday evenings were, after prolonged debate on the "unwarrantable liberty" of taking away ratepayers' rights, defeated.

Voluntary effort to relieve the emptiness and boredom of unemployment took a number of forms. From 1930 the Independent Methodists and the Primitive Methodists held special weekly weekday afternoon services, usually with soloists to entertain and sometimes with tea and buns to refresh them. Their children were sometimes admitted free to the local cinemas. In 1930 Spion Kop was levelled to make football possible and in 1931 football leagues for the unemployed were organised. By 1934 there were 12 Unemployed Clubs and in 1935 the Warren Social Club, of which Cllr J. G. Arkley was president, on the Central Estate was opened by the Mayor.

> *... H.H, the club's "top" man at billiards, challenged the Mayor to a game, and Major Graham at once accepted. The members and spectators were greatly impressed by the mayor's display, and he was applauded at the close...*

The Mayor was either tactful or a good loser: possibly both. In 1935 there was an Unemployed Billiards League and gifts to 200 needy families were provided at Christmas by Basingstoke Girl Guides.

At the same time the Central Hotel and the Lord Clyde continued to pay Club dividends, always providing "harmony" at their annual Smokers' meetings. Both the Central Hotel ("Klondyke") and St Barnabas' Hall accommodated shows for rabbit and guinea pig fanciers.

In addition to gardening, self-help flourished in the gathering of coal from the pit heap on the shore at Blackhall Rocks (Plate 76 p. 236). It was possible to carry two sacks beneath the crossbar of a bicycle although this made pedalling impossible. The answer was to push the handlebars or to pedal velocipede-wise from a carrier over the rear wheel. The distance by road or along the sands at low tide was three miles or so, and excitement was provided by local unemployed miners who resented the "theft" of "their" coal. NDM actually remarked in 1934 on the absence of pithead fights. NDM also noticed in May 1935 that those who preferred the even more laborious effort of scraping coal, washed from outcrops on the sea-bed, from the high tide mark:

> A SURPRISE FOR THE COAL-GATHERERS
>
> *Sea-coal gatherers at Hartlepool, who make it their daily routine to visit the sands before most people are awake, received a pleasant surprise this morning, when they found that not only was there coal on the North Sands, but that the beach was littered with pit-props. From 6.30 up to 9 o'clock there was a steady procession of men to and from the sands, each carrying his share of props, and more are still being washed ashore, People at first thought that a vessel had gone ashore, but the explanation of where the props had come from is still a mystery.*

Presumably no one cared, and any legal niceties concerning flotsam or jetsam were ignored.

There was also provision for self-improvement by attendance at lectures, although the Study Centre of 1930, patronised by Major Ropner, was not aimed at the unemployed. It is difficult to believe that the WEA had ceased to exist but for whatever reason it was no longer reported.

Only petty crime was reported: serious crime was either nonexistent or undiscovered. In 1930 Central Estate cyclists were fined for having no front or rear lights or reflectors and a Bell Street motor cyclist for having no license. A Union Road thief from his mother-in-law's gas meter was freed because his neighbours refused to identify him though he was immediately re-arrested on another charge. Another Union Roader was fined for being drunk and disorderly after leaving the Quoit Alley on Montague Road.

In 1931 a Rokeby Street unemployed man was fined for £14 arrears on affiliation orders and there were fines in Hart Road and Romaine Park for no lights on a lorry and improper seating on a motorcycle pillion. A young Union Road man was fined for substituting a hand-held flash lamp for a proper cycle light, and in 1932 an affray in Stephenson Street was reported at length.

"LIKE LITTLE CHILDREN"

An amusing experiment took place at the Hartlepool Police Court this morning in a case in which... summoned... for assault. P. alleged that G. called him abusive names and threw an acetylene lamp, which struck him in the back, as he was cycling along Stephenson Street. G. said P. made an offensive noise with his mouth, but P. maintained that was impossible, as he was smoking a cigarette. P, handed the defendant a cigarette and told him to make the noise with the cigarette in his mouth. G. tried, but no noise resulted, and the magistrate ordered the evidence to proceed. G. was finally bound over and ordered to pay 4s. costs. The Mayor (Coun F.J. Carr): The case should never have been brought. The pair of you seem to have gone on like children instead of men with common sense.

In 1933 two mothers in Hart Road were bound over for taking part in their children's quarrels and in 1934 an Arch Street chimney-on-fire was fined 2/6d. In the same year there was an amazing encounter in Clyde Street.

A MIDNIGHT INCIDENT

... P.C. Gyllenspetz said he was called to Clyde Street about midnight, where he found Mr and Mrs J.G and their eight year old daughter... standing in the middle of the road. Mrs G. told him that she went into the house about 10.30 and locked the door from the inside. Mr G. who was already in the house, locked the back door. Later she went upstairs to put the child to bed and her husband followed her. On looking out of the window he saw L. climbing over the yard wall, and although he ran downstairs to prevent L. entering, the latter forced the door. L. then bundled the family into the street. The constable added that, with the assistance of another constable, he forced the door and found L. in the back kitchen with the door shut. He appeared to be looking round for something, and had eaten the G's supper. As both G. and L. are mutes, the services of Mr Frank Hastings had to be called to interpret the evidence. Through him L. said that G. invited him into the house. L. was sent to prison for one month...

Not all is clear. G. and L. must have been previously acquainted, if not related: otherwise coincidence has been pushed too far.

Someone in Hart Road was fined four shillings for riding a child on the crossbar of his bicycle. In retrospect I can only marvel that I myself had been cross-barred to school and back for two years, twice a day, twice a week and must have been seen by scores of policemen without reproach. Indeed it was common practice.

In 1935 there was a positive crime wave on the Central Estate. A former Union Road schoolmate of mine was fined for shooting with both an air rifle and an air pistol. Footballers in Cleveland Road (2/6d) and cyclists on the Rokeby Street footpath (5/-) were fined. One of the footballers was a Clyde Street 17-year old:

> *... P.C Greenlees said he, H. was in company with another boy near the Throston Bridge police box. They were on opposite sides of the road and were kicking a ball to each other. H. took a kick at the ball and tripped, and only the quick braking of a car averted an accident. When the constable approached H. and the other boy ran away, but later they were caught, still playing football on the Central Estate.*

One Union Road mother was fined for striking another who intervened in their children's quarrel. Another Union Roader, accused of stealing coal which (he said) "rolled down the embankment", was discharged for lack of evidence and corroboration and a dog "ran amok" at Hart Road School without a name or address on its collar although it seemed docile. Two boys in Hart Road were charged with stealing a quantity of wood slabs, valued at 6d, from a timber yard. The boys were cautioned and the case dismissed. All these summonses were the work of a new police constable, Greenlees, who may have been officious. Other constables arrested boys from Hart Road for alleged thefts of wood from the Propyard and a boy from Cleveland Road who claimed that in brilliant moonlight he had no need of a bicycle lamp.

Inevitably there were accidents but only one was fatal: in 1934 a woman's body was found on the North Sands, although she may not have been local. In 1929 a Hart Road lady running for a bus to Bell Street was knocked down by a motor cyclist and a milk van collided with a mourning car emerging from West View Cemetery after a funeral. In that same year there was fire in the Propyard but the catastrophe of January 1922 was not repeated because of the precautions taken in consequence. In 1930 a greenhouse on an allotment on Warren Road caught fire and was extinguished with buckets of water carried from the tram depot. The same thing happened a year later but this time water was carried from Hall's Farm. The Fire Brigade was present on both occasions but frustrated by the dryness of the neighbouring beck. It could, however, directly extinguish an after-midnight fire upstairs at the Lord Clyde Hotel because mains water was conveniently available. In 1933 part of a wrecked aeroplane was washed up on the North Sands. In 1934 a horse coming from Watson Street put its head through a lorry windscreen in Bell Street. The driver was slightly cut but the horse was unharmed. A 12-year old boy from Romaine Park lost an eye whilst playing with an air rifle.

Meanwhile NDM continued to chronicle and comment cautiously on the sad succession of international events which culminated in the outbreak in 1939 of the Second World War.

The rise of Hitler to power in Germany in 1933, German conscription and the Reichstag Fire in 1935, the Italian invasion of Abyssinia in 1934, their joint intervention in the Spanish Civil War and the continuously victorious conquest of China by

Japan which culminated in the Axis, the Anti-Comintern Pact, of 1936 were ill-matched by the impotence of the divided League of Nations and the persistence of American neutrality. British foreign policy was paralysed between hatred of Nazism/Fascism and fear of Stalinist Communism. British imperialism, challenged by the problems of De Valera's Ireland, Gandhi's India, the Palestine Mandate also split public opinion. There was no more national consensus on remedies for the world-wide economic slump between free trade and protectionism than there was between rearmament and disarmament, pacifism or militarism.

All these issues were aired and debated in the columns and correspondence columns of the NDM and in countless political party and trade union meetings in the Hartlepools. Political (and religious) matters were forbidden to the Henry Smith School Debating Society (of which I was Secretary 1933-35) but hot exchanges abounded in classrooms and corridors and several teachers who favoured the cause of the League of Nations and collective security allowed their views to be known. In 1935 Sixth Formers were old enough to vote in the League of Nations Peace Ballot and the only matter of dispute was whether or not the failure of arbitration and negotiation should or should not be followed by recourse to war.

On the Central Estate there was at least one activist who spent a great deal of time preaching to me on the righteousness of the socialist cause. He was an unemployed shipyard worker of Geordie origins, "victimised", he believed, for political and trade union activity. He had been a WEA student and had a large collection of left-wing books and pamphlets which he was very eager to lend. His socialism derived, I now recall, not from Marx, whom he never mentioned, but from a deeply-felt moral imperative of fairness a against individual and collective greed and "the policy of grab". His stories of childhood poverty and educational deprivation strongly resembled those of Keir Hardie, the founder of the Labour Party. His information on national politics, international relations in general and the "iniquities" of British foreign and imperial policies from the end of the 19th century onwards was impressive and he could and always would hold forth eloquently on iniquities of the Boer War, the recruitment of indentured Chinese labourers to gold mines in the Transvaal (i.e. slave labour), the arms race, the private manufacturers and dealers in arms (most notably Sir Basil Zaharoff of Maxim-Nordenfelt-Vickers), the ostracism of Soviet Russia after the 1917 Revolution, and, most vehemently, the appeasement of Japan in Manchuria, of Mussolini's Italian invasion of Abyssinia and of Hitler's German rearmament.

He was equally impassioned against British Conservative and Liberal prime ministers and foreign secretaries, whose treacheries and hypocrisy he recited at length. Even Labour's first and second prime minister, Ramsay Macdonald, was only tolerable until the "betrayal" of 1931 when he abandoned the Labour party to become head of the so-called "National" Government" with Conservatives and Liberals. I canvassed these opinions with my father and with my Form VI history master. The former, although also a Labour voter, was both more moderate and more patriotic. The latter, just as sceptical and even better informed, taught me that politics and international relations were ruthless and cynical contests for power in which morality was an elusive, if not illusory, component.

Otherwise, on the Central Estate, Stephenson Streeter Cllr Arkley defeated Arch

Streeter W. Lawson in 1929. In January 1930 Hart Ward Conservative and Unionist Association held a meeting in Hart Road and in March a Whist Drive and Dance, not in the Central Hotel in Cleveland Road but in the Central Hotel, Musgrave Street, West Hartlepool. In the same year Thomas Pailor was (at last) elected Councillor for St. Hilda's Ward. He was dedicated to becoming the scourge of unnecessary expenditure. In 1931 former boatbuilder-turned-undertaker John Metcalfe of Arch Street (Plate 77 p. 236), like Cllr. Arkley a craftsman-turned-shopkeeper, was elected Councillor for Hart Ward. In 1933 former Cllr. Chambers, who had been its representative for six years, was again defeated for the Middleton Ward and in 1934 ill-health forced Cllr Bulmer to retire. In September 1935 the Hart Ward Conservative and Unionist Association took a hundred children by bus for sports, sweets and novelty bags to Blackhall Rocks. In the same year only two votes deprived would-be Cllr. Chambers of victory.

In so far as General Election results are indicators, the majority was solidly Conservative. Howard Gritten's majority was even safer in the National Government elections of 1931 and 1935 than it had been in 1929. NDM advert Nov 12 1935:

> *The Issue Is Clear!*
> *NATIONALISM V. SOCIALISM*
> *Nationalism Stands for Safety and Progress*
> *Socialism - Chaos - Disaster*
> *CHOOSE WISELY AND VOTE FOR GRITTEN*

The last Liberal MP, William Jowitt, had been defeated in 1924. Councillor Scott-Cowell, the local Liberal candidate and Captain Goatcher, Labour, were defeated.

Plate 72 - Edward Prince of Wales (later King Edward VIII) with Canon F. T. Salter, July 3 1930

Plate 73 - Prince of Wales at St Hilda's, Sir William Gray behind with Mayor

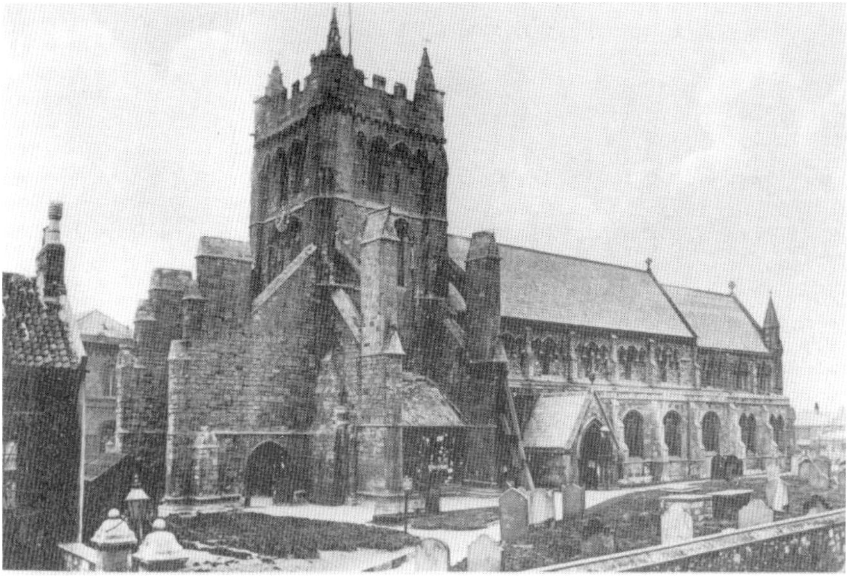

Plate 74 - St Hilda's Church (c. 1192-1240) with the "new" chancel

Plate 75 - Brus Arms West View 1939

Plate 76 - Seacoal gathering

Plate 77 - Councillor John Metcalf

Chapter 11: 1935-1945.

In 1935 I went off to university and although I spent all my vacations on the Central Estate and all my leaves during the war 1939-45 (including hours in the backyard air raid shelter) and remained in close contact until my mother left Hartlepool in 1949, my contact was obviously less close and intimate. Indeed it was not until the late 1960s that I was irresistibly drawn back and, increasingly convinced that I had been fortunate in my background and childhood, resolved to write the history of my birth-place both as a professional historian and as one who belonged. This has involved some conflicts of loyalty which I have done my best to resolve.

By 1935 the Central Estate was almost half a century old and established in its habitat and its ways. Although emigration and immigration continued, its population was basically stable, and although there were novelties and changes in employment it continued to be the semidetached suburb of a shipbuilding industrial town, its population predominantly respectable working class. Although originally conceived as an overspill area for Hartlepool, necessitated by expansion and to accommodate the surplus created by slum-clearance, it never ceased to attract "outsiders" from other parts of the north, all other parts of the country, from the rest of the United Kingdom, and from beyond. Consequently it came to have its own character and loyalty of which its inhabitants were both conscious and proud.

The years 1935-39 saw gradual improvement in the national economy with corresponding reductions in the numbers of unemployed. Rearmament played its part in this and the Central Estate profited in one sense from the erection of a factory (the Palliser Works, Plate 78 p. 245) in 1937 for the production of magnesium (for incendiary bombs, etc) from sea-water, although this was not public knowledge at the time. What was known was that it was constructed on the sand banks next to the Old Cemetery and rapidly swallowed Sandy Park, our playground for so many games. It also constructed a huge pipeline into the sea, obstructing free passage along the North Sands. It offered some employment but it was not until well after the outbreak of war on September 3rd that something like full employment returned for the first time since 1918. Volunteering and conscription created vacancies in the work force. Unfortunately, but equally predictably, aerial bombardment also returned and the Central Estate, because of its proximity to shipyards and engineering works, again at least had its share.

The Prime Minister Neville Chamberlain was due to broadcast at 11.00 a.m on Sunday September 3rd Sept 3 and it was beyond belief, not to say reason, that the message would be that we were not at war with Germany. Expecting to hear immediate air raid sirens (as did happen in London) I walked round the Central Estate with friends and was both surprised and pleased to discover a large gang of men with picks and shovels digging for an air raid shelter on spare ground behind Hart Road School. It was a beautifully warm and sunny morning and I felt patriotic and proud that at last we had done what was right. Having already made blackout shutters (as required by governmental order) from discarded wooden venetian blinds and sheets of black paper, I walked round the Central Estate again at night, officiously tapping on windows which still leaked light.

A few days later workmen arrived to demolish the wooden shed which had housed bicycles and a mangle and other washing-day apparatus in our backyard and to erect a two-brick-thick air raid shelter with a reinforced concrete roof six inches thick. Then for eight months there followed the anticlimax of the so-called "phoney war" and the prospect of a possible phoney peace, shattered in May 1940 by the German invasion of France and the beginnings of the blitz on London. By that time I had joined the army and was training to be a subaltern in the Royal Artillery by day and manning the coast (at Filey in Yorkshire) at night against threatened invasion, with rifles without bullets and four point five inch howitzers without shells or charges, salvaged from a World War I museum. "Dad's Army" was not confined to what became the "Home Guard", then beginning to recruit "Local Defence Volunteers.

The real war hit the Central Estate in September 1940 when two sticks of bombs fell in the West View area killing one man and wounding two children. In May 1941 two mines fell on the Palliser Works. In March 1941 it also hit Hartlepool with parachute mines in the sea, and in May with bombs killing twelve people in the town centre. In December 1942 bombs on the Central Estate hit the Central United Club and nine people were killed in Union Road. The house in neighbouring Stephenson Street, in which I had lived 1922-26, was so damaged by the same bomb as to become uninhabitable. Its occupants were immediately offered shelter by a family on the opposite side of the street until repairs were completed - a matter of weeks, not days.

West Hartlepool, being bigger and with still more engineering works and a steel mill, etc, as well as docks, suffered even more. In 1940 bombs fell not only on the town centre but on the Steelworks and the shipyard at Graythorp. In both towns there fell every size and variety of high explosive bomb, incendiary bomb and land mine. In addition to the resulting deaths and injuries, local volunteers and conscripts were killed, wounded or imprisoned in every land, sea and air campaign from the battles of Britain and France, to North Africa, Italy, mainland Europe, and in the Middle and Far East from Alamein to Jerusalem, Singapore, Burma and beyond.

NDM took the war in its stride. On Dec 12 1939 it proclaimed that blackout time was from 4.7 p.m. to 7.51 a.m and reported:

CYCLED ON PATH IN BLACK-OUT

A 16-year-old newsboy who was stated to have ridden a cycle for 120 yards on the footpath in Hart Road was fined 5s. at the Hartlepool Juvenile Court this morning. Inspector Walker said the offence was magnified by the fact that it took place during the black-out, when the footpath should be reserved for the use of pedestrians. Ald. R. H. Davison (chairman) said this type of offence would be dealt with much more severely in future...

On the same day there was a leading article:

WAR IN THE AIR

... Fortunately, the oft-predicted mass attack on Great Britain by German machines has not yet materialised... But at least it can be said that, on the balance, Allied machines have shown themselves to be the better... up to this stage...

Such is the position in the present state of tentative air warfare. It would be idle to deny that Allied and enemy air power has now reached a condition of potential effect that the warring governments are manifestly unwilling to launch wholesale attacks on civilian centres just now because of fear of reprisals...

Allied machines may have been better, but as bitter experience was to show for the next two or three years, there were far fewer of them. Blitzkrieg against armies in the field and blitz against civilians in towns, including the Hartlepools, soon followed. Meanwhile

NDM (Dec 15,1939) reported:

SERVING THE COUNTRY

Mrs M. E. C... Arkley Crescent, West View, Hartlepool has her husband, a son aged 18 years and three brothers in the Army. Her husband served in the Navy in the Great war, and she was a W.A.A.C. (Women's Army Auxiliary Corps).

On the same day, "In the Hartlepools" recorded the whereabouts of the Member, Howard Gritten; a daytime, not blackout, coast road fatality to a cyclist, and a knock down injury to a pensioner in the town centre; egg-laying trials ("the last which will be held until after the war"), and the presentation of First-Aid Certificates to 80 casualty workers in Hartlepool. On December 20th a Stephenson Street lorry owner was fined for having no rear light.

... a cyclist complained that he had collided in the black-out with the lorry as it stood by the roadside. Defendant said that as far as he knew the light had been on, and he wondered whether it had been extinguished when the cyclist collided with it.

O December 29 NDM reported a Hartlepool Town Council debate on whether employees who joined His Majesty's Forces should have their pay made up to pre-war standards whether married or single. "Hartlepools Day By Day" simultaneously reported:

CHRISTMAS AND A.R.P.

A.R.P was "Air Raid Precautions" for which Wardens had been appointed to every ward.

During the past few days, through the press and over the air, we have heard a good deal about Christmas with the B.E.F, (British Expeditionary Force: in France), *the Navy, the RAF... and the evacuees, but what of the A.R.P. stalwarts? Without relaxing their vigilance they, too, had a merry Christmas. A glimpse into most of the air raid wardens' posts and dugouts in the Hartlepools will show that they are, indeed, at the moment "better 'oles". These people have proved that the drawing-room mantelpiece is not the only place for Christmas cards, nor the nursery the only home of festoons and tinsel.*

Many of the posts are gay places where the helmeted men have found opportunities for enjoying themselves. During off-duty hours there have been supper parties and dances...

Not, presumably, on A.R.P. premises. A year later, on Dec 12 1940, NDM reported:

HARTLEPOOL RECTOR'S BROADCASTS

It is safe to assume that before the week is ended millions of people will have heard the voice of Canon Salter, Rector of Hartlepool - familiar to our readers as "The Window Cleaner" - broadcasting these short, homely spiritual talks which precede the 8 o'clock

BBC news bulletin... It has been necessary for the Rector to travel daily and stay overnight...

On Dec 14 1940 a leading article commended the Mayoress (of West Hartlepool)'s happy thought to include the children of local soldiers, sailors and airmen as beneficiaries of her Christmas Cheer Fund.

> *... During the past year hundreds... have been called from their ordinary jobs for service in the ranks. This Christmas they will not have very much to spare from service pay to send presents home, unless, of course, they belong to the fortunate few whose peace-time incomes are made up. But that is not their fault, so no soldier's child should be deprived of the gift the Mayoress offers because its parents are afraid of that much maligned word charity...*

By Dec 2 1941, although its layout remained the same, NDM had switched to a much larger type-face, without a change of font. Bearing in mind that newsprint was by then severely rationed and news itself severely censored, NDM may have been making a virtue of necessity. The first leading article cautiously suggested that in invading Russia in addition to conquering Europe, the British Empire and the Americas, Hitler might have bitten off more than he could chew. Nearer to earth NDM reported:

> *"CASH AND CARRY SUCCESS"*
>
> *On a small scale Hartlepool will begin midday meals for school children tomorrow. The St Barnabas Hall has been requisitioned for this purpose, and this is situated within a few hundred yards of the present "cash and carry" centre in Hart Road. Miss E. Trechman, supervisor of the communal feeding arrangements for Hartlepool Corporation... states that the "cash and carry" system for adults has proved very successful. "On most days we are working to full capacity, especially towards the week-end. In the beginning people asked mainly for soups and puddings, but now they are taking the full course."*

The "cash and carry" centre can have been none other than the former Primitive Methodist Chapel, redundant since the completion of its successor in 1938. It was later promoted to the status of "British Restaurant", where meals could be eaten as well as purchased, before its eventually inevitable post-war demolition (Plate 71 p. 217).

Still on Dec 2 1941 NDM reported:

> *RAILINGS "REPRIEVE" SOUGHT*
>
> *Iron railings surrounding many public as well as private places are likely to be removed in West Hartlepool in the interests of the war effort. The Ward Jackson Park... and the Esplanade and foreshore have all been considered as places which could sacrifice their railings without prejudice to public safety. The Park and Recreation Committee has decided, however, that the railings around the Park and Burn Valley Gardens should be retained...*

Parallel agonising decisions must also have been made in Hartlepool. It was the shortage of iron and steel that prompted these sacrifices of amenity, just as the appeal for aluminium saucepans to make more Spitfires prompted my mother to donate our egg-poaching pan. The contributions of railings and saucepans did not, presumably, determine the ultimate victory but may have contributed to the uplift of civilian morale when there was little else to inspire it.

On Dec 24 1941, shortly after the Japanese bombardment of Pearl Harbour added the USA to the "united front" of Britain and Russia, transforming it to the "united nations", the leader pronounced that "the English-speaking races... must jointly act as the policemen of the world... "

In the adjoining column to this momentous pronouncement, was this item of news:

THE BOROUGH HALL

A proposal that the Corporation should organise Borough Hall dances on its own account may come before Monday's meeting of Hartlepool Town Council. Some members hold the view that if the Council decided to run their own dances instead of letting the hall regularly to outside organisations, the profits would result in an appreciable relief of the rates. The equivalent of a threepenny rate has been mentioned as a possible reward for municipal enterprise in the matter.

Presumably this was a nonstarter: there might have been losses as well as profits.

By the time the war ended in 1945 Hartlepool was politically changed. In the July general election the Labour landslide included victory for Hartlepool's first Labour MP, David Jones, and local elections also produced the first Labour majority on the Borough Council. R. S. Boswell of Stephenson Street had at last become a Labour town councillor for Hart Ward but C. Chambers had regained a seat on the other side (Plate 69 p. 216). The victory was narrow indeed. On the issue of whether the Corporation should sell land for housing to a private builder for private sale, which had earlier been given council consent, or be retained for council housing for rent, the division was so even that the mayor - not Labour - could give a casting vote in favour of the original agreement.

The Council was divided on the sale of land for an extension to the Palliser Works and on the need to pay for councillors' attendances at conferences. Warren Road allotments were still being flooded and there was to be a site meeting with representatives of the Allotment Holders' Association. Policeman (now Sergeant) Ogleby was actually commended "on this occasion" for arresting a seaman who had stolen a motorcar. The Town Clerk stated that at the last meeting of the Joint Consultative Committee (i.e. with West Hartlepool County Borough Council):

... the question of the hardness of the water supply to the Hartlepools was discussed. The discussion had arisen as a result of a suggestion from a local firm that the hardness of the water was detrimental to industrial development. Arrangements were now being made for a deputation to meet the Hartlepool Gas and Water Company...

It is unlikely that anything was achieved. The limestone aquifers could not be changed and water-softening, although technically feasible and commercially available (long used by the L.N.E.R railway company) was expensive.

Later in 1945 the Town Council's meeting headline was explosive:

HARTLEPOOL'S POLICE FORCE
COUNCIL AND ABSORPTION THREAT

In view of the threatened absorption of the Hartlepool Borough Police Force in the

Durham County Constabulary, Hartlepool Watch Committee is to consider whether it would be preferable to establish a join force with West Hartlepool, "with our force as the basis"

... Ald. Carr asked if the committee appreciated that, if the Police Bill was passed... there was little or no likelihood of small forces such as Hartlepool being allowed to exist independently, and that this would mean a further loss of an important service from the control of the Council.

The chairman of the Watch Committee agreed but Cllr. Boswell doubted under the terms of the Bill it would be possible to make arrangements with West Hartlepool. He was right: but it is significant in view of previous attitudes to West Hartlepool that it should be canvassed as the lesser of two evils. At the same meeting it was also suggested and agreed that the Hartlepools might combine to form an Accident Prevention Council representative of all peoples interested in accident prevention.

Could it be that after six years of world war historic attitudes were changing? Certainly not as regards some things.

BOROUGH HALL QUESTIONS

Coun. Aird asked why the application for an occasional license for a Darts League competition at the Borough Hall was not granted.

Ald. Jacques said the committee felt that as the competition closed at 9.30 p.m. there was sufficient time for any person to get refreshment afterwards. Moreover they had to take into consideration the extra work an occasional license would involve.

An amendment by Coun. Mrs Smith to refer back a recommendation that the Ladies' Voluntary Committee be charged a fee of £2 2s for a whist drive and dance at the Borough Hall was defeated. She suggested that the Committee should have the hall free.

Ald. Lightfoot seconded the amendment.

Ald. Wood said to do as suggested would create a precedent, and Ald. Jacques said they had to look at the question from the ratepayers' point of view. Bills had to be paid.

On the other hand, it sounded as though allotment holders were being positively spoiled:

The Town Clerk reported that a total of 258 allotment-holders on Hart Road and Sturrock's Field had been circularised regarding the new allotments, and that 171 applications had been received. Tenants on war allotments are to be included in the applications for these allotments. The allotment-holders are to be asked to include the cost of removal in their claims for compensation...

The Borough Engineer was instructed to provide all available transport for the allotment-holders each Saturday afternoon and Sunday morning until the transfer of all buildings, etc, to the new site is completed... .

Allotment-holders are to be permitted to erect greenhouses and tool sheds and to keep homing pigeons (long distance) and poultry, but no pigs.

A possible reason for this change of heart from habitual resistance to allotment-holders demands to generosity and permissiveness had been revealed earlier in the proceedings:

THE TRADING ESTATE

In reference to the proposed trading estate, the Town Clerk reported that he had received the report of the district valuer stating that he was prepared to offer, on behalf of the Board of Trade, the sum of £8,000 for the whole of the site, the board to bear half the cost of the extension of Winterbottom Avenue, the cost of the new sewer in that road, and the cost of making up the pavement on Warren Road adjoining the land. The offer was accepted.

Cllr. Boswell, an allotment holder of many years standing, may also have been influential.

The Trading Estate of cheap sites for light industries, not the old heavy staples of shipbuilding, had been planned before the war but had become irrelevant whilst it was fought. The prospect of peace and demobilisation of the millions in the armed forces naturally revived it.

More explosive headlines followed:

The County Borough of Hartlepool
Amalgamation Moves May Soon Be Renewed

Recent references to amalgamation may lead to more definite moves before very long. Public men in both the Hartlepools are convinced that sooner or later the twin towns will join hands in their own interests and become the County Borough of Hartlepool.

"JOHN CITIZEN" went on:

Any move to that end is certain to meet with opposition - some has already been newly expressed - but the hint which the Member for the Hartlepools gave last week is a timely indication of how the old controversy will probably develop unless it is settled by mutual agreement.

"A voluntary amalgamation" said Mr David Jones, "may be a better result then some form of compulsion which may come about when the Boundary Commission starts on its work."...

In view of previous articles on the subject, it is not my purpose here to stress the importance of taking the long view, of sinking old prejudices in favour of a common future: but rather to illustrate, by recalling amalgamation moves of the past, how frequently the project has been thwarted by a short-sighted refusal to appreciate that unity in municipal matters would lead to strength in many other directions.

The story of the amalgamation moves of the past 80 years is largely the story of the development and growth of West Hartlepool. A recurring measure of the rapid and large paces with which West Hartlepool has outstripped in size and importance its older and smaller neighbour.

It has to be remembered that less than 100 years ago the prosperous citizens of Hartlepool, proud of centuries of civic independence, used to look across the bay at a little hamlet nestling around Stranton Church and wondered how on earth the 300 inhabitants managed to make a living without docks and ships and fish.

Then almost overnight, as it were, the hamlet grew into a village, the village into a town, and the town into a flourishing port with new docks, new railways, and all the other aids, artificial and natural, needed to challenge at that time the supremacy of Liverpool itself and almost put old Hartlepool out of business...

When amalgamation was first mooted there were actually five townships - Hartlepool, Middleton, Throston, and Seaton Carew. As long ago as 1857 Hartlepool sought to take over the districts which later came under the authority of the Middeton and Throston Boards. But nothing came of this and during the next 20 years, while Hartlepool continued to lose population and prestige, West Hartlepool advanced its mushroom growth, looking round eagerly all the while for more leberstraum (sic).

Plate 78 - Steetley Magnesite (formerly Palliser) Works 1960

Plate 79 - Bathing Pool Storm Damage 1953

Plate 80 - Lock's Plan for Hartlepool 1948

Plate 81 - Brus Arms, late 40s

West View now expanded into West Hartlepool before the 1967 Union of the Hartlepools

Plate 82 - The Ropery prior to demolition 1967

Plate 83 - Arch St / Union Rd prior to demolition

Plate 84 - Match Factory Fire Aug 30 1954

Plate 85 - Chick Henderson before World War II (1939-45)

Plate 86 - Chick Henderson during World War II

Plate 87 - Nuclear Power Station 1987

Plate 88 - Hartlepool Marina

Plate 89 - John Ward

Chapter 12: 1945-99

In 1967 the presumably inevitable but long-delayed amalgamation of the two Hartlepools was at last brought about irrespective of diehard thoughts on both sides. A bonfire had been lit on the Town Moor in 1952 when the House of Lords rejected West Hartlepool's proposals for amalgamation, but Hartlepool now lost its Borough Council and became part of the County Borough of Hartlepool. The date of merger, ironic or not, was April 1st and the fact that the local MP had switched from Labour to Conservative in 1959 and back to Labour in 1964 was apparently irrelevant. As for the Central Estate, to avoid confusion with streets in former West Hartlepool, three street names were changed: Lambton Street became Stapleton Street, Gray Square (in Romaine Park) became Gibb Square and Hart Road became West View Road. Contrariwise, the names of West Hartlepool's Bell Street, Pease Street, Rokeby Street and Watson Street were changed. In this respect at least, justice may have been a little more than evenhanded.

Meanwhile much was changing. In 1948 the Cement Works chimney (unused since the closure, under Trechman's will in 1939) was demolished and the remnant of Low Warren Farm not already sold for West View housing development became the "New" Friarage Field (originally adjacent to the Henry Smith School) for Hartlepool Rovers (Rugby Union). In 1951 the Cement Works (Plate 65 p. 215) were demolished, the Civic Restaurant in the former Primitive Methodist Chapel was closed and it served out the rest of its time (before demolition) as a drill hall for the Territorial Army. In 1952 the Ferry ceased to operate and in 1953 storms damaged the Bathing Pool beyond repair and the last trolley bus ran to Hartlepool. In 1955 Trinity Church was demolished and in 1956 the guns were removed from the Heugh Battery. In 1958 it housed archery rather than artillery, and the Ropery works closed. The Cement Works site was levelled and seeded, reverting to its 19th century role as a playground. In 1959 application was made to demolish Sir Cuthbert Sharp's birthplace in the High Street and the Queen's Cinema became a Bingo Hall. In 1962 the Palladium ceased to be a cinema. In 1962 came the heaviest blow of all. Gray's Shipyard and Central Marine Engineering Works closed down. Hartlepool had apparently run out of steam.

Patched up from war damage in the early post-war years, with the successful development of light industrial and service employments on the Trading Estate, Hartlepool and the Central Estate also hoped to resume pre-war coal and steel exports, timber imports, fishing and shipbuilding. As during and after World War I, however markets had been lost and new competitors with labour- and cost-saving advantages taken their place. Ship tonnages had so increased that the local 8-10,000 tonnage building limit had become obsolete and the local shipyards could no longer compete with Poland or East Germany, Japan or Korea. In 1948 the town planning consultant Max Lock reported that the problem of blight could only be remedied by wholesale reconstruction (Plate 80 p. 246). The docks, he said, were rambling and obsolete. There was a lack of modern warehousing and bad road access. Shipbuilding and marine engineering were bound to contract. Strong local patriotism inhibited amalgamation. There was a thriving club life and adequate pubs and cinemas but cultural and recreational facilities were poor and scattered against the need for neighbourliness. There was hardly a building of architectural merit and the large percentage of houses with shared WCs, no bathrooms and no gardens were ripe only for immediate clearance. A mile-wide industrial belt cut the town off from the sea and there was heavy pollution, notably from the Palliser Works. Hart Road School should be demolished and Hart Road Cemetery should include a park and public garden. The Lord Clyde Hotel (already vacant) might be licensed as a restaurant. There was a high percentage of small, un-prosperous round-the-corner shops and no main shopping focus. The long-term policy for the Central Estate was total clearance. Low-lying, hedged in between the railway embankment, industry and timber yards it was unsuitable for housing. There were no open spaces, parks or gardens, playgrounds or playing fields, health centre, cinema, library or community centre and only one (St Barnabas) surviving centre of worship. It was a brutal verdict, naturally provoking determined opposition. Why could it not be rebuilt and its community rehoused?

West View, on the other hand, was deemed prosperous and expandable. By 1939 it had already extended to the Horse Shoe Arch, opposite which the Brus Arms dispensed hospitality, and up Warren Road as far as Howbeck Hospital. In 1946 a Nursery School was added and in 1949 houses were built between the Brus Arms and the new King Oswy Drive (Plate 81 p. 246). 1951 saw the building of shops on Warren Road, and the installation of a telephone kiosk outside West View Post office, by which time Hart Ward was large enough to be split in two. In 1952 West View got its own Primary School and in 1953 shops were opened opposite the Brus Arms. In 1954 an Infant School was opened and a Child Welfare Centre. A School Clinic and a United Services Club were authorised and in 1956 not only a Baptist Sunday School Hall but another pub, the Touchdown, in close proximity to the New Rovers Field (which also had its bar), not to mention a Children's Section at the West View Library. 1957 saw the sale of land for shops in King Oswy Drive and the opening of a Baptist Chapel and in 1958 permission was granted for a Working Men's Club and the opening of a Secondary Modern School. The same year saw the closure of the Ropery (Plate 82 p. 246) and 1959 the laying of the Foundation Stone for a Methodist Church. In 1961 a Community Centre was opened. By 1967, the year of amalgamation, West View, the child of the post-World-War I extension of the Central Estate, had dwarfed its parent. Moreover it was now contiguous with expanding West Hartlepool: there was no longer even the semblance of the old municipal boundary by the tramsheds at Greenland.

During the same period Hartlepool was shrinking physically as well as in terms of employment: the 1931 population of 21,000 had shrunk to 17,000 by 1951. Although continuously replaced by new housing (naturally at much lower density and greater amenity) demolition of what was now deemed slum property began in 1949 on the Town Wall and continued in 1951 on the High Street itself. In the same year the Council issued compulsory purchase orders on houses in no less than five streets, and, in 1952 not only on three more but also closed two pubs and demolished a third. In 1955 seven more pubs went and in 1956 the demolition of the whole of Middleton was virtually completed. In the same year properties in six more streets were compulsorily purchased. Five more streets went in 1959, the Lighthouse Battery was sold and demolished and notice was given of the demolition of the Naval Barracks. At the same time the timber ponds were filled in, presumably because the import of pit props (a second staple trade) for the collieries had ceased. In 1964 railway services between West Hartlepool and Hartlepool disappeared and the Central Marine Engine Works crane, as well as the Sheer Legs (an earlier giant crane) were demolished (Plate 39 p. 134). It was a shrunken and impoverished Hartlepool which amalgamated in 1967. The only employment boosts were North Sea oil exploration and car imports.

In relation to the closure of shipyards and collieries and the contemporaneous decline of the fishing industry, all of them beyond national and some beyond international control, municipal boroughs were helpless beyond begging or demanding aid. Hartlepool Corporation could and did collaborate in the development of the Trading Estate from 1946 but it is apparent from the lists of demolitions, new houses and new streets that reconstruction on a massive scale was the top priority. As far as possible Hartlepool was being rebuilt, as Max Lock had recommended.

What of the Central Estate, which he had condemned to obliteration? In 1952 permission was given for a Royal Observer Corps post to be erected on Spion Kop and in 1953 the rebuilt Central United Club was officially opened. In 1955 permission was given for a sawmill on Hart Road, in 1958 for the erection of a grandstand at the New Rovers Field, and in 1965 for workshops on Spion Kop, when it was levelled and seeded. On the other hand in 1950 the farm labourers' cottages at Low Warren Farm were demolished and in 1951 Clyde Street was closed. The Rope Works (Plate 82 p. 249) closed in 1958 and the Creosote Works in 1964. In 1961 the Golf Club was moved a mile further north to High Warren and away from the expanding Periclase works and in 1965 St. Barnabas Hall was demolished. As an integral part of Hartlepool the Central Estate could expect nothing else.

The union of the two Hartlepools in 1967, important and sensible though it was in economic and administrative terms, could not alter long term trends. In that very year Warren Terrace and Beaumont Street were demolished and so were the battery on Spion Kop (in the interest of a new factory by Steetley) and the west side of Union Road. In 1972 the old Destructor chimney on Spion Kop was demolished. Even more emphatic was the demolition of Throston Bridge (Plate 18 p. 37) in 1973 which symbolised the death of the link to the collieries (of 1835) and the staple of coal exports. Blackhall Colliery closed in 1981, Horden Colliery in 1986. In 1978 the demolition of housing became wholesale and in 1979 the great stone railway bridge across Hart (now West View) Road which had carried the line to Old Hartlepool was demolished. This destroyed the great triangle of embankments which had surrounded Hall's Low Warren Farm, leaving the iron bridge for the line from former West Hartlepool to the former collieries and Sunderland, looking at houses as far as the eye could see in place of the former countryside with its meadows, fields and allotments.

The "Klondyke" (Central) Hotel went in 1981, forty years after the death of C. T. Watson, and a few years before its centenary. In 1982 all but one of the kipper houses on West View (former Hart) Road were closed and Union Road was closed to traffic. Vincent Street, Hutton Street and Rokeby Street as well as Hart Road School, the only building of architectural merit apart from St. Barnabas Church on the estate, were demolished. After 1984 all that survived were houses on West View Road ("Railway Cottages") and what had been Romaine Park. Heortnesse Road, the former magic route to the North Sea and Sands, became a cul-de-sac when the railway arch was demolished in 1991. What remained of the railway embankment was planted with trees, most of which did not survive, but the greening of the Cement Works site showed that Max Lock's environmental suggestions were not wholly ignored. In 1989 a government grant of £500,000 to turn derelict land into a park was made and in 1996 £10.3m were added to improve the Headland - the "new" name for Old Hartlepool - including West View and the Central Estate. In 1987 the sixtieth anniversary of the West View Housing Estate was celebrated, although as will be recalled, the first West View houses date from the early 1920s. West View in the meanwhile had been nicknamed "Coney Island", which seemed to detach it from the Central Estate. Coney Island nevertheless valiantly maintains a sense of community with meetings and publications. In 1998 St. Barnabas Church was demolished, the last distinguishable symbol of what had been the old Central Estate.

Similar developments proceeded in both parts of the new Hartlepool from 1967. On the Headland the Queen's cinema was demolished (1967), the Swingbridge to Middleton (1968), the Palladium, having served out its time as a bingo hall (1969) demolished and Brougham Street Methodist Church closed. In 1972 it was the turn of the coal staiths and Galleys Field school and in 1976 the Comet Cinema in Northgate which, built in 1938, had never been opened as such, but during the war served less entertaining but perhaps more useful purposes. In 1977 the Henry Smith School was closed and in 1982 demolished, although its name was later transferred to a new comprehensive school in the West View area. In 1983 Richardson Westgarth's was demolished and, in 1987, St. Hilda's Hospital. Virtually nothing demolishable was left.

Demolition was no less rife in former West Hartlepool, which had already lost its Match Factory (by fire Plate 84 p. 248) in 1954 and its airport in 1957. In 1967 the Gaiety Cinema went, in 1968 the Swainson Dock was filled in and the Queen's Rink closed; in 1969 the partial demolition of Stockton Street and Church Street (main thoroughfares) began; in 1970 the Cerebos salt-mine at Greatham closed; in 1971 the chimney of the Paper Mills (closed in 1965) went and in 1972 the Northerns Cinema, also finally a bingo club, was demolished; in 1973 Christ's Church (Ward Jackson's creation) and the Wesley Church, both distinguished buildings in the very town centre, were closed; in 1974 the Empire (sometimes a cinema but primarily a theatre and built as such) was demolished; in 1976 the Water Works went and in 1977 the Steelworks, formerly a major employer, stopped production; in 1978 the Convent and in 1979 the breakwater, Ward Jackson's challenge to rival Liverpool, was offered for sale at £1.00 *(sic)*. In 1980 the Water Works tower, another distinctive landmark, went; in 1981 the Middleton Gasometer went and in 1982 the Tramsheds were demolished. By this time the old town centre of Lynn St. and Musgrave St., etc., had also disappeared. What was left?

Quite a lot: the positive side to so much demolition gave unprecedented opportunity for archaeological excavations. 1963 witnessed Romano-British remains, 1964 a Bronze Age burial urn, 1967 and 1968 medieval kilns and Saxon timber dwellings, worked flints, stone coffins and pottery. In 1969 the Gas Works site produced more late medieval pottery and the spring on the Fish Sands - the origin of Hartlepool's 18th century claim to be a spa - an iron bound wooden pipe and several pieces of planking. In 1970 an iron arrow head was found, in 1972 a skeleton from 2700 BC, in 1973 medieval wall foundations, in 1975 flint tools and in 1976 a Saxon graveyard. A

12th century dock was revealed in 1981 and, beneath the demolished Henry Smith School, the church of the medieval Franciscan Friary in 1982. A jet necklace was found in 1985 from c. AD 2-300 and in 1987 a rectangular house from the Iron Age, and round houses from the Bronze Age. In 1995 the skeleton of a red deer killed with a wooden spear from c.3000 BC and in 1994 a fish weir from c. 3700 BC confirmed that Hartlepool had been inhabited from Neolithic times. Subsequent discoveries may, as they doubtless should, discover Palaeolithic forbears. It is, however, quite certain that the Hartlepool monkey - if there ever was one - did not drop from local trees.

There were also personal achievements of more than local note. Hartlepool-born dance-band singer Chick Henderson's recording of "Begin the Béguine" in 1939 was the first to sell more than a million copies (Plates 85-86 p. 248). He was killed in action in 1944. In 1952 Teddy Gardner was publicly honoured for his British, British Empire and European Flyweight boxing championships and in 1965 the injured Hartlepools United footballer, Brian Clough, was appointed manager and achieved promotion to the Third Division for the team before departing to a long and distinguished sequence of First Division managerships.

It was in 1957 that Reg. Smyth(e), born in Union Road on the Central Estate on July 10 1917, responding to an invitation to create a cartoon character for the "Daily Mirror" with "northern" appeal, created "Andy Capp", the unemployed and unemployable lay-about who, with his long-suffering wife Flo, ultimately became world-famous, uniquely (so far) the only Central Estatian - or for that matter Hartlepudlian - to do so (Appendix H, p. 288). "Andy" appeared in 1600 newspapers - in the "Mail" from 1991 - including 100 in USA as well as in China, Russia ("Isvestia") and Turkey. He should be commemorated with a plaque in Union Road.

In 1967 it was confirmed that there would be a Hartlepool nuclear power station (Plate 87 p. 249). In 1968 the new Throston Grange Estate expanded and in 1969 construction began of a new General Hospital (alongside the former Howbeck Workhouse), a new College of Further Education and a new College of Art were opened. In 1970 no less than HRH Princess Anne opened the Middleton Grange Shopping Centre to replace demolished shopping facilities, and in 1972 the Duchess of Kent opened the new General Hospital. Hartlepool was, not unsurprisingly, voted Floral City of Britain jointly with Bath in the same year. Civic pride had revived but did not, presumably, swell when the Local Government Act expelled it from the County of Durham and forced it into the new County of Cleveland, carved out from the old North Riding of Yorkshire, in 1974. Eligibility for grants from Teesside may, however, have been beneficial, although in 1987 the Boundary Commission refused Hartlepool permission to quit Cleveland. In 1976 there was an additional industrial estate at Tofts Farm and in 1977 the "Mail", renamed from "Northern Daily Mail" and transformed from a broadsheet to a tabloid in 1959, celebrated its centenary. New horizons were heralded in 1979 with the arrival of HMS "Warrior", Britain's first armoured battleship (though a sailing ship) to be restored, a substitute for shipbuilding. More promising, in 1989, was the sanctioning of a marina, and in 1992 an undertaking by the Imperial War Museum to build a maritime division there. This was, unfortunately cancelled in 1995 but by then HM the Queen had opened the Marina and Maritime Heritage Centre. In 1994 the new Historic Quay and a pub and restaurant at "Jackson's Wharf" were added. By this time Hartlepool had a new Central Library in York Road, in the following year a superstore at the Marina itself and in 1996 the refurbished Christ Church in the refurbished Church Street became the new Art Gallery, with its neighbouring old Library and municipal offices also refurbished into modern offices. The old "Northern Daily Mail" office and works had been demolished and, much enlarged and modernised, rebuilt in situ, and the old Wesleyan Chapel, so long a conspicuous ruin, had become an indoor swimming pool, fitness club, pub, nightclub and fast food outlet.

Clearly there had been a fundamental rethink of the town's basic orientation from manufacture to tourism, a turning back of the clock to pre-industrial Hartlepool's role as seaside resort, not only on the Headland and at Seaton Carew but in the very town centre itself. What in the 1920s and 30s had been a desperate but ill-funded palliative to mass unemployment in the form of relief work, had become the new pivot of the town's economy. Having demolished and partially rebuilt the old town centres, the city fathers, aided by their MPs, had successfully attracted the necessary resources of millions of pounds to finance a transformation. This proceeded irrespective of the 1974 and 1996 changes of county boundaries, although the disappearance of the County of Cleveland without re-incorporation into the County of Durham made Hartlepool a county in its own right in the latter year. The new Civic Centre in Grange Road which symbolised the union of the Hartlepools in 1967, which was opened by HM the Queen in 1977, became the sole centre of local authority. The succession of Peter Mandelson in 1992, to Ted Leadbitter as Member for Hartlepool, may have helped.

The changes were much more visible in what had been West Hartlepool than on the Headland because there was more space and even more to be done. The Headland docks could not accommodate a marina as well as continue to function as a port (Plate 88 p. 249). There was no room for the palatial Bingo Hall, Watersports Centre, Bandstand, multi-screen Cinema, Virtual Reality Centre and fast-food chicken and pizza outlets, all of which were rapidly added to the resort attractions. Even less was there room for the Marina Asda superstore which must have competed with the refurbished and expanded Middleton Grange Shopping Centre. The Headland had to be content with a Social Club and the restoration and resiting of the 1856 Crimean War Trophy - a muzzle-loading gun - from Sebastopol, in 1991. I am, in this first year of the Third Millennium, happy to learn that the balance of funding is visibly being restored.

The Central Estate fared better. The Council had ignored Max Lock and rebuilt it. By 1980 replacement houses for former residents were built on the Old Boys Field and the former Propyard, and in 1989 there was a grant of £500,000 for the creation of a Central Estate Park. Later additions from Union Road to the West View Road - Lancaster (formerly Cleveland) Road junction was planned more spaciously and to higher building standards, aimed at the more expensive private (mortgage) level. This may or may not have promoted the growth of neighbourliness between the two parts, but survival was the name of the game.

It was in 1970 that I myself revisited Hartlepool after a gap of some seventeen years and I naturally sought the reasons, indeed the justification for the destruction of what I by now realised had been a good place in which to be born and nurtured. I canvassed the views of surviving friends and their parents and heard little but angry lamentation. It could and should have been avoided, but wrong if not wicked decisions had, it was said, been made by the old Borough Council. It was agreed that because of the war many people had left and would never return but it was contended that enough remained to ensure survival of the community. Had the resources poured into destruction been expended on resuscitation all could have been well. I was also assured by John Ward himself that when he left the Central in 1956 it was still thriving and viable (Plate 89 p. 252).

The Council was faulted for dumping problem families on the Estate after compulsory purchase of land and buildings had been decreed, and for boarding up windows and doors when houses were vacated. "Look at Bell Street", they told me, and certainly the houses remaining on the seaward half of the street from Arch Street to Hart Road were still in very good repair and spotlessly maintained. The same was true of some houses in Arch Street (including our own at No. 72) as well as those which were preserved in West View Road but by now the process of destruction was clearly irreversible. Fired with indignation I sought out and questioned a retired Borough Sanitary Inspector who had served from 1936 to 1976. What he said was that improvement grants had been offered but failed: owner occupiers not interested, and "up and downers" with a common tap, yard, and WC (sic) were unsuitable. Installation of baths would have been difficult and indoor WCs impossible. So, although he did not mention it, would have been the provision of gardens. There had been no option but clearance by Compulsory Purchase Order. Union Road, he said, had been the worst.

I now think he was right. It is true that similar housing was preserved in former West Hartlepool (and elsewhere) but it is (or was when I last saw it in 1998) conspicuously inadequate by contemporary standards. By those standards the rebuilt Central Estate survives, rejuvenated, unlike other "villages" within the old towns like Stranton and Middleton which have been totally obliterated from once thriving communities. Neighbourliness must survive even in post-industrial society but whether there are any survivors or descendants of the heydays of the 1920s and 30s only the sequence of decennial census releases from 2001 to 2101, in the absence of Ward's Directories, will reveal. There must be some, as well as newly-establishing "dynasties". Perhaps another local-born historian will resume the fascinating search.

As already observed, in one sense there was nothing unique about the Central Estate. New towns and new suburbs have been created from Neolithic times onwards, especially during the Industrial Revolution, and all must have shared many or most of the experiences of amalgamation and assimilation described. What was unique was the precise time, position and circumstances of the coming together and the rapid creation of a community. As old Hartlepool-born Mrs. Kettlewell said: "The Central was a Village". She might have added: "because that's what its people wanted it to be, and made it".

Appendices

Appendix A - Glossary

Dialect.

Although firmly located on the North East coast between Northumbrian Geordieland and North Yorkshire, and therefore having a native twang somewhere between the two, Hartlepool was also a port in which much of the population was seafaring. Foreign sailors (etc.) frequently settled and brought their Scandinavian or German, etc., names, accents and vocabularies with them. Even more important, when the docks and railways were built there was a large and permanent influx of Irish labourers with their families. As detailed in Chapter 2, the Central Estate population was widely recruited from many native and foreign sources, and although there was a predominant recognisable local lingua franca, common to Hartlepool and West Hartlepool, usages could be very local, certainly between the Central Estate and Hartlepool town (as shown below) and possibly from street to street. Some oddities may have been individual neologisms, repeated because their originators were bullies. For instance it would not have paid Stephenson St. boys to pronounce "Robinson" as other than "Robberson" and Robertson as other than Rob'nson: JL's displeasure would have been palpable.

Consequently Hartlepool was an island in a sea of permanent accents and, like Liverpool and Hull differed in vocabulary and pronunciation from inland areas not more than three miles away. In the colliery villages the musical quality of Geordie persisted but in Hartlepool the tone was flat and pronunciation emphatic. Most pronounced was the ending of words ending in "a" or "er", e.g. . pianner, mutheh, sisteh: Anner, Berther, Steller; Aatheh, Chahlie, Petch. Aspirates were always dropped and elisions were crude, with the "r" sound predominant; e.g. "get on" would be "gerron", "get away" would be "gerraway and "put him" "purrim". The letters "ing" were always shortened to "'n". Vowels also were emphatically flat: e.g. "butter" was "b<u>u</u>tter" not "battah", and "matter" was "matteh" not "mettah" . The glottal stop was not used. Double negatives were obligatory: e.g. "I 'aven' got none", "'E won' give yer nowt". Emphasis was emphasised by vowel distortion, e.g. "'Tes naat!" for "'Tis not!". Irony was endemic. Almost every statement was deliberately exaggerated or diminished.

Anyone who violated any of these rules would be persecuted as "stuck up", i.e. a show-off, but there was a sort of bilingualism between street talk and talk in school. Double negatives or the use of slang words were punished and words ending in "ing" had so to be pronounced. All the teachers at the Elementary Schools were of local origin and it was only at the grammar school or via the radio that non-northern ("posh") accents were heard.

* Not used in downtown Hartlepool.

v. Todd's Geordie Words and Phrases: Frank Graham: ISBN 0 85983 103 5: 1977

A **adrumal**: wilful(?) mispronunciation of "admiral".
Ah!: "I!": Geordie "Aa"
Ah never: I did not.
'Amsam: helter-skelter.
Anty: Anthony.
(H)'airy werm: (worm): caterpillar.
'alf a mo: wait a minute.
'ardluns: hardly.
'arf a dollar: half-a-crown: silver coin worth two shillings & sixpence: 15p.
'ave a lend: borrow.
Autocar: the train that ran between Hartlepool and West Hartlepool. In the 20s it was an engine between two carriages: in the 30s it was a single carriage with its own small steam engine underneath the wheels, made by Sentinel.
Awwy!: "Come on!": pronounced "A(h)wee!": cf Geordie "Howway".
Aye: Yes!
Aye aye: a greeting, presumably of nautical origin. Tone of voice could also make it a warning.

B **bad:** poorly: Geordie "baad".
bairn: small child: Scottish and Geordie
***banana legs:** bandy-legged.
bairn: baby, child: Scottish.
***balley:** diminutive of "ball".
***banana crane:** swan-necked mechanical crane: sited near the Harbour entrance.
***bantie:** bantam (hen or cock).
bare 'ammer: naked.
bare buff: naked.
bat: blow (e.g. "Gi'm a bat in the gob"): Geordie
***Barny's:** St. Barnabas Church.
beaut: beauty, e.g. "What a beaut!" - e.g. a butterfly or a fish.
big fish: cod or haddock.
bile: boil: painful sore: Geordie
***bimmeller:** good, first-rate.
blackclocks: black beetles: Geordie.
blow: pronounced to rhyme with "How": exclamation of frustration.
blower: a sheet of metal placed in front of a kindling fire to create a draught. A sheet of newspaper spread over it increased the area from which air was excluded and increased the draught.
blummun': blooming: usually ironic and pejorative: e.g. "Yeh blummun' rotter!".
bob: shilling (now 5p, then 12 pence).
bobby-dazzler: brightly coloured: also Geordie.
bog: lavatory: defecate.
boily: bread soaked in hot water or milk: for invalids or after total tooth extraction: replacement by false teeth was delayed for months to permit gums to harden.
booler: iron hoop for trundling, with a stick or iron hook.
bray: talk, chatter.
bray: thrash: e.g. "A(h)ll bray you": "Me da'll bray us": Geordie.
brazzent: brazen: referring to girls only.

bubboo(s): sweet(s): presumably derived from French 'bon-bon'.
buggerlugs: a term of endearment or reproach according to tone of voice.
bullet: sweet, i.e. sweetmeat, confection: Geordie.
bulliker: large spherical marble: presumably from 'ball', with hint of 'bollock'.
bustin f'r a: desperately needing to urinate.
but!: conjunction, but placed at the end, not the beginning of a sentence, e.g. 'Can't see you Thursday. See you Friday, but!': also Geordie (i.e. Newcastle) usage.
By!: polite form of oath, omitting e.g. "Christ!": used by mothers rather than boys.

C

cack: cacka: excrement.
***cakey:** diminutive of 'cake'.
canny: strongly approve, right, good: e.g. 'canny lad/lass' - nice boy/girl: Geordie. Scottish/Northumbrian
catty: catapult.
carbine: calcium carbide (to generate acetylene for bicycle lamp).
***Cementies:** Cement Works.
charrer: pronounced "sharrer": char á banc.
Chasey: chasing: a game: identical with "tiggy" i.e. "tag".
chuck: bread, food: cf W. Hartlepool "scran": colliery "bait".
chuck: throw.
chuck: term of endearment.
Chucky: diminutive of Charles, Charlie.
chuddy: chewing gum.
ciggy card: ciggies: cigarette cad(s).
clag: stick on e.g. with saliva: Geordie.
claggy: sticky: Geordie
clart: damp or wet dirt, soil, etc.
clart on: mess about.
clart'n about: messing about: Geordie.
clarty: dirty, muddy.
clemmy: brick or stone missile.
clip: clout: Geordie.
Cock!: boy: form of address to a boy, frequently disparaging e.g. "Watch it, Cock!".
cock-eyed: cross-eyed.
cog: a hoist, e.g. by proffering a shoulder to a would-be wall-climber.
Connie: Cornelius.
cossy: swimming costume.
***cowbag:** rotter.
cow's platter: cow dung.
cowd: cold
coxarusa: Hartlepool game in which boys ran across between end lines with initially only one to stop them; by means of a rugby tackle.
cuddy: cuddy whiffer in West Hartlepool: left-handed.

D

da(h): dad, daddy, father e.g. "Me da".
Deelevo: game: see below: derived from "deliver"?
dafty: fathead, foolish person
dicky deadeye: crack-shot with stone: or the missile used.
diddler: threepenny bit: a small silver coin.

Diddler: nickname for an undersized boy: cf "Tich" in West Hartlepool.
***dilly:** silly.
Dilly: Hilda.
***dingy:** mad: pronounced with hard "g".
dogger: small green or immature crab.
dollar: five shilling coin: five shillings.
Ducky: the inevitably nickname of anyone named "Swan".
dummy tit: child's comforter, usually coated with syrup or treacle.
dumper: cigarette end.

E

Eeee!: expression of disgust, disbelief.
***Everys:** claim for every possible privilege in a game of marbles: cancelled by earlier cry of "Nowts!"

F

fa'ther: accent on first syllable: FAther, rhyming with 'gather'.
fesst: first
fessy: first: cf seccy (second), thirdy, etc. Shouted by whoever caimed first to have spotted the Autocar, or an aeroplane or whatever.
fewndral: funeral.
fit as a lop: fit as a flea: Hartlepool, not Central Estate usage
flamer: very wicked person: Hartlepool, not Central Estate usage.
flower: pet name for a little girl: e.g. "My flower!"
flat iron: the simplest form of iron: a piece of iron shaped like a perpendicular Gothic window, about 9 inches long, with an iron handle superimposed. It was heated on the top of the oven and operated with a thick wrapping of cloth round the handle for protection against burning. Many households had two which were used in succession, one heating whilst the other was used. A superior alternative consisted of a hollow iron body into which shaped cast iron blocks, heated to redness inside the fire, could be placed in succession. By 1925 gas-fired irons were available and by 1930 electric irons. It is pertinent to recall that by 1930 there were also light aluminium wringers with small (2") diameter rubber rollers to replace huge Victorian mangles with their 6" diameter wooden rollers and their huge and dangerously exposed cogged wheels.
***flashie:** flash-lamp: torch.
fly: sharply clever.
***Fly Jack and be Gone:** game.
fond: foolish: only used together with the word "brazzent" (brazen), e.g. "She's brazzent fond!"
front-room: sitting room or parlour as distinct from kitchen or bedroom. also Geordie.
***Full Foller:** shout in game of marbles to prevent "Everys".
funnun': funning, joking: Geordie "funnin".

G

gaffer: boss
"Game's poxed!": cry of foul play.
Garn!: "Go on!": exclamation of disbelief.
get: arrive: come: e.g. "She can't get!" = "She won't be able to come".
get/git: unpleasant person: prob. "bastard".
get wrong: get into trouble.

gi'e: give; e.g. "Gi'es a bullet!": Give me a sweet: also Geordie.
gill: (pronounced "jill"): half a pint.
***glasseyes:** wearer of spectacles: derogatory: Hartlepool equivalent was "four eyes".
gob: mouth: presumably Irish origin.
gobby: mouthy; too talkative.
God's 'onour!: solemn affirmation: "On my oath": usually marked by finger drawn across throat.
goes with: is fond of: boy's initials followed by girl's: chalked on wall or fence: pejorative: always vehemently denied and almost certainly untrue in any case
goke: the core of an apple: "Gi'e 's 'e' goke!" was the invariable greeting to anyone eating an apple. cf Geordie "gowk".
***Golden Things:** game; see below.
***gospel's e's gob:** he's greedy.
gran: grandfather/grandmother.
Greenland: border with West Hartlepool: gasworks, railway embankment, level crossing: probably ironic: cf "Egypt", "California", "Spion Kop".
gritty big: great big.

H

(h)amsam: at random; wantonly extravagant, helter-skelter.
(h)'oney: endearment for both sexes: Geordie "hinny".
(h)'oss muck: horse manure. There was a great deal of it on every street and road and enthusiastic gardeners (or their children) collected it in buckets or small barrows for its fertilising richness, thus saving labour for street sweepers.

I

***Illy Illy Arky:** game.
Ironies: ball bearings used in bulliker games
***Itchybay:** game: hopscotch.

J

***Jack Show the Light:** game.
jammy: easy, lucky.
jamrag: sanitary towel.

K

kali: effervescent sweetmeat.
kep: catch: also Geordie.
Keps: catches: a game with a small soft-ball.
kid: boy: e.g. "ou' kid" = my brother.
kidder: younger or elder brother: any other person addressed.
kidcatcher: school attendance officer.

L

lace: thrash; e.g. "Me dad'll lace us!"
***Lampy:** nickname for lamplighter.
lass: e.g. "ou' lass": sister, wife.
lav: lavatory.
leather: a strap.
leathered: beaten (with a strap).
Levo: game: see below.
like: slight emphasis on preceding statement: e.g.. A(h) went t' Sunday School, like".
***Little Apple:** Little Chapel: Primitive Methodist Church on Hart Road: derisory.
longstand: small boys were sent into a plumber's or ironmongery shop to ask for a "longstand". The shopkeeper would tell him to "Wait!", which he did, until the penny

dropped.
loopy: mad: also Geordie.
lucker: look here: also Geordie "lukka".

M

mam: mammie: mother.
me: my: e.g. "Me mutheh!"
mebbies: may be, perhaps.
Mick: Roman Catholic. "Left-footers" in West Hartlepool, because the left foot was put forward in genuflexion.
mind!: verbal exclamation mark: e.g. "A(h) won' be there t'morrer, mind!": = "Don't forget!"
mingy: pronounced "minjy": mean: stingy.
moggy: cat.
***moonlight moggy:** cat.
***Montykitty:** game: cf Geordie "Moont the cuddy", ie "Mount the horse".
mucky mixture: derisory reference to cheap sweets.
my oath!: affirmation of truth.

N

nab: catch.
nark: annoy: e.g. "That narks ye(h)!".
naw: no
never: did not do: e.g. "A(h) never did nowt! = I didn't do anything.
nixey: nothing.
nixey push: nothing.
nob: head.
not 'alf: not half: strong emphasis e.g.: "Did yer get the cane?" "Not 'alf!"
nowt: nothing

O

oit: pronounced oyt: oik: foolish person: e.g. "Ye(h) daft oit!".
'ole: sexual intercourse.
'(h)op ut!: hop it!: clear off!
'oss muck: horse manure
owld girl: mother: not disrespectful.
owld feller: father: not disrespectful.
ou' lass: my wife/sister.
owt: anything

P

Pallad: Palladium: Hartlepool cinema.
pagged out: out of breath.
pease pudd'n 'n' ducks: take-away meal, usually served from back doors in back lanes: made from ham-flavoured split peas or polenta and faggots: i.e. food for the poor.
peg leg: wooden leg.
penk: nose.
***penny bebber:** boy's small, peaked cap: school cap: cf large peaked cap, also worn by workmen; and by some women, notably fishermen's wives.
pess ahff!: piss off!: an example of emphasis by vowel distortion.
pillick!: rude dismissal: e.g. "Pillick yer tits!"
pisspottical: stupid: West Hartlepool usage.
pit yacker: collier.

pittle: urinate: also Geordie.
play war: complain: rebuke, verbally chastise.
plodge: paddle.
ploat: pluck: hit: also Geordie.
plonker: audible kiss.
pocket billiards: playing with own testicles, ie masturbating.
***Polly Polly Wallflowers:** song accompanying a game.
pooly: poorly, indisposed.
prop ends: short off-cuts from pit props, hawked for kindling from back door to back door.
pullet: hen: presumably from French poulet.
pully-up mat: carpet made on sacking from strips of cloth pulled through and knotted with a hook. The sacking was stretched to tightness in a home-made wooden frame.
Puss in the Corner: game.

Q

Queenie: game played in Hartlepool, not on Central Estate.
quid: £1 sterling.

R

rag out: angry.
Raggy Arsed Old Buggers: R.A.O.B.: Royal & Ancient Order of Buffaloes.
ramsammy: at random, wantonly extravagant, helter-skelter.
Ring o' Roses: game with song, possibly dating from Black death 1349. (See Games below).
raspberry: rude noise made by blowing through lips on protruding tongue, with emphatic dismissive gesture.
rasper: fart
***raz:** rude dismissal: contraction of "raspberry": e.g. "Give 'im the raz!".
roundy: rounded: only applied to "roundy coal", a piece of coal rounded like a pebble by wave action.
rotter: unpleasant, dishonest person.

S

Sammy: possibly "Psalmy": the nickname of the Rev. F. T. Salter who wrote a weekly column in the "Northern Daily Mail".
sandshoes: gym shoes, pumps.
Sante(h!): Santa (Claus).
scabby: repellent: no reference to strikebreaking.
scallion: scally onion.
seccy: second: cf fessy, thirdy, fourthy...: the first one to spot e.g. the Autocar or an aeroplane would shout: "Fessy autocar!". "Seccy" etc would follow on.
Seppy: Septimus.
Sham: Hartlepool, but not Central Estate, game: see below.
***shigs:** shares.
Shotty In: game of football on small pitch: see Games below.
shuggyshoes: fairground swing-boats, possibly suggested by shape which resembled a large shoe: cf Geordie "shuggyboats".

Sido: pronounced "Sydo(h)": nickname for Sidney.
skelp: verb: to skin or scalp: e.g. "A'(h)'ll skelp yeh!"
skew-whiff: lop-sided: also Geordie.
skinch: flinch: down Hartlepool, however, it meant a dispensation from certain rules.
slop: police constable: also Geordie.
sneck: door-latch: also Geordie.
sod: a term of abuse. As with all the four and six letter words, it was learned and used by small boys without knowing what it meant.
***snottybob:** dirty-nosed.
snot rag: handkerchief.
soapy: stupid.
soda lunch: effervescent sweetmeat: powder sucked through a tube of licorice from a cylindrical paper container: accompanied by two small thin cakes an inch in diameter.
spelk: small sliver of wood, usually requiring removal from a finger with a needle: also Geordie.
split: verb: to betray.
spuggy: sparrow: also Geordie.
***Spy Sheep:** game: see below.
spud: potato: fathead.
starved: very cold.
steelies: ball bearings used in "bulliker" games.
***"Step Over the Cotton, Please":** game: see below
struggling bar: on their first day at work in the shipyard or engine works beginners were sent to the Tool Store to ask for the "struggling bar". They were given a hefty piece of iron or steel which was rejected, time after time, because it wasn't heavy enough... until the penny dropped.
stumer: fathead.
suck 'ole: toadie, sycophant.
suck-in: deceit.
suck up: crawl, flatter.
swaller: swallow:exclusively the inhalation of tobacco smoke: e.g. "Can ye do the swaller?" - a point of honour: a whole cigarette had to be inhaled without vomiting.

T

tab: cigarette: also Geordie..
tab-end: cigarette-end.
taffy: toffee: also Geordie.
taddy: tadpole.
***tanner meg:** sixpence halfpeny.
tarry wagga: rope impregnated with creosote: glowing end used to ignite fireworks.
tart: girl: sweetheart: common girl but NOT a whore.
tash: moustache.
taataas: goodbyes: also walks: e.g. "The bairn's going taataas.: also Geordie.
taty: potato: fathead.
"'Tes naat!": It is not!!: an example of emphasis by vowel distortion.
***Thee Jolly Sailor Boys:** game; see below.
Tiggy: game: tag: see below.

***Tippy Finger:** game; see below.
tishy paper: tissue paper
tittle: mild expletive: e.g. "Garn, tittle!" = "Get off with you!"
***Tonker:** nickname.
toss off: masturbate.
tret: treated; e.g. "She tret me rotten!": also Geordie.
***Tug o'Bay:** game: see below
tungy: (tunjy): turnip.
tussy pegs: infantile teeth: baby talk.
twist: ice cream cone.

U

us: me: e.g. "Don' 'it us".

W

wet week: (wet weak?): description of an inadequate person.
what fettle?: how are you?: also Geordie.
whey aye: of course: also Geordie.
window breaker: peg top with large top and thin cylindrical spindle: airborne when struck hard with whip.
won' 'alf: won't half: e.g. "'A won' 'alf get wrong!" - "I won't half get into trouble!"
***won't can: wouldn't could:** won't/wouldn't be able to...
wot cheer?: greeting: possibly also a warning: "Watch 'ere!"

Y

yarn: dirty story.
yarpin' on: harping on: going on and on about something.
ye(h): you.
yeh: yes.
yesst: yeast.
young 'un: older or younger brother.

Appendix B - Rhymes

Ah hah, ah hah, ah hee,
I saw three ladies pee,
They peed so fast
They made me laugh,
Ah hah, ah hah, ah hee.

Annie Buck
'Ad a fuck,
In a truck,
Full o' muck.

A sol, a sol, a soldier I will be,
To fight for the co(u)nt, to fight for the co(u)nt.
To fight for the co(u)nt-ery,
Two pis, two pis, two pistols on my knee,
F' cu, f' cu, f' curiosity.

- presumably learned from fathers or brothers who had fought in the 1914-18 War.

Bulliker Bill from (H)averton (H)ill,
Never worked and never will.

- Haverton Hill, near Stockton-on-Tees, had a shipyard at which some Hartlepudlians were employed.

I am the ghost of Joshua Harold,
I was stabbed in the night by a rusty carrot!

If a feller wants a job,
Shave the whiskers of 'is nob,
Follow the swallow back 'ome.

Ikey Mo' the King of the Jews,
Sold 'is wife for a pair o' shoes,
When the shoes began to wear,
Ikey Mo' began to swear.

I slit the sheet and the sheet slit me,
Slit was the sheet that was slit by me.

- dictated slowly to an innocent who had to repeat it slowly until word perfect, but followed by the command to recite it at top speed, it earned a rebuke for "swearing" if the spoonerism erred into a four letter word. In the same category was:

I chased a bug around a tree,
I'll get his blood -
'E knows Ah will.

In nineteen 'undred and six,
Me fa'ther was choppun' sticks,
He missed the stick,

And 'it 'is prick,
In nineteen 'undred and six.

or:

...'E missed the block,
And 'it 'is cock...

The Lord said unto Moses,
All Jews shall have big noses,
Except Aaron, and he shall have a square 'un,
Except Peter, and he shall have a gas-o-meter.

Mick said to Mike:
'Can y'r mother ride a bike
With her feet on the handle bars?,
With her tits in a sling,
And a finger up her thing,
And a bell up her arse
Going ding!, ding!, ding!'

Once upon a time,
The dogs shit lime,
The elephants chowed tobaccer.

There was a young lady of Spain,
Who cocked her leg over a train,
The train went canny,
And tickled her fanny,
There was a young lady of Spain.

....Where has he gone to?: he's gone down the lane,
'Ere's Daddy Fordham coming with the cane.

-"Daddy Fordham" was the "kidcatcher" ie School Attendance Inspector.

Appendix C - Songs

Ailey Pailey. "Christmas" "carol", sung by waifs hoping for pennies: a mournful ditty sung with great feeling.

"Ailey, pailey, snow on the ground, (Hartlepool version: "It hailed, it hailed, it snowed...)
The wind blew bitter and cold,
A poor young sailor boy, tattered in rags,
Came up to a lady's door.
The lady sat at the window so high,
And fixed her eyes upon him,
'Come in, come in, my kind-hearted child,
You shan't go out any more,
For as long as I live, shelter I give
To a poor young sailor boy'.
'My father, my father was lost on the sea,
My mother she wept and she cried,
She died of a broken heart,
And left me behind.'
'For as long as I live, shelter I give
To a poor young sailor boy!'

"'Oo's that at the door, oo's that at the door?",
Said the fair young maiden,
"Oo's that at the door, oo's that at the door?",
Said the fair young maiden.
"It's Bulliker Bill, it's Bulliker Bill,
It's Bullikker Bill the sailor,
It's Bulliker Bill, it's Bulliker Bill,
It's Bulliker Bill the sailor".
"O lay on the mat, O lay on the mat",
Said the fair young maiden...
"Bugger the mat, Ah can't fuck that,"
Said Bulliker Bill the sailor...
"It lies between me thighs",
Said the fair young maiden...
"And what's between yer thighs?",
Said Bulliker Bill the sailor...
"A nice pin cushion",
Said the fair young maiden...
"And I've got a pin that'll stick in yer cushion",
Said Bulliker Bill the sailor...
"And what if we get a kid?",
Said the fair young maiden...
"We'll strangle the bugger, and fuck for another",
Said Bulliker Bill the sailor...
"And what if the police get t' know?",
Said the fair young maiden...

"Bugger the police and fuck the Force",
Said Bulliker Bill the sailor...

Bye-bye Blackbird: a parody using the same tune.

There was a man, 'e was no good,
'E took a girlie in a wood,
Bye-bye, blackbird;
Sucked 'er fingers, sucked 'er thumb,
Sucked 'er belly, sucked 'er bum,
Bye bye, blackbird!

The Corporation Muck-Cart.

The corporation muck-cart, was full up to the brim,
The corporation driver fell in, and couldn't swim;
He sank to the bottom, just like a little stone,
He swam to the top, just like a little dog.
They laid him on a stretcher, they laid him on a bed,
They rubbed 'is belly with 'alf a clemmy, and this is what he said:
"Rule Britannia, Britannia rules the waves,
Britons never, never, never, shall be slaves".

Horden version:

"My father 'ad a bull dog, it's name was "Dirty Dick".
It died of influenza and a gumboil on its prick".

Go to Shields before yer go to Jarrer,
Only tuppence'apenny in the boat,
Fried fish, potato chips, saveloys and polony,
Donkeys on the sands only penny a ride.

Sung to the tune of "Go to sleep, my little piccaninny". Shields was North (or South) Shields and Jarrer was Jarrow. A West Hartlepool version was:

Go to Shields, to Tynemouth and to Jarrer,
It's only tuppence ha'penny in the boat,
Fried fish, taty chips, sausages and polony
Your Mammie's little illy-billy coo!"

Ol' King Cole was a merry old soul,
A merry old soul was 'e.
'E called for a light in the middle o' the night,
To go on the WC.
The light shone on the closet door,
The candle took a fit,
Ol' King Cole fell down the 'ole,
And swallered a bucket of shit.
"Oh bring me back my candle.
Oh bring me back my light,
Oh bring me back my shovel.
To shovel away the shite".

Cowardy, cowardy custard,
Three bags o' mustard!

Ha-ha-ha, ih-he-he,
Elephants's eggs up a rhubarb tree,
Follow the swallow, back 'ome!"

If a feller wants a job,
Shave the whiskers off 'is nob,
Follow the swallow, back 'ome.
- "Follow the Swallow" was a song hit of the early 1920s.

I've seen it, I've seen it,
I've been right between it,
The 'airs on 'er dicky dido
Reach down to 'er knees.

(eg) "Jacky Woolford" is a funny 'un,
Got a face like a scally onion,
Got a nose like a bruised tomato,
And legs like pit props."

- "pork chops" in West Hartlepool which had no perpetually visible stacks of pit props. Sung to the tune "The Ash Grove."

The Lord Mayor of Hartlepool
Was walking on the shore,
When he came across a funny sight
He'd never seen before.
There was this little feller,
Sitting on the sand,
Holding a banana in his little hairy hand.

Obviously a West Hartlepool song referring to the (alleged) hanging of the monkey by Hartlepool fishermen who (allegedly) believed it to be a French spy. Sung to the tune of "Darkies' Sunday School". See Appendix: "Who Hung the Monkey?"

Rain, rain power down,
Knock a little feller down.

As I was going to Strawberry Fair,
Singing, singing 'Buttercups and Daisies'...
Rifle, rifle, Tommy got 'is eyeful.
Rifle, rifle, ——— 'ad 'is 'ole.

Ripe bananas, like y'r father's
Cock y'r leg over the stool, boys!

Who's that knocking at the window?,
Who's that knocking at the door?
If it's ——— and his wife

We will stab him with a knife,
If you'll only put your shoulder to the wheel.

Vote, vote, vote for Mr ———,
Put old ——— in the dock,...
If you'll only put your shoulder to the wheel.

- sung at election time and the name used varied according to the party. A (superior?) West Hartlepool variant was:

Who's that knocking at the window,
Who's that knocking at the door?
If it's ——— let him in,
If it isn't' punch his chin,
And he won't come a-knocking any more!"

Appendix D - Physical "Accomplishments"

Belching: achievable at will by "swallowing the breath": competitive.

"Double-jointed" thumb: some boys, who claimed to be "double-jointed", could make the joint below the thumb protrude so far as to suggest that it had come out of its socket.

Funny faces: achieved by going cross-eyed, pulling down or pulling wide the eyelids, opening the mouth with upper teeth protruding.

Handstand: upside down on the pavement, followed by walking on hands.

Spitting: accuracy in pinpointing a spot or stone on the ground was prized and might even be praised. The accompaning comment was: "Pick the bones out o' that!"

TOH: a loud noise was made (competitively) by placing the tongue in the centre of the upper gum, with the mouth open, and making the "toh" sound as the tongue was thrust downwards.

Urinal competition: who could squirt highest up or over the wall.

Whistling: everyone could whistle but some boys could produce a piercing shriek with or without the use of a finger, or fingers, in the mouth.

Appendix E - Street Games

The number of games obviously devised for playing in streets was large and a tribute to the ingenuity and inventiveness of generations of children of the Industrial Revolution who had no immediate access to fields. From age 4 or so, children "played out" from after breakfast until dinner time, from after dinner until teatime and after teatime until bedtime. School was an interruption, although there were games at playtime in the school yard, but only from 9.00 a.m to 4.30 p.m.

Aeroplanes: these were made from sheets of folded notepaper and flown competitively. In a suitable breeze they could fly 50 metres or more.

Bay: The place in which games started and finished, usually on the pavement opposite a (gas) street lamp. The people in the adjoining house invariably protested - in vain in the long run - against the noise.

Bomber: On sale at a penny each were truncated cones of iron with a hemispherical top. They were split in halves and held together by a piece of string in diametrically opposed vertical grooves. The whole thing was barely an inch (2.5 cm) long. A percussion cap was placed in the middle and when dropped, usually immediately behind someone, it exploded with a loud bang.

Bulliker: on a corner piece of land a large marble was placed about 10cm from the wall and a ring in the ground marked round it. The competitors stood a metre or so away and tried to dislodge it with another large marble thrown full force. The missile then had to hit the wall. Those who had large steel ball bearings had a great advantage.

Car numbers: It was said and believed that anyone who collected a thousand registration plate letters and numbers of cars passing by and sent them to an address - unspecified - in Leeds would be given a bicycle. The fact that letters and numbers could be invented and that legs had been pulled came as a surprise.

Catapult: Elastic came from a variety of sources eg knickers, rubber bands, golf balls and toy shops. Missiles varied from paper pellets to stones. Removing the cover from a golf ball and winding onto a stick the elastic, first very thin and then twice as thick, took a long time. The core of white lead, encased in a thick black rubber ball, was very heavy for its size (about an inch in diameter) and was itself an effective missile.

Chasey: another name for "tiggy": tag.

Comb and Paper: a piece of paper, preferably grease-proof against saliva, placed on a comb and held against te pursed mouth, amplified the voice and gave it a brazen quality. One could only hum, but it was effective, especially when two or three hummed in unison. The idea was quickly taken up by toy manufacturers who dispensed with the comb and substituted a disc of plastic for the paper. Early versions were named "kazoos" and were distributed as "free gifts" by comic papers. Soon afterwards toymakers produced what were called "submarines", in which the periscope, which contained the plastic disc, was perpendicular to the mouth tube, with a thread and insert to keep it in place. Further refinements were trumpet shaped appendages which, however, made no ifference to the "music". From the early 30s onwards, most streets had so-called "jazz bands in which children, disguised in coloured "uniforms", paraded and marched behind banners and a stick-wielding strutting "leader" and blared out their versions of the latest tunes, always in unison: no redeeming harmony. Competitions were organised, as for example at the Hartlepool Carnival, and "trophies" awarded. The last parade I witnessed was in the early 1970s when the demolition of the Central Estate was taking place.

Cricket: "stumps" were chalked on a convenient wall on unbuilt corner sites. "Runs" were counted - and dismissals invariably disputed. Usually there were only two players.

Diabolo: girls only: the "devil on two sticks": a wooden bobbin shaped like converging cones was thrown upwards from a string between two sticks, one held in each hand. The bobbin had to be caught as it fell and re-launched as soon as possible.

English: a game of marbles for several boys in which marbles had to be holed in the ground from a distance of about a metre propelled by one forefinger. The winer was he who holed the last marble and then scooped the whole lot.

French: a game of marbles for several boys in which marbles had to be holed in the ground from about a metre propelled by one forefinger. Each player could claim all he had holed unti he missed.

Full Foller: a game of marbles for two, played along street gutters, with the drains as hazards. Using only a forefinger, the object was to hit the opponent's marble. If the marble was unplayable the player shouted "Everys" or "Strides" which allowed him to stride out the distance between the marbles and shoot from the equivalent distance on the other side, but if his opponent got in first with the cry "Full Foller" it had to be played from where it was. Since the trophy was only the one marble there was seldom an enduring fight.

Fly: a game of leapfrog in which the distance from the mark increased with every successful leap. The jumper was not allowed to use the shoulders of his crouching opponent as a fulcrum.

Fly Jack And Be Gone: a game of tag ("tiggy") in which the players each held on to a finger of he who was "on", who stood against the wall with his back to the others. If he said: 'Fly Jack and be - come back", the players were allowed to try to kick his backside whilst still holding on to a finger. As soon as he said the whole sentence the players ran off and the game of "tiggy" followed. The first one caught, who would be the next one "on", joined hands with him and they hunted together. Each one tagged joined the line until the last one was caught.

Footer: football, usually with a small soft ball. The "pitch" was either a backstreet, narrow enough to be the goal or an unbuilt corner plot on the wall of which a goal could be chalked. The coveted position was goalkeeper and anyone who scored got the job until someone else scored against him. This version, known as "Shotty-In", could be played by as few as two players. If and when a full-sized football became available, the game was played on open ground behind Hart Road School, in a playing field at "Greenland" or on a flat stretch at the top of the sandbanks known as

"Sandy Park". The goal was marked by discarded caps or jackets. The only rule I recall was that whenever anybody scored the opposing team shouted "Offside!" and the game only resumed after threats of fisticuffs had been made and repudiated.

Golden Things: another variant of "Tiggy". The boys who were "on" each chose an object - aeroplane or roundabout or whatever, and their leader advanced to the kerb behind which the others stood in the Bay and said: "Fool, fool, come out of school, And find a golden aeroplane" - or car or horse or whatever. The others then guessed. If right, the race across to the other pavement started and the tagging, if any, took place. If not, the dialogue was repeated until someone got it right.

Guessies: a game for two, outside a shop window. "On", standing on the street by the kerb, gave the initials of a sweet (or other object) in the window. His rival on the pavement had to guess the object. If and when he got it right, "On" galloped across the street to the other pavement. If he got there without being tagged the game began again. If not, roles were reversed.

Guns: pistols which fired single percussion caps were very cheap: only a few pennies. Repeater pistols which fired percussion caps in continuous rolls were more expensive: perhaps 6d or a shilling. Like kites and tops they appeared only seasonally in the shops. Pellet-shooting airguns were available but beyond Central Estate means.

Hop, Skip and Jump: a variant of leapfrog in which the distance from the starting line increased every time a player failed to make a clean leap. He was moved forward a foot or two and then became the frog and the last successful leaper decided how many hops, skips and/or jumps had to be made for the next leaper. A "skip" was a hop on the other foot. A the "jump" had to include the frog, with feet landing more or less together.

Illy Illy Arkie: another variant of "Tiggy": He who was "on" put his hands together and closed his eyes as if in prayer, reciting "Illy, illy arkey, my black darkie, purrum ("put him) in a cage. Amen!". During this recital the other players scattered - though never beyond the bounds of a particular street. The first caught was the next "on".

Itchy Bay: hopscotch, played both on a pavement in straight lines or in the middle of the road on a chalked spiral.

Jack Show The Light: a variant of "Spy Sheep" in which Black Sheep commanded the hidden side to flash a lamp to show they had been found.

Judge: A small boy (or an innocent newcomer) was persuaded to be the "judge" in a mock court scene. The brief proceedings were ended with the cry: "What will you have, Judge? The answer was "Muck!" and he was showered with street refuse.

Keps: catches with a small soft ball: the two players started close together but gradually moved further and further apart, throwing the ball higher and higher until it was above the roof-tops. Scores were not usually counted: the winner was self-evident. Continuous ball bouncing and bouncing against the wall from the edge of the pavement was also competitive.

Nicky Knocky Nine Doors: The back doors of two adjacent houses were tied together with rope and both kicked hard. The kickers fled as soon as wrathful sounds emerged. In downstreet Hartlepool there was a rather subtler prank. A safety pin, with a thread through the hole and a small stone tied a foot or so below, was skewered into the top of a window pane. Another thread tied immediately above the stone was used to jerk it against the window from a safe distance. To begin with, a single pull rattled the window. Subsequently the number of pulls was increased.

Levo: probably contraction of "Relieve-o": a variant of hide-and-seek played in the dark. From the "bay", normally a lamppost, one of the rival teams dispersed and after an interval was hunted by the other. Prisoners were taken by tagging and guarded in the bay. They were all released if one of the hiders crept up in the dark and ran through the bay shouting "Levo". When all were taken the roles of the teams were reversed,

Mill on Fire: an innocent young (or credulous older) victim was persuaded, as "Fireman", to shout "Mill on Fire" as he crawled through the straddled legs of the other boys in line who urinated (or pretended to) on him.

*__Montykitty:__ local version of Geordie "Mount the Cuddy". The cuddy was a horse which bucked to unseat its rider. He who was "on" adopted the leapfrog position with his hands against a wall and when another boy leapfrogged onto his back he had to unseat him by bucking. When he succeeded the second boy adopted the leapfrog position immediately behind him and locked his arms around the other's waist. Each boy in succession leapfrogged on and tried to work his way forward whilst being bucked. Consequently the length of the horse continually increased and the bucking became more and more violent. As he worked his way forward they sang: "Montykitty, montykitty, one, two, three. Fall off, fall off, fall off me!"

Nigger: a variant of leapfrog in which the leaper had to land with his heels smiting the road exactly together.

"On". He who was to be on in games of tiggy, etc, was chosen by one of several ritals. The simple one was: "The one who's 21's on" and the acknowledged leader would count round the ring of boys. If he himself was 21 there was great laughter. More elaborate was to count round the ring reciting:

"Icketty, Picketty, eye solicketty,
Bombadairy jig,
Every man that has no hair
Ought to wear a wig.
Pig's snout, all out,
I am in, and YOU ARE OUT!"

This eliminated one possible boy and the rhyme continued until only one was left. Naturally the leader who did the counting excluded himself.

Polly Polly Wallflowers: one of the few games in which girls were allowed to join. Boys and girls alternately in a ring with arms extended and hands joined danced round a central spot, singing:

"Polly, polly wallflowers, growing up so high,
We all little children, we all go to die,

Except (eg) Jacky Woolford, he's the only one,
Ohfershe, ayeforshee, turn your head around again".

The named child, still holding hands, did an about turn and faced outwards. When everybody faced outwards the game could be reversed, ending with all facing inwards.

Puss in the Corner: a very lively variant of "tiggy", in which a boy stood at each corner of a square and had to run across without being tagged by the puss in the middle.

Queenie: Hartlepool game: a ball was bounced from a high wall. He who was "on" had to guess who caught it.

Quoits: played by older boys in back streets or on flat hard ground. The iron peg and rings were presumably "trophies" from the shipyard.

Ring a Ring o' Roses: a variant of "Polly, polly wallflowers" in which the song was:
"Ring a ring o' roses,
A pocket full of posies,
Atishoo, Atishoo,
We all fall down".

Only the pre-named victim actually fell and then turned outwards. Like "Polly Polly Wallflowers", with the similar hint of death, this may have been a folk-memory of the Black Death of 1349 which killed at least a third of the population, or the Great Plague of 1665.

Secret language: Words were distorted according to a simple formula, eg: "Can you ride a bike?" would become: Annacar o(w)eryou iaride a ikabar"?

SHAM: Hartlepool game. A stone-throwing battle between rival youth gangs. However, on the Central Estate in 1928 and 1929 there were pitched battles between Union Roader and Stephenson Streeter gangs using broom handles with protruding nails at the end.

Shotty In: see above Footer.

Skipping: Only very occasionally would boys and girls skip together. A long rope was needed through which each had to run in turn without hitting it as it whirled round.

Slides: In frosty weather these were made on the pavement or road by the act of sliding itself. The point of the ensuing competition was who fell first. They were, of course, dangerous, particularly to adults, who sometimes sprinkled ashes on them, glaring as they did so.

Snowfights/Snowmen: self-evident. There was never a winter without snow by the week.

Spy Sheep: another variant of "Hide and seek" in which the side which lost the "on" process went off to hide. One of the other side, which remained behind in the "bay", was appointed "Black Sheep" and accompanied the fugitives, calling out the names of the streets and back lanes as they went in search of a hide. When the hide was chosen, he returned to the bay and accompanied the searchers, again calling out the names of the streets and lanes they searched. When the searchers were close to the hideout he shouted "Ball's Busted!" to warn them and they then all raced back to the bay. The team of the first one back was the winner. This was the theory. In practice there was usually at least one interloper from another street who shouted false information and "Ball's Busted!". This was countered with shouts of "False Alarm". if this did not work the shout was: "The game's poxed!"

Statues: another of the rare games in which girls joined in. He or she was "on" stood with his/her back to the players, who were ten yards or so behind, and called: Two, four, six, eight, ten, STATUE!". As he/she turned round everyone was supposed to freeze into a pose and anyone deemed to have "skinched" (ie moved) was out. As soon as he/she faced away again, everyone had to hop forward, until "STATUE!" was again called.

"Step over the cotton, please!" Two boys crouched by the kerbside on the street and one of them extended a forefinger as though holding a line. When an adult approached the other boy asked him or her to step over the cotton. The problem was not to laugh at the resulting gymnastics.

Three Jolly Sailorboys: Yet another variant of Tiggy. The three boys who were "on" stood on the street by the kerbside of the bay, in which the rest stood. The following dialogue ensued:

"Three jolly sailor boys, come to see the world".
"What can you do?"
"Eat black puddn's as well as you!"
"Show y'r motion!"

Those who were "on" then performed a pre-agreed mime of some familiar activity, and if the others guessed right, the chase to the opposite pavement began, the jolly sailor boys tagging as many as possible. Roles were then reversed.

Throw Out Your Luggage: a small boy was appointed porter to the train which consisted of all the rest in single file with arms imitating pistons and connecting rods. When the train stopped in the Bay the porter shouted: "Throw out your luggage!" and the pebbles or bits of dirt previously collected were thrown at him.

Tiggy: tag: one boy chased another and as soon as the former touched the latter the roles were reversed.

Tippy Finger: yet another variant of Tiggy. He who was "on" faced the wall and put his hands behind his back, linking his thumbs and extending his fingers. Someone touched one finger and on turning round he had to guess who it was. Whoever was named had to say: "What have I to do" and would be told to go to a named shop or corner and count ten or twenty or turn round three times or whatever. If the guess was right the command had to be obeyed before the tigging could begin. If wrong the joyful cry was: "Go yourself and count them"!

Tops 'n' Whips: not competitive: always on the pavement: very seasonal - springtime only.

Tug O'Bay: another variant of tiggy. He who was "on" had to stay on the road and could only run on to the pavement at a specified point, usually the end of the street. His opponent, after a few feinted starts, had to race along the pavement to the point, and after a pause, back to the starting point.

Water pistol: water squirt: squeeze bulb with nozzle: pistol with plunger: transparent plastic tube filled with water at high pressure, squirting more powerfully at longer range.

Zeppelins: these were flattened rings of paper about an inch in width and four, or five, inches long. Before launch, the sides of the rings were parted so that the shape became an elongated oval. For the launch, a small stone was placed inside the front end and the whole thing was flung as high as possible into the air in the same direction as the wind was blowing. In a suitable breeze the contraption whirled round, looking like an airship or zeppelin, as well as moving forward. Races were therefore possible.

Girls' Games

Ball bouncing and catching:

"One, two, three a-lary,
Four, five, six a-lary,
Seven, eight, nine, a-lary,
Ten, eleven, twelve a-lary".

This was chanted as accompaniment to ball bouncing. At "a-lary" the ball was jumped over as it bounced. It was competitive and could be carried out at various speeds.
"Two, four, six, eight, ten".
This was chanted as the ball was thrown from the edge of the pavement high up the wall. Before catching it the hands had to be whirled round each other with fingers extended ten times before the ball was caught. There were many variants.

Checkers: A ball and four cubes, made of light stone and only an inch in diameter or length, were thrown into the air and caught in succession of number.

Skipping: This was done singly or in pairs, facing or back to back, with one rope. One of the girls would count, say from one to twenty and then the speed of the rope would be doubled. The speed of the jumps might or might not be doubled at the same time. Single skippers would cross their hands for a few jumps. A group of girls would use a long rope and run through the turning rope in succession. Anyone who failed became one of the rope turners. In West Hartlepool two skips to one turn of the rope were called "double-unders". Two girls holding each end of two ropes, swung in unison, was called "doublers". Each rope had to be skipped separately. Also in West Hartlepool, girls would line up in two groups of three. The first three danced up singing:

"We're three gypsies, riding, riding, riding,
We're three gypsies, riding y. o. u.

The other three returned with:

"What y'r coming here for, here for, here for,
What y'r coming here for y.o.u.?

The answer was:

"We've come here to marry, marry, marry,

We've come here to marry y.o.u.
The others turned their backs, flicked their skirts up and down to show knickers, and sang:
"You're blue, black and dirty, dirty, dirty,
You're blue, black and dirty, y. o. u.
Roles were then reversed.

Seashore and Sandbank Activities

Crabbing: A small-meshed net was attached loosely to the rim of an old bicycle wheel and suspended from the promenade or pier with a length of clothes line. The bait was a cod's head scrounged from the Fish Quay. Very occasionally it worked.

Fires in tins: Tins and pieces of wire could be found on the old fifty feet high refuse Tips on the shore. On the top of the sandbanks were iron spikes surrounding the Battery on which holes could be hammered on opposite sides of the tops of the tins using a brick or stone as a hammer. The wire was threaded through the holes and secured by twisting so that the tin could be swung around, and the bottom and sides were pierced for ventilation holes. A walk along the shore invariably yielded pieces of wood, bark, candle ends, solidified tar and small pieces of sea-coal washed up from the sea-bed. Cinders could be found on the Tips. With a sheet of newspaper (brought for the purpose) and a match a fire could be kindled in the tin, building up from small to larger pieces of wood etc to coal, coaxing each layer by swinging the tin vertically at arm's length to enhance the draught. The tins were than carried up to the Battery where there was a Mess Room in which chestnuts could be roasted and cigarette ends smoked. When the fires were out (sometimes with liquid assistance), the tins were hidden in the long and coarse grass.

Fires on the shore: A squarish fireplace was made from bricks or stones and fired and fuelled as above. Sea-water (and other liquids) was boiled in tins and the salty residues marvelled at.

Fishing: Fishing lines could be bought for sixpence or a shilling, and a trace with three hooks for ninepence. Sinkers were home-made from scrap lead melted in a pan and poured into a mould of damp sand made with a tablespoon. A big nail made the hole for attaching the sinker to the line. At the other end of the line was tied a short stick which was hurled round the head before the line was cast: no fishing rods! Bait - usually herring or mackerel - was scrounged from friendly trawlermen on the Fish Quay. The fishing could be done at high tide from anywhere along the Promenade, but the favourite venue was the New Pier which stretched out over 200 metres into the sea.

Fishing: net: Small boys fished for small fish (sticklebacks and tadpoles) with small nets from the beck which flowed through a field on Warren Road. They were taken home in jamjars carried with a loop of string round the neck, with a small amount of weed inside, and invariably died.

Kite-flying: This was also very seasonal, not long before or after tops and whips. Kites were home-made, either diamond shaped or with a curved top and covered with brown paper or wallpaper. Tailings were made from strips of newspaper rolled up and tied in sequence to the string at the base of the kite. If the wind was strong, a duster or a handkerchief was tied to the end of the tailings to prevent the kite from veering too wildly. If the wind was strong the kite would fly without assistance, but if there was little or no wind, someone had to hold the kite aloft whilst its owner walked to a suitable distance and then ran to create enough breeze to get the kite off the ground. A kite which did not fly was ceremoniously destroyed: "A' put me foot through ut!" There was competition for size and splendour of decoration and for height attained, but no Chinese style battles to cut rivals down with abrasive strings. Box kites were available in the shops but were beyond means of Central boys.

Plodging: When the sea was warm enough, boys (and girls) paddled either in the pools left by receding tides or along the beach itself. The slope of the beach was very gentle and at low spring tides would be as much as a quarter of a mile broad. Boots or shoes were tied together by the laces and slung round the neck. Splashing was the only available aggression.

Roly-poly: The sandbanks on the shore were steep enough for children to roll down them from various heights. It was a brief pastime because nausea rapidly ensued.

Sandcastles: These were normally made by small children with buckets and spades, but older boys hollowed out intersecting tunnels in the firm wet sand beneath the surface near the tidemark, and watched the tide as it destroyed them.

Sea-coaling: Every tide deposited a thin layer of coal fragments from the sea-bed at high watermark. They could gently be scraped off the firming sand with a flat stick when the tide receded, and collected in buckets which were emptied into sacks. After drying they made good fires. For the unemployed there might be no other source of fuel and there were threats or fights to determine proprietary rights to stretches of beach.

Slinging: A sling of the type used by David against Goliath was easily made from a square of thin leather, pierced on opposite sides for the two strings, one several inches longer than the other. The longer was wound round the forefinger and the shorter held between thumb and middle finger. A stone was placed inside the leather. The sling was than spun vertically at arm's length and the shorter string released. The targets were usually seagulls though none was ever hit.

Swimming: The beach had a very bad reputation for drownings, and parental warnings deterred most.

Tracking: Spying on courting couples on the sandbanks.

Winkling: Beyond Throston Bridge the sands yielded to rocks and there were winkles in the pools (as well as seaweed, starfish and small inedible crabs). Jam jars with string handles were used to take the winkles home, where mothers might be willing to boil them. The meat was extracted from the shells with a pin.

Appendix F - Phrases

"Ah believe yeh: thousands wouldn't!". Polite disbelief.

"Ah rah rah chickarahrah,
Rooney, pooney, ping pong pynee,
Para, parawacky, Chinese chicks!" Said (and believed to be) Chinese.

"A'l tell me Father o' you. 'E won' 'alf bash yer."
"Garn! My Father's bigger 'n 'im!"

"A'poth of wot y'aven't got!": halfpenny worth

"A'poth of wot ye gerra lot of!"

"A'poth o' mucky mixture!"
- advice to small boys going into a sweet shop to ask for a halfpenny worth of sweets.

"'Appy as a dog with a bellyful o' piss and a street full o' lamp posts".

"Ask no questions, get no lies!". Warning.

"Aye tiddley 'ossmuck, grab (or crab?) shite!" Verbal equivalent of a drum-roll.

'Bashy strawbenger!' The first to spot a man wearing a brimmed Panama hat was entitled to punch his companion. See also *'Punch Panama!'*: possibly despised as upper-class raiment.

**"Ow's yer belly for spots?"* Friendly greeting: reply: *'Same as your's for doorknobs'.*

"Bustin' for a ...". Needing to urinate.

"Go canny!" Go carefully.

"Cheap at 'alf the price and y'r money back". Response to any reference to price.

"Constantinople's a very hard word. Can you spell it?" Almost inevitable failure was greeted with jeers: *"Can't spell "it" - I-T.* In the middle '20s there was a popular song "Constantinople" in which the word was spelled out no less than three times.

"E's gospel's 'e's gob." His gospel is his mouth - i.e. he's greedy:

**"E's got the can't-'elp-uts"*. He's irresponsible, eg can't help himself.

C O N T E N T S Cows Ought Not To Eat Nasty Turnip Skins - Sunday School joke about the meaning of the "Contents" page in the hymnal.

"Copt yer bending!" Anyone caught bending was (not always) gently kneed in the behind.

"'Cos for!": because: derisory answer to *"What for?"*

"Could'n 'it a cow's arse with a shovel". A bad shot: *'couldn't hit a barn door with a spade'.*

"Daddy can A' smoke, Ah've got long trousers?" Inevitable greeting when a boy first appeared in long trousers.

"Daft as a brush!" Unexplained but vivid simile.

"Don' say Ah never give yer nowt!" Emphasis on gift of sweetmeat (etc).

"Dropped 'e's false teeth". Reference to any third party who dropped anything.

"F.P x feet". These were metal plates at ground level on walls showing the proximity of "Fire Points", i.e. water mains available for fire-fighting. The first boy to spot a particular one would say: *"Father's prick, 6 feet (or whatever) long!"*

"Fish 'n' a pennorth, twice, please!". Typical order at a fish and chip shop; sometimes shortened into *"One and one, twice, please!"*, or even *"Twice, please!"* A satisfying and nourishing meal for threepence was indeed a bargain, especially from the shop in Watson Street which was superior to the one on Hart Road.

"First 'e only thought, but when 'e looked, 'e 'ad!": joke about involuntary excretion.

"For after!": ironic answer to the question: *"What's that for?"*

"Gi'e 'm a bat in the gob!". Give him a smack in the mouth.

"Gie's a bullet!" Give me a sweet!: a suitable riposte was: *"Them wot ask don't get, them wot don't ask don't want!"*

"God's honour!" Solemn affirmation, usually accompanied by a throat-slitting sign.

"I laughed so much I could 'ave pee'd;
In fact a drop did come!"

"Like a fanny (or fart) in a fog!" Lost!

"Gi'e 's ''e goke!" Give me the core of your apple.

"Know Peter?"
"Naw!"
"Peter Knight before y' go to bed". Anticipating the later *"Knock-Knock!"*

"Y'r money or y'r life. Yer baccy or y'r pipe". Mock threat, with the right forefinger sticking out from a clenched fist in imitation of a pistol.

"Know the yarn about the two slugs?"
"Naw!"
"Dear (deer), dear! (deer)"

Medal: anyone deemed to merit praise, even if ironic, had a thumb moistened with saliva imposed above his heart and drawn downwards for two or three inches. Anyone deeming himself to merit praise, even if ironic, awarded himself with a similar gesture.

"My oath!" Solemn affirmation of truth, preceded or followed by emphatic expectoration.

"Neely's (nearly's) on'y 'alf way". Dismissive comment.

"Open y'r hand 'n' close y'r eyes, and see what God'll send yer!" Invitation to receive a gift which might - or might not - be undesirable.

Ow! me bad back!... (leg, arm, chest, etc)!" When assaulted, victims frequently claimed that the place hit was already wounded.

"Pick the bones out o' that!" Challenge after emphatic statement, followed up by emphatic expectoration.

**"Prick, suck it till yer sick, & when y' get t' the bone, chow like 'ell!".* Ironic advice.

"Put that in y'r pipe 'n' smoke it!" Emphasis on unexpected/unacceptable statement.

"Put y'rself be'ind y'rself 'n' give y'rself a push!": derisory advice.

"Run up a shutter!": derisory advice

Sedgefield: The Durham County Lunatic Asylum. Typical remark: *"Ye'll finish up in Sedgefield!"*

"Spit in y'r eye 'nd choke ye(h)!: threat: never carried out.

'Them wot ask don't get, them wot don't ask don't want!' Response to a supplicant.

"Third time catchy time!" Third time, out.

"Tough guy! Tough as (h)'ens' piss! Derogatory dismissal.

"Up the bump". Pregnant

"E walks with a stutter and speaks with a limp, the man with the wooden eyelash".

"Waste not, want not,
"Pick yer nose 'n' eat ut!"

"Wha' do they call yer?" What is your name?

"Why is a mouse when it spins?"
"Because the higher they fly the fewer!"

"Well!" To anyone using this conjunction the reply was:
"Two wells make a river, and you in the middle would make it bigger!"

"Where ye bin?" To this question the inevitable reply was:
"There and back to see 'ow far it is"!

"Which would yer rather do: run a mile, suck a bile, or eat a plate o' scabs?"

"Who knows?": "God knows, and 'E won't split!" (i.e. reveal).

".....'s got the winnots. 'E winnot work!"

"Yer nowt else!" Additional emphasis to a rebuke eg *"Yer a blummun' rotter! Yer nowt else!"*

Appendix G - Who Hung the Monkey?

Hartlepool is better known for the story that its fishermen inhabitants, confronted with a monkey, sole survivor of a French shipwreck during the Napoleonic Wars (1801-15), hung it on the shore as a French spy, than for its true history. The hung monkey is now an inseparable part of Hartlepool's image, not without value when all publicity, especially to promote tourism, is good. But is it true? Could it really have happened?

There is no contemporary record, although Sir Cuthbert Sharp, Hartlepool-born and -resident, including the Napoleonic period and author of the "History of Hartlepool" published in 1816 and still an invaluable record, does not mention it. Nor do contemporary French naval histories. Nor does anyone else until the 1840s. Moreover, similar tales are told of Boddam near Aberdeen, Mevagissey in Cornwall and Chalvey in Berkshire.

In the 1840s, as outlined in Chapter 1, Hartlepool and the future West Hartlepool were locked in rivalry for railways, coal exports, timber imports and shipbuilding, a rivalry which persisted at least until 1967 when the two boroughs were merged. It was a brilliantly malicious invention or transposition of the same sort as tales of "Irish" or "Polish" (etc., etc., etc.) stupidity, presumably by a would-be West-Hartlepudlian.

Appendix H - Reg. Smythe Creator of "Andy Capp"

In March 1995 through the good offices of a mutual friend I was able to meet Reg. Smythe and to tape-record his Hartlepool recollections. It was a delightful experience which I here transcribe with minimal editing. We were spontaneously friendly, sharing as we did our persistent local accent and our devotion to Hartlepool and the Central Estate.

Reg. was born on July 10 1917 at the Cleveland Road (ie respectable) end of Union Road where the bus (tram) used to stop. I myself had been born a month earlier on June 12 at 68 Arch Street, just round the corner from Union Road. Hence our warm and cordial mutual interest. At age 1, however, Reg's parents moved to Alliance St, Hartlepool, just round corner from Galleys Field School. He first attended Baltic Street and then Galleys Field schools. Consequently he had no early recollections of the Central Estate, but many of the Hartlepool Independent Chapel, of which he was a choir boy, of the Boys Brigade, of Maypole dancing on the Town Moor and of schoolmates (several of whom I myself knew at Henry Smith's School). One of them had recently died of a heart attack when his house in Friar Terrace, as well secured as Fort Knox, was attacked by hooligans, a sad, said Reg, change in Hartlepool, which was now always rough on Saturday nights).

Both his father and mother were old Hartlepudlians, his father, from Alliance Street. A boat builder at Pounder's on Hart Road who moved his family to Sunderland for two years in search of employment, was related to the painter Christopher Smyth, newsagent in Northgate, later well reputed as a local historian and JP, although there was little family contact. It was because of the two years in Sunderland that he had not gone to Henry Smith's School. He had been downgraded a class on return, although if he had gone there he might well have finished up working in an office. When he left school in 1931 his first job was as an errand boy for a butcher in Vane Street and then for a grocer at the bottom of Friar Terrace. When he got to age sixteen he got the sack because the employer would have had to pay Unemployment Benefit stamps of two shillings on top of his four shillings and sixpence a week. From that time he was "on the dole". He had spent quite a bit of time on the Central Estate where he met a new mate at a party who invited him to join "our gang". There was also a girl (who I also knew and admired) "to knock around with". He was in those days, he said, "a boy for the little girls". There were no jobs in Hartlepool, so he joined the army, the Northumberland Fusiliers, aged nineteen, in 1936.

He returned to Hartlepool after the war in 1945, having mainly served in the N. African Western Desert. His mother then lived at 1 Arch Street on the Central Estate, to which he had used to come back on leave and have a drink at the "Klondyke". But he didn't stay long in Hartlepool because there was still no work, so he went to London.

A London job was also hard to find, so he joined the Civil Service, Postal Section, which, as usual, had a table tennis team and a dramatic group which he joined. This latter needed a poster for the Notice Board and, said Reg., "I'll have a go if you like". Someone said: "Why don't you take it up for a living?" and that's how it started. I'd never been at art school or anything like that. I went to see an agent and he said: "You won't be very good as a commercial artist but, if you like, have a try at cartooning and I'll try and sell them for you". He sold the first batch to "Everybody's Weekly". He said I must have a pen name, and when I said my name was Smyth he said he would put an "e" on it, "which sounded a bit posher", especially because it was working class humour.

He started freelancing and the "Daily Mirror" had a feature called "Laughs at Work", always illustrated by cartoons. After some time they said it could be a permanent job for the somebody who had most accepted for the next month. Reg. got the job.

Then there was a promotion drive in the North because circulation was dropping. A cartoon appealing to Northern people was needed and he, Reg., known to be from the North, was asked "to do something". He was up in Hartlepool seeing his mother when the Art Editor wrote to him. He "got the idea" as he was driving, overnight, back to London. He couldn't think of anything "sharp and gimmicky" but conceived the character of "Andy Capp" who was a handicap to his wife. It was a terrible pun: and in those days everyone wore a cap. Andy's wife, Flo, was Reg's mother but Andy Capp wasn't his father, He didn't drink as much as Andy and wasn't such a lay-about. His father didn't have Andy's flair as "the last of the Cavaliers" who had no conscience at all. Andy was an amalgamation of three men Reg had known in Hartlepool (not the Central Estate), little fellows with caps on, OK when sober but very dangerous when drunk. If you looked at them sideways they'd be at you. They would no more work than carry shopping, or wheel prams, which nowadays is unbelievable. They hadn't been indoctrinated by TV adverts or women's lobbies.

Andy was a success straight away and although it began as a regional character it began to sell abroad, now in 1600 papers, a thousand in the States and the rest spread round the world including China, Russia (Isvestia) and Turkey. This shows there's not much difference between Hartlepool and Ankora in terms of matrimonial relationships.

Reg. returned to live in Hartlepool, despite the fact that it was thirty years behind the times, in 1976 because he tired of the rat-race in London where it took two hours to get into work by car. So he started going by tube, waiting hours on crowded platforms for doors to open and with two changes of train. "To Hell with this", he said, and here he was, nineteen years later and still working. Andy, "born" in 1957 (when Reg was already 40 years old), was still going strong and more successful than ever, most especially in Sunday 'comics' in the United States . He reckoned it was the market for nostalgia. Good money was hard to turn down, especially with syndication by the million, and no cartoon of his had ever been turned down. There weren't many new jokes but variations on old jokes were enough. He had never been on the staff of the "Daily Mirror", always insisting on being freelance. Andy didn't go out of fashion because he was old-fashioned in the first place, and was now accepted as part of the establishment, like St Paul's. He, Reg., was nothing but for Andy who was his "dancing bear". It had been a matter of luck, of being there to be pushed into it at the right time. (I ventured to dispute this: one needed more than luck to become internationally famous.) Yet his life in Hartlepool had been a perfect preparation for it. The CMEW (Central Marine Engine Works) crane and the pit props in the Propyard on Cleveland Road appeared in his cartoons. There were only three settings for Andy, the sofa, the pubs and the football ground.

Reg. was 78 when I interviewed him. He said that despite bad eyes he could still draw. It kept him busy and out of trouble and otherwise he wouldn't know what to do. He had two years of cartoons in reserve. His existing contract would end in 2 yrs, time but he couldn't see packing it in.

In fact he "packed it in", from the cancer from which he must already have been suffering, on 13th June 1998. The very many tributes showered upon him were indeed well earned. He was the only Central Estate-born (and Hartlepudlian) to have achieved world-wide fame.

Appendix I - Tables

Table 7 - Streets, Households (H) and Shops 1(S)

	YEAR								
	1891	1900	1902	1912	1921	1924	1929	1933	1935
	H	H:S	H:S	H:S	H:S	H:S	H:S	H:S	H:S
Arch St	//////	26:10	49:12	46:9	39:9	46:10	47;12	48:12	47:12
Beaumont St	//////	//////	4:1	4:1	4:1	4:1	3:0	3:0	3:0
Bell St	//////	25:2	27:3	23:3	23:4	25:5	21:4	22:3	19:3
Clevelnd Rd[2]	20	75:10	77:10	69:11	52:8	56:8	58;8	59:6	51:7
Clyde Place	6	6:	6:	5:1	-:-				
Clyde St	7	13:1	13:1	11:0	-:-				
" Back Terr	3	-:-							
Hart Rd[3:4:5]	//////	51:4	67:4	110:13	101:9	119:9	130:9	136:7	129:10
Hutton St	//////	//////	//////	7:0	-:-	-:-	-:-	12:0	12:0
Lambton St		10:	10:	10:0	-:-	-:-	-;-	9:0	9:0
Pease St	4	9:	10:0	9:0	10:1	10:2	10:1	7:1	6:1
Rokeby St	//////	//////	//////	39:0	-:-	-:-	-:-	46:1	45:0
Romaine Park	//////	//////	//////	//////	//////	//////	//////	42:0	42:0
Stephenson	//////	51:5	60:6	45:3	42:3	44:3	43:3	43:5	42:4
Union Rd	//////	42:1	48:0	31:0	26:1	42:2	46:1	49:2	48:1
Warren Rd	6	-:-							
Warren Terr	7	-:-							
" Back Terr	3	-:-							
Vincent St	//////	//////	12:0	-:-	-:-	-:-	-:-	17:0	15:0
Watson St	28	85:7	103:12	64:8	56:10	66:7	65:8	66:8	65:7
Watt St		36:0	37:0	32:1	25:1	31:0	31;0	31:0	30:0
West View	//////	//////	//////	//////	//////	87;1	92:1	92:1	92:1
Totals[6]	84	429:40	523:49	517:50	390:47	530:48	561:47	582:46	655:46
Households per shop		10.7	10.6	10.3	12.0	8.3	8.4	7.9	7.0
Population[7]	465	2145	2615	2610	2585	2120	2244	2328	2620

Notes:

////// Not yet built. -:- Not recorded.

1 'Shops' includes agents, dressmakers, offices, overseers, pawnbrokers, pubs and surgeries.

2 Includes Balmoral Terrace.

3 Includes Clyde Terrace and Warren Terrace from 1900.

4 Also includes Roseburn and Pirie Terraces in 1902.

5 Also includes Wilster Terrace in 1912.

6 Assuming continued occupation 1913-33.

7 Estimated after 1891: to 1912 5 per household: 1931-35 4.

From 1900 Hart Road included the Cement Works, the Ropery, the Galvanising Works and the Farm: the School and Primitive Methodist Chapel: and St Barnabas Church from 1904.

Table 8 - Occupations

Source	**Census**	**Wards Directories**							
Occupation	**1891**	**1900**	**1902**	**1912**	**1921**	**1924**	**1929**	**1933**	**1935**
Accountant						1	1		
Agent				1					
Analyst		1	1	1	1	1	1	1	1
Architect						1			
Army pensioner	1								
Asst overseer		1	1	1	1				
Asst foreman					1				
Baker						1		1	1
Bank clerk							2	1	
Barman	1	1	2				2	1	1
Beer retailer		1	1	1	1	1	1	1	
Bicycle dealer				1	1	1			1
Blacksmith	5	10	10	14	11	8	7	10	8
" apprentice	2								
Boatbuilder		4	3	7	9	10	8	9	6
Boarder/lodger	13								
Boilermaker/smith	15	18	27	21	21	20	22	24	17
Boiler examiner								1	1
Bookbinder					1	1	1	1	1
Bookmaker								1	1
Boot make/repair		4	5	2	2	2	1	1	1
Brass finisher	1	3	5	4	4	8	7	4	4
" moulder	1		1	3	4	2		3	3
Brewer						1			
Bricklayer	2	4	4	7	2	5	1	7	6
Bridgeman						1	1		
Builder		4	2	2	2	2	1	1	1
Bus conductor									1
Bus driver								3	2
Butcher	2	5	7	5	2	6	7	8	8
Butcher journeyman									
Caretaker	2	1	1	1					
Carpenter		4	2					2	
Cartman	1	2	2	4	1	2	3	3	3
Cashier		1	1						
Caulker		6	3	3	2	4	3	3	3
Cement burner						1	1	1	1
" man	1								
" engineman	1								
" miller	4	1	2	2			1	1	1
" millwright	1								
" nightwatch	1								
" teemer	1								
" tester					1	2	1		1
" worker		7	17	8		1	3	4	5

Source	Census	Wards Directories							
Occupation	**1891**	**1900**	**1902**	**1912**	**1921**	**1924**	**1929**	**1933**	**1935**
Cemetery supt									1
Chargeman:	1					1	3	2	2
Checker				1		1	3		
Chemical worker								1	1
Civil engn'r ret'd	1								
Clerk:	2	5	7	11	4	14	12	14	14
Clerk to Justices								1	1
Clothier	1	1	2						
Coalman								1	1
Coal merchant	1			3	2	1	1	2	2
Coal trimmer	1	10	7	16	11	17	15	17	18
Coke drawer			1						
Commercial agent							1	1	
Companion	1								
Compositor	1		1	1	1	1			
Conductor bus								1	
Conductor tram	1	1				1		1	
Confectioner		3	3	1	1	1		3	3
Cooper		1	2						
Coppersmith		3	5	3	3	2	1	3	3
" appr.	1								
Craneman		5	4	4		4	5	4	4
Curate				1		1		1	
Customs: ret'd	1								
" watcher				1					
Cutler		1							
Dairyman		3	1	1	1	2	1	1	1
Dealer: general	1	1	1						
Delegate					2	2	1	1	1
Deputy surveyor								1	
Die cutter				1	1	1	1		1
Dining Rooms					1				
Dockman								3	3
Diesinker		1	2						
Dock gateman				1				2	1
Dock pilot					1				
Dockmaster's asst				1					
Domestic servant	6								
Donkeyman									1
Draper		4	1	4	3	6			1
Draughtsman			2			2	1	1	
Dredging master								1	1
Dressmaker	1	4	3	11	1				
Dressmaker appr	1								
Driller mar eng	1								
Driller	2	4	6	11	4	9		8	8

Source	Census	Wards Directories							
Occupation	**1891**	**1900**	**1902**	**1912**	**1921**	**1924**	**1929**	**1933**	**1935**
Dripping refiner							1	1	
Driver							2	2	
Electrical eng'r			1						
Electrician		1		1	1	5	5	5	5
Engine driver		2	2	1	1		2	5	5
" man		1	2	2	1	1	1		1
Engineer		8	8	3	1	3	4	6	10
Examiner								1	
Farm labourer				1					
Farm servant(male)	4	1							
Farm manager				1	1				
Farmer	1	1	1	1	1	1	1	1	1
Felter							1	1	
Fireman		1	1	6		2	6	12	7
Firewood dealer									1
Fish curer				2		2	1	3	1
Fisherman				3	1	2	3	2	2
Fishmonger/merchnt	1			2				2	2
Fitter	9	26	26	26	36	43	35	37	39
" apprentice	2								
Foreman:	1	12	8	15	8	10	10	10	7
Forgeman	1	5	6	3		4	2	3	3
French polisher						2	2	1	1
Fried Fish dealer		2	2	3	3	4	3	2	2
Funeral furnisher							1	1	1
Fruiterer		2	2						
Furnaceman		3	5	1	1	2	2	2	1
Galvaniser		1	1	1					
Ganger				1					
Garage proprietor							1		
Gardener						2		1	1
Gas meter inspctr				1	1	1			
Gas worker							3	2	1
Gateman							1	1	1
Gravedigger							1		
Green keeper								1	1
Grocer		6	7	6	5	9	6	6	7
Grocer asst	1	2		3	3	4	3	3	
" errand boy	1								
Guard		2	1	2	2	5	4	4	3
Gunsmith								1	1
Hairdresser		1	1	2	1	1	2	2	1
Hardware dealer									1
Hardwareman		1	1	1			1		
Haulage contractor							1		1
Hopperman						1			

Source	Census	Wards Directories							
Occupation	**1891**	**1900**	**1902**	**1912**	**1921**	**1924**	**1929**	**1933**	**1935**
Horsekeeper			1	1					
Hosier		1							
Innkeeper		2	2	2	2	2	2	2	2
Insurance agent		1	3	1	1	3	2	1	1
" supt			1						
Inspector: train							2	3	2
Iron dresser				1	1	1	1		
Joiner	2	11	11	17	11	14	13	14	12
Joiner ship	3								
" appr	1								
Labourer: boiler	2								
" cement	17	1							
" coal	1								
" dock	1								
" eng	1								
" farm	4								
" helper/holder up	2	4	5	11	3	2	3	5	4
" fitter	1								
" horse	1								
" iron	1								
" paint	1								
" plater	2		1			3		2	4
" shipyard	13								
" striker	1			2					
" waterwks	1								
" subtotal	48	66	72	37	3	11	25	38	45
Lamplighter								1	1
Laundress			1						
Lithographer			1						
Lodgings	1	1	1						
Machinist/man	4	14	16	10	4	9	7	17	17
" appr.	1								
Manager		2	5	4	4	6	4	5	5
Manageress		1		1					
Marine engineer	1	1		8	5	7	5	7	4
" " appr.	1								
" chargeman	1								
" eng bldr	1								
" engineman	2								
" store dealer								1	1
Mariner		5	4				1	1	3
Marker off		1							
Mate		1	1	1	2	3	2	3	
Metal worker							1	1	
Millwright	2	1	3			2	2	3	2
Milkman/seller	1			2	2	1	1	1	1

Source	Census	Wards Directories							
Occupation	**1891**	**1900**	**1902**	**1912**	**1921**	**1924**	**1929**	**1933**	**1935**
Miner								7	7
Mooring man			1						
Motorman				1					
Motor driver								1	
Motor mechanic						1		1	4
Moulder	4	16	25	24	16	19	21	19	17
" :iron appr.	1								
Newsagent			1	1	2	3	2	2	2
Office boy	2								
Own means	6								
Packer				2	1	2	1		2
Painter				3	1	3	3	5	7
Patternmaker		9	7	5	6	5	4	6	6
Patternmaker appr									
Pawnbroker									
Pharmacist						1	1	2	1
Piano maker						1			
Pilot								1	
Pipe fitter							2	1	1
Picture framer					1				
Platelayer		1		6		2	3	3	4
Plater	4	13	16	16	10	10	13	14	13
" appr.	1								
Plumber		1	1	5	2	3	4	5	5
" appr.		1							
Police insp.(rtd)				1					
Police man		1	1	1	1	5	7	7	6
" officer								1	1
" sgt		1	1	2	2	1	2		
Porter						1	1	2	1
Postman						1	1	2	2
Post Master		1	1	1	1	1	1		
Printer		1				1	1	2	1
Professional golfer						1	1		
Rent collector					1	1			
Rigger								1	
	1	0	2	2	1	4	9	3	5
Rivetter		13	21	12	10	10	9	10	10
Rolleyman						1			
Roper				1					
Salesman						2	2	2	2
Sanitary inspector					1	1		1	1
Sawyer				3	2	1	3	6	4
Scholar	49								
Schoolteacher					1	3	1	1	1
Screwing machine	1								

Source	Census	Wards Directories							
Occupation	**1891**	**1900**	**1902**	**1912**	**1921**	**1924**	**1929**	**1933**	**1935**
Seaman	1				1				
Secretary		1	1	2	1	1			
Sheet iron	1								
Sheet metal						1	1	2	2
Shipsmith		1	1	1					
Ship steward									
Shipwright	1	3	13	10	9	10	9	9	6
Shop assistant				1			2	1	1
Shopkeeper		5	9	13	31	15	20	13	13
Shunter		2	2	6		1	2	2	1
Signal fitter				1					
Signalman		3	4	2	3	2	5	3	1
Slater	1			1		1	1	1	1
Slinger									1
Spar maker				1					
Stamper					2	2	1	1	2
Steam gauge maker				1	1	1			
Steward			1					2	1
Stocktaker						1			
Stonemason/sculptr		1	1	2	1				1
Storekeeper	1	3	5	2	1	1	1	1	1
Striker	1			1	1	1	1	1	1
Superintendant							1	1	
Supervisor						1	1		
Surgeon/doctor		2	2	1	2	2	2	2	4
Tailor			1						
Tax collector						1			
Teemer		1	2	5	2	3	5	5	5
Timekeeper			1	2	3	3	4	4	4
Tinsmith		1	1	1	1	2	1		
Toolmaker			1	1					
Tool grinder						1			
Town clerk						1			
Traveller						1	1		
Trawlermaster						1	3	2	2
Tram conductor						1			
Tram driver			3						
Tugboatman							1		
Tugmaster							1	2	2
Turner		6	4	8	6	7	4	5	4
Turner steel			2						
Unspecified: Mr		8	8	17	13	15	23	38	52
" Mrs	6	18	28	22	33	30	34	54	91
" Miss	4	5	3	1	2	3	2	3	5

Source	Census	Wards Directories							
Occupation	**1891**	**1900**	**1902**	**1912**	**1921**	**1924**	**1929**	**1933**	**1935**
Vanman	1	1	1	1	1	1	1	1	2
	1	0	2	2	1	4	9	3	5
Visitor	1								
Wagon inspector			1						
Waitress	1	2							
Warehouseman						1	1		1
Watchmaker		1	1	1					
Watchman		2	1			1	1		
Waterman		1	1						
Welder								1	1
Weighman			1	4	1	1	2	2	
Window cleaner									1
Wire rope maker	1	1	1	1					
Wiredrawer		4	5	5	1	2	2	1	1
Wireless engineer									1
Wireless operator								1	1
Wireman					1	1			

Bibliography

Published Sources

1881 Census
1891 Census
Compass: Holy Trinity Parish Magazine: Dec 1972
Compass: Church of England & Non-conformist Churches: April/May 1973: 1974-6, 1976-78:
Hartlepool Borough Council: Court & Election Book 1866-83: 1904
    Improvement Committee Minute Book 1886-1901
    Improvement & Property Minutes 1912-21
    Minute Books 1866-83: 1904-67:
    building plans 1852-1948:
    abstracts of accounts 1902-41:
    Improvement Committee minutes from 1896
Hartlepool Free Press Jul 1855
Kelly's Hartlepool & West Hartlepool Directory 1887
Northern Daily Mail files 1883-1939
Report of Royal Commission on Housing of Working Classes 1885
South Durham & Cleveland Mercury 1890-91
South Durham Herald & Stockton Journal: 1867: 1889-91
Sunderland News & N. of England Advertiser: Mar 1855
Tate's Description of Hartlepool & Seaton Carew: Christopher & Jennet, 1816: republished Hartlepool Archaeological & Historical Society 1985
Ward's Directories of Hartlepool: 1900/1902/1912/1921/1924/1927/1929/1933/1935
Lock: The Hartlepools, A Survey & Plan: West Hartlepool Corporation: 1948

Taped Recollections: 1979-80

Bill Boagey: Bombardment, Dec 16th 1914: MSS
Frances Kettlewell
Bob Moore
Mary Baines (née Perry)
Jenny Robson
Jean Scott
Mary White (née Shires)
Reg Smythe
Bob Tyson
Monica Watson

Correspondents

Ernest Chambers
Alan Dixon
Harry Elliott
Bill Hunter
C. Lovell
Hilda McGuire
Morris Marshall
Mary Newton
Dorothy Smith
John Ward

Hartlepools' Books

Cowley: Air Raids On The Hartlepools: Ord 1945
Etherington: Our Patch: South East Durham: Printability, Wolviston: 1993
Dodds: Hartlepool: Victoria County History of Durham: 1928
German Raid on the Hartlepools: Sage: pre-1920
Gill: The Hartlepool Story: Gill: Printability Publishing, 1990
Hartlepool Charter Celebrations Brochure: Borough Council: 1951
Hartlepool Headland Urban Village: Headland Local History Group: Hartlepool Borough Council
Hogg: "Richies": Richardsons, Westgarth & Co. Ltd: Hartlepool Borough Council: 1994
Hogg: Central Marine Engine Works 1884-1961: Hartlepool Borough Council: 1995
Hogg: The Furness Legacy to the Hartlepools 1895-1995: Printability Publishing, 1995
Hunter: Down Memory Lane: 1981
Lock: The Hartlepools, A Survey & Plan: West Hartlepool Corporation: 1948
Martin: Historical Notes on West Hartlepool and its Founder: 1924
Museum of Hartlepool: Allison & Alderson Associates, Leyburn
Museum of Hartlepool: Allison & Alderson Associates, Leyburn
O'Heugh: Central Estate Recollections: Northern Daily Mail 1959
Screeton: Who Hung the Monkey? Printability 1991
Sharp: History of Hartlepool 1816: Hartlepool Borough Council 1978
Smith and Mincher: West View's Coney Island: Printability Publishing, 1991
Souvenir Guide to Happy Healthful Hartlepool: 1932-34: Printability, Wolviston: 1994
Waggott: Jackson's Town: West Hartlepool & Its Founder: Hartlepool Borough Council: 1980
Ward: Hartlepool Chronology: Atkinson Print: 1985
Hartlepool Chronology: Printability Wolviston: 1999
Dawn Raid: Printability Wolviston: 1989
The Cement Works: MSS
The Creosote Works: MSS
Notes on the Hartlepool Trading Estate: MSS
The Ropery: MSS
Memories of Hartlepool 1979: MSS
Notes on the Central Estate 1979: MSS
LNER Creosote Works: MSS
Ward/Herdman: Centre Circle, PO Box 182, Hartlepool TS26 0XL: 2000
Warren Cement Works
Vanishing Windmills of Hartlepool
Barracks
Central Estate
Central Estate & Beyond
Andy Capp Uncapped
Wood: West Hartlepool: Victorian New Town: Hartlepool Corporation: 1967
Victorian Delights: Evans Bros 1967

Illustrations

Colley: Let's Go back To My Place: Memory Lane Prints: 1989
Yesterday Once More: Colley: 1990
Shades of the Past: Colley 1992
Sands of Time: Colley: 1994
A Hartlepool Portrait: Colley: 1995
You Must Remember This: Colley: 1997
Ferriday: Hartlepool As It Was: Hendon: 1977
Vintage Hartlepool: Hendon: 1978

Hartlepool in the 1930s and 40s: Hendon: 1988
Hartlepool 1946-1997: Chalford: 1997
The Book of Hartlepool: Barracuda: 1987
Ed. Harrison & Almond: Industrial Archaeology in Cleveland: Cleveland County Libraries: 1978
C. Lovell:
Mennear: Hartlepool In Old Picture Postcards: European Library - Zaltbommel/Netherlands: 1985
Spaldin: Shipbuilders of the Hartlepools: Hartlepool Borough Council: 1986

Maps

Ordnance Survey: 1857: Alan Godfrey Maps, Gateshead 1989
1861-3: David and Charles
1896: West Hartlepool: Alan Godfrey Maps
1914: Alan Godfrey Maps, Gateshead
Hartlepool AZ Street Plan: Geographers' A-Z Map Co, Sevenoaks: 1996
Sharp: History of Hartlepool 1816: Hartlepool Borough Council 1978

Relevant Studies

Briggs: Victorian Cities (Ch 6, Middlesborough: The Growth of a New Community): Penguin 1990
Chalklin & Havenden: The Making of Some New Towns c. 1600-1720: Rural Change & Urban Growth 1500-1800
Cook & Stevenson: Longman Handbook of Modern British History: 1714-1980 (1983)
HMSO 1977 Guide to Census Reports Gt Br 1801-1966
Hoole: Railways of Gt Britain Vol 4, North East: David & Charles: 1974
Hudson: Coming Back Brockens: Jonathan Cape: 1994
Muthesius: The English Terraced House: Yale 1982
Newman & Foster: The Value of a Pound 1900-1993: Gale Research International, Ltd, 1995
Rogers: This Was Their World: BBC: 1972
Todd: Geordie Words and Phrases: Frank Graham 1977
Tomlinson: North Eastern Railway, Rise & Development: Longmans Green: 1914

Videos

Charter Celebrations 1201-1951: RTV Communications 1992
Hartlepool Headland Urban Village: Headland Local History Group: RTV Communications: 1995
Hartlepool Video: Ward & Martin: 1990 Revision: RTV Communications
Hartlepool Remembrance & Renaissance: Ward & Martin: RTV Communications 1991
Hartlepools 1896-1996: A Century of Change: RTV Communications 1996
Images of Hartlepool Headland: Hartlepool Borough Council: RTV Communications 1994
Middleton: A History: Martin, Craven, Allen: RTV Communications 1992
Millennium Video: Martin: RTV Communications:

Index

A

B

C

I

J

K

L

M

N

O

P

Q

R

S

T

U

V

W